The Great Texts of the Bible

The Great Texts of the Bible

EDITED BY

JAMES HASTINGS

JOB · PSALMS I · XXIII

VOLUME III

Wm. B. Eerdmans Publishing Company
Grand Rapids, Michigan

Library of Congress Catalog Card Number: 58-13517

Published by special arrangement with Charles Scribner's Sons.

PRINTED IN THE UNITED STATES OF AMERICA

CONTENTS

TOPICS.

CONTENTS

TEXTS.

Job.

Psalms.

THE UNSELFISHNESS OF TRUE RELIGION.

LITERATURE.

Bradley (G. G.), *Lectures on the Book of Job*, 34.
Brooks (P.), *New Starts in Life*, 36.
Davies (D.), *The Book of Job*, i. 59.
Godet (F.), *Old Testament Studies*, 183.
Kemble (C.), *Memorials of a Closed Ministry*, 209.
Ker (John), *Sermons*, i. 98.
Rattenbury (J. E.), *Six Sermons on Social Subjects*, 53.
Shore (T. T.), *Some Difficulties of Belief*, 211.
Simeon (C.), *Works*, iv. 314.
Spurgeon (C. H.), *Evening by Evening*, 22.
Watkinson (W. L.), *The Ashes of Roses*, 191.
Christian World Pulpit, xvii. 241 (Perowne).

The Unselfishness of True Religion.

Then Satan answered the Lord, and said, Doth Job fear God for nought?
—Job i. 9.

BEFORE the throne of Jehovah are gathered "the Sons of God."
We meet the phrase elsewhere in the Old Testament, and we find
it again in this Book, as used to designate beings of other than
human mould, employed as God's ministers of mercy or of
judgment, whose creation dates from a period older than that of
the material earth and of us its inhabitants. Among these
beings, who come to do homage to their Lord, is one who bears
the title of "the Adversary," or "Opposer," *the Satan*, as the word
stands in the Hebrew, who reports himself as fresh from travelling to and fro on the surface of the earth. Jehovah Himself calls
his attention to one, of whom He speaks as *my servant Job*, and
bears His own testimony, a more than human testimony, to his
goodness. He repeats, reminding some of us perhaps of similar
repetitions in the oldest of classic poets, the very words in which
the author had introduced him : "Hast thou considered," he says,
"my servant Job? for there is none like him in the earth, a
perfect and an upright man, one that feareth God, and escheweth
evil." But "the Adversary," clearly a malignant spirit, has his
answer ready. "Doth Job fear God," he asks, "for nought?"
He insinuates at once a doubt, and more than a doubt, as to Job's
motives. "Hast thou not," he goes on, "made an hedge about
him, and about his house, and about all that he hath, on every
side? Thou hast blessed the works of his hands, and his substance
is increased in the land. But put forth thine hand now, and
touch all that he hath, and he will renounce thee to thy face."
I myself, he seems to say, could be as pious as Job, were I as
prosperous as he. "It is easy," says a character drawn by a
modern satirist, "to be virtuous on a handsome income, on so

3

many thousands a year." The temptations of poverty are obvious, and strike the eye. Satan sees them at a glance. Those of wealth, which wrung from the Great Teacher the words, "How hardly shall they that have riches enter into the kingdom of God," are more subtle and hidden. Satan read the one, Jesus Christ the other.[1]

I.

THE ACCUSER.

1. The word "Satan," or "adversary," or "accuser," supplies one aspect only of Satanic character. He is here presented not as the "tempter," the one who *suggests* evil *to* man; but as the "accuser," the one who *insinuates* evil *about* man. No one name sums up the whole character of the fallen angel. It is as an "accuser" that he appears here. Job was a perfect and an upright man, one who feared God, and turned away from evil. The devil in the capacity of tempter had very little elbow-room in the life of Job. Hence he appears here as the false accuser of the man whom he could not successfully tempt.

¶ We must be careful not to impose upon the Book of Job or this prophet conceptions belonging to a more advanced period. The Satan of these books is no mere "evil spirit," the real enemy of God though His unwilling subject. There is no antagonism between God and the Satan. The idea that the "attacks of Satan are aimed primarily at the honour of God"; that his purpose is to deny that God is "ever disinterestedly served and sincerely loved by any being whatever"; and that "the object of the trial of Job is precisely to demonstrate to him the contrary"—such an idea is altogether at variance with Old Testament conceptions. The Satan is the servant of God, representing or carrying out His trying, sifting providence, and the opposer of men *because* he is the minister of God; hence Job's afflictions, represented as inflicted by the Satan in one place, are spoken of as due to the hand of God in another, "thou hast set me on against him, to destroy him" (ii. 3), just as Job's friends "came to condole with him over all the evil that the Lord had brought upon him" (xlii. 11), and of course everywhere in the poem the Almighty is assumed to be the author of Job's calamities both by the sufferer and by his friends. The angels and Satan among them are the

[1] Dean Bradley.

ministers of God's providence. The Satan being the minister of God's trying providence, which is often administered by means of afflictions, it was an easy step to take to endow him with the spirit of hostility to man which such afflictions seemed to reflect. This step is taken in the Book, though not very decidedly.[1]

2. What are the signs of the "Satan" character?

(1) The first sign is *a want of regard for one's fellow-creatures.* —This is a faint enough way of putting it, so far as Satan is concerned, the spirit that moves through the world, deceiving and destroying, of whom Christ has said, "He was a murderer from the beginning, and abode not in the truth, because there is no truth in him." With no belief in principle or goodness, he can cherish no reverence and feel no pity. All may be treated remorselessly where all are so contemptible. The belief and the moral nature must in the end come into harmony; and where a spirit sets itself only to doubt and deny, it sets itself also to tempt and seduce. It must prove its own theory valid. Hence, probably, what otherwise seems insanity—the temptation of the Son of God, in whom there was no shade of sin. The mocking and sceptical spirit, which feels nothing but hollowness within, sees nothing else around and above it, and believes it possible to drag all that seems to be higher down to its own level.

¶ The possession of reverence marks the noblest and highest type of manhood and womanhood: reverence for things consecrated by the homage of generations—for high objects, pure thoughts, and noble aims—for the great men of former times, and the high-minded workers amongst our contemporaries. Reverence is alike indispensable to the happiness of individuals, of families, and of nations. Without it there can be no trust, no faith, no confidence, either in man or God—neither social peace nor social progress. For reverence is but another word for religion, which binds men to each other, and all to God.[2]

¶ It was about 6.20 a.m. when we reached the canal bridge at Tel-el-Kebir. Two or three hundred Highlanders, a squadron of cavalry, and some odds and ends of mounted corps had just arrived. The seamy side of a battle was here painfully apparent; anything seemed to be good enough to let off a rifle at. Dead and wounded men, horses, and camels were on all sides. Some of the wounded had got down to the edge of the water to quench their

---

[1] A. B. Davidson.　　　　　[2] S. Smiles, *Character*, 14.

thirst; others were on the higher banks, unable to get down. Many of our officers dismounted and carried water to these unfortunates, but the men were not all similarly disposed. I heard an officer ask a man who was filling his canteen at the canal to give a drink of water to a gasping Egyptian cavalry soldier who was lying supporting himself against the battlement of the bridge. " I wadna wet his lips," was the indignant reply.[1]

(2) The next consequence to the spirit which has no belief in unselfishness is *the want of any centre of rest within itself.*—The condition of Satan is thus described, in verse 7, " And the Lord said unto Satan, Whence comest thou ? Then Satan answered the Lord, and said, From going to and fro in the earth, and from walking up and down in it." Incessant wandering, "going about," "seeking rest and finding none," is the view given of him in Scripture. There is the constant endeavour to find a fixed point, and inability to discover it; and this may be the truth intended to be conveyed in that strange but significant narrative (Matt. viii. 28) where the evil spirit is urged from place to place by the conquering power of good, till it is driven to beg for a refuge in the lowest and most grovelling forms of creation,—to find itself, even here too, rejected, and cast forth naked and shelterless. This is most certain, that if the heart does not give quiet, no place in the universe can, and the personal head of evil has been for ages making the attempt to find that quiet in vain.

¶ The place both of the past and future is too much usurped in our minds by the restless and discontented present. The very quietness of nature is gradually withdrawn from us; thousands who once in their necessarily prolonged travel were subjected to an influence from the silent sky and slumbering fields, more effectual than known or confessed, now bear with them even there the ceaseless fever of their life; and along the iron veins that traverse the frame of our country, beat and flow the fiery pulses of its exertion, hotter and faster every hour. All vitality is concentrated through those throbbing arteries into the central cities; the country is passed over like a green sea by narrow bridges, and we are thrown back in continually closer crowds upon the city gates.[2]

(3) There is still another effect to be remarked of this want of belief in unselfishness—*the failure of any real hold on a God.*—

[1] *Autobiography of Sir William Butler*, 235.
[2] Ruskin, *Seven Lamps of Architecture* (*Works*, viii. 246).

It was so with the great spirit of evil. He could not deny God's existence. This was too plainly forced in upon him and felt by him, but he had no just views of a God of truth and purity and goodness, else he had never continued so to resist Him. He had a belief that made him tremble, but that never stirred him up to lay hold on God, because he saw only heartless power seated on the throne of the universe. It is within the sphere of every spirit to make and maintain its own world and its own God, and the God it makes bears the character of its world.

¶ The sneerers and scoffers at religion do not spring from amongst the simple children of nature, but are the excrescences of overwrought refinement, and though their baneful influence has indeed penetrated to the country and corrupted many there, the fountain-head was amongst crowded houses where nature is scarcely known. I am not one of those who look for perfection amongst the rural population of any country; perfection is not to be found amongst the children of the Fall, be their abode where it may; but until the heart disbelieve the existence of a God, there is still hope for the possessor, however stained with crime he may be, for even Simon the Magician was converted. But when the heart is once steeled with infidelity, infidelity confirmed by carnal reasoning, an exuberance of the grace of God is required to melt it, which is seldom or never manifested; for we read in the blessed Book that the Pharisee and the Wizard became receptacles of grace, but where is mention made of the conversion of the sneering Sadducee? and is the modern infidel aught but a Sadducee of later date?[1]

¶ What *In Memoriam* did for us was to impress on us the ineffaceable and ineradicable conviction that *humanity* will not and cannot acquiesce in a godless world: the "man in men" will not do this, whatever individual men may do, whatever they may temporarily feel themselves driven to do, by following methods which they cannot abandon to the conclusions to which these methods at present seem to lead.[2]

II.

The Accusation.

The accusation is put in the form of a question; and a question may be more incisive than a statement. There are few forms of

---

[1] George Borrow, *Letters to the Bible Society*, 128.

[2] Professor Henry Sidgwick, in *Memoir of Tennyson*, i. 302.

speech which can be so suggestive as the interrogatory.   This is a
commonplace in the Satanic art of suggesting evil.   It is also a
convenient cover for cowardice; although it was not so in this case,
as it is supplemented by a bold and specific assertion.   The literal
and perhaps the most forcible rendering of this question is "Doth
Job serve God *gratis*?"   This is the exact significance of the
Septuagint translation.   It is the form, too, in which the irony
of the Hebrew is best expressed.   The suggestion is that in the
case of Job there was no disinterested goodness, no unselfish piety.

1. *It is an insinuation, not only against Job, but against all
men.*—The view embodied in Satan's words is one which we have
heard whispered, or loudly spoken, or taken for granted, now and
here, as there and then.   There is no such thing, we are told, as a
love of goodness for its own sake.   There is always some ulterior
aim, some selfish motive.   Even religion, we hear, even the religion
of Christ, is a mere matter of selfish interest.   It is nothing more,
even when sincere, than a selfish device to escape from pain, and
enjoy happiness hereafter.   "Doth Job fear God for nought?"
You see how far the words extend.   They cover a wider range
than that of the character of one child of Adam.   They go down
to the very springs of human nature; down to the very essence
and even the existence of goodness itself.   "Can men and women
care for goodness and mercy, or for truth, or for righteousness, for
their own sake?"

Job was a typical saint.   According to Divine testimony there
was "none like him on the earth."   If Job's piety had turned out
to be selfish and self-seeking, what hope could there be of others?
So much hinged upon this.   The vindication of Job would also
be a vindication of human piety at its best.   It was well worth
Job's suffering to expose the Satanic fallacy.   It was worth all the
endurance to turn back the edge of that cruel suspicion, not only
against Job, but also against men of Job's spirit throughout the ages.

¶ Every one who values the highest interests of his race must
look with deep pity upon the efforts of many whose chief aim it
seems to be to depreciate humanity, and to show their ingenuity
only by repeating, in every varied form, the old question of the
mocking spirit, "Doth Job fear God for nought?"   There is a
literature which makes it its pleasure to depict affection that it
may trace its slow decline, and to analyse human nature that it

may exhibit its meanness, which when it paints goodness gives us the superficial gilding of a paltry amiability, and puts heart after heart into its crucible that it may reduce all to dross. It passes with many for deep knowledge of the world, and finds its refrain from some worn-out men of pleasure who repeat "vanity of vanities" with another aim than the "Preacher," and from some younger men who affect the worn-out style as lending them, at an easy price, the air of insight and old experience. After all, it is a shallow philosophy, and unhappy as shallow, which degrades human nature and casts doubt on the Divine, and leaves us to infer that dust and ashes are all that is.[1]

¶ I cannot but enter the most emphatic and earnest protest I am capable of uttering against the dreary mechanical utilitarianism which would resolve even secular life into one vast scheme of selfishness. The world, all that is best and noblest in the world, does not act from purely selfish motives. There are grand lives lived, there are noble deaths died, by statesmen, by soldiers, by sailors, by clergymen, by doctors, by travellers, by common stokers on our railways, and common miners in our coal pits, for the sole love of England, or of Humanity, with no tinge of a base self-seeking nature in the hearts that thus labour and thus fall. Not from any cold-blooded calculations of gain come such lives and deaths, but from the influence of the Spirit of God, from which cometh every good, true, noble, brave thought and deed that ever glows in the soul of man, and burns itself into action upon earth.[2]

¶ Miss Anna Swanwick, the translator of the dramas of Æschylus, formed a class of shop girls and servants. Once when she was trying to interest them in Milton, some one suggested that instruction in arithmetic would be more useful, considering their work and future. She thought not, but resolved to leave it to themselves to decide. So at their next meeting she put the question to them, Which do you prefer—instruction in the poets or in book-keeping? and, not to hasten their decision, left them to discuss it among themselves, telling them that she would come back for their answer. When she returned she found that only two of the girls were in favour of what bore upon their ordinary work; all the rest wished what would take them away from it or lift them above it.[3]

2. *It is also an accusation against God.*—The arrow launched

---

[1] John Ker, *Sermons*, 112.

[2] T. Teignmouth Shore, *Some Difficulties of Belief*, 212.

[3] W. L. Watkinson, *The Ashes of Roses*, 195.

at Job flies farther: in the end it reaches God Himself. If Satan is right, it is not only that there is no such thing as disinterested goodness, but God Himself is robbed of His highest and noblest attribute. If He can no longer win the hearts, and retain in joy and sorrow the reverential affection of those on whom He showers His benefits; if He can no longer inspire anything but a mercenary love, He may be all-powerful still, but there are surely those among our fellow-creatures, whom some of us know or have known, who must come before Him in our homage. Heaven and earth are no longer full of His glory. Vital is the question which the challenge stirs, and rightly has it been said, that in the coming contest, Job is the champion, not of his own character only, but of all who care for goodness, and of God Himself.

¶ If the prologue be an integral part of the poem, we have here the key to the interpretation of Job. In the incisive words of A. B. Davidson: "This question—Doth Job serve God for nought?—is the problem of the book." But the difficulty is just to read the poem in this light. And the learning and insight which Davidson and his great *confrères*, Delitzsch and Dillmann, have applied to the problem throw the difficulty into still clearer relief. It is not merely that the bearing of Job is different; but the whole centre of interest changes. In the poem, the Satan and his cynical assaults on human goodness vanish. It is no longer Job's piety, but God's justice, that is in question. As even Godet admits, "The Being who is brought to the bar of judgment is in reality not Job, it is Jehovah. The point in debate is not only the virtue of Job; it is, at the same time, and in a still higher degree, the justice of God." And Job is now the Prometheus who boldly joins issue with the Almighty. The problem of the poem is to reconcile faith in God with the inequalities of His Providence. And it ends in God's appearing, not to reveal to His steadfast servant the meaning of His sufferings, but to vindicate His own character as worthy of trust and love.[1]

III.

THE ANSWER.

Job's life, as it is traced in the glowing, indignant, faith-inspired words of his complaint, is the triumphant answer. Job

[1] A. R. Gordon, *The Poets of the Old Testament*, 204.

does fear God for nought: that is, his integrity is no vulgar barter for wages, as Satan supposes, but deeply founded in the truth of things—so deeply that he takes leave of friends, of family, of life, even of God Himself, as he has hitherto regarded God, in order to be true. And if Job, a man like ourselves, has wrought out the answer, then the answer exists in humanity. There is such a thing as disinterested piety, and it contains whole worlds of faith and insight. Or, to gather the history before us into a sentence: There is a service of God which is not work for reward: it is a heart-loyalty, a hunger after God's presence, which survives loss and chastisement; which in spite of contradictory seeming cleaves to what is Godlike as the needle seeks the pole; and which reaches up out of the darkness and hardness of this life to the light and love beyond.

1. We must admit that there are some forms in which certain doctrines have been presented and enforced which would seem to sustain the charge. And it is, perhaps, because we have dwelt too much on these aspects of the religious life that the thought has caused some vague uneasiness to ourselves.

(1) Has there not sometimes been too great a tendency to make our individual salvation the sole and exclusive object of the Christian life? In some manuals of devotion, and in books which treat systematically of the religious life, this is painfully apparent. Take, for example, that treatise which has for many reasons justly obtained the reverence of ages, Thomas à Kempis' *De Imitatione Christi*. This selfish aspect of Christianity is the one blot on that otherwise luminous and noble work. "His one view of the duty of man," writes Farrar, "is to be self-absorbed in accomplishing his own personal salvation, in securing his individual safety amid universal conflagration, to save himself on some plank of prayer or self-denial out of the fiery surges of some devouring sea." [1]

But let us not err on the other side any more than on this. Selfishness is certainly an evil, when it leads us to subordinate spiritual things to those which are temporal: but if understood as implying a supreme regard to our eternal interests, it is good and commendable; for it is that very disposition which was exercised

[1] T. Teignmouth Shore, *Some Difficulties of Belief*, 219.

by Mary, when she dismissed from her mind all inferior considerations, and chose that good part which should never be taken away from her. In this sense Christians are selfish ; and it may justly be said of them that they do not "serve God for nought." For they desire, above all things, the salvation of their souls. They know what they have done to offend their God, and what God has done to save them, and what promises of mercy He has given to all who repent and believe His Gospel. And, knowing these things, they desire to avail themselves of the opportunity afforded them, and to secure to themselves the proffered benefits. And is this wrong? If so, what can all the invitations and promises of the Gospel mean? Why did Peter say, "Repent, and be converted, that your sins may be blotted out"? or why did our blessed Lord say, "If any man thirst, let him come unto me, and drink ; and out of his belly shall flow rivers of living water"?[1]

(2) There is another point, which is perhaps of still more practical importance to ourselves; for it not only seems to justify some of the accusations against our faith as being selfish, but it does tend in many of us, perhaps, really to give our religious thoughts and aspirations a selfish tinge. There is no word which we use more frequently in religious phraseology than the word "Salvation." "To be saved" is beyond all question the very end and object of every religious, anxious soul, so far as it can be summed up in so brief a formula. "To save us" Jesus Christ died. "To save perishing souls" is the one great practical end for which the Catholic Church of Christ exists. Is there not too great a tendency in many of us always to speak and think of that salvation which Christ purchased for us with His precious blood as solely an escape from some future punishment? Have we not read and heard too, frequently, appeals to men to accept Christ as their Saviour from punishment and from hell? Yet such is only a fragment—possibly to some extent a distorted fragment—of the glorious Gospel of Jesus Christ. If we regard the atoning sacrifice of the Son of God as merely a means by which we are to escape some future pain, there may be a strong tinge of selfishness in our faith. There is a more awful thing than pain, or punishment, or hell itself, so far as we use the word merely to

[1] C. Simeon, *Works*, iv. 317.

indicate a place of torture—there is sin, the most awful thing in the universe of God. It is to save us from sin that Christ died. Sin and Self, these are the tyrants we are groaning under; it was to deliver us from these that Christ came.

¶ Salvation is not putting a man into Heaven, but putting Heaven into a man. It is not putting a sinful man into a law-abiding community, but writing the law of God in his heart and mind. The real question is not, What will we do under outward compulsion? but, What will we do by inward choice? Salvation is not the change of circumstances, but that central change in us, that change of the heart, of its attitude, its intentions, and its choices, which will make it the conqueror under all circumstances in life's battles.[1]

2. But now let us directly face this question of the disinterestedness of religion.

(1) And first of all, it is a fact that, in the long run and in the large view, prosperity and the service of God are bound together. That is the idea of life. That is what our sense of justice demands. And no man must deny that fact as it applies itself to his own life. It is not by burning his barns and killing his cattle that Job will get rid of his difficulties and answer the question of his motive in serving God.

¶ It is remarkable to see how really the Bible has two classes of utterances. On the one hand it has such promises as offer blessings to obedience and assure men that if they serve God they shall prosper. On the other hand there are such words as those of Jesus in which He frankly told His disciples that in the world they should "have tribulation" in proportion as they belonged to Him. It is very interesting to put these two sorts of utterances together and ask what will be the total impression which is the resultant in the mind of him who believes them both. No doubt he will decide that what they mean is the certainty that righteousness will come to happiness in the end, but will have to pass through much of suffering upon the way. And, if he be wise, the practical rule by which the man will try to live will be the forgetfulness of consequences altogether, the ceasing to think whether happiness or unhappiness is coming, and the pursuit of righteousness for its own sake, the being upright, brave, and true, simply because uprightness, bravery, and truth are the only worthy conditions of a human soul. Great is the condition of a man who

[1] M. D. Babcock, *Thoughts for Every-Day Living*, 11.

thus lets rewards take care of themselves, come if they will or fail to come, but goes on his way true to the truth simply because it is true, strongly loyal to the right for its pure righteousness.[1]

¶ Carlyle took occasion to relate how when he was a child of four his parents had given him an earthenware " thrift pot," a sort of bottle without mouth, but slit in the side to slip pennies in. Somehow he was left alone in the house; there came to the door a beggar-man, pale, weary, worn, and hungry, dripping with wet. " I climbed on the kitchen table," says Carlyle, " and reached down the thrift pot from its shelf and gave him all that was in it—some fourpence.   I never in all my life felt anything so like Heaven as the pity I had for that man."   How different this from " the inward satisfaction and pride resulting from a virtuous action ! "[2]

(2) But we think, and rightly, of the Christian as looking for blessing not in this life but in the life beyond the grave.   " I shall be happy in Heaven," says the servant of Christ ; " I can wait.   The glory and the bliss that are to be revealed are well worth waiting for.   I can suffer for these few years, sure of the freedom from suffering which I am to have for ever and ever." What multitudes of souls have fed upon this certainty.   What multitudes are feeding on it now and gathering great strength and patience.   And we can see at once that this expectation of celestial reward has left behind much of the danger of the anticipation of reward to be received on earth.   In the first place it never can be so distinct and definite.   It cannot take clear concrete shapes to the ambitious desires, like houses and lands and bags of money, and the visible, audible tokens of men's esteem. Being of necessity less sharp and distinct before the imagination, the prizes of the celestial life may well appear more spiritual and the terms of their attainment may seem less arbitrary, more essential.   Thus they may be the means of higher and purer inspiration.

¶ To ask to see some fruit of our endeavour is but a transcendental way of serving for reward ; and what we take to be contempt of self is only greed of hire.[3]

(3) And, after all, character is the essential reward and true ambition of a noble life.   For then we pass beyond all of what

---

[1] Phillips Brooks, *New Starts in Life*, 39.
[2] *Mrs. Brookfield and her Circle*, ii. 435.
[3] R. L. Stevenson, *A Christmas Sermon.*

are commonly meant by consequences, and our thought is fixed
upon intrinsic qualities as the true result and recompense of
struggle after righteousness. "If I do these brave things I shall
be brave." "If I resist this temptation to impurity I shall be
pure." Bravery and purity as real possessions of the soul; as real
as, indeed far more real than, houses and oxen and bags of gold
—these make the new ambition.

In the lower stages of personal religious experience, as in the
earlier stages of national religious development, the bargaining
temper of the patriarch Jacob may be condoned; but in the
higher stages, which cannot be delayed without serious loss,
the huckstering spirit has entirely passed away. "Now when
Simon saw that through the laying on of the apostles' hands the
Holy Ghost was given, he offered them money. . . . But Peter
said unto him, Thy silver perish with thee, because thou hast
thought to obtain the gift of God with money." In our day
dollars and divinity are associated without causing any special
shock, but to men full of the spirit of Christ the association was
sacrilegious; the attempt to obtain spiritual power with money,
or to get money out of spiritual virtue, was equally impious.
The strong language of Peter shows that profit and piety are
utterly irreconcilable in religious thought and motive, although
they are often and naturally coincident in practical life.

¶ James Smetham's painting, poetry, and study of literature
did not lead to conventional success; yet toward the end of life
he wrote: "In my own secret heart I look on myself as one who
has got on, and got to his goal, as one who has got something a
thousand times better than a fortune, more real, more inward,
less in the power of others, less variable, more immortal, more
eternal; as one whose feet are on a rock, his goings established,
with a new song in his mouth, and joy on his head." Here is the
exceeeding great reward of devout souls, however carnal fortune
may fail.[1]

(4) Have we yet reached the end? Is there a higher motive
still? There is a motive, or perhaps we ought to say a range
of motives, which yet more completely casts aside and leaves
behind the taint of mercenariness while it still presents a true
prize to the uplifted eye of the struggler with his sins and

[1] W. L. Watkinson, *The Ashes of Roses*, 197.

the seeker for goodness. This range of motives is inspired by two ideas. One of these ideas is the honour which man by his holiness may render to God. The other is the help which man by his holiness may render to his fellow-man.

You go to your Christian friend, your fellow-student, your fellow-merchant, your fellow-man. You say to him, "You are serving God." And he replies, "Yes, certainly I am, and I am always trying to serve Him more and more"; and then you ask Satan's question, "Is it for nothing that you serve Him? Do you serve God for nought?" And he replies again, "Oh no, He pays me bountifully." And then you say, "Tell me what He gives you." And the answer comes, "He gives me the privilege of honouring Him and helping my fellow-men." What then? It may be that these rewards seem to be no reward to you. It may be that you look into his face as if you looked upon an idiot, and wondered what distortion of the mind could let him care for things like these. But none the less you see that he does care for them. They make for him a great enthusiasm. They are his "exceeding great reward."

¶ It is not your business and mine to study whether we shall get to heaven, even to study whether we shall be good men ; it is our business to study how we shall come into the midst of the purposes of God and have the unspeakable privilege in these few years of doing something of His work. And yet so is our life all one, so is the Kingdom of God which surrounds us and enfolds us one bright and blessed unity, that when a man has devoted himself to the service of God and his fellow-man, immediately he is thrown back upon his own nature, and he sees now—it is the right place for him to see—that he must be the brave, strong, faithful man, because it is impossible for him to do his duty and to render his service, except it is rendered out of a heart that is full of faithfulness, that is brave and true.[1]

Jesus came
And laid His own hand on the quivering heart,
And made it very still, that He might write
Invisible words of power—"Free to serve!"
Then through the darkness and the chill He sent
A heat-ray of His love, developing
The mystic writing, till it glowed and shone

[1] Phillips Brooks, *Addresses*, 10.

And lit up all her life with radiance new,—
The happy service of a yielded heart.
With comfort that He never ceased to give,
Because her need could never cease, she filled
The empty chalices of other lives.
And time and thought were thenceforth spent for Him
Who loved her with His everlasting love.[1]

[1] F. R. Havergal, "Under His Shadow" (*Poetical Works*, 789).

THE DEEPS OF GOD.

LITERATURE.

Barton (G. A.), *The Roots of Christian Teaching as found in the Old Testament*, 103.

Bigg (C.), *The Spirit of Christ in Common Life*, 53.

Burrell (D. J.), *The Wondrous Cross*, 154.

English (W. W.), in *Church Sermons*, No. 29.

Eyton (R.), *The Search for God*, 1.

Hadden (R. H.), *Selected Sermons*, 47.

Hutton (A. W.), *Ecclesia Discens*, 11.

Leach (C.), *Old Yet Ever New*, 290.

Macintosh (W.), *Rabbi Jesus*, 31.

Matheson (G.), *Times of Retirement*, 234.

Moffat (H. B.), in *Sermons from the " Pulpit,"* No. 141.

Momerie (A. W.), *Defects of Modern Christianity*, 337.

Ritchie (A.), *St. Ignatius' Pulpit*, 150.

Russell (A.), *The Light that Lighteth every Man*, 149.

Simeon (C.), *Works*, iv. 372.

Terry (G. F.), *The Old Theology in the New Age*, 43.

Vaughan (J.), *Sermons* (Brighton Pulpit), xviii. No. 1128.

Voysey (C.), *Sermons* (1876), No. 9.

Cambridge Review, vi. Supplement, No. 132 (Robertson).

Christian World Pulpit, xxxix. 333 (Hocking); lxiv. 401 (Gibbon).

Church of England Magazine, xxii. 356 (Ayre); xxiii. 421 (Webster).

Church of England Pulpit, liii. 2 (Lias).

THE DEEPS OF GOD.

Canst thou by searching find out God?
Canst thou find out the Almighty unto perfection?—Job xi. 7.

1. THESE words occur in the first speech of Zophar the Naama-thite. What is Zophar's creed? It is that wherever there is suffering, there is sin, real and tangible sin, proportional to that suffering. God governs this world by rewards and punishments, and those rewards and punishments are distributed here below with unerring justice. It follows therefore that Job, this seeming saint, is really a man of heinous sin.

And having said this to his brother in his pain, and dis-charged that which, he honestly believes, Job's words had made the duty of others (v. 3), by speaking sharply where sharp words were needed, he points Job to the high and mysterious nature of the God against whom he is in rebellion. "High," he tells him, "that nature as Heaven, deep as the deep underworld; it stretches beyond the bounds of earth, and is broader than the broad sea. His power, too, is irresistible, and His eye sees at a glance concealed iniquity. How small before Him the wisdom, or rather the ass-like folly and petulance of man."[1]

2. The words of the text are sometimes read as a question whether God be discoverable by the efforts of the natural mind. The margin, "Canst thou find out the deep things of God?" suggests that the question is not whether God be discoverable at all, but whether He be wholly discoverable; not whether He can be found, but whether He can be comprehended. No Hebrew writer would have thought of putting the question whether God could be found or was knowable; the question, however, whether He could be wholly known, whether there were not deeps in His

[1] Dean Bradley.

21

nature unfathomable by the mind of man, was a question which, with a view to right conduct under trying providences, many felt themselves compelled to put.

More literally rendered it would read—"Hast thou arrived at the inner deeps of God, or arrived at the outermost bounds of Shaddai." Zophar challenges Job, and asks whether he has reached either the centre or the circumference of Deity? Had he either arrived at the inner thought or purpose, or scanned the unlimited range of the operations, of God? The one presents the microscopic, and the other the telescopic, aspect of investigation. Zophar asks whether in either direction Job had found out God. The question is not whether Job had found God, but whether he had found out, that is, comprehended, God. Then by a series of graphic images he seeks to impress upon Job the fact that, compared with God's omniscience, his very knowledge was utter ignorance. His perceptions at best were dull and very limited. Poor ignorant man, how could he comprehend Him who was infinite, or judge Him who was far beyond the scope of his investigation?

¶ "Canst thou by searching find out God?" No; and why? Because I never begin to search for Him until I have found Him; God alone can create the search for God. That is the great difference between things material and things spiritual. In material things the search precedes the finding; in spiritual things the finding precedes the search. When a man goes out to seek for gold you may infer that he is materially poor, but when a man goes out to seek for God you may conclude that he is spiritually rich. In the case of the gold we see the shadow before we touch the substance; in our experience of God we first touch the substance and then see the shadow. When a child stretches out its hand and cries for the moon it is seeking something which it will never find; but when a man stretches out his hand and cries for holiness, he is seeking something which he has found already. No man can pray for the Divine Spirit except by the *voice* of that Spirit. Why is our Father so eager that we should pray for the Kingdom? Is it because our prayer for goodness will *make* us good? No, it is because our prayer for goodness proves us to be good already. When did Abraham begin to search for the land of Canaan? When he got into it. He wandered up and down seeking the promised country; and he was there all the time, folded in her bosom. So is it with us.

We long for Canaan when we stand in Canaan. We cry for love when we have learned love. We pray for purity when we have tasted purity. We feel our distance from God when God is at the door.[1]

I.

THE DEEPS OF GOD.

Literally the verse reads: Canst thou find the deeps of (or, that which has to be searched out in) God; canst thou reach to the perfection (the outmost, the ground of the nature) of the Almighty? The word is the same as that translated in xxxviii. 16 "*recesses*" of the sea.

1. *God is not to be fully comprehended in His Being.*—Our knowledge of God, in this life, must be a constant "moving forward in the twilight"; fragmentary, and perhaps unequal; but by His grace increasing, as we "follow on to know"; starting from a venture, demanding an effort; and to the end of this life a knowledge only in part. But after this life, if we have endured and persevered unto the end, there will be a change. "Then shall I know even as also I have been known." When the things which keep us back have loosed their hold on us; when sin and indolence and doubt are done with; when all the anxieties that we have allowed to fret us and divide our hearts here are put away for ever; when, through whatsoever discipline, in this world or beyond it, God has wrought His perfect work in us; then will the broken and faltering effort pass into an unhindered energy, and we shall know Him even as also we are known. Even as from the first He has known us; as, when He made us His, when He called us to Himself, when He gave us our work to do, He knew us; as now, in all the discipline of life, in all His dealings with us, His gaze penetrates at once the inmost depths of our being; so shall we be ever moving forward, with intensity then undivided and unwearied, in the realization of His infinite truth and goodness.

Some measure of the knowledge of God is within the reach of all who really desire it and will really strive for it. Through

[1] G. Matheson, *Times of Retirement*, 235.

many ways He is waiting to reveal Himself more clearly to every one of us—through conscience, through nature, through the Bible, through the lives of the poor and of those who suffer patiently, through all moral beauty, and above all in the life and teaching of our Lord. Through all these ways, it may be, hints and glances of His glory have already come to us; through all these ways we may know in part, and follow on to know continually more. But, undoubtedly, there is need of venture—the venture of faith, to commit ourselves to Him; to trust the light we see, even though we see it faintly and unsteadily. Knowledge will never grow in that cold and sceptical mind which Dr. Newman has described so well; the mind "which has no desire to approach its God, but sits at home waiting for the fearful clearness of His visible coming, whom it might seek and find in due measure amid the twilight of the present world."

¶ How my mind and will, which are not God, can yet cognize and leap to meet Him, how I ever came to be so separate from Him, and how God Himself came to be at all, are problems that for the theist can remain unsolved and insoluble for ever. It is sufficient for him to know that he himself simply is, and needs God; and that behind this universe God simply is and will be for ever, and will in some way hear his call. In the practical assurance of these empirical facts, without "Erkentnisstheorie" or philosophical ontology, without metaphysics of emanation or creation to justify or make them more intelligible, in the blessedness of their mere acknowledgment as given, lie all the peace and power he craves. The floodgates of the religious life are opened, and the full currents can pour through.

It is this empirical and practical side of the theistic position, its theoretic chastity and modesty, that I wish to accentuate. The highest flights of theistic mysticism, far from pretending to penetrate the secrets of the *me* and the *thou* in worship, and to transcend the dualism by an act of intelligence, simply turn their backs on such attempts. The problem for them has simply vanished—vanished from the sight of an attitude which refuses to notice such futile theoretic difficulties. Get but that "peace of God which passeth understanding," and the questions of the understanding will cease from puzzling and pedantic scruples be at rest.[1]

¶ It is neither what we seem to understand about God that feeds our love, nor the fact that He is infinitely beyond our

[1] W. James, *The Will to Believe*, 135.

understanding, but the fact that we can ever progress in knowledge and love, and always with a sense of an infinite "beyond." It is at the margin where the conquering light meets the receding darkness that love finds its inspirations. If we are forced to conceive Him human-wise, we know that the conception is but an idol or picture; that if He is all that, He is also infinitely more. To the savage He is but the biggest and strongest of men; to the rationalist He is but the most intelligent and moral; to faith He is the hidden Infinite, of which these are but the finite symbols.[1]

> The splendours of the Summer sunset-glow
>   Shot blood-red through the intercepting trees:
>   And, fretful that my vision could not seize
> Unblurred, the hues beyond, or fully know
> The gorgeous scene that was obstructed so,
>   In haste my discontentment to appease
>   I climbed my tower, when lo! I missed the trees!
> Too dazzling was the sight! The charm did go!
>
> I must not seek all things to understand:
>   If 'mid the tangled mystery of my days,
> And cares that mar delights on every hand,
>   I catch but gleams of glory through the maze,
> I'll wait till in the All-revealing Land
>   The full effulgence meets my tutored gaze![2]

(1) The intellect by itself is utterly at fault in the search for God.

¶ Jacob begged that he might know his Benefactor's name, but it was not conceded to him. God wraps Himself in mystery. He partly reveals and partly conceals Himself. His purpose is to keep man, not in ignorance, but in lowly reverence. Wonder is an element of worship. God is not angry with man for his reverent curiosity; He rather stimulates it to the utmost; but there are limits which He will not let us overstep. He says, "Thus far shalt thou come, and no farther." We have no line with which to measure the Infinite. "Who can by searching find out God? who can find out the Almighty unto perfection?"

> No answer came back, not a word,
> To the patriarch there by the ford;
> No answer has come through the ages
> To the poets, the saints, and the sages,

---

[1] George Tyrrell.   [2] Thomas Crawford, *Horae Serenae*, 65.

Who have sought in the secrets of science
The name and the nature of God
But the answer that was and shall be,
" My name! Nay, what is that to thee?"[1]

Yet God does reveal Himself. He is not the unknown and unknowable. His revelations come to the heart and the conscience; they come in the experiences of life; and they come really rather than verbally. When God has wrestled with Jacob and blessed him, Jacob knows God, although His name is withheld. He knows His power and His grace; knows Him as the source of blessing; knows how wonderful and adorable He is. For the rest, mystery does not repel men from God, it attracts them to Him; and in view of the infallible assurances of the soul we may reverently say even of God, " What's in a name?" If the Hebrews could do nothing better, they could at least now call upon the " God of Jacob." They could encourage one another by saying, " The name of the God of Jacob defend thee." The contents of that designation, the experience which it recalled, were full of inspiration. " Therefore, to whom turn I but to Thee, the ineffable Name?"[2]

¶ It is really time for men of science to be warned off the grounds of philosophy and psychology as peremptorily as they warn religion off the territory of science. A purely materialistic student of the facts of science is simply impudent when he applies his scientific methods to things spiritual. It is as absurd as the old application of theological methods to science. Let him say what he *knows* about his "atoms," but when he attempts, as Tyndall says he attempts, "to leap beyond the bounds of experiment" and guess at the cause of his "atoms" he is just in the position in which Tyndall places us—"that of a man attempting to lift himself by his waistband." But after all what a testimony to the need of a revelation is all this! What is it all but what Job said long ago, "Who can by searching find out God?" The last word of science must be atheism, if science denies all that is not scientifically demonstrable; and just for that reason when science has said her last word, religion says her first, "In the beginning was the Word and the Word was God." I look on Stuart Mill's "Life" and Tyndall's manifesto as two valuable contributions to the evidence of Christianity; the one showing man's moral need, the other his intellectual need of a revelation *ab extra.*[3]

---

[1] J. Hay, *Israel.*   [2] J. Strachan, *Hebrew Ideals,* ii. 67.
[3] *The Life of Archbishop Magee,* ii. 11.

(2) Our knowledge of God is a recognition by our whole personality.

¶ God is for me that after which I strive, that the striving after which forms my life, and who, therefore, *is* for me ; but He is necessarily such that I cannot comprehend or name Him. If I comprehend Him, I would reach Him, and there would be nothing to strive after, and no life. But, though it seems a contradiction, I cannot comprehend or name Him, and yet I know Him—know the direction toward Him, and of all my knowledge this is the most reliable.

You know God not so much by means of reason, not even by means of your heart, as by the complete dependence felt in relation to Him—something like the feeling which a suckling babe experiences in the arms of its mother. It does not know who holds it, who warms and feeds it ; but it knows that there is somebody who does this, and, moreover, loves this person.[1]

¶ Maeterlinck's cardinal doctrine will, I conjecture, prove to be something like this. What should be of most account for us all is not external fact, but the supra-sensuous world. "What we know is not interesting"; the really interesting things are those which we can only divine—the veiled life of the soul, the crepuscular region of sub-consciousness, our "borderland" feelings, all that lies in the strange "neutral zone" between the frontiers of consciousness and unconsciousness. The mystery of life is what makes life worth living. "'Twas a little being of mystery, like every one else," says the old King Arkel of the dead Mélisande. We are such stuff as dreams are made of might be the "refrain" of all M. Maeterlinck's plays, and of most of his essays. He is penetrated by the feeling of the mystery in all human creatures, whose every act is regulated by far-off influences and obscurely rooted in things unexplained. Mystery is within us and around us. Of reality we can only get now and then the merest glimpse. Our senses are too gross. Between the invisible world and our own there is doubtless an intimate concordance; but it escapes us. We grope among shadows towards the unknown. Even the new conquests of what we vainly suppose to be "exact" thought only deepen the mystery of life.[2]

> I cannot find Thee! Still on restless pinion
>   My spirit beats the void where Thou dost dwell;
> I wander lost through all Thy vast dominion,
>   And shrink beneath Thy light ineffable.

[1] Tolstoy, *Thoughts on God* (*Works*, xvi. 410).
[2] A. B. Walkley, in Maeterlinck's *Treasure of the Humble*, xii.

I cannot find Thee! E'en when most adoring,
  Before Thy throne I bend in lowliest prayer;
Beyond these bounds of thought, my thought upsoaring,
  From farthest quest comes back: Thou art not there.

Yet high above the limits of my seeing,
  And folded far within the inmost heart,
And deep below the deeps of conscious being,
  Thy splendour shineth: there, O God! Thou art.

I cannot lose Thee! Still in Thee abiding,
  The end is clear, how wide soe'er I roam;
The Hand that holds the worlds my steps is guiding,
  And I must rest at last in Thee, my home.[1]

2. *God is incomprehensible in His Providence.*—How small and insignificant are the mysteries of Nature in comparison with the problems of human life! Almost every month sees some fresh triumph of scientific research. It looks as if, by persistent and certain processes, man were to wrench from Nature her most precious secrets, as if in the end matter must confess itself beaten, as if all physical forces would ultimately bow before the dominion of the intellect and the mind. How different it is in the sphere of human experience! Sin remains; sorrow remains; pain remains; death remains. What more do we know about any one of them than the world knew in its infancy and childhood? They, too, like the earth and the air, the rocks and the seas, have their own secrets, but they hold them fast.

Sin—why upon this man does it swoop down with over-mastering might, and hold him in its relentless clutches, and crush and lacerate his soul, till it passes out of shape and festers and dies? And why does it leave that other man alone or touch him so rarely and gently that the wound heals up almost at once?

Sorrow—here is some polished voluptuary, whose life is one stream of apparent happiness, who never feels the cankerworm of care and weariness and desolation, to whom remorse and bitter-ness and anguish are strangers, and there is some simple, pious, reverent soul from whose mind perplexities and griefs and dis-tresses are never absent.

[1] Eliza Scudder.

Pain—how wayward, how partial, how erratic is its empire! This man with his magnificent physique and indomitable strength has neither been chastened by its discipline nor has smarted under its sting, while that poor body, lying in uncomplaining solitude in some cheerless back-room, remembers hardly anything else.

And Death, vastest, richest, final mystery of all—look at it from which standpoint you like, on the one hand "the grisly Terror," on the other

> That golden key
> That opens the palace of eternity

—need one of us travel beyond a very small and solemn circle to realize the strange scope and cruel incidence of its grim visitations?

> If I could answer you—
> If I could give you any light
> On this dark question, true,
> I should have more than human sight.
>
> I cannot understand
> The strange, sad mystery to-day,
> Here in the shadowland,
> Where knowledge only leads astray.
>
> I also sometime trod
> This path where hidden danger lies,
> And sought to find out God
> Where heights of human wisdom rise.
>
> But now I only see,
> Though all around is cold and dim,
> One Light that shines on me,
> And as I look away to Him—
>
> Lo! in the Light divine—
> Wherever falls its living ray—
> I see that all things shine
> Undimmed, and night is changed for day.[1]

3. *God is incomprehensible in His Grace.*—Grace is more than pity with tearful eye; more than mercy with outstretched hand;

[1] E. H. Divall, *A Believer's Songs*, 94.

it is an "arm made bare"—an omnipotent arm, bared for a mighty task. God's love finds its supreme expression in His grace as manifest on Calvary. It is His power to save. Here is the solution of the problem, "How can God be just and yet the justifier of the ungodly?" and of that other, "How shall a man be just with God?"

¶ To measure the heart of the Infinite, we must get the dimensions of the cross. We call it the "accursed tree." Rather, it is the tree of life; its roots deep as hell, its crown in heaven, its branches, laden with the fruits of life, reaching out to the uttermost parts of the earth. On the cross the only-begotten Son of God tasted death for every man. From the cross He offers redemption to the uttermost, not to respectable sinners only, but to thieves, harlots, and reprobates. By the cross He saves utterly; nailing our indictment there, blotting out our sin, sinking it into the depths of an unfathomable sea, washing us, though stained as scarlet and crimson, until we are whiter than snow. This is the measure: God so loved the world that He gave His only-begotten Son to suffer and die for it. That "so" is spelled with two letters, but it is vast enough to girdle the sin-stricken world and bind it back to God.[1]

II.

Our Attitude to the Deeps of God.

1. **Reverence.**—It goes without saying that, while faith in its essence must ever be the same, the particular standpoint of our fathers is not that of their children. They dwelt upon the depravity of human nature, the horror of sin, the holiness of God, the helplessness of the soul, the sovereignty of the Divine Mercy, and the unsearchable purpose of the Divine Will, themes full of awe and majesty. Therefore they humbled themselves before God and cast their souls upon His pity. They sought anxiously for a ground of pardon, and searched themselves for signs of the Divine calling. They dared not boast of His favour, but they walked humbly before Him and hoped for His salvation. Theirs was an inward, intense, and lowly religion. We are inclined to dwell on the possibilities of human nature, the wide hope of the Incarnation, the revelation of the Divine Fatherhood, the compass

[1] D. J. Burrell, *The Wondrous Cross*, 162.

of God's love, the full assurance of faith, the joy of the present life, and the glory of the life to come. ·Our religion is, therefore, more outspoken, unfettered, high-spirited. About the saint of the former day it was written, "he feared God"; but of our good man you read in his biography that he was a "bright" or a "happy" Christian.

It is futile to recall days which are gone, or to reproduce their moods; for the time spirit bloweth where it listeth, and, rightly used, it is the spirit of God. We have cause to be thankful, because we have learned not to despair of our race, to think of our fellow-men as brethren, and to remember that a man has more to do in this world than save his own soul. Our religion is less morbid, gloomy, introspective, and selfish; but there are times when, looking out through the palms upon this expanse of blue, one wearies for the strong salt air of the Atlantic and the grandeur of the hills when the sun shines through the mist. One is haunted with the conviction that if in our day we have gained joy and charity, we have lost in devoutness and humility, and that we have almost bidden good-bye to reverence.

¶ Reverence is the eyelash that lets us endure the sun, which lost, we must make up our minds to darkness for the rest of our lives, and give up for ever all thoughts of the vigour and health and pure richness of life which sunlight only gives.[1]

2. **Thankfulness.**—To one who sees the spiritual order of the world and recognizes the sublime chances of spiritual fortune which it offers, there is no need of special causes of gratitude; such an one thanks God daily that he lives. Times and seasons for special thanksgiving are wise and necessary; for men need to be reminded of what they have received, and they need to have provision made for the special expression of their gratitude; but the grateful man does not depend on days and festivals for his thought of God's goodness and care for him; these thoughts are always with him, and the song of thanksgiving is always in his heart. For all sweet and pleasant passages in the great story of life men may well thank God; for leisure and ease and health and friends may God make us truly and humbly grateful; but our chief song of thanksgiving must be always for our kinship

[1] *Phillips Brooks*, 52.

with Him, with all that such divinity of greatness brings of peril, hardship, toil, and sacrifice.

¶ An old man in Nottinghamshire came to me one Sabbath as we were going into church, and said: "Do you think, Sir, you could bring in that prayer about giving thanks this morning? I am eighty years old to-day, and I should like to thank God for all the mercies He has been pleased to send." He had one small room in a poor cottage; his income was three shillings a week; he had no relatives and few friends; he was often ailing and always infirm, needing two sticks to lean on, and yet he was not only content, but happy. He was a Christian in spirit and in truth, and the last words he spoke to me, just before his death, were these: "I am not dying in darkness, I am dying in the light of life."[1]

Lord, in this dust Thy sovereign voice
    First quicken'd love divine;
I am all Thine,—Thy care and choice,
    My very praise is Thine.

I praise Thee, while Thy providence
    In childhood frail I trace,
For blessings given, ere dawning sense
    Could seek or scan Thy grace;

Blessings in boyhood's marvelling hour,
    Bright dreams, and fancyings strange;
Blessings, when reason's awful power
    Gave thought a bolder range;

Blessings of friends, which to my door
    Unask'd, unhoped, have come;
And, choicer still, a countless store
    Of eager smiles at home.

Yet, Lord, in memory's fondest place
    I shrine those seasons sad,
When, looking up, I saw Thy face
    In kind austereness clad.

I would not miss one sigh or tear,
    Heart-pang, or throbbing brow;
Sweet was the chastisement severe,
    And sweet its memory now.

[1] Dean Hole.

Yes! let the fragrant scars abide,
Love-tokens in Thy stead,
Faint shadows of the spear-pierced side
And thorn-encompass'd head.

And such Thy tender force be still,
When self would swerve or stray,
Shaping to truth the froward will
Along Thy narrow way.

Deny me wealth; far, far remove
The lure of power or name;
Hope thrives in straits, in weakness love,
And faith in this world's shame.[1]

3. **Patience.**—This is the question to which a man must get the answer before he can work against evil and on the side of enduring good, viz.: not, Why does evil exist? but Why has not God thrown a clear light upon the problem of its existence? That is the question which he is bound to face or he must be for ever useless—he can never understand God's ways or know God Himself. There is a mighty and loving Being whose object is to educate us into likeness with Himself. That is the fundamental postulate. Why then has He not told us what we want to know, viz., why there is evil at all? The Christian answer is that He has given us this problem to work at for the sake of our education, in order that through thinking about it and working at it, certain powers, which we call spiritual, might be developed—powers by which we draw near to Him now, and shall come to be like Him hereafter. God did not set us this hard sum to work at merely in order to puzzle us. He set it us in order that we might in our working at it, even through our sense of despair in solving it, become what He meant us to be, that we might be trained in inmost character. When we become like Him, when the conditions of this life are changed into those of the fuller life, the fog will lift, and by means of the fuller life the question will be answered and the problem solved. In the meantime the very question which we took to be a kind of hindrance, because we could not find the answer to it, turns out to be a means of education—is calling out our strongest powers, is preparing us for finding the answer in another life. This is the Christian theory: and,

[1] J. H. Newman, "Occasional Verses."

starting from it, vast numbers of men and women are working for good against evil at the present day; they have their share of those difficulties with a monopoly of which frivolous critics often credit themselves; they feel those difficulties amid surrounding evil and intensified sufferings, and feel them acutely; but nevertheless they go on living their lives in a useful and a noble fashion; and they recognize that the very existence of this insoluble problem, when once they take up arms and play the man, does help them, does educate them, does call out from them nobler powers and more enduring virtue, and a more resolute patience than were otherwise possible.

¶ Patience, thou blessed attribute! How could we get on without thee? How we would worry and fret this miserable life away but for thy benign help. It is among the ranks of the poor and lowly that we see that grace in most frequent and most beautiful operation. I never return from visiting my poor sick people without learning a lesson of thankfulness from them. They are so patient under suffering, so thankful for the least attention, so submissive to God's sovereign will. I suspect that it still holds true that "God hath chosen the poor of this world, rich in faith, and heirs of the kingdom which He hath promised to them that love Him." [1]

I, and the Bird,
  And the Wind together,
Sang a supplication
  In the winter weather.

The Bird sang for sunshine,
  And trees of winter fruit,
And for love in the springtime,
  When the thickets shoot.

And I sang for patience
  When the tear-drops start;
Clean hands and clear eyes,
  And a faithful heart.

And the Wind thereunder,
  As we faintly cried,
Breathed a bass of wonder,
  Blowing deep and wide. [2]

[1] *Dr. MacGregor of St. Cuthberts*, 127.
[2] A. C. Benson, *Lord Vyet and Other Poems.*

Trust Inextinguishable.

LITERATURE.

Askew (E. A.), *The Service of Perfect Freedom*, 68.
Bennie (J. N.), *The Eternal Life*, 179.
Caird (E.), *Lay Sermons and Addresses*, 285.
Dawson (G.), *The Authentic Gospel*, 264.
Donne (J.), *Works*, iv. 537.
Hall (N.), *Gethsemane*, 237.
Halsey (J.), *The Spirit of Truth*, 79.
Newman (J. H.), *Parochial and Plain Sermons*, iv. 117.
Pusey (E. B.), *Sermons from Advent to Whitsuntide*, 91.
    „   „   *Selected Occasional Sermons*, 41.
Spurgeon (C. H.), *Metropolitan Tabernacle Pulpit*, xxi. (1875), No. 1244.
    „   „   *Grace Triumphant*, 300.
Voysey (C.), *Sermons*, iii. 17.
Christian World Pulpit, xliv. 184 (Munger), 369 (Farrar) ; lxxiii. 372
    (Sparrow) ; lxxv. 189 (Abey).
Church of England Pulpit, xxxvii. 97 (Farrar).

Trust Inextinguishable.

Though he slay me, yet will I wait for him.—Job xiii. 15.

1. These words, in their strange mixture of faith and unfaith, of trust and mistrust may be taken as summing up the argument of Job in the book called by his name. That book is one of the most remarkable in the Bible, not merely for its great literary qualities, for the imaginative grandeur of its pictures of nature, and the boldness and directness of its expression of the facts of human life, and the emotions they excite in us, but above all for the vivid way in which it brings before us what we may call the great perennial debate between man's soul and God. It describes the struggle between the doubts that beset man as to the existence of any Divine justice or goodness and the faith that sustains him against such doubts, and ultimately enables him to triumph over them.

This book has special reference to a stage in the development of the creed of Israel when the belief in a simple justice of rewards and punishments—the belief that goodness is directly followed by success and happiness, and ill-doing by failure and misery—began to be shaken by the experience of life. It was observed that the facts of human existence did not support the idea of any such immediate distribution of rewards and punishments, and the minds of men began to be distressed and perplexed by the problem, whether the whole conception of God as a righteous Judge was to be abandoned, or whether, on the other hand, a deeper justice could be discerned in the apparent injustice, and the old faith could be widened and elevated so as to overcome the new difficulties raised against it. And the intensity of the conflict was made greater by the fact that as yet there was no thought of a future life, or at least of a future life that had any joy or energy in it.

Yet—and this is the characteristic feature of the poem—through all his doubt and distress, through all his suffering and the agony of mind it produces, Job is exhibited as maintaining his faith in God; and in the end his integrity is vindicated by God against those who have denied it merely on the ground of his misfortunes. The aim of the writer, therefore, is to show that there is a point of view from which the difficulties in question may be removed, or transcended, that they are not fatal to faith but only trials of it, from which it may emerge purer and stronger than ever.

2. In the verses preceding the text Job resolves to appeal to God. But he knows how terrible will be the risk of this great enterprise. "I will take my flesh in my teeth, and put my life in my hand!" he cries,—a fine proverbial expression for running all hazards even to the last, of which Shakespeare gives a noble variation in King Henry VIII., when describing the people of England under oppressions which break the sides of loyalty, as

Compell'd by hunger
And lack of other means, in desperate manner
Daring the event to the teeth.

Then comes our text. And first about its meaning. We have so fine a rendering in our Authorized Version that we cannot surrender it without pain. And, indeed, many competent scholars refuse to surrender it. They still read the verse, "Though he slay me, yet will I trust in him." But properly translated and rightly understood, it means something quite different. In the Revised Version there is a rendering differing from the accepted one—"Though he slay me, yet will I wait for him," it reads. But with their usual timidity the Revisers have thrown the really correct translation into the margin, and the passage ought to stand, as it there stands, "Behold, he will slay me; I wait for him; I will maintain my ways (or, I will argue my cause) before him." So that instead of being the utterance of a resigned soul, submissively accepting chastisement, it is rather the utterance of a soul that, conscious of its own integrity, is prepared to face the worst that Providence can inflict, and resolved to vindicate itself against any suggestion of ill desert. "Behold, He will slay me. Well, I wait for Him in the calm assurance of the purity of my motives and the probity of my life. I will accept the blow, because I can do no other, but I will assert my blamelessness."

¶ What Cheyne has happily called "an inspired mistranslation" has to be given up. For many reasons, one regrets this, and yet I personally believe that the Revised Translation expresses a mightier faith than even the sacredly familiar translation of the Authorized Version—"Though he slay me, yet will I trust in him." Here I unhesitatingly affirm that "waiting for" God in these circumstances is a higher type of faith than "trusting in" Him.

Job, in saying "Though he slay me, yet will I wait for him," practically says, "Though He slay me, yet will I not try to escape from Him, or evade Him, I will wait for Him. If I am to be slain, it shall be with my face, and not my back, toward Him; and if I am to fall, I will fall at His feet!" Was there ever a more daring expression of faith than that?[1]

3. Yet, the words, as usually understood, have an historic claim in their favour which cannot be disputed. Even the Apostles do not spurn the use of the Greek words of the Old Testament, though they do not accord with the proper connexion in the original text, provided they are in accordance with sacred Scripture, and give brief and pregnant expression to a truth taught elsewhere in the Scriptures. Thus it is with this utterance, which, understood as the Vulgate understands it, is thoroughly Job-like, and in some measure the final solution of the Book of Job. It is also, according to its most evident meaning, an expression of perfect resignation. We admit that if it is translated: "behold, He will slay me, I hope not," *i.e.* "I await no other and happier issue," a thought is obtained that also agrees with the context.[2]

¶ Now, as no history is more various than Job's fortune, so is no phrase, no style more ambiguous than that in which Job's history is written; very many words so expressed, very many phrases so conceived, as that they admit a diverse, a contrary sense; for such an ambiguity in a single word, there is an example in the beginning, in Job's wife; we know not (from the word itself) whether it be *benedicas*, or *maledicas*, whether she said Bless God, and die, or, Curse God: and for such an ambiguity, in an entire sentence, the words of this text are a pregnant and evident

[1] D. Davies, *The Book of Job*, i. 295.
[2] F. Delitzsch, *Commentary on the Book of Job*, i. 214.

example, for they may be directly and properly thus rendered out of the Hebrew, "Behold he will kill me, I will not hope"; and this seems to differ much from our reading, "Behold, though he kill me, yet will I trust in him." And therefore to make up that sense, which our translation hath (which is truly the true sense of the place), we must first make this paraphrase, "Behold he will kill me," I make account he will kill me, I look not for life at his hands, his will be done upon me for that; and then, the rest of the sentence ("I will not hope") (as we read it in the Hebrew) must be supplied, or rectified rather, with an interrogation, which that language wants, and the translators used to add it, where they see the sense require it: and so reading it with an interrogation, the original, and our translation will constitute one and the same thing; it will be all one sense to say, with the original, "Behold he will kill me (that is, let him kill me), yet shall not I hope in him?" and to say with our translation, "Behold, though he kill me, yet will I hope in him": and this sense of the words, both the Chaldee paraphrase, and all translations (excepting only the Septuagint) do unanimously establish.[1]

4. May we take the text both ways? As Delitzsch says, each translation teaches a good lesson and a scriptural. So perhaps we may—the vindication first and the trust after. They show us, in a striking way, the two sides of one great truth.

I.

VINDICATION.

1. In order to understand the real sentiment underlying this exclamation we must have a correct conception of the theory of the Divine action in the world common to that age. For let us remember that this is a dramatic poem ; that Job is a real personage in the sense in which Shakespeare's Hamlet is a real personage; and that the author of the poem is simply putting into his mouth a protest against the sentiments current in his day as formulated by the "friends" who came to condole with him in so extraordinary a fashion. And if the boldness of his self-vindication sounds somewhat too audacious, and, to some, seems to verge even upon the blasphemous, it must be borne in mind

[1] John Donne, *Works*, iv. 539.

that it is the God of the contemporary theologians who is thus challenged, not the Father in Heaven whom our Lord revealed.

The struggle represented for us with so much dramatic power and vividness in this poem is Job's struggle for reconciliation between the God of the theologians of his day and the God of his own heart. And is not this a modern as well as an ancient struggle? Does not *our* heart often rise within us to resent and repel the representations of Deity that some forms of theology give? Do we not say to ourselves, " *This* God cannot be *our* God for ever and ever"?

Job had to answer to himself, Which of these two Gods is the true one? The God of my contemporaries, who is ever on the watch for a slip or an offence that He may punish it, and who seems often to punish when there is no offence; or the God of whom my own heart speaks to me, who doth not afflict willingly, and whose chastisements are all kind? If the God of the theological imagination were the true God, he was prepared to hold his own before Him. This Divine Despot, as the stronger, might visit him with His castigations, but in his conscious integrity, Job would not blench. " Behold, he will slay me; I will wait for him. I will maintain my cause before him."

¶ A favourite theme of Greek tragedy was the conflict between fate and freedom, between Divine necessity and man's free will, between the despotism of nature's inexorable laws and the passionate longings of the human soul. And in the story of Prometheus, or Forethought, we have this conflict most vividly set forth. Because Prometheus brought fire from heaven for the benefit of mortals, Jupiter was angered and caused him to be chained to a rock on Mount Caucasus, where for thirty thousand years a vulture was sent to feed upon his liver, " which was never diminished, though continually devoured." His offence was that he had brought a heavenly boon to men; and he would not cry " Peccavi" any more than Job would in order to secure release. " He whose God-like crime it was to be kind, he who resisted the torments and the terrors of Zeus, relying upon his own fierce soul," is in this respect the counterpart of Job in his suffering. " Each refuses to say he is wrong merely to pacify God, when he does not see that he is wrong. As Prometheus maintains this inflexible purpose, so Job holds fast his integrity."[1]

[1] J. Halsey, *The Spirit of Truth,* 83.

2. Let us dare to follow our own thoughts of God, interpreting His relation and providence towards us through our own best instincts and aspirations. This is what Jesus taught us to do. He revealed and exemplified a manly and man-making faith, as far removed as possible from that slavish spirit which is so characteristic of much pietistic teaching. Christ said, Find the best in yourselves and take that for the reflection of God—the parental instinct, for instance, with its patience, its unselfishness, its self-denying love. Reason from that up to God, He says. "How *much more* shall your heavenly Father!"

¶ John Sterling with us. Talked over many people. Much discourse on special providences, a doctrine which he totally disbelieves, and views the supporters of it as in the same degree of moral development as Job's comforters. Job, on the contrary, saw further; he did not judge of the Almighty's aspect towards him by any worldly afflictions or consolations; he saw somewhat into the inner secret of His providence, and so could say, "Though he slay me, yet will I trust in him." We must look for the hand of His providence alike in all dispensations, however mysterious to us. Every movement here has its first impulse in Heaven; though, like a pure ether, it may be contaminated or altogether changed by collision with the atmosphere of this world, yet its origin is Divine. Thus, on the ruins of the doctrine of particular providences may be built up our belief in the constant superintendence and activity of our Infinite Father; and though some highly extolled species of faith may lose their value for us, we shall, instead of them, see our entire dependence on Omnipotence for every gift, however trifling, and feel that He doeth all things transcendently well.[1]

3. It is pleasant to know from the last chapter, that before the drama closes Job comes to truer thoughts of God and a more spiritual knowledge of himself. He perceives that his heart, in its blind revolt, has been fighting a travesty of God and not the real God. Then, as soon as he sees God as He is, and himself as he is, his tone changes again. The accent of revolt is exchanged for that of adoring recognition, and the note of defiance sinks into a strain of penitential confession. "Who is this that hideth counsel without knowledge? Therefore have I uttered that which I understood not. I had heard of thee by the hearing

[1] Caroline Fox, *Journals and Letters*, i. 236.

of the ear" (the things that Eliphaz the Temanite, and Bildad the Shuhite, and Zophar the Naamathite had said to him about God); "but now mine eye seeth thee." The vision brought him back by one bound to God and himself. "Wherefore I abhor myself, and repent in dust and ashes."

¶ The sentiment that the highest bliss might be found in love without return is no other than that which has nourished in all time the noblest forms of human love and devotion. It is the sentiment which inspired with sublime passion the well-known words of Saint Teresa: "Thou drawest me, my God. Thy death agony draws me; Thy love draws me, so that, should there be no Heaven, I would love Thee. Were there no Hell, I would fear Thee no less. Give me naught in return for this my love to Thee; for were I not to hope that I long for, then should I love Thee even as I do now." Not until the passion of self-abandonment has touched the point at which the words, "Though he slay me, yet will I trust in him," are the simple and natural expression of pride and joy, is that height of exaltation reached the attainment of which includes the highest possibilities of love and sorrow. For "love's limits are ample and great, and a spacious walk it hath, but with thorns not lightly to be passed over." The call to love, rightly understood, is, in truth, a call to self-renunciation, as indeed is every call to lead the higher life. The soul to whom such a call comes is directly confronted with the necessities of sacrifice, for devotion to another in its highest form leads to the way of the Cross. Only through much suffering may the Saint attain the fulfilment of the promise of the spiritual life and see Him face to face, yet in her triumph she cries, "Give me naught in return for this my love to Thee!"[1]

Couldst thou love Me when suns are setting,
  Their glow forgetting
  In thought of Me;
Couldst thou refrain thy soul from fretting
  For days that used to be?

Couldst thou love Me when creeds are breaking,
  Old landmarks shaking
  With wind and sea;
Couldst thou restrain the earth from quaking,
  And rest thy heart in Me?

[1] Lady Dilke, *The Book of the Spiritual Life*, 162.

Couldst thou love Me when friends are failing,
  Because fast paling
  Thy fortunes flee;
Couldst thou prevent thy lips from wailing,
  And say, " I still have Thee " ?

Couldst thou love Me when wealth is flying,
  The night-blast sighing
  Through life's proud tree;
Couldst thou withhold thy heart from dying,
  And find its life in Me?

Couldst thou love Me when tears are welling
  Within thy dwelling
  Once glad and free;
Couldst thou escape their flood's high swelling,
  And reach thine ark in Me?

Couldst thou love Me when storms are roaring,
  Their torrents pouring
  O'er mart and lea;
Couldst thou on larger wings be soaring,
  And hear all calm in Me?

Couldst thou love Me when death is nearing,
  A mist appearing
  In all but Me?
If then thy heart cast out its fearing,
  Thy love shall perfect be.[1]

II.

TRUST.

1. How often have these words been the vehicle of a sublime faith in the hour of supreme crisis ! In the moment of their darkest necessity and deepest anguish pious hearts have adopted this as the formula of their unwavering confidence in and submission to the Infinite Wisdom ; and in the hour when their life's path has been strewn with the wreck of all that was delightsome in their eyes, and all that was dear to their hearts, have cried, with unfaltering tones, " Though he slay me, yet will I trust in

[1] George Matheson, *Sacred Songs*, 168.

him." And from this usage of centuries the words have acquired a sacredness, and are invested with associations, that make it very difficult to break the spell they hold over our devout affections by any attempt to show that they do not stand for the writer's original thought, and are far from representing the suffering patriarch's real state of mind.

¶ There is a story, in Swedish history, of a king who was mad with rage; and, in his madness, sent for one of his prisoners to be brought before him. Then the king drew his dagger, and passed it through the arm of his victim; and the poor wounded man just drew the dagger out, kissed it, and gave it back to the brutal hand which had smitten him. Now, hating such loyalty, as I do, yet how one wonders at the passionate beauty of that deed ! Marvelling that the man could so worship such a creature, yet how perfect was his loyalty to him ! That man might have written, Though Thou slay me, yet will I trust in Thee. It was the *king's* dagger that struck him, and he was the king's subject, so he just drew out the dagger, kissed the bloody blade, and gave it back.[1]

2. Now, taking the text in this sense, we notice first that it is very easy to praise God when all things prosper. Praise and prosperity usually go together. Just as all my good luck comes from God's providence, so God's mercies perfect my praise. But that is no sign of faith. Even the Gentiles do that. To be thankful when there is something to be thankful for—there is nothing in that. To look pleasant when things are pleasant is but common graciousness. Not to smile when the sun shines would be churlish. To dance when the music is good is inevitable to those who are well attuned—there is nothing in that. But there are some men who are gracious when all things are ungracious, sweet when things are sour, bright when other people are in the dark. The good economist keeps his candle for the time when it is most needed; then his little light comes into eminent service. He puts his lamp out while other people's lamps are shining; then, by and by, when the unwise virgins are all in the dark, this cheery soul lights his lamp.

(1) Do we trust God in the presence of the *evil* that is in the world, and in the darkness that accompanies it ? Conscience affirms right and duty as supreme realities, but God pays no heed

[1] G. Dawson, *The Authentic Gospel*, 269.

to them and lets the righteous suffer—this is the puzzle of the
ages, and it is as far from solution to-day as ever.   Conscience
still holds men to duty, but what is the profit?   The righteous
suffer and die and pass away under the natural laws of God with
no advantage over the wicked.   Nature—and to the Jew nature
was God—looked down on good and evil alike, and by no law, by
no variation of its forces, showed that the good had any advantage
over the evil.   The wise avoid evil; the foolish incur it: but ask
the light, the rain, the dew; ask gravitation and chemical affinity
and electricity if they distinguish between good and evil men.   To
the Jew these things were God—he knew no difference between
an agent of God and God Himself; and thus the terrible contradiction involved God.   We blunt the force of it by referring evil
to nature; but the Jew saw things more nearly as they are.   Here
was God in the conscience demanding righteousness, and here was
God in nature ignoring righteousness.   His intense sense of God
deepened the problem and made it awful as a fact.

¶ It is not the mere existence of evil, but the amount of evil
in the world that really depresses us and seems like a load too
heavy to be lifted up.   And if we could realize to ourselves that
the purposes of God are known to us in part only, not merely as
regards another life, but also as regards this; if we could imagine
that the evil and disorder which we see around us are but a step or
stage in the progress towards order and perfection, then our conception of evil would be greatly changed.   Slowly, and by many
steps, did the earth which we inhabit attain to the fulness of life
which we see around us.   I might go on to speak of this world as
a pebble in the ocean of space, as no more in relation to the
universe than the least things are to the greatest, or to the
whole earth.   But, that we may not become dizzy in thinking about
this, I will ask you to consider the bearing of such reflections,
which are simple matters of fact, on our present subject.   They
tend to show us how small a part, not only of the physical but
also of the moral world, is really known to us.   They suggest to
us that the evil and suffering which we see around us may be only
the beginning of another and higher state of being, to be realized
during countless ages in the history of man.   That progress of
which we think so much, from barbarism to civilization, or from
ancient to modern times, may be as nothing compared with that
which God has destined for the human race.   And if we were
living in those happier times, we should no more think seriously

of the misery through which many have attained to that higher
state of being than we should think of some bad dream, or dwell
on some aberration or perversity of childhood when the character
had been formed and had grown up to the stature of the perfect
man.[1]

> I questioned: Why is evil on the Earth?
> A sage for answer struck a chord, and lo!
> I found the harmony of little worth
> To teach my soul the truth it longed to know.
>
> He struck again; a saddened music, rife
> With wisdom, in my ear an answer poured:
> Sin is the jarring semitone of life,—
> The needed minor in a perfect chord.[2]

(2) But the test can be closer; other *calamities* come pouring
in upon Job with true epic swiftness. His family is swept out
of existence. To the Jew this meant more than to us—not more
grievous, but as taking away the hope of the Messiah. Under
this hope the family had become a Divine institution, and so an
intenser, if not a dearer, relation; it embraced his whole world;
he had no thought, or life, or hope outside of it. When our
children die we quench our tears with the hope of meeting them
again; but to the Jew it was the overthrow of his life, the
blotting out of his world. Job also endured this test, evolving in
his communings with himself a full belief in another world, where,
if he should find personal vindication, he might also find what
was dearer to him.

¶ Forty-three years ago, four men were left to starve on a
southern isle, whither they had gone in the hope of preaching the
Gospel to some of the lowest savages which the earth contains.
Three of them slowly died of hunger; the fourth, Captain Allan
Gardiner, survived them in a prolongation of agony. When the
winter was over a ship touched on that bleak shore, and his
remains were found near the entrance of the cave which had
given rude shelter. Can you imagine a lot more lonely or
horrible? Here was a noble and holy man, filled with the
burning and the sole desire to make known the love of Jesus
Christ to the miserable Fuegians, and God allowed him to starve
to death in lonely anguish on a desert isle. And did his faith
fail in that extremity of horror? Not for one moment. At the

[1] B. Jowett, *Sermons on Faith and Doctrine*, 44.　　[2] Francis Howard Williams.

entrance of the cave, in red paint, he had painted a rude hand pointing downward, and under it the words, " My soul, trust thou still upon God." The diary containing his last words, as for weeks he slowly starved to death, is written with the sunshine of joy and peace in God. " Asleep or awake," said one of his starving companions, " I am happy beyond the poor compass of language to tell." The very last words which Allan Gardiner wrote in his diary were these : " I know not how to thank my gracious God for His marvellous loving kindness." Many a man, many a king, many a prince, many a millionaire, might give all that they had ever done and all they had ever possessed to die a death like that. And did these saintly heroes die in vain ? No ! Their very deaths brought about that Patagonian mission on which their labours had been spent.[1]

¶ The Electoress Louise Henriette von Oranien (died 1667), the authoress of the immortal hymn, " *Jesus meine Zuversicht* " [the English translation begins, " Jesus Christ, my sure defence "], chose these words, " Though the Lord should slay me, yet will I hope in him," for the text of her funeral oration. And many in the hour of death have adopted the utterance of Job in this form as the expression of their faith and consolation. Among these we may mention a Jewess. The last movement of the wasted fingers of Grace Aguilar was to spell the words, " Though he slay me, yet will I trust in him." [2]

(3) Again, *reverses of fortune* often come on the good and honest with giant strides because of sickness, because of fraud, or the failure of others, because of unforeseen calamities ; and then, oh ! the anguish of heart-breaking anxieties which a man must feel, if not for himself, at least for those whom he loves. What is he to do ? What form is his faith and fortitude to take ?

¶ There is a grandeur which has always touched my heart in the young man struggling with the storm of fate, in Œdipus nobler and grander in his blindness and exile than on the throne, in Marius sitting among the ruins of Carthage, and Belisarius begging for his obolus in the streets of Constantinople. Strip a man of everything that he possesses, rain all sorts of blights and sorrows and afflictions on his head as on the head of Job, let him die by lonely martyrdom, after long imprisonment, amid the alienation of all for whom he has spent his life, like St. Paul ; let him be pelted and spat upon by the boys in the streets of his own city ; or, like Savonarola, cast into the flames after recanta-

[1] F. W. Farrar.   [2] F. Delitzsch, *Commentary on the Book of Job*, i. 214.

tion, enforced by the hideous torture of his fellow-men, and what remains to him? The grandest of all things remains to him, as an inalienable and abiding possession—himself. Not all the vaunted legions of men and devils can rob a man of himself and his immortality, of his peace with God, the glory-cloud of God's presence in the temple of every pure and noble soul.[1]

¶ Our earth holds no more glorious scene than that of men and women who have passed from a mansion to a cottage, from abundance and servants to simplicity and necessity, and who have widened their influence as the path of life narrowed. Here is a man who, through no fault of his own, has lost all his goods. Gone the splendid house, the carriages, the positions of honour. Gone his pictures, his wife's piano and all her jewels. He lives in a tiny little house. He who always rode now walks. He still stands in the aisle of the church on Sunday morning; his beautiful face is more handsome at seventy than it was in the prosperous days when he was fifty. Never was he so useful, never did his word and example count for so much. Having no more duties as director of companies he has more time to visit the poor, to teach boys in the mission school, to serve the needy, to carry the flower and the cup of cold water to Christ's little ones. He never repines. The note of victory is in his voice when he refers to the old days. Once he ruled over things and bonds and stocks and markets. Now he rules over souls, and has time to spare. His last days have been his best days, through poverty. His happiest years have been his despoiled years. Once he made his gold to shine through Christian generosity; now he makes his coppers to shine. Yesterday, in the brown sear field, where the plough had made havoc, where the gleaners had carried away the last ear of corn, there stood in the corner of the field a bunch of wild asters, blooming up to the very edge of frost and winter, their brave beauty challenging the north wind! It was my old friend, with his stout heart, his finely-chiselled face, his beautiful, Christ-like life, flinging out his challenge to poverty, disaster, revolution, and standing victorious over all life's troubles. When the sunset gun shall boom for him the end of that man will be peace.[2]

(4) But there are even closer tests, harder trials and heavier burdens. So long as a man is strong he can endure; the crucial test is made in weakness. He can endure poverty, standing erect in the strength of manhood; he can bear death—it is the common lot. But there is one thing a man cannot endure, simply

[1] F. W. Farrar.   [2] N. D. Hillis, *The Contagion of Character*, 266.

because it takes away the strength to endure. *Disease* is the intolerable thing in human life, because it is the reversal and negation of life. It confuses or destroys our field of action ; it takes the world from under our feet; it is a subtraction from our powers; it colours and distempers the action of the mind; it saps the will, dulls or exaggerates the sensibilities ; and because it does all this, it unfits us beyond all else for resistance.

> Not in the hour of peril, thronged with foes,
>   Panting to set their heel upon my head,
>   Or when alone from many wounds I bled
> Unflinching beneath Fortune's random blows ;
> Not when my shuddering hands were doomed to close
>   The unshrinking eyelids of the stony dead ;—
>   Not then I missed my God, not then—but said :
> " Let me not burden God with all man's woes ! "
>
> But when resurgent from the womb of night
>   Spring's oriflamme of flowers waves from the sod ;
>   When peak on flashing alpine peak is trod
> By sunbeams on their missionary flight ;
> When heaven-kissed earth laughs, garmented in light ;—
>   That is the hour in which I miss my God.[1]

3. Now while the problem of the Book of Job is always a problem, it does not always press upon men in exactly the same way. The existence of evil and the fact of death, poverty, and disease are still felt to be hard to bear and harder to explain. But the great perplexity of our day is due to the decay of authority. This age has been called the age of criticism, an age in which every belief and institution inherited from the past is called upon to show its credentials, and in which, at least for educated men, there is no possibility of evading the duty of examining them, and endeavouring to the best of their ability to distinguish what is accidental and changeable from that which is essential and of permanent value. What, then, is the best course for those who are born in such a time to follow ?

(1) There are many at the present day who tell us that, in view of the progress of science and the results of critical inquiry, the only rational course is to adopt an Agnosticism which gives

[1] Mathilde Blind, *Poems*, 140.

up as hopeless the whole problem of religion; that is to say, all the great problems of human life and destiny. Guided by a very narrow view of science, they advise us to repudiate the great heritage of religious thought and life which has been accumulated by all the labours and sacrifices of the past, because it centres in a belief for which, in their view, scientific evidence is wanting. They think, like Job's wife, that the difficulties which try our faith are a sufficient reason for renouncing it altogether.

¶ If a thinker had no stake in the unknown, no vital needs, to live or languish according to what the unseen world contained, a philosophic neutrality and refusal to believe either one way or the other, would be his wisest cue. But, unfortunately, neutrality is not only inwardly difficult, it is also outwardly unrealizable, where our relations to an alternative are practical and vital. This is because, as the psychologists tell us, belief and doubt are living attitudes, and involve conduct on our part. Our only way, for example, of doubting, or refusing to believe, that a certain thing *is*, is continuing to act as if it were *not*. If, for instance, I refuse to believe that the room is getting cold, I leave the windows open and light no fire just as if it still were warm. If I doubt that you are worthy of my confidence, I keep you uninformed of all my secrets just as if you were *un*worthy of the same. If I doubt the need of insuring my house, I leave it uninsured as much as if I believed there were no need. And so, if I must not believe that the world is Divine, I can only express that refusal by declining ever to act distinctively as if it were so, which can only mean acting on certain critical occasions as if it were *not* so, or in an irreligious way. There are, you see, inevitable occasions in life when inaction is a kind of action, and must count as action, and when not to be for is to be practically against; and in all such cases strict and consistent neutrality is an unattainable thing.[1]

(2) There are others who tell us that the only safe course is to shut our ears to every doubt and difficulty, and simply to adhere to every element in the faith. They bid us follow Job's friends in simply reaffirming the forms of doctrine we have inherited, and refusing to pay any regard to the new questions which our new experience—the experience of a world which, both in knowledge and in action, has been carried far beyond any previous generation—inevitably presents for our consideration.

[1] W. James, *The Will to Believe*, 54.

(3) Both these alternatives are counsels of despair, and they both lead to a narrowing of human life and thought; in the one case by a scepticism which gives up as hopeless all endeavour to throw light upon the ultimate meaning of our lives, and abandons all those beliefs in which the best of our race have found their greatest support and stimulus; in the other case by making our religion an adherence to the tradition of the past rather than an immediate living experience of the present.

The spiritual life of man cannot detach itself from its religious root without withering and decaying; but neither can it continue to exist without growing. Neither Scripture nor reason gives any encouragement to such a desperate alternative between " all " and " nothing," between Agnosticism and a faith which is fixed once for all and has no possibility of growth.

For us, as for Job, it is the greatest of all the supports of spiritual life to believe in the rational character of the system of things in which we are placed, or, in other words, in the wisdom and goodness of the power which manifests itself in our own life and in the life of the world. For us, as for him, the essence of religion lies in the simple elementary creed that there is a Divine purpose in our existence, and that, if we make ourselves its servant and instrument, it will be well with us, but, if not, it will be ill with us. Now, as then, the great source of religious energy is to feel that the cause we serve is the good cause, and that the good cause is the cause of God. The simple consciousness expressed already in the song of Deborah, that the " stars in their courses fought against Sisera," that is, that the whole system of things is leagued against evil, and makes its ultimate triumph impossible, has been the great solace and support of religious men in all ages.

¶ The ideal end for man, as it exists in the mind of God, is only gradually being revealed to him, so that every height he attains to discloses a higher yet behind it:

> We climb, life's view is not at once disclosed
> To creatures caught up, on the summit left,
> Heaven plain above them, yet of wings bereft;
> But lower laid as at the mountain's foot.

We press on towards a phantom light that for ever flies before us, bidding us aspire, but not suffering us to attain; or perhaps we should rather say that the goal of our journey is, as it were, a to-morrow that never comes, or the last of all the lamps upon a winding road, where each appears the last until the traveller draws near it, and sees another coming into view. We pass therefore, not merely from what seems bad to what seems good, but also " from what once seemed good, to what now seems best," not merely, that is, from what we are, towards what we think we ought to be, but also from what we once thought we ought to be towards a more recent ideal of ourselves.[1]

[1] A. C. Pigou, *Robert Browning as a Religious Teacher*, 73.

LIFE BEYOND DEATH.

LITERATURE.

Albertson (C. C.), *Death and Afterwards*, 31.
Barton (G. A.), *Christian Teaching in the Old Testament*, 209.
Campbell (R. J.), *City Temple Sermons*, 161.
Cooper (T. J.), *Love's Unveiling*, 105.
Denney (J.), *The Way Everlasting*, 175.
Jerdan (C.), *Pastures of Tender Grass*, 408.
Maclaren (A.), *Expositions* : Esther, Job, 43
Munger (T. T.), *The Freedom of Faith*, 237.
Newton (J.), *The Problem of Personality*, 116.
Peck (G. C.), *Ringing Questions*, 31.
Wilson (P.), *The Great Salvation*, 263.
The Christian World Pulpit, xlii. 105 (Varley); xlvii. 259 (Fielding);
    lxxi. 249 (Ruth).
The Church of England Pulpit, lxii. 251 (Synnott).

LIFE BEYOND DEATH.

If a man die, shall he live?—Job xiv. 14.

JOB has just given utterance to an intense longing for a life beyond the grave. His abode in Sheol is thought of as in some sense a breach in the continuity of his consciousness, but even that would be tolerable, if only he could be sure that, after many days, God would remember him. Then that longing gives way before the torturing question of the text, which dashes aside the tremulous hope with its insistent interrogation. It is not denial, but it is a doubt which palsies hope. But though he has no certainty, he cannot part with the possibility, and so goes on to imagine how blessed it would be if his longing were fulfilled. He thinks that such a renewed life would be like the "release" of a sentry who had long stood on guard; he thinks of it as his swift, joyous "answer" to God's summons, which would draw him out from the sad crowd of pale shadows and bring him back to warmth and reality. His hope takes a more daring flight still, and he thinks of God as yearning for His creature, as His creature yearns for Him, and having "a desire to the work of his hands," as if His heaven would be incomplete without His servant. But the rapture and the vision pass, and the rest of the chapter is all clouded over, and the devout hope loses its light. Once again it gathers brightness in the nineteenth chapter, where the possibility flashes out starlike, that "after my skin hath been thus destroyed, yet from my flesh shall I see God."

¶ When standing in the shadows, the words of Ingersoll seem none too melancholy: "Life is a narrow vale between the mountain peaks of two eternities. . . . The skies give back no sound. . . . We cry aloud and the only answer is the echo of our wailing cry." Such were the great infidel's words at his brother's open grave. O, how many anguished hearts, like his, have cried up into the skies and for answer caught only the echo of their own lamentation ! In the "narrow vale" how many pilgrims have lost their way ! Against those unyielding peaks how many souls have bruised and broken their wings ! Earth's most fevered search and bitterest agonies are in that ancient phrase : "If a man die, shall he live again ? " [1]

¶ In a sad poem, entitled "The Great Misgiving," William Watson voices modern unsettlement and belief on this question. Writing there of our life as a feast at which we have banqueted, he asks why the worms should not have their feast too upon us, once we are done with it all. In soul-withering doubt, he estimates that it is impossible to know, when we have done with this life, whether we shall pass into the ampler day with its heavenly light, or whether we shall slip into new prospects, or fall sheer— a blinded thing ! His closing words, sounding like the shutting of the iron gate of a prison-house on man's soul, are—" *There* is, O grave, thy hourly victory ; and there, O death, thy sting ! " [2]

> Though bleak winds blow and earth grows drear,
>   When autumn's golden days depart,
>   We scan the skies
>   With fearless eyes,
> For winter brings no blight to him
>   Who holds the summer in his heart.

> Though death's chill shadows hover near,
>   And billows wild about us roll,
>   In faith's sweet calm
>   We lift our psalm,
> For death no terror wears for him
>   Who mirrors heaven in his soul. [3]

The answers to Job's question may be reduced to three, according as the inquirers are guided by Reason, the Old Testament Scriptures, or the Revelation in Christ.

I.

The Answer of Reason.

The greatest philosophers of Greece speculated on the nature and destiny of man. They felt there was something Divine in

---

[1] G. C. Peck, *Ringing Questions*, 35.   [2] P. Wilson, *The Great Salvation*, 265.
[3] Mary B. Sleight.

human nature, as well as something which seemed to them to be only of the earth. The mortality of the body they could not deny, nor did they wish to do so. They conceived of it not as the necessary expression and organ of the soul, but as a burden, a prison, a tomb; it was their one hope and desire that man's immortal part might one day be delivered from it. The Greek philosophers, too, as well as the great poets, rose above that moral neutrality which characterizes the instinctive faith in man's survival. They saw rewards and punishments in the once un-distinguishing future. Heroic men were admitted to some kind of blessed existence in Elysian fields; while the conspicuously bad—giants, tyrants, lawless profligates—were tormented in some kind of hell. Such ideas, however, were confined to a limited circle; they did not interest themselves in the common people; and however much we may admire the nobleness of the poets and philosophers of Greece, it is not to them, any more than to the priests of Egypt, that the world is indebted for the hope of immortality.

1. The foundation of a belief in a future life is embedded in human nature. In the transient course of things there is yet an intimation of that which is not transient. The grass that fades has yet in the folded and falling leaves of its flower that perishes the intimation of a beauty that does not fade. The treasures that are frayed by the moth and worn by the rust are not as those in which love and faith and hope abide. There is a will that in its purpose does not yield to mortal wrong. There is a joy that is not of emulation. There is a freedom that is other than the mere struggle for existence in physical relations, and is not determined in its source or end by these finite conditions.

¶ I have heard that the mortar in the walls of Sancta Sophia, at Constantinople, still retains some traces of the perfume with which it was mixed when built a thousand years ago. But let us make the figure complete. Suppose the fragrance of a rose had the same property in relation to the rose that the spirit has in relation to the body. What if the fragrance controlled the rose? What if it were endowed with such a superior nature as to be able to disseminate a rich, rare, and wondrous perfume even though the rose were faded, and fallen, and broken, and dead? What if the odour had a consciousness of its own, apart from the flower, able to say as the rose falls to fragments, " I am an odour still ! " Would we not regard it as somewhat less likely that such a fragrance could perish for ever—could be diffused into nothing ? [1]

¶ Huxley's consciousness of the difficulties involved in his views on life and destiny caused him to advocate a resolute front against the prospect of future nothingness. " We are grown men, and must play the man "—

Strong in will
To strive, to seek, to find, and not to yield.

He admits that a ray of light may perchance steal in upon the dreadful gloom :

It may be that the gulfs will wash us down,
It may be we shall touch the Happy Isles.

The natures that will find comfort in this scanty outlook are few indeed, and later teachers of the evolution school have revolted against its dismal predictions. Mr. Fiske says, " For my own part, I believe in the immortality of the soul, not in the sense in which I accept the demonstrable truths of science, but as a supreme act of faith in the reasonableness of God's work." Le Conte is more emphatic still. He holds that, without spirit—immortality—this increasingly beautiful cosmos, which has run its ageless course with manifest purpose and value, would be precisely as though it had never been—an idiot tale signifying and portending blank nothingness. [2]

2. The instinct of immortality is reinforced by man's innate sense of justice. He feels that something is needed to complete this life elsewhere. Immortality has been named " the great prophecy of reason "—a phrase which is in itself an argument. We cannot look into ourselves without finding it. The belief is a part of the contents of human nature : take it away, and its most unifying bond is broken ; it has no longer an order or a relation ; the higher faculties are without function : eyes, but nothing to see ; hands, but nothing to lay hold of ; feet, but no path to tread ; wings, but no air to uphold them, and no heaven to fly into.

¶ I do not know that there is anything in nature (unless indeed it be the reputed blotting out of suns in the stellar

[1] C. C. Albertson, *Death and Afterwards*, 41.
[2] S. Parkes Cadman, *Charles Darwin and other English Thinkers*, 76.

heavens) which can be compared in wastefulness with the
extinction of great minds: their gathered resources, their matured
skill, their luminous insight, their unfailing tact, are not like
instincts that can be handed down; they are absolutely personal
and inalienable, grand conditions of future power unavailable for
the race, and perfect for an ulterior growth of the individual. If
that growth is not to be, the most brilliant genius bursts and
vanishes as a firework in the night. A mind of balanced and
finished faculties is a production at once of infinite delicacy and
of most enduring constitution; lodged in a fast-perishing organism,
it is like a perfect set of astronomical instruments, misplaced in
an observatory shaken by earthquakes or caving in with decay.
The lenses are true, the mirrors without a speck, the movements
smooth, the micrometers exact: what shall the Master do but
save the precious system, refined with so much care, and build
for it a new house that shall be founded on a "rock"?[1]

¶ Kant, the great moralist, based his demonstration of the
doctrine of immortality on the demands of the conscience.
Conscience bids us aim at perfection. But perfection is not
reached upon the earth. If the earth be all, if death ends everything, then we are overweighted in our moral nature. Conscience
needs an enduring arena for its operation. Conscience demands
immortality.

> The facts of life confirm the hope
> That in a world of larger scope—
> What here is faithfully begun
> Will be completed, not undone.[2]

¶ If no atom of matter is ever lost, no unit of force ever
wasted—if nothing is destroyed, although all is changed—will the
Father fail to preserve the gift of immortality in His children?
Every true gift of God preaches this sublime truth. We have felt
sometimes, when we have listened to beautiful music, that it must
be an echo from those "choirs invisible" of which our great
composers have often dreamed. And as of music, so of poetry;
for the real poet is by nature a seer and a prophet, and his noblest
lines are full of the consciousness of the Eternal. He takes his
illumination from—

> The light that never was on sea or land.

Whichever way we look, into whatever realm of life we enter,
the immortal truth is seen shining more and more brightly unto

[1] James Martineau.   [2] T. E. Ruth.

the perfect day.   Life, not death—restoration, not ruin—growth, not decay,—these are our rich inheritance and possession.[1]

> For love, and beauty, and delight,
> There is no death, nor change; their might
> Exceeds our organs', which endure
> No light, being themselves obscure.[2]

3.   There is in every soul a crystal skylight opening out toward the upper realms ; but if we do not keep it clean the vision of those realms will grow dim until it is obscured from us altogether. Sincerely and practically to believe that we are immortal, we must more or less feel ourselves immortal; but this feeling of immortality will seldom visit the bosom of the man who does not honestly try to live on earth the life of heaven.   Emerson has truly said that from a low type of moral life a slaughter-house style of thinking invariably results—a style of thinking, that is, which butchers men's fairest ideals and noblest hopes, because it cannot realize how fair and noble they are.   Spiritual things are not likely to be discerned by the animal man.

¶ It is the hardest thing in the world for a child to believe that the dead are no more.   Wordsworth has shown us this with beautiful simplicity, in his poem of the little cottage-girl, to whom the sister and the brother lying in the churchyard were as really alive and pleased with the songs she sang to them, as were the two who dwelt at Conway and the two who had gone to sea.

> Whatever crazy sorrow saith,
> No life that breathes with human breath
> Has ever truly longed for death.

> 'Tis life, whereof our nerves are scant,
> Oh, life, not death, for which we pant,
> More life, and fuller, that I want.[3]

II.

The Answer of the Old Testament.

1. In the Old Testament a great forward step is taken.   We feel that we have left the twilight for the dawn.   Among heathen races faith in immortality rested on conceptions of man's nature,

---

[1] Henry White.   [2] Shelley.   [3] Tennyson, "Two Voices."

in the Old Testament it rests on God's character. He is the Eternal Righteousness, and His faith is pledged to man whom He calls to live in fellowship with Himself. All things may seem to be against a man; his friends may desert him, circumstances may accuse him; but if he is righteous, God cannot desert him, and if he must die under a cloud, even death will not prevent his vindication. His Redeemer lives, and one day he shall again see God. And to see God is to have life, in the only sense which is adequate to the Bible use of the word.

¶ It is quite true to say that Israel had hardly any ideas about the future, and shrank in horror from those it had; but Israel had God, and that was everything. Israel knew that there was One only, the living and true God, from everlasting to everlasting, infinite in goodness and truth; Israel knew that God had made man in His own image, capable of communion with Him, and only blessed in such communion; to Israel, to see good was all one with to see God; with God was the fountain of life, in God's light His people saw light. This faith in God was greater than Israel knew; it could not be explored and exhausted in a day; it had treasures stored up in it that only centuries of experience could disclose, and among them was the hope of immortality. The believing nation of Israel, like Bunyan's pilgrim, unconsciously carried the key of promise in its bosom, even when it was in the dungeon of Giant Despair.[1]

> "Oh, little bulb uncouth,
> Ragged and rusty brown,
> Have you some dew of youth?
> Have you a crimson gown?"
> "Plant me and see
> What I shall be,—
> God's fine surprise
> Before your eyes!
>
> A body wearing out,
> A crumbling house of clay!
> Oh, agony of doubt
> And darkness and dismay!
> Trust God and see
> What I shall be,—
> His best surprise
> Before your eyes!"

[1] J. Denney, *The Way Everlasting*, 182.

2. The Old Testament revelation is at the best hazy. The descriptions given of Sheol are numerous and depressing. Man existed in it, but did not live. He had no communion there either with the living God or with living men. It was a pale transcript of life, but not life in reality. It was a realm of darkness, dust, and endless silence, unbroken by the vision of God or the voice of praise. The best men shrank from it with horror. The feeling with which they regarded it will be sufficiently illustrated by these lines from the Psalm of Hezekiah : " I said, in the noontide of my days I shall go into the gates of Sheol. . . . I shall not see the Lord, even the Lord in the land of the living : I shall behold man no more with the inhabitants of the world. . . . But thou hast in love to my soul delivered it from the pit of nothingness, for thou hast cast all my sins behind thy back. For Sheol cannot praise thee, death cannot celebrate thee : they that go down into the pit cannot hope for thy truth. The living, the living, he shall praise thee, as I do this day : the father to the children shall make known thy truth."

¶ It goes without saying that Job's most far-reaching and comprehensive declaration falls unspeakably short of that abolition of death, and bringing of life and immortality to light, accomplished by the gospel of Christ ; but what it lacks in fulness and breadth, it gains in the burning intensity and glow out of which it springs, and the sublime motives which urge and impel him, not only to speak, but also to covet a monumental and immortal pulpit for his words. His sayings form a window through which we look into his soul ; a lit lamp by whose clear ray we see the workings of his mind, and enter into partnership, not only with his ideas, but with himself, as those ideas are born in his soul, and take their place in his life.[1]

III.

THE ANSWER OF CHRIST.

1. When Christ entered on His ministry of teaching, He found certain doctrines existing in Jewish theology ; they were either imperfect or germinal truths. He found a doctrine of God, partial in conception ; He perfected it by revealing the Divine

[1] J. Clifford, *Daily Strength for Daily Living*, 318.

Fatherhood. He found a doctrine of sin and righteousness turning upon external conduct; He transferred it to the heart and spirit. He found a doctrine of judgment as a single future event; He made it present and on-going. He found a doctrine of reward and punishment, the main feature of which was a place in the under and upper worlds where pleasure was imparted and pain inflicted; He transferred it to the soul, and made the pleasure and pain to proceed from within the man, and to depend upon his character. He found a doctrine of immortality, held as mere future existence; He transformed the doctrine, even if He did not supplant it, by calling it *life*, and connecting it with character. His treatment of this doctrine was not so much corrective, as accretive. He accepts immortality, but He adds to it character. He puts in abeyance the element of time or continuance, and substitutes quality or character as its main feature. Hence He never uses any word corresponding to immortality (which is a mere negation—unmortal), but always speaks of *life*. The continuance of existence is merely an incident, in His mind, to the fact of life. It follows inevitably, but is not the main feature of the truth.

¶ A little child whose angel still beholds the face of the Father, does not repine over the past, or sigh for the future. The very law of innocence and perfection, whether in child or angel or God or perfect man, tends to exclude the sense of time. Continuance becomes a mere incident; the main and absorbing thought is quality of life. When Christ speaks of eternal life, He does not mean future endless existence; this may be involved, but it is an inference or secondary thought; He means instead fulness or perfection of life. That it will go on for ever is a matter of course, but it is not the important feature of the truth.[1]

¶ Dr. Young of Kelly (the famous chemist who first extracted paraffin oil from shale) died on 13th May 1883. On the Sunday following his funeral, Dr. Robertson preached at the evening service in Skelmorlie United Presbyterian Church, Dr. Goold of Edinburgh preaching in the forenoon. Mr. Boyd, the minister of the church, writes: " In the course of his sermon Dr. Goold insisted strongly that the doctrine of immortality is taught in the Old Testament, and quoted a number of passages in support of his position. Dr. Robertson had arranged to preach in the evening from the text, ' Christ hath brought life and immortality

[1] T. T. Munger, *The Freedom of Faith*, 265.

to light through the gospel,' and the psalms, hymns, and anthem had been chosen with this text in view. But after the forenoon service he came to me in anxiety and said, 'I must change my subject; if I preach the sermon I intended, Dr. Goold will think I am controverting his teaching.' All afternoon he was restless, evidently thinking over other sermons, but unable to fix on one. When the hour of evening service had come he told me that he was still undecided. I replied, 'Keep to your subject, the choir cannot now change the hymns.' He consented to do so. It was evident that he had`taken the position that immortality was not clearly taught in the Old Testament. With great tact he succeeded in avoiding the appearance of contradiction between him and the morning preacher, by saying in well-chosen words, which I cannot reproduce, something to this effect: 'Doubtless there are references to the doctrine of immortality in the Old Testament, as was so well put before you in the forenoon. But just as he whose death we are this day remembering with sorrow found embedded in the caverns of the earth the dark substance by which he has illuminated the homes of rich and poor in many lands, so did Christ bring to light the doctrine of a future life. The shale was in the earth long before, but it was Dr. Young who revealed its illuminating power. Even so the doctrine of immortality, embedded in Old Testament passages, was practically unrevealed until He came who brought life and immortality to light.'

"I can give you no idea of the beautiful touches by which Dr. Robertson wrought out the thought I have only indicated; but so skilfully was it done that I think no one in the church ever dreamt of anything but completest harmony between the two preachers."[1]

.2. Christ put the copestone on the doctrine of immortality by illustrating it in His own person. He could point to Himself as the living embodiment of His teaching. He came and entered into the living stream of our life. He was linked on to the past; human experience moulded His human character; He goes to the marriage feast; He meets sin, and disease, and death and sorrow; He is buffeted by the waves of this troubled world; He is a man of sorrows and acquainted with grief. And then, as He passed through death, sin and sorrow have no power to leave their marks upon His nature; He corresponds now to all that is spiritual, peaceful, heavenly in human nature. He dwells with

[1] Dr. James Brown, in *Life of W. B. Robertson of Irvine*, 428.

the spirit of man, and passes out of our sight ever to live to make
intercession for us. So it has been, so it is with each of us. God
puts each individual soul into this wide-reaching life, whose tides
sweep by us out of a past lost in the mists of history, and which
eddy away into eternity. We are attached as it were to this
great life and we never can cease to be, or lose our personality.
To this life we correspond as natural bodies; to the life hereafter
we shall correspond as spiritual bodies. And so we draw life
from our surroundings.

¶ Christ makes poetry of the suggestions we see in the world.
The demands we see in human nature He sets to Divine music.
We know simply the letters of the alphabet of life; some lofty
souls can see certain notes of music. He arranges the letters and
the notes in such marvellous melody that the angels burst into
anthems, and the singers by the crystal sea sing a new song, and
the earth hears the echo of heaven's triumph. Death is abolished.
In Christ immortality is revealed. He was dead, and behold, He
is alive for evermore. Because He lives, we shall live also. His
resurrection involves ours. Our continuity is implied in His.
We cannot die while He lives.[1]

¶ In some of the cathedrals of Europe, on Christmas Eve, two
small lights, typifying the Divine and the human nature, are
gradually made to approach one another until they meet and
blend, forming a bright flame. Thus, in Christ, we have the light
of two worlds thrown upon human destiny. Death, as the
extinction of being, cannot be associated with Him; He is life—
its fulness and perfection, and perfect life must be stronger than
death. The whole bearing of Christ towards death, and His
treatment of it, was as one superior to it, and as having no part or
lot in it. He will indeed bow His head and cease to breathe in
obedience to the physical laws of the humanity He shares, but
already He enters the gates of Paradise, not alone but leading a
penitent child of humanity by the hand. And, in order that we
may know He simply changed worlds, He comes back and shows
Himself alive; for He is not here in the world simply to assert
truth, but to enact it.[2]

¶ When Livingstone asked the natives in Central Africa as to
what became of their noble river, they, having no idea of the sea,
replied, " It is lost in the sands." We know another wonderful
river, the river of human life which rushes through these metropolitan streets, spreads far and wide, and flows on through ages—

[1] T. E. Ruth.   [2] T. T. Munger, *The Freedom of Faith*, 268.

the mystic river whose bubbles are cities, whose music is language, whose jewels are thoughts, whose shells are histories. What becomes of this river of life ? Says scepticism sadly, " The clergy-man, the undertaker, and the sexton see the last of it in the sands." But we can never be content with such a solution, which is no solution. The Lord Jesus alone enables us to give a bright inter-pretation to the dark problem. He has brought life and immor-tality to light. He has put into our lips the great cry, " The sea ! The sea ! " Beyond the sands of time we behold gleams of the great bright ocean of eternity, and through the mist comes the music of many waters. Our Lord was manifest in the flesh, He died, was buried, and rose again that He " might deliver all them who through fear of death were all their lifetime subject to bondage." We take our harp from the willow. Our mourners are musicians, our graves are filled with flowers, our epitaphs are hallelujahs.[1]

3. Our future life is secure in Christ. Linked to Him we cannot perish. Christians believe in their own resurrection, because they believe in the resurrection of Christ. But faith does not depend upon—it does not originate in nor is it maintained by —the resurrection of Christ, simply as a historical fact. The resurrection of Jesus is not simply a fact outside of us, guaranteeing in some mysterious way our resurrection in some remote future. It is a present power in the believer. He can say with St. Paul— Christ liveth in me—the risen Christ—the Conqueror of Death— and a part, therefore, is ensured to me in His life and immortality. This is *the* great idea of the New Testament whenever the future life is in view. It is indeed very variously expressed. Sometimes it is *Christ in us*, the hope of glory. Sometimes it is especially connected with the possession, or rather the indwelling, of the Holy Spirit. " If the Spirit of him that raised up Jesus from the dead dwelleth in you, he that raised up Christ Jesus from the dead shall quicken also your mortal bodies through his Spirit that dwelleth in you." It is easy to see that the religious attitude here is precisely what it was in the Old Testament, though, as the revelation is fuller, the faith which apprehends it, and the hope which grows out of it, are richer. Just as union with God guaranteed to the Psalmist a life that would never end, so union with the risen Saviour guaranteed to the Apostles, and guarantees to us, the resurrection triumph over death.

[1] W. L. Watkinson, *The Education of the Heart*, 25.

¶ "*March* 11*th*, 1870.—I have been astounded by a most influential member of the Church saying to me, 'What is it to me whether Christ worked miracles or rose from the dead! We have got the right idea of God through Him. It is enough, that can never perish!' And this truth is like a flower that has grown from a dunghill of lies and myths! Good Lord, deliver me from such conclusions! If the battle has come, let it; but before God I will fight it with those only, be they few or many, who believe in a risen, living Saviour. This revelation of the influence of surface criticism has thrown me back immensely upon all who hold fast by an objective revelation. Nothing can possibly move me from Jesus Christ, the living Saviour, the Divine Saviour, the Atoning Saviour, whatever be the philosophy of that atonement." [1]

¶ The ancients fabled that Orpheus the god of music was drowned, and his lyre lost in the sea; hence water is musical. What the Greeks meant by this legend it is impossible to say; but perhaps they intended it to signify that the secret of harmony has perished from the world. Be that as it may, when the Son of God plunged into this gulf of dark despair, He recovered more than the lost lyre of Orpheus: He gave us again the secret of spiritual and eternal music, whatever may be the confusions and discords of earth and time. [2]

---

[1] *Memoir of Norman Macleod*, ii. 321.
[2] W. L. Watkinson, *The Education of the Heart* 26.

I Know that my Redeemer Liveth.

LITERATURE.

Clifford (J.), *Daily Strength for Daily Living*, 305.
Davidson (A. B.), *Waiting upon God*, 79.
Davies (T.), *Sermons and Homiletical Expositions*, 30.
Lockyer (T. F.), *Seeking a Country*, 41.
Magee (W. C.), *Christ the Light of all Scripture*, 207.
Metcalf (R.), *The Abiding Memory*, 77.
Price (A. C.), *Fifty Sermons*, xi. 209.
Ramage (W.), *Sermons*, 245.
Robertson (F. W.), *Sermons*, 1st Ser., 147.
Spurgeon (C. H.), *Metropolitan Tabernacle Pulpit*, ix. (1863), No. 504 ;
    l. (1904), No. 2909.
Stone (H. E.), *From Behind the Veil*, 89.
Thomas (J.), *Myrtle Street Pulpit*, ii. 49.
Christian World Pulpit, xxx. 188 (Johnson), 345 (Boardman).
Churchman's Pulpit : Easter Day and Season, vii. 294 (Keble).
Homiletic Review, New Ser., xvi. 358 (Davis).
Sermon Year Book, ii. 48 (Skinner).

I Know that my Redeemer Liveth.

But I know that my redeemer liveth,
And that he shall stand up at the last upon the earth:
And after my skin hath been thus destroyed,
Yet from my flesh shall I see God:
Whom I shall see for myself,
And mine eyes shall behold, and not another.
My reins are consumed within me.

                                        Job xix. 25-27.

1. THE author of this book was a poet who felt the iron of suffering pass deeply into his own soul, and had been driven by the cold consolations of well-meaning, though unsympathetic, friends into open revolt against the God of popular imagination. He has fought his way through despair and doubt, if not to clear light on the problem of suffering, yet to a freer and nobler faith in the living God. And in the poem he has opened his heart, and spoken out all the feelings that passed through his soul in his agony of grief, till he found rest again in God.

2. The hero of the poem is depicted as suffering under the load of accumulated sorrows, until he regards death as the only possible release from trouble. Again and again Job returns, fascinated, to this thought. But as he gazes into the misty depths of Sheol, the horror of death seizes him. The place of the dead is

a land of darkness and murk,
A land of thick darkness and chaos,
Where the light itself is like pitch.

It is a land, too, whence there is no return. Therefore in Sheol Job can no longer hope to see the vindication of his rights, but must go down to posterity as a godless man. The thought is intolerable, and he revolts against it. The first gleam of a hope beyond breaks from ch. xiv.—a passage of almost midnight gloom. Job is mourning over man's brief and troublous life and swift, untimely end.   There is hope of the tree, if it be cut down, that it will sprout again.   Its root may be old and decayed, and its stock cut down to the ground ; yet at the scent of water it will bud, and put forth boughs like a fresh, young plant.

> But man dieth, and is laid in the dust ;
> He yieldeth his breath, and is gone.
> As the waters fail from the sea,
> And the river dries up and is vanished,
> Till the heavens be no more, he shall not awake,
> Nor be roused out of his sleep.

But the hope of the tree suggests to the despairing soul a possible hope for man as well.   If man too may die and live again, God may perchance bring him down to Sheol, to hide him there till His wrath is past, and then " appoint him a set time and remember him."   If he could only entertain this hope, he should wait patiently, and endure the cruellest pains, all the days of his warfare, till his release came; and when at last God called, he would answer joyfully, and forget the misery of the past in the bliss of his new life with God.   It is a hope, however, too high for him to grasp; and he is plunged into deeper darkness than before.

> The waters wear the stones,
> The floods wash off the dust ;
> So Thou destroyest man's hope—
> He sleepeth, and riseth no more.
> Thou prevailest against him for ever ;
> Thou changest his face, and dost banish him.

And the lot of the dead man in Sheol is utterly miserable.   He knows nothing more of what passes in this upper sphere.   He cannot follow the fortunes even of his dearest ones.

> His sons are honoured, but he knoweth it not ;
> They are brought low, but he marketh it not.

Nor is the sleep of the dead unbroken rest.   He sleeps—" perchance to dream ! "   Though he knows nothing of his friends on earth.

> Yet his own flesh hath pain,
> And his own soul mourneth.

The sorely wounded sufferer seeks to move his friends to pity by the spectacle of all his accumulated woes: his glory stripped away, his hope plucked up by the root, his path enshrouded in darkness, his dearest friends estranged from him, and no one to hear his cry and bring him redress, for it is God that hath "subverted his rights." But the friends are cold and pitiless as God Himself. In his despair Job turns for his vindication to posterity. If only he could write his defence in a book, or engrave it on the rock with iron stylus and beaten lead, future generations would read it, and judge justly, and attest his righteousness. But the record on the rocks is impossible. Thus he turns once more to his Witness in heaven.

> But I know that my Goel liveth,
>   And as Afterman on my dust
> He will stand as Witness before me,
>   And lift up His voice in my cause.

> Then God shall I see in spirit,
>   Mine own eyes will look on His face;
> No more estranged shall I see Him.
>   My reins are consumed at the thought.[1]

¶ It has been wisely said that "there is a Gethsemane in every noble life." Sometimes our path seems like a lane full of windings, where steep banks shut out light and air. But if we look up, we can never fail to see the fair blue hills of our Land of Promise rising high against the sky. The thorny wreath is sharp, but we shall exchange it by and by for that crown of glory which fadeth not away. . . . Christ's crown of thorns broke into blossom long ago, and its sweet odours of healing float through our daily lives, and are wafted over the earth by every wind that blows. So shall our sorrows burst into bloom, if only we are patient, steadfast, immovable, always abounding in the work of the Lord. . . . The sweetness and sanctity of the Christian life lie in the firm conviction that a gentle, unfaltering, though invisible hand is weaving for us that crown of thorns which we are bidden to wear.[2]

¶ We reach here the Mont Blanc of this poem of poems; the highest range tracked by this inspired and victorious hero. There in his Gethsemane he triumphs. From that moment "the prince of this world comes, and finds nothing in him" out of which he

---

[1] A. R. Gordon, *The Poets of the Old Testament*, 204.   [2] Henry White.

can extract a ray of hope for his attacks. When the cup, charged to the full with bitterness, is in the sufferer's hand, and he is ready to say, "If possible let it pass on to another," an access of power arrives, enabling him to hold it with a firm grasp, and say, "Not my will, but Thine, O living Redeemer, shall be done. I am convinced of the blessedness of the final issue. I am content. I am victorious." [1]

¶ An interesting analogue to Job's solution of the problem may be found in Sophocles' ripest tragedies. Æschylus had regarded misfortune as the penalty paid for wrong-doing, with the view of working out the sinner's moral discipline. On the other hand, Sophocles views suffering *sub specie aeternitatis*, in the light of the eternal harmony of things. Thus the grievous sorrows Philoctetes had to bear are conceived to have been laid upon him "by the care of one of the gods," that he might be held in reserve, and braced in character, for his appointed task in the overthrow of Troy; and when Heracles at length reveals the purpose of the gods, he accepts his destiny with courage and joy. The tragedy of Œdipus ends in the same atmosphere of peace. The sorely-afflicted hero finds himself now reconciled to heaven, surrounded by the love of devoted children, and honoured by the friendship of kindly Athens and its chivalrous king, and gently yields his life to the touch of the gods, his destiny thus finding "a perfect end." In both these dramas, then, Sophocles "views the problem of human suffering with the eye of faith, and in proportion as he sets before him an ideal of an all-powerful Divinity, who is merciful, loving, and gracious, so does it become easy for him to bear patiently with the evil and suffering in the world, in the serene belief that, were man's vision wide enough, he would see joy and sorrow to be parts of one harmonious whole." [2]

In considering this great declaration, let us note—

I. The Meaning of Job's Words.
II. The Faith that they enshrine.
III. The Ground of Job's Conviction.

I.

JOB'S WORDS.

In interpreting this passage we must distinguish between what it meant to Job and what it means to us who are able to

---

[1] J. Clifford, *Daily Strength for Daily Living*, 308.
[2] Mrs. Adam, in *Early Ideals of Righteousness*, 42.

turn upon it the blaze of the light of New Testament revelation,
where life and immortality are brought to light in the Gospel.
In thinking of Job, we must bear in mind the gloomy, hopeless
doctrine of Sheol in which he had been nurtured, and which he had
expressed so often. Even after the previous outburst of xiv. 13,
we find him still speaking of Sheol in xvi. 22 as the place whence
he shall not return. He could hardly pass suddenly from such
views into the *full* meaning of xix. 25 as *we* interpret it. And the
subsequent discourses render it evident that he did not. If Job
had realized all that we do in this text, the discourse would have
ceased here; for this is the last word that even the New Testament can say. But we do not find any change in Job's gloomy
outlook. In fact, the third cycle is, in some respects, most
pessimistic of all. Probably Job intended little more in this
verse than he did in xiv. 13, that is, to express a firm conviction
that God would vindicate him, and even if it should be delayed
until his spirit had gone to Sheol and the flesh rotted from his
bones, yet the vindication must come. God would call up his
spirit from its abode of gloom, and he would answer, and would
witness his vindication on the earth. But this is a germinal
truth. It was intended by the Spirit of God to be so. The Old
Testament prophets and sages often wrote far more profoundly
than they knew. And this text was one of those which, pondered
over by the saints of later days, opened up with new meaning,
until it led to the brighter hopes of later Judaism, many of which
received the sign-manual and royal imprimatur of the Great
Master, whose life and Resurrection are here faintly foreshadowed.

> Could I but see His face,
>   And hear His voice,
>   Oh! then I think
> My heart would well forth love,
>   As from a fountain full,
>   And service would be my delight!
>
> Yet if He showed His face
>   And spake to me,
>   Should I in truth
> Arise to love and serve
> Him as I ween? Alas!
> I trust not my deceitful heart,

E'en if I saw and heard
       Him as I wish,
       Would not dark doubts
Ere long invade my soul?
And I should wondering ask—
Was't true that He appeared and spake?

E'en so, my Lord, 'tis so;
       And therefore I
       Will be content,
That Thou Thyself reveal
By making strong, true, glad
My foolish, sad, inconstant heart.

And when my sinful heart
       Is purified,
       Made fair and fit
For Thine abode: Oh! then
My Lord, show Thou Thy face
And speak: so shall I love and serve.[1]

1. What are we to understand by the term " redeemer "?
We find that the word is frequently used of God as the deliverer
of His people out of captivity, and also as the deliverer of
individuals from distress.   Among men the *Goel* was the nearest
blood-relation, on whom it lay to perform certain offices in connexion with the deceased whose Goel he was, particularly to
avenge his blood, if he had been unjustly slain.   Job here means
God is his Goel.   The passage stands in close relation with ch. xvi.
18, 19, where he means God is his " witness " and " sponsor " or
representative.   It is probable, therefore, that there is an allusion
to the Goel among men—Job has in God a Goel who liveth.
This Goel will vindicate his rights against the wrong both of men
and of God.   At the same time, this vindication is regarded less
as an avenging of him, at least on others, than as a manifestation
of his innocence.   This manifestation can be made only by God's
appearing and showing the true relation in which Job stands to
Him, and by Job's seeing God.   For his distress lay in God's
hiding His face from him, and his redemption must come through
his again beholding God in peace.   Thus the ideas of Goel and
redeemer virtually coincide.

[1] D. W. Simon in *Life*, by F. J. Powicke.

¶ "Whoever alters the work of my hand," says the conqueror called Sargon, "destroys my constructions, pulls down the walls which I have raised—may Asshur, Nineb, Raman and the great gods who dwell there pluck his name and seed from the land and let him sit bound at the feet of his foe." Invocation of the gods in this manner was the only resource of him who in that far past feared oblivion and knew that there was need to fear. But to a higher God, in words of broken eloquence, Job is made to commit his cause, seeing beyond the perishable world the imperishable remembrance of the Almighty. So a Hebrew poet breathed into the wandering air of the desert that brave hope which afterwards, far beyond his thought, was in Israel to be fulfilled.[1]

2. Job says that this redeemer liveth. The term "liveth" is emphatic. Job may die, but his Vindicator cannot die. The order of the world, of which Job has caught a glimpse in his own life, is eternal. Job's cause, the truth for which he so strenuously fought, is undying;.for it is the expression of an infinite life which rules above all mortal destiny. Job sets the life of his Vindicator over against his own death. It is by bearing this opposition in mind, by emphasizing the undying life of the Vindicator over against the mortality of the vindicated that we see the fulness of the hope to which Job rises at this point in his conflict.

¶ Historical events and characters to some extent sway the hearts of men. Trafalgar and Nelson quicken "every man this day to do his duty." But Nelson is dead, and Trafalgar among the things of the past. Waterloo and Wellington kindle a memory of uusurpassed British bravery, but Wellington is no more, and Waterloo is not a living force in the national life of to-day. Calvary lives because its Hero lives, "I am he that liveth and was dead, and behold, I am alive for evermore. Amen. And have the keys of hell and of death." He further says, "I live, and ye shall live also." The widow says of her departed husband, "Had he been alive, things would have been very different with me from what they are." The orphan says of the sainted father, "Had he been alive, I should not have been compelled to ask you this favour." Faith leans on a living bosom, and draws its comfort from a living heart.[2]

> O Thou the Lord and Maker of life and light!
> Full heavy are the burdens that do weigh
> Our spirits earthward, as through twilight gray
> We journey to the end and rest of night;

[1] R. A. Watson, *The Book of Job*, 232. [2] T. Davies, *Sermons*, 35.

Tho' well we know to the deep inward sight,
Darkness is but Thy shadow, and the day
Where Thou art never dies, but sends its rays
Through the wide universe with restless might.

O Lord of Light, steep Thou our souls in Thee!
That when the daylight trembles into shade,
And falls the silence of mortality,
And all is done, we shall not be afraid,
But pass from light to light; from earth's dull gleam
Into the very heart and heaven of our dream.[1]

3. Job looks for a vindication of his character, when this Redeemer standing upon his dust takes up his cause. It can scarcely be that Job has any hope of deliverance in this life. He regards himself as already on the verge of the grave: every temporal prospect has vanished. Besides, if this were his expectation, he would be abandoning his own position, and adopting that of his friends. Job then looks for a vindication beyond the grave. Does he mean that apart from his body, stripped of flesh, he will see God; or that, clothed in a new body, looking out from restored flesh, he will yet see God? The expression "from my flesh," "out of my flesh," is ambiguous; and we can judge of Job's thought only from the context and general scope of the book. But when we look at these, we conclude that what Job has in view is a real spiritual vision and not a resurrection of the flesh.

This corresponds best to the whole tone and movement of his thought. For obviously, he is expecting a Divine vindication of his integrity only after he lies in the dust; and it is not likely that, with this great hope suddenly invading his mind and taking instant but full possession of it, he would at once begin to speculate on whether or not, when he had shuffled off the mortal coil in which he was entangled, he should be clothed upon with "flesh" in some new and higher form. Such a speculation would have been well-nigh impossible at such a time. That Job, rising from his long agony, his long inquest, to a sudden recognition of a great light of hope burning behind the dark curtains of death, and so far streaming through them as to give him courage to

[1] R. Watson Gilder.

sustain a burden otherwise intolerable, should instantly fall into a curious speculation about "in the body," or "out of the body," would be contrary to all the laws which, as experience proves, govern the human mind at a crisis such as that at which he had arrived. Most probably he neither knew when, or in what form, the great deliverance for which he hoped would be vouchsafed him, nor did he curiously inquire how, or in what form, it would find him when it came. All he knew was that, somehow, after his mortal body had been destroyed, God would redeem him; but whether he would then be in a body or out of a body, he cannot tell and does not speculate.

¶ "Why does He not," as Carlyle said in his blind agony, "Why does He not do more?" Why does He not turn back the rolling seas of wickedness, construct a world without earthquakes, states without injustice and oppression, cities without knavery, villages without poverty and disease, homes without envy and disorder, and churches without selfishness and impurity—that is to say, why does not God make a world of puppets, and arrange everything on the principles of *mechanics*, making men perforce good and pure and true, as a well-made and properly-regulated watch is constructed to keep time with the sun; instead of creating man on the basis of a sovereignly free and dignifying choice, the necessity of personal virtue, the supremacy of law, the discipline of experience, and the evolution of the riches of character by trial? "Take for an example of suffering and patience, the prophets who spake in the name of the Lord. Behold, we call them blessed which endured; ye have heard of the patience of Job, and have seen the end of the Lord, how that the Lord is full of pity and merciful." Resist the diabolical sophistry which identifies a cloudless sky with an existing sun, affirms the unseen to be the non-existent, and the unhappy to be the unholy. God is love. That is His nature, the essence of His being; not an accident, an occasional emotion, or a passing mood; and therefore, He is, as Job saw and felt, the Redeemer and Vindicator of all souls that sincerely seek Him and diligently serve Him; the guarantee that defeated and humiliated and oppressed man will be set free, and exalted to behold the triumph of eternal righteousness; and the witness that man is at present, and here in this world, scarred and defaced with evil though it be, the object of God's pitiful sympathy, redeeming care, and constant protection.[1]

[1] J. Clifford, *Daily Strength for Daily Living*, 317.

Why should I wish to see God better than this day?
I see something of God each hour of the twenty-four, and
    each moment then,
In the faces of men and women I see God, and in my own
    face in the glass,
I find letters from God dropt in the street, and every one is
    signed by God's name,
And I leave them where they are, for I know that where-
    soe'er I go,
Others will punctually come for ever and ever.[1]

4. In spite of death Job holds that in some way he will
witness his own vindication. By the phrase, "mine own eyes
shall behold, not those of another," he does not, of course, mean to
assert that no one but himself will be cognizant of his vindication; but that, come when it may, he himself must be cognizant
of it; that, even though it should come when men account him
dead, he shall be alive unto God and to the action of God on
his behalf.

5. Job pants for this manifestation, until he almost faints.
The words "my reins consume me" are an exclamation, meaning,
"I faint." The reins are the seat of the deepest feelings and
experiences, especially of those toward God. Job began with
expressing his assurance that he should see God, but as he
proceeds, so vivid is his hope that it becomes almost reality, the
intensity of this thought creates an ecstatic condition of mind, in
which the vision of God seems almost realized, and he faints in
the presence of it.

¶ There is a deep pathos in the way in which Job assures
himself of his personal participation in the coming triumph of
moral truth. He says, with pathetic repetition and fond emphasis,
"I shall see God; whom I shall see for myself, and mine eyes
shall behold, and not another." Then, as though overcome by the
glorious vision, he ejaculates, "My reins are consumed within me."
Parallel to this are the words of the hymn—

> I thirst, I faint, I die, to prove
> The greatness of redeeming love,
>   The love of Christ to me.[2]

[1] Walt Whitman.
[2] J. Thomas, *Myrtle Street Pulpit*, ii. 57.

II.

JOB'S FAITH.

"I know that my redeemer liveth." It seems clear that in expressing himself thus Job attains to the thought of a future life, a life of blessedness in the presence of God. But this is not an easy thought for him. It is new and unfamiliar and strange. It is a vision that breaks upon him for a moment and then disappears. If he could only have held it fast, if he could have planted his foot upon it, then his trouble had been gone, the mental perplexity would have disappeared, and he would have been able to rest in patience till the great vision came. But he gets only a passing glimpse of the truth; the clouds soon gather, and he is plunged back again into his fear and perplexity.

1. Job represents humanity struggling into the light of a larger faith. Great moral truths are never discovered by nations or races, but by individual men. And yet even the wisest and most forward-looking men but rarely discover a truth much in advance of the thoughts and yearnings of their own race, in their own generation. As a rule, the new truth is in the air of the time; many have some dim consciousness or presentiment of it, and are groping after it, if haply they may find it. And at last one man, one happy man, prepared for the achievement by the peculiar bent of his nature, or gifted with the vision and the faculty Divine, or driven onward by peculiar personal experiences into untrodden regions of thought, grasps the present and widely-diffused but evasive truth, and compels it into a definite and permanent form.

(1) Of this common process of discovery we probably have an illustration in the case of Job. There are many indications that, both in the patriarchal age, *i.e.* the time of Job himself, and in the Solomonic age, *i.e.* the time of the Poet to whom we owe this *divina commedia*, the thought of a better and more enduring life, a strictly *moral* life, hidden from men by the darkness of death, was in the atmosphere; that the best and highest minds were reaching after it and yearning for it. And in Job this general thought took form, this common yearning rose to articulate

expression, this widespread hope became a living and vitalizing
faith. His personal experience, the wrongs and calamities he
endured, the doubts and conflicts these miseries bred in his heart,
prepared and qualified him to become the interpreter of the
general heart of his time, to discover the truth which alone could
satisfy it. It was simply impossible for him, since he believed
the great Ruler of men to be just and unchangeable, to conclude
that the God whom he had done nothing to offend was really
hostile to him, though He seemed hostile, or that He would
always continue to *seem* hostile to him, never acknowledging his
integrity. And as he had lost all hope of being redeemed and
vindicated in this life, as therefore he could no longer admit the
present to be a strictly retributive life, he was compelled to look
for, till he discovered, a retributive life beyond " the bourn."
Fading out of this world, he looks for, and finds, a juster and a
better world to come.

> Then what this world to thee, my heart?
> Its gifts nor feed thee nor can bless.
> Thou hast no owner's part
> In all its fleetingness.

> The flame, the storm, the quaking ground,
> Earth's joy, earth's terror, nought is thine,
> Thou must but hear the sound
> Of the still voice divine.

> O priceless art! O princely state!
> E'en while by sense of change opprest,
> Within to antedate
> Heaven's Age of fearless rest.[1]

(2) The life of humanity on earth is exactly typified by all
that part of the drama of Job's life which lies between its
prologue and its epilogue, between its supernatural beginning
and its supernatural ending. Through all that long story of a
man—full, as it is, of tragic interest—what is the very sorest
trial to which it has ever been subjected, to which it still is and
always must be subject ? It is not merely the calamities, the
sorrows of life, which come to all; it is the added suffering of the

[1] J. H. Newman, *Verses on Various Occasions*, 20.

mystery of these sorrows. It is the thought of the apparent
carelessness and capriciousness with which the joys and the pains
of existence seem to be scattered among the children of the
common Father. It is that suffering in this life seems to be
neither penal nor yet remedial, but seems to come, as the rains of
heaven fall and the winds blow, on just and unjust alike. It is
that there is so much apparent waste and gratuitous suffering, so
much purely useless and purposeless agony. It is that human
lives seem wasted by myriads, poured out on the earth like water,
seemingly unregarded, unpitied, unaided, unrequited. Suffering
humanity, wherever it still retains its faith in a Divine Lord and
Ruler, is still haunted by this question: "Why is it thus with
us?" Like Job, too, it has been sorely vexed by false comforters,
would-be friends who preach and lecture and rebuke and exhort,
but who cannot console, because they cannot solve that enigma
with which every sufferer finds himself confronted: "Why, if
God is good and just, does He thus afflict me?" Surely the
analogy is perfect here. Humanity seems to have still the old
choice presented to it: to curse God and die; or to die believing
in and blessing Him, and yet with a thousand reasons why it
should not believe in, why it should not bless or praise, the Being
who thus seems causelessly to afflict it. And the message—the
inspired message of this type of our race to all who strive to
believe in a Father, though they have no visible and sensible
proof of a Father's love—is this: "Believe as I did, although such
proof be lacking. Believe as I did, in spite of all the seeming
disproof that you see and feel. Believe that God is your Father;
believe that He will—indeed, must, because He is your righteous
Father—do for you what He has done for me. Believe that for
you, too, there is an avenger; one who will yet give you victory
over all that now afflicts you. Believe that you shall yet see for
yourselves the loving Father who is hidden from you now.
Believe that a day is coming for you when you will discover that
there was a need for all you mourn under; when you will receive
from your Father double for all that He has done unto you."

> The throb of Thy infinite life I feel
>   In every beat of my heart!
> Upon me hast Thou set eternity's seal!
>   For ever alive, as Thou art.

I know not thy mystery, O my God,
  Nor yet what my own life means,
That feels after Thee, through the mould and the sod,
  And the darkness that intervenes.

But I know that I live, since I hate the wrong,
  The glory of truth can see;
Can cling to the right with a purpose strong,
  Can love and can will with Thee.[1]

(3) The cry of the patriarch is the utterance of the desire of humanity.   But it is more ; it is a prophecy; it points forward to the completed drama of another life, in which once more appears, as in this older drama, the supernatural controlling the natural.   Once more we see, behind the veil of the material and the visible, the Divine power that rules and overrules all things for good.   We see once more a righteous sufferer, holy, harmless, undefiled, whose whole life was spent in absolutely perfect submission to the will of his Father in Heaven, and who was yet a man of sorrows and acquainted with grief, and whose sorest sorrow and deepest grief sprang from the intensity of His sympathy with His sorrowing and suffering fellow-men.   We see Him rejected, despised, hated of those He loved so well, dying at last a death of shame and agony, which was regarded by those who inflicted it as the just punishment for offences against the laws of His country and His God, and we hear from Him in the moment of His supremest agony just that appeal to the justice and to the love of God which suffering has wrung from the heart of the righteous sufferer in all ages: " My God, my God ! why hast thou forsaken me ? " [2]

¶ Just as science tells us that each order in creation—each successive type in the long evolution of living creatures—gives, in some rudimentary organ or function, its mute mysterious prophecy of the higher type that is to follow it, so that each type is at once a prophecy and a fulfilment of a prophecy, an accomplishment of a past foreshadowing, a foreshadowing of a coming future—so in the slow evolution of redeemed humanity, all along its course, there may be seen like tokens and prophecies of its completion; prophecies all the more real, because they are not read in words, but in facts and events ; profound analogies,

[1] Lucy Larcom.   [2] W. C. Magee, *Christ the Light of all Scripture*, 223.

marvellous correspondences between what has been and what is, and again between what is and what we are told is yet to be; successive and ever clearer indications of the one great design that runs through all the ages; prophecies, as the buds are of the spring—as the flowers are of the summer—as the dawn is of the sunrise; prophecies which are, therefore, a far weightier evidence for Christianity than any number of merely verbal predictions, because they are predictions which could not possibly have been interpolations of later date, made to fit the events after they had occurred; prophecies entirely free from questions of dates, or authorship of books, or verbal niceties of translation, because they are interwoven through the whole structure of the sacred books—nay, throughout the whole structure of human history—of human life itself—which they illustrate and explain. As the cross in the ground-plan of some great cathedral shows that its idea from the first must have been Christian, whereas the external cross placed upon it might have been but the after-thought of later builders; so this prophetic structure of all sacred history is in itself a far greater, a far more certain word of prophecy than any single word or words of this or that individual prophet.[1]

2. Job turned from the harsh theories of men to the mercy of a Divine Vindicator. He had expected sympathy from his friends. They were men of his own age and standing; they were religious men, men of very sincere, though perhaps of somewhat narrow, piety; and, more than that, they were wise, thoughtful, experienced men, accustomed to trace the working of God in providence and to find the principles by which His dealings with men were regulated. They were men with whom it had been the pleasure in happier days of Job to converse upon the great mysteries of human life and destiny. And these men, when they heard of their friend's trouble, did not desert him. They were mindful of the claims of friendship. They knew that Job needed their help, and so they made an appointment, and rose up each man from his place, and came to see Job and to comfort him in his affliction, and sat with him there seven days and seven nights in silence, respecting the sacredness of his grief. And yet we know that these men, so good, so faithful, so promising, failed Job utterly in the hour of his trouble. He had to say that they were like a deceitful watercourse, which the travelling caravan in the desert

[1] W. C. Magee, *Christ the Light of all Scripture*, 215.

hastens to in order that it may be refreshed with water, and finds that the water has disappeared. So they had been to him. He had waited for their coming, he had waited after they came for their speaking, and when they spoke, and when he was able to hear the thoughts that were in their hearts with regard to him, he found that they were miserable comforters, that they could give him no help. And it is just then, when he has touched this lowest depth of despair, that he comes to see how near he is to the fountain of all hope and consolation. Why should he wish this impossible wish? What good would it do him to have his words recorded and read by future generations? Ah! was it not that deep in his heart, though he hardly knew it, there was a conviction of a day of witness somewhere else than upon earth, that those thoughts and words which had passed through his mind were all known to One? And that thought now breaks through his darkness, and he leaps up to meet it with this exclamation: " But I know that my redeemer liveth, and that he shall stand up at the last upon the earth." It is Job's appeal from the sympathy of man, which was refused, to the sympathy of God, which at last he dared to claim and to trust.

> Into the heaven of Thy heart, O God,
>   I lift up my life, like a flower;
> Thy light is deep, and Thy love is broad,
>   And I am not the child of an hour.
>
> As a little blossom is fed from the whole
>   Vast depths of unfathomed air,
> Through every fibre of thought my soul
>   Reaches forth, in Thyself to share.
>
> I dare to say unto Thee, my God,
>   Who hast made me to climb so high,
> That I shall not crumble away with the clod;
>   I am Thine, and I cannot die!

¶ There have been four typical notes of despair in the region of literature. The first and most intense is the voice of Omar Khayyám. It is despair absolute, despair of life all round, despair whose only relief is to drown itself in wine. The second is the Book of Ecclesiastes. I would call it despair of *results*. It does not deny that it is a pleasant thing to see the light of the sun; it does not dispute that there is a time to dance as well as a time to weep; but it asks, What is the good of it? does it not all end in vanity? The third is the cry of Pascal. It is despair of everything finite—finite reason, finite love, finite pleasure; the only possible joy is joy in God. The fourth is that dramatic portraiture which we call the Book of Job. I would describe it as the despair of old theories. It is the least despondent of the group. It does not say that the world is bad; it does not say that life is vanity; it does not even say that finite things cannot bring joy. What it does say is that all the past theories to explain the evils of the universe have been utterly powerless to account for these evils, but none of them is fit to sustain the weight of human woes, and that all of them put together are inadequate to wipe the tear from a single eye.[1]

3. Job turned from the God of providence to the God of his conscience. Job had no idea of a distinction in the Godhead, such as we have. This was not yet revealed to him. And what he says of his Redeemer, he says of God generally. A fuller revelation has taught us that God the Redeemer is God manifested in His Son; and what Job says here of his Redeemer standing on the dust is fulfilled in the Son. Yet this distinction, as already said, was not one known to Job. God is his Redeemer. In the next verse he himself explains this to be his meaning: "I shall see God." He shall vindicate him against the wrongs which he suffers, against the suspicions of men, against the aspersions of Satan; yes, and against another thing—against the hardships that have fallen upon him from the general providence of God, where evil and disease and death are now elements of the current of events.

One of the most singular positions into which Job is driven by the riddles of his history is this: he divides God into two. One God, the God of outer providence, who rules, and whom events obey, persecutes him, holds him guilty, and refuses, with ears obdurately closed, to listen to the appeals of His creature for a hearing and an adjudication: "Oh that I knew where I might find him! that I might come unto his place! I would fill my mouth with arguments. Wherefore hidest thou thy face, and holdest me for thine enemy?" But behind all this is a God who knows his innocence, a heart conscious of his rectitude: "My

---

[1] George Matheson, *The Representative Men of the Bible*, 350.

witness is in heaven, and he who can bear testimony to me is on high." And the suffering saint appeals to the one against the other, from the providence of God to the heart of God, from the Ruler of the universe to the gracious Redeemer: "Mine eye poureth out tears unto God; that he would maintain the right of a man with God, and of a son of man with his neighbour!"

¶ There are strange riddles in life, strange mysteries of providence, irreconcilable with our ideas of God—the miseries of the just, early deaths, earthquakes and shipwrecks swallowing up innumerable lives. Our spirits are bounded by iron walls on every side, cabined and confined; and we are mostly content to have it so. We are so familiar now with mystery that we are scarcely stirred by the most appalling occurrences; we are so used to the inexplicable, and so absorbed in what is around us, that the narrow limits of our knowledge hardly trouble us. But to an eagle spirit like Job's this caging was unbearable; and he spread his wings and dashed himself against the bars of his cage demanding knowledge—resolved to come even unto God's place, and pluck out the mystery from the darkness; demanding that the events of God's providence should be made to correspond with this idea of God, and sure that if he know not now he shall know hereafter, when God will descend from the heavens, and stand upon the earth, to unravel the mysteries of his life here, and to proclaim his innocence and God-fearing way.[1]

¶ Wherever a landscape-painter is placed, if he paints faithfully, he will have continually to paint effects of mist. Intense clearness, whether in the North after or before rain, or in some moments of twilight in the South, is always, as far as I am acquainted with natural phenomena, a notable thing. Mist of some sort, or mirage, or confusion of light, or of cloud, are the general facts; the distance may vary in different climates at which the effects of mist begin, but they are always present; and therefore in all probability it is meant that we should enjoy them. Nor does it seem to me in any wise difficult to understand why they should be thus appointed for enjoyment. In former parts of this work we were able to trace a certain delightfulness in every visible feature of natural things which was typical of any great spiritual truth; surely, therefore, we need not wonder now that mist and all its phenomena have been made delightful to us, since our happiness as thinking beings must depend on our being content to accept only partial knowledge, even in those matters which chiefly concern us. If we insist upon perfect intelligibility

[1] A. B. Davidson, *Waiting upon God*, 86.

and complete declaration in every moral subject, we shall
instantly fall into misery of unbelief. Our whole happiness and
power of energetic action depend upon our being able to breathe
and live in the cloud ; content to see it opening here and closing
there ; rejoicing to catch, through the thinnest films of it, glimpses
of stable and substantial things ; but yet perceiving a nobleness
even in the concealment, and rejoicing that the kindly veil is
spread where the untempered light might have scorched us, or the
infinite clearness wearied.[1]

> "Only the Dark ! . . . Only the Mystery ! . . ."
>   He said. "Only beyond, above, before ! . . .
>   Only—O Captives of the wave-walled shore !—
>   Only the incommensurable sea ! . . .
> Only, for eyes that all too wisely see
>   The sun at midday, and are blind therefore,
>   Only the Dark—where, lambent to the core,
>   Gyre the great stars' deepening galaxy ! . . .
> Only of ignorance the ancient wrong ;
>   Only of life the viewless counterpart ;
>   Only of truth the secret undivined ;
> Only—new ranges for the feet of song,
>   New loves of the inextinguishable heart,
>   New powers of the imperishable mind ! . . ."[2]

4. Job turns from the present to the future, from his present
misery and perplexity to a coming vindication. For, after all, as
Job would have said to himself, this horrid confusion and contradiction must come to an end. There are not two Gods. The God
who deals with me so harshly in providence and the God who
speaks to me in my heart are one Being, and He must make His
ways plain ; He must reveal Himself, and declare Himself to be
upon my side. Where that will take place, or how, or in what
state of being, or whether in the body or out of the body, Job could
not have told ; but somehow and somewhere in the future God will
be seen, God will vindicate his case, and Job will be there to see
Him.

¶ God is better to us than our best desires, and gives a larger
blessing than our fullest prayers. The incised rock and molten
lead are not to hand, but a place is given to the suffering preacher
in that "finer world of books within the world," yea, in that *finest*

---

[1] Ruskin, *Modern Painters* (*Works*, vi. 89).

[2] George Cabot Lodge, "The Noctambulist" (*Poems and Dramas*, ii. 154).

book-world of all—the Bible—so that, instead of speaking in one language, he speaks in hundreds, and where he might have reached the eyes of only a few solitary pilgrims he now addresses the hearts of myriads and shall have an increasing congregation for evermore. "God is not unrighteous to *forget* our work of faith and labour of love," and fervency of missionary desire ; but treats us with ineffable generosity, and rewards our poor and faltering work with unsearchable riches—

> No life is lost, no hope is vain,
>   No prayer without a sequent deed ;
> He turns all seeming loss to gain,
>   And finds a soil for every seed.
> Some fleeting glance He doth endow,
>   He sanctifies some casual word,
> Unconscious gifts His children show,
>   For all is potent with the Lord.[1]

III.

JOB'S CONVICTION.

1. "I know." Job holds fast the living truth in his own life, and in so doing, lays fast hold of God. He will not deny the clear convictions of his spirit within him, and take refuge in the conventional platitudes of his friends. Their utterances are honoured and hoary, and sanctioned by high authority. The canons of the Fathers and the visions of the orthodox are set in array against him ; and he has nothing to set against them except his consciousness of passionate sincerity and great living convictions of righteousness that have taken his life by storm, and made it their own. Yet this is enough. It is the living man, not the formulated creed, that stands nearest to God. In the truth that lived and conquered in his own life Job became assured of the living supremacy of the God that would vindicate that truth.

Job's assurance is based on his own past experience, on his life with God, on his consciousness of being a God-fearing man, and on his ineradicable convictions in regard to the nature of God and His relations to men. Job's circumstances cause his principle to appear in its barest form : the human spirit is conscious of fellow-

[1] J. Clifford, *Daily Strength for Daily Living*, 323.

ship with God, and this fellowship, from the nature of God, is a thing imperishable, and, in spite of obscurations, it must yet be fully manifested by God. This principle, grasped with convulsive earnestness in the prospect of death, became the Hebrew doctrine of immortality. This doctrine was but the necessary corollary of religion. In this life on earth the true relations of men and God were felt to be realized; and the Hebrew faith of immortality— never a belief in the mere existence of the soul after death, for the lowest popular superstition assumed this—was a faith that the dark and mysterious event of death should not interrupt the life of the person with God enjoyed in this world.[1]

¶ You cannot miss the ring of conviction in the man's speech. It resounds in every line, and fills the air with its thrilling music. He says what he knows. He believes, and therefore speaks. It is the grand outleap of his whole soul in emphatic declaration, defiant faith, and fearless appeal, "rising with the aspiration of a flame, the beneficence of a fountain," and the certainty of unclouded midday sunshine. "*I know.*" It is not desire or caprice, wish or will, faith or hope, but unwavering, absolute knowledge, whose voice arrests our listening ear, and directs our expectant thought.[2]

¶ By Reason the limits of the finite may be transcended in knowledge, as for the dying saint they are in practice, and men may be certain that, could they comprehend as God comprehends, they should see the Eternal made manifest through the fleeting shadows of time. For there is but one Single Subject within which all knowledge and all reality fall. With and in that Single Subject philosophy and faith alike assure us that we are one. And so when his simple creed, pictorial, it may be, but symbolical of the deeper meaning of reality, bids the humblest soul in his greatest and last extremity be assured that his Redeemer liveth, it may be that there has come to him an insight in form only different from that of the profoundest thinker.[3]

> Jesus my Redeemer lives,
> Christ my trust is dead no more;
> In the strength this knowledge gives
> Shall not all my fears be o'er,
> Though the night of Death be fraught
> Still with many an anxious thought?

[1] A. B. Davidson, *Job*, 293. [2] J. Clifford, *Daily Strength for Daily Living*, 312.
[3] Lord Haldane, *The Pathway to Reality*.

Jesus my Redeemer lives,
  And His life I once shall see;
Bright the hope this promise gives,
  Where He is I too shall be.
Shall I fear then ?   Can the Head
Rise and leave the members dead ?

Close to Him my soul is bound
  In the bonds of Hope enclasp'd;
Faith's strong hand this hold hath found,
  And the Rock hath firmly grasp'd;
And no ban of death can part
From our Lord the trusting heart.[1]

¶ Starting with the existence of an all-strong, all-wise, and all-loving God, Browning endeavours to prove the doctrine of a future life by pointing to the incompleteness of the present one. Infinite wisdom united with Omnipotence cannot make anything imperfect; but man in his earthly life is imperfect; therefore that life can only be a part of a scheme which is as yet unrevealed in its entirety :

                    I search but cannot see
What purpose serves the soul that strives, or world it tries
Conclusions with, unless the fruit of victories
Stay one and all stored-up and guaranteed its own
For ever !

If it be answered that, for all we know, the life of humanity as a whole, in its gradual development towards an as yet unconceived end, may be perfect in itself, without the need of a future life for individuals, Browning would rejoin that in the temple which God builds, not merely the edifice itself, but every separate stone composing it, must be without spot or blemish; for He is not subject to human limitations, and need not sacrifice the part to the whole. Consequently, Browning believed that if the individual's earthly life can be shown to be incomplete, the existence of Heaven is proved.[2]

2. Job reached his conviction by the painful path of suffering. As we look back upon the history, and as we read the book, we can see in what way Job was a gainer by his discipline.   And we find it in these verses if we find it in any part of the book.   It

---

[1] *Lyra Germanica*, 93.
[2] A. C. Pigou, *Robert Browning as a Religious Teacher*, 55.

was just this, that he had learned a new view of God. He had learned a great new truth. He had not perhaps been able to grasp it as fully as he would afterwards, but it had dawned upon him, this thought of God as a Father and a God who would reveal Himself more fully in a future life; and the words that were wrung from him in that hour of his deepest trouble were put here for the admonition of all the ages; and saints of God who came after him, and followed sympathetically his history and his words, saw there a new light, a light that was strange to them, as it was to him, a light upon the far-distant horizon that cheered their souls through those dark ages that were to elapse until the coming of Christ. The dim and uncertain light led them on till at last the Sun of Righteousness came, bringing life and immortality to light.

¶ On any morning of the year, how many pious supplications, do you suppose, are uttered throughout educated Europe for "light"? How many lips at least pronounce the word, and, perhaps, in the plurality of instances, with some distinct idea attached to it? It is true the speakers employ it only as a metaphor. But why is their language thus metaphorical? If they mean merely to ask for spiritual knowledge or guidance, why not say so plainly, instead of using this jaded figure of speech? No boy goes to his father when he wants to be taught, or helped, and asks his father to give him "light." He asks what he wants— advice or protection. Why are not we also content to ask our Father for what we want, in plain English?

The metaphor, you will answer, is put into our mouths, and felt to be a beautiful and necessary one.

But why is the metaphor so necessary, or, rather, how far is it a metaphor at all? Do you think the words "Light of the World" mean only "Teacher or Guide of the World"? When the Sun of Justice is said to rise with health in its wings, do you suppose the image only means the correction of error? Or does it even mean so much? The Light of Heaven is needed to do that perfectly. But what we are to pray for is the Light of *the World*; nay, the Light "that lighteth *every man that cometh into the world.*"

You will find that it is no metaphor—nor has it ever been so.

To the Persian, the Greek, and the Christian, the sense of the power of the God of Light has been one and the same. That power is not merely in teaching or protecting, but in the enforcement of purity of body, and of equity or justice in the heart; and this, observe, not heavenly purity, nor final justice; but, now, and here, actual purity in the midst of the world's foulness,—practical justice in the midst of the world's iniquity. And the physical strength of the organ of sight—the physical purity of the flesh, the actual love of sweet light and stainless colour—are the necessary signs, real, inevitable, and visible, of the prevailing presence, with any nation, or in any house, of the " Light that lighteth every man that cometh into the world." [1]

Without, as I heard the wild winds roar,
And saw the black clouds their floods outpour,
  As the lightnings flashed,
  And the thunders crashed,
And the hurricane's force waxed more and more,
  I said, as I looked from my window warm,
  " Heaven never on me send such a storm ! "

Then came a dark day, when fierce and fast,
Down fell on my head the blinding blast !
  Yet tho' sore assailed,
  I nor shrank nor quailed,
For tho' loud the gale raged, as 'twould rage its last,
  The struggle I waged, as I journeyed on,
  Awoke in me powers before unknown !

I felt my hot blood a-tingling flow;
With thrill of the fight my soul did glow;
  And when, braced and pure,
  I emerged secure
From the strife that had tried my courage so,
  I said, " Let Heaven send me or sun or rain,
  I'll never know flinching fear again ! " [2]

¶ Be content to wade through the waters betwixt you and glory with Him, holding His right hand fast; for He knoweth all the fords. Be not afraid, therefore, when you come to the black and swelling river of death, to put in your feet and wade after Him. The death and resurrection of the Son of God are stepping-stones and a stay to you; set down your feet by faith upon these stones, and go through as on dry land. [3]

 [1] Ruskin, *The Eagle's Nest* (*Works*, xxii. 203).
 [2] Thomas Crawford, *Horae Serenae*, 17.   [3] Samuel Rutherford.

ACQUAINTANCE WITH GOD.

LITERATURE.

Dinwoodie (J.), *Outline Studies*, 126.
Maclaren (A.), *Expositions*: Esther, Job, 49.
Morgan (G. C.), *Christian Principles*, 22.
Parkinson (R.), in *Practical Sermons*, i. 39.
Raleigh (A.), *The Way to the City*, 229.
Salmond (C. A.), *For Days of Youth*, 193.
Simeon (C.), *Works*, iv. 418.
Spurgeon (C. H.), *Evening by Evening*, 129.
Vaughan (J.), *Sermons in Christ Church, Brighton*, 1st Ser., 42.
Christian World Pulpit, lxx. 289 (Horton); lxxx. 140 (Tattersall).
Church of England Magazine, xliv. (1858) 344 (Clayton).
Church of England Pulpit, xxx. 1. (Kerr-Smith); xlii. 175 (Naylor);
   xliii. 133 (Maturin).
Clergyman's Magazine, 3rd Ser., xii. 159 (Burrows).
Preacher's Magazine, xii. 81 (Whittleton).

ACQUAINTANCE WITH GOD.

**Acquaint now thyself with him, and be at peace:
Thereby good shall come unto thee.**

Job xxii. 21.

IN the sense in which the speaker meant them, these words are
not true. They mean little more than "It pays to be religious."
What kind of notion of acquaintance with God Eliphaz may have
had, one scarcely knows, but, at any rate, the whole meaning of
the text on his lips is poor and selfish. The peace promised is
evidently only outward tranquillity and freedom from trouble, and
the good that is to come to Job is plainly mere worldly prosperity.
This strain of thought is expressed even more clearly in that
extraordinary bit of bathos, which with solemn irony the great
dramatist who wrote this book makes Eliphaz utter immediately
after the text, "The Almighty shall be thy defence and—thou
shalt have plenty of silver!" It has not been left for commercial Englishmen to recommend religion on the ground that
it produces successful merchants and makes the best of both
worlds.

These friends of Job's all err in believing that suffering is
always and only the measure of sin, and that one can tell a man's
great guilt by observing his great sorrows. And so they have two
main subjects on which they preach at their poor friend, pouring
vitriol into his wounds: first, how wicked he must be to be so
haunted by sorrows; second, how surely he will be delivered if
he will only be religious after their pattern, that is, speak platitudes of conventional devotion and say, "I submit." That is the
meaning of the text as it stands. But there is a higher sense in
which it is true.

I.

ACQUAINTANCE WITH GOD.

1. The knowledge of God which the Bible insists upon as essential to peace and salvation, consists in personal or heart acquaintance with Him—such acquaintance as involves transformation of character and radical change of spiritual environment, as well as change of relationship to God, thereby introducing man into a new and blessed life of peace and enjoyment of all good. "Acquaint now thyself with him"—not with His works, not with His ways, not even with His words, life-giving and soul-uplifting though these be—but with Himself! We must be on intimate terms with God. To know Him, as to know a man, we must "live with" Him, must summer and winter with Him, must bring Him into the pettinesses of daily life, must let our love set to Him, must be in sympathy with Him, our wills being tuned to make harmony with His, our whole nature being in accord with His. That is work more than enough for a lifetime, enough to task it, enough to bless it.

¶ We and God have business with each other; and in opening ourselves to His influence our deepest destiny is fulfilled.[1]

¶ When we speak of "knowledge of God," do we not always mean something very far short, from the nature of the case, of comprehension? Surely we do. In one sense we never "know" God. In another, as all Christians believe, "This is Life Eternal, to know Thee, the only True God." Knowledge of God, in the sense of comprehending Him, is always impossible. Do we really comprehend even each other? Do we not feel each other just as we feel God? and then take our feelings to pieces and find that they include, or are based on, a recognition of certain qualities in the person who excites them? And is not this recognition really knowledge—such knowledge as may be expressed in propositions? And if so, how does it differ in kind—I admit that it differs enormously in degree—from the knowledge that we have about God? Certainly our highest knowledge of God is only apprehensive, yet it is knowledge, as far as it goes, and it may be set forth in propositions. Even the most shadowy Theism includes

[1] William James.

at least one tremendous affirmative proposition—however this may be qualified. And this proposition makes this Theism a Theology as well as a Religion. Nor can I see any à priori difficulty in supposing that God may have furnished the mind of primitive man with some feeling or instinct about Himself—a feeling which would be irrational if not based on knowledge of some kind. Why should He have done this less easily than He has given *all* men the sense of right and wrong? Does not this sense of right and wrong itself imply God? Is it not a law? and does not a law imply a Law-giver?[1]

2. Personal acquaintance with God is possible.

(1) Jesus Christ confidently and constantly affirmed the possibility of soul-saving personal acquaintance with God, and maintained that His disciples actually enjoyed such acquaintance or experimental knowledge. His appeals to His disciples were all based on the assumption that they knew God after a spiritual manner, and were thereby distinguished from the world which knew Him not. Indeed, so prominent is experimental knowledge of God as the basis of true discipleship in the Gospels, and especially in the Fourth Gospel, that it may be regarded as the supreme condition of eligibility to the privileges and blessings of the Kingdom of God.

(2) The Apostles confirm our Lord's teaching on this point. John's First Epistle is practically a positive affirmation and doctrinal setting forth of the great truth that all true believers personally and experimentally know God. "Hereby we do know that we know him." "We know that we are in him." "I write unto you . . . because ye know him." "He that knoweth God heareth us." "That we may know that is true." Paul says: "That I may know him" . . . "the Gentiles that know not God"—distinguishing between them and believers who do know Him. "I know whom I have believed."

(3) Further, good men in all the Christian ages, belonging to many lands, of various races and nationalities, while differing in regard to a thousand things, and perhaps having very little in common so far as material surroundings are concerned, have harmoniously testified, as a fact of experience, that they knew God. Men of purity of life, of force of character—distinguished

---

[1] *Life and Letters of H. P. Liddon*, 233.

among their fellows in many instances for probity, benevolence, intelligence, and usefulness—positively affirm with unswerving confidence, persistence, and absolute absence of unworthy motive that they know God; that they enjoy spiritual commerce and personal communion with Him; that He constantly reveals Himself in their consciousness and to their spirits in peace and power and answer to prayer.

¶ God can reveal Himself, and can be known. Spirit with spirit can meet; to a person a Person can speak. Had man's attitude remained normal his apprehension of God would have been continuous and, to the extent of its widening range, unclouded. There are faculties in man which render him capable of this. But, as things are, the knowledge of God has been arrested and confused and sometimes destroyed. The light shining in the darkness has been as good as lost. Yet it has been universal, and hints of the truth have never been altogether absent from any age or race of men; and in Israel a medium of revelation was found, chiefly in its great moral personalities—the prophets—which enabled God to let the real truth of His being and character shine forth with increasing clearness. In this way preparation went on for the final unveiling of God in Christ as Spirit, light, and love.[1]

¶ I dare say that you remember the often quoted saying of Lessing, that "the Christian religion had been tried for eighteen centuries, and that the religion of Christ remained to be tried." It seems rather boastful and extravagant, but it expresses the spirit in which any new movement for the improvement of theology must be carried on. It means that Christians should no longer be divided into Churchmen and Nonconformists, or even into Christians and non-Christians, but that the best men everywhere should know themselves to be partakers of the Spirit of God, as He imparts Himself to them in various degrees. It means that the old foolish quarrels of science with religion, or of criticism with religion, should for ever cease, and that we should recognize all truth, based on fact, to be acceptable to the God of truth. It means that goodness and knowledge should be inseparably united in every Christian word or work, that the school should not be divorced from the Church, or the sermon from the lesson, or preaching from visiting, or secular duties from religious ones, except so far as convenience may require. It means that we should regard all persons as Christians, even if they come

---

[1] *Life of Principal David W. Simon,* 339.

before us with other names, if they are doing the works of Christ.[1]

¶ Can man by searching find out God? Yes! There is no need to seek Him in the unreachable heavens, or in the depths of the invisible darkness to look for Him. He is here in the life, and intelligence, and beauty of Nature. He is here in the conduct of the world. He is here in the sense I have of my own righteousness before Him. He is here in the sense of an absolute justice, even though that justice punish me. He is here, O God! how deeply, dearly, how intensely, in my undying, unquenchable trust that He is mine and I am His for ever.[2]

¶ I have just read that testimony by Goethe that you have quoted from Professor William James. I am about seventy-four —his age. My circumstances have not been nearly so favourable as his, but I am thankful to be able to speak much better of life in this world than he does. I have had many sorrows, and though I am not of sanguine disposition, life has been a joy to me, and is so still. Two great beliefs give me rest from the worry and dissatisfaction which torment so many: (1) that God is a Person. I cannot define the specific sense in which He is a Person. And (2) that God is *Love*. He *must* be love. An Agnostic will confess that if there be a Creator He must at least be the equal of His highest creation. It is a logical absurdity to say that any creature can love more than God loves. If, therefore, there is anything in creation that I cannot harmonize with love, it is because of my limited faculties. All must be right. When this, the great burden of Bible teaching, is heartily received, how much of perplexity and pain is taken out of the life![3]

3. Acquaintance with God is man's highest and most glorious privilege. Do we not count it a privilege to know earth's great men and women? How often have we heard the note of pride in the voice when one has been able to say of some distinguished person, "I know him; I am acquainted with him; I am on terms of familiarity with him, even of affection!" And there is a glow on the face, and a light in the eye, which seems to give the lucky man a reflected glory. When we admire some one greatly, we count it an honour to know him personally, and especially to be known by him; and we can conceive no higher privilege than to

---

[1] *Life and Letters of Benjamin Jowett*, ii. 362.
[2] Stopford A. Brooke, *Sunshine and Shadow*, 7.
[3] *John Brash: Memorials and Correspondence*, 70.

live on terms of intimate fellowship with him. What, then, must be the nature of his privilege who walks with God as did Enoch, who is the friend of God as was Abraham? There cannot possibly be a higher privilege than that.

When the light is in the west,
When the day goes home to rest,
When the busy pulse of city life in mart and lane beats low,
Then in earth's garden lonely
I hear Thy footsteps only,
And the ancient words to me are new, "Be still, and thou shalt know."

Thou hast been walking here
Each hour of every year;
'Twas not the evening coolness brought Thy presence to my side:
But in my heart's great flutter
The day was darkness utter,
And I missed thee in my madness, and I passed Thee in my pride.

Thy holy, heavenly will
Must bid my heart be still
Ere it can catch a note so low as ripples in Thy rest;
For in its constant quiver
I cannot hear the river
That glides, to make Thy city glad, from gardens of the blest.

Why should I wait for even
To snatch a glimpse of heaven,
When the river from the garden can refresh the heated way?
Let but Thy stillness stealing
Impart its sweet revealing,
And through the fire I'll walk with Thee in coolness of the day.[1]

4. If you would know God, you must study Him in the person, and the character, and the life, and the work of His Son. As Christ Himself expresses it, Christ is "the Word." And as a man's words represent and declare the man,—so that you cannot know the man, the invisible mind of the man, but by the words he speaks,—so Christ represents and declares the invisible Father.

[1] George Matheson, *Sacred Songs*, 6.

¶ For us Jesus Christ is the Revealer. What men know of God apart from Him is dim, shadowy, indistinct; it lacks certainty, and so is not knowledge. I venture to say that there is nothing between cultivated men and the loss of certain knowledge of God and conviction of His Being but the historical revelation of Jesus Christ. The Christ reveals the inmost character of God, and that not in words but in deeds. Without Him no man knows God; "No man knoweth the Father save the Son, and he to whom the Son will reveal him." [1]

¶ This morning I arose a little after seven o'clock, in possession of my reason and of my health, and not without aspirations of soul towards the communion of God; but poor and heartless when compared with those experiences of the Psalmist, whose prayers prevented the dawning of the morning, and his meditations the night-watches; and my soul being afflicted with downwardness, and wandering of spirit, and coldness of heart, towards the God of my salvation, in the morning, which is as it were a new resurrection, it was borne in upon my mind that it arose in a great measure from my not realizing with abiding constancy the Mediator between me and God, but breaking through, as it were, to commune with Him in my own strength—whereby the lightning did scathe my soul, or rather my soul abode in its barrenness, unwatered from the living fountain, in its slavery unredeemed by the Captain of my salvation, who will be acknowledged before He will bless us, or rather who must be honoured in order that we may stand well in the sight of the Father. [2]

5. What do we lose if we have not this personal acquaintance with God?

(1) Without acquaintance with God our thoughts of Him will be false thoughts. We shall have no just view of His real character. Some think Him harsh, stern, tyrannical. They regard the law as severe, and its penalties as unjust. They say that His government is arbitrary, and He Himself unworthy of confidence. Therefore, when they are disappointed, baulked in their expectations, denied their hearts' desire, when trouble finds and sorrow lays a heavy hand upon them, they curse God. "Father, forgive them; for they know not what they do." How mournful is the lament of Jesus: "O righteous Father, the world hath not known thee"! The world had not understood God, and

---

[1] A. Maclaren.   [2] *Life of Edward Irving*, i. 255.

men had misrepresented Him; had charged Him with folly; had blasphemed His holy name; had taken it in vain; had wandered far into the darkness of unbelief. But Jesus knew the Father, and therefore, though His face was marred more than any man's, and His form than the sons of men; though He was the "man of sorrows and acquainted with grief"; yet with the shadow of the cross heavy upon Him, He kept bright in His faith and serene in His trust; and He could pray, "O righteous Father, the world hath not known thee: but I have known thee, and these have known that thou hast sent me. And I have declared unto them thy name, and will declare it: that the love wherewith thou hast loved me may be in them, and I in them."

¶ None can have low thoughts of Thee, but they that know Thee not.[1]

¶ From Tungwa we went to Makuta. One afternoon I was strolling about the town. Seeing some women making pottery, I went over to them and sat down under the gables of the house, for the sun was hot. We soon changed the subject of conversation, although they were much interested in what I told them of making pots in England. Then we talked of the work at Tungwa, and how some there had learned of Jesus and were trusting in Him. I was speaking of the love of God, and how anxious He was to change our hearts and to fit us to go and live with Him in the Blessed Home above; how ready He was to help and bless all who sought Him, when the sister of one of the Tungwa lads who had been with us some time, and is now a member of the Church, spread out her hands and cried most pathetically, "Oh God! where are You, that I may know You?" My eyes fill up even now, somehow or other, as I think of her cry. We talked on for some time, and I tried to assure her that He was very near, and would hear her whenever she spoke to Him. Then we talked of Jesus and His great love, and the other women joined in, much interested, and wished that there was some one to teach them at Makuta.[2]

(2) A man without the knowledge of God is simply so far an imperfect man. He is only partially educated, only partially developed. He is like a person who has not the colour sense and cannot see the beauty of the autumn leaves; or like a person who has a defect of the brain and cannot put two ideas together; or

---

[1] Andrew Wellwood.   [2] *W. Holman Bentley*, 320.

like a person who, having had a very narrow experience, can form no opinion of things beyond his ken, and judges the whole world by the little town in which he lives or the people according to the neighbours whom he knows. A man without a knowledge of God is simply a man who has left out of his study the most important and also accessible of all truths, that piece of knowledge which is not so much a branch of the tree as the root of the tree itself, the knowledge upon which all sound living and all sound thinking must ultimately depend; for one who has missed God in the universe has found himself in a universe which has no key, no meaning, no goal, nothing intelligible, and his own mind therefore reflects the meaninglessness and the chaos of the godless universe in which he imagines that he lives.

> Acquaint thyself with God, if thou wouldst taste
> His works. Admitted once to His embrace,
> Thou shalt perceive that thou wast blind before:
> Thine eye shall be instructed; and thine heart,
> Made pure, shall relish with divine delight
> Till then unfelt, what hands divine have wrought.[1]

II.

The Peace which comes from Acquaintance with God.

Personal acquaintance with God brings peace to the soul. This peace is twofold :—

1. *It is peace with God.*—The enmity of the carnal mind is slain, Divine love has vanquished the spirit of opposition, all barriers are broken down; the soul glides from the storm-swept sea of doubt, fear, and uncertainty into the calm haven of God's assured forgiveness and acceptance. The disquieted conscience finds rest from upbraiding; being justified by faith, the believer now has peace with God through our Lord Jesus Christ. There is therefore now no condemnation to him, he has passed out of death into life.

¶ From a boy I had been led to consider that my Maker and I, His creature, were the two beings, luminously such, *in rerum*

---

[1] Cowper.

natura. I will not here speculate, however, about my own feelings. Only this I know full well now, and did not know then, that the Catholic Church allows no image of any sort, material or immaterial, no dogmatic symbol, no rite, no sacrament, no Saint, not even the Blessed Virgin herself, to come between the soul and its Creator. It is face to face, "solus cum solo," in all matters between man and his God. He alone creates; He alone has redeemed; before His awful eyes we go in death; in the vision of Him is our eternal beatitude.[1]

> Dear Angel, say,
> Why have I now no fear at meeting Him?
> Along my earthly life, the thought of death
> And judgment was to me most terrible.
> I had it aye before me, and I saw
> The Judge severe e'en in the Crucifix.
> Now that the hour is come, my fear is fled;
> And at this balance of my destiny,
> Now close upon me, I can forward look
> With a serenest joy.[2]

2. *It is also the peace of God.*—God's peace is not merely a negative thing, not merely the removal of enmity and dispersion of wrath. It is like music. Harmony is the perfection of sound, not the absence of sound. The return of the soul in penitence and faith to God, and its union with Him in peace leads at once to harmonious commerce and reciprocal affection between the two spirits—finite and infinite. As the Divine Rewarder lifts upon those who diligently seek Him the light of His countenance all tumult subsides, peace at once takes possession and establishes its sovereignty. The immutable promise is, "Thou wilt keep him in perfect peace, whose mind is stayed on thee; because he trusteth in thee." The perfect attitude of trust, with the mind unwaveringly stayed upon God as the sure support and never-failing help, secures perfect permanent peace.

¶ The central thought of religion is of a peace that is beyond the unrest of life, of a harmony that transcends all its discords, of a unity of purpose which works through all the conflict of the forces of nature, and the still more intense conflict of the wills of men.[3]

[1] J. H. Newman, *Apologia Pro Vita Sua*, 195.
[2] J. H. Newman, *Verses on Various Occasions*, 244.
[3] Edward Caird.

Acquaint thyself with God!
    Know thou His tender love;
So shall the healing sunshine fall
    Upon thee from above.
Acquaint thyself with God!
    In Him alone is peace,—
Rest for the weary child of time,
    And everlasting bliss.

Acquaint thyself with God!
    Choose thou the better part;
So shall His heavenly sunlight be
    The day-spring of thy heart.
Acquaint thyself with God!
    He bids thee seek His face,
That thus thy youthful soul may taste
    The sweetness of His grace.

Acquaint thyself with God!
    In Jesus and His cross
Read there that love which makes all loss
    But gain, all gain but loss.
Acquaint thyself with God
    In childhood's joyous prime;
So shall thy life a foretaste prove
    Of heaven's long summer-time.[1]

III.

The True Good which comes from Acquaintance with God.

1. Eliphaz was only thinking, on Old Testament lines, that prosperity in material things was the theocratic reward of allegiance to Jehovah. But we have a better meaning breathed into his words, since Jesus has taught us what is the true good for a man all the days of his life. Acquaintance with God is, not merely procures, good. To know Him, to clasp Him to our hearts as our Friend, our Infinite Lover, our Source of all peace and joy, to mould our wills to His and let Him dominate our whole selves, to seek our well-being in Him alone—what else or more can a soul need to be filled with all good? Acquaintance with God brings Him in all His sufficiency to inhabit otherwise empty hearts. It changes the worst, according to the judgment of sense,

[1] *Hymns by Horatius Bonar*, 162.

into the best, transforming sorrow into loving discipline, interpreting its meaning, fitting us to bear it, and securing to us its blessings.   To him that is a friend of God,

> All is right that seems most wrong
> If it be His sweet will.

¶ Good—a little word, but how pregnant! What manifold treasures are wrapped up in it! Spectrum analysis has revealed wondrous things to us concerning God's starry hosts; but who will analyse for us this single word " good " as it comes from the Father's lips and leaps from His heart ? [1]

¶ The infinite goodness which I have experienced in this world inspires me with the conviction that eternity is pervaded by a goodness not less infinite, in which I repose unlimited trust.[2]

2. "Thereby good shall come to thee." Good of every kind, and especially of the *best* kind. In fact, the state itself is the good begun. No good can ever come to a man from without, in the shape of possession of any kind, which can for a moment be compared with the blessedness of *being good*. There is a beautiful prayer in one of the Psalms to this effect. " Do good, O Lord, unto those that *be* good." That short sentence is a religious philosophy as well as a prayer. For until a man is *good*, good of the highest kind God cannot do him. He can fill his veins with health, and his coffers with gold, and his rooms with pictures, and his gardens with flowers, and his fields with fruits, and his life with comfort and outward peace ; but one thrill of the holy peace of this text, and of the Saviour's legacy, he can never have, so long as he is unthankful and evil. These things are just hung about him, or thrown in his way ; they are not *in* the man himself.[3]

¶ The beginning of religion seems to me to be, first, resignation, and, secondly, trust in God. " O rest in the Lord." This is a true word for the departing one as well as for the survivor. " The souls of the righteous are in the hands of God, and there shall no torment touch them." "Peace I leave with you, my peace I give unto you : not as the world giveth, give I unto you." It is weak and wrong to rebel against the order of nature, which is also the will of God, or to seek to know things which no one has ever known. Sympathy is a precious help, but our chief support must be the thought of God.[4]

[1] J. E. Robinson.   [2] E. Renan, *Recollections of my Youth*, 329.
[3] A. Raleigh, *The Way to the City*, 237.   [4] B. Jowett, *Life and Letters*, ii. 449.

Songs in the Night.

LITERATURE.

Bardsley (J. W.), *Illustrative Texts*, 133.
Matheson (G.), *Leaves for Quiet Hours*, 51.
Melvill (H.), *Sermons at Cambridge*, 21.
Oosterzee (J. J. van), *The Year of Salvation*, ii. 504.
Robertson (S.), *The Rope of Hair*, 28.
Spurgeon (C. H.), *Metropolitan Tabernacle Pulpit*, **xxvi.** (1880), No. 1511 ; xliv. (1898), No. 2558.
Wagner (G.), *Sermons on the Book of Job*, 260.
Church of England Magazine, x. 169 (Grant).

SONGS IN THE NIGHT.

But none saith, Where is God my Maker,
Who giveth songs in the night?

Job xxxv. 10.

1. SOME men are always disposed to look at the bright side of life, and others at the dark. The tempers and feelings of some are so cheerful and elastic that it is hardly within the power of ordinary circumstances to depress them; while others are of so gloomy a temperament that the least adversity serves to confound them. But if we can divide men into these classes, when reference is had simply to their private affairs, we doubt whether the same division will hold, we are sure it will not in the same proportion, when the reference is generally to God's dealings with our race. In regard to these dealings, there is an almost universal disposition to look on the dark side, and not on the bright; as though there were cause for nothing but wonder that a God of infinite love should permit so much misery in any section of His intelligent Creation. Few are ready to observe what provision has been made for human happiness, and what capacities there are yet in the world of ministering to the satisfaction of such as prefer righteousness to wickedness.

¶ Here are two men, who both seem to have deserved success; both have worked hard, and one to-day is rich and the other is poor. All the chances came to the one, and all the hindrances to the other. There is something obviously unfair and unjust in all this. So the world thinks. O world, so swift to judge, so slow to understand! I know that some get that which they never worked for, and some work for that which they never get; and if money were the real end of existence and the real standard of success, then your plaint about inequality would be a true one. But it is not. You say all the chances came to one. Not so. There were some chances that came to them both, the chance to be honest

and meek and merciful and pure in heart, and these are the things
that fit men to enter into and possess the true success, the
kingdom of heaven; and finding that is finding happiness. So,
then, human happiness depends on our relation to God.[1]

2. No one can deny that, if we look upon the earth merely as
it is, the exhibition is one whose darkness it is scarcely possible to
exaggerate. But when we seek to gather from the condition of
the world the character of its Governor, we are bound to consider,
not what the world is, but what it would be if all that that
Governor has done on its behalf were allowed to produce its
legitimate effect. And when we set ourselves to compute the
amount of what may be called unavoidable misery—that misery
which must still remain even if Christianity possessed unlimited
sway—we should find no cause for wonder that God has left
the earth burdened with so great a weight of sorrow, but
only of praise that He has provided so amply for men's happiness.

¶ Elihu, in seeking to justify God's ways with man, pressed
his argument unduly in the context, and made it appear that God
is so high and great that the guilt or innocence of a petty human
being is of no moment to Him. So now he proceeds to alter his
course, and to feel his way to some higher explanation of the
unredressed miseries of life. His words deserve full attention.
"True," he says, "a voice of wailing goes up from earth, a groan
of suffering under injustice and oppression. But it is a mere cry
of pain, not a turning to God, man's Maker, to Him who *giveth
songs in the night*, brings, *i.e.*, a joyful sense of sudden deliverance
in the very darkest hour of tribulation. God would have men
cry to Him with something more worthy of those whom He has
made in His own image than the mere inarticulate cries of *the
beast of the earth, the fowls of heaven*. He has taught us more
than the one, He has made us wiser than the other. Empty
moans, empty cries, will not reach His ear. Thy passionate
words give thee no claim, Job," he seems to say, "on God; and
thy prayers to Him, have not risen above mere childish brute-like
cries of pain."[2]

3. Though for wise ends a certain portion of suffering has
been made unavoidable, the Divine dealings with man are, in the

[1] P. C. Ainsworth, *The Blessed Life*, 54.
[2] G. G. Bradley, *The Book of Job*, 296.

largest sense, those of tenderness and love, so that, if the great
majority of our race were not determined to be wretched, enough
has been done to ensure their being happy.   And when we come
to give the reasons why so much wretchedness is found in the
world, we cannot assign it to the will of God; we must charge
the whole of it on man's forgetfulness of God, on his contempt or
neglect of remedies divinely provided; in short, we must offer in
explanation the words of our text, " None saith, Where is God my
Maker, who giveth songs in the night ? "

¶ The note of praise once reached, its office is, even humanly
speaking, no less serviceable than that of prayer.   It is the
attitude of mind that gives courage for the attack of things
difficult.   The healthy soul cannot accept the view, taken by
many of the devout, that our mortal state is so sunk and wretched
that, should we look closely into it, we must remain for ever
inconsolable.   By no man have such as these been reproached
more than by Dante, who had had himself much cause for
sadness.   To the sorrowful he assigns the shades of the fourth
circle of hell, and out of their darkness they cry unto him—

> Tristi fummo
> Nel aer dolce che dal sol s'allegra,
> Portando dentro accidioso fummo;
> Or ci attristiam nella belletta negra.

Fretful were we in the sweet air which is gladdened by the
sun, bearing within us a smoke of Accidie; now we are fretting
ourselves in the black mire.[1]

> My son, the world is dark with griefs and graves,
> So dark that men cry out against the Heavens.
> Who knows but that the darkness is in man ?
> The doors of Night may be the gates of Light;
> For wert thou born or blind or deaf, and then
> Suddenly heal'd, how would'st thou glory in all
> The splendours and the voices of the world !
> And we, the poor earth's dying race, and yet
> No phantoms, watching from a phantom shore
> Await the last and largest sense to make
> The phantom walls of this illusion fade,
> And show us that the world is wholly fair.[2]

[1] Lady Dilke, *The Book of the Spiritual Life*, 180.
[2] Tennyson, *The Ancient Sage*.

I.

THE SONG.

1. Shakespeare says that music is "the concord of sweet sounds." But it is more, just as poetry consists of something more than harmonious words. Music is the language of the unseen and eternal; and song is the accord of the heart with this, the utterance of eternity. Of course there are evil songs, which show that the heart of the singer is in accord with the dark nether world of evil; but good and holy songs show that the heart of the singer has caught the strains and chords of the bright, blessed world of God and the holy angels.

¶ All deep things are Song. It seems somehow the very central essence of us, Song ; as if all the rest were but wrappages and hulls! The primal element of us; of us, and of all things.[1]

¶ You must have the right moral state first, or you cannot have the art. But when the art is once obtained, its reflected action enhances and completes the moral state out of which it arose, and, above all, communicates the exultation to other minds which are already morally capable of the like.

For instance, take the art of singing, and the simplest perfect master of it (up to the limits of his nature) whom you can find— a skylark. From him you may learn what it is to "sing for joy." You must get the moral state first, the pure gladness, then give it finished expression; and it is perfected in itself, and made communicable to other creatures capable of such joy. But it is incommunicable to those who are not prepared to receive it.[2]

¶ Music, heard by my inner ear, accompanied me at all times and during all my walks, and I created for myself a singular test by which to know if a piece of music was beautiful or not. There was a spot, a bench under a tree by the side of a very small waterfall, where I loved to sit and "think music." Then, going in my mind through a piece of music such as Beethoven's "Adelaide," or the Cavatina from "Der Freyschütz," I could imagine that I heard it in the air surrounding me, that the whole of nature sang it, and then I knew that it was beautiful. Many pieces would not stand that test, however hard I tried, and those I rejected as indifferent.[3]

[1] Carlyle, *Heroes and Hero Worship.*
[2] Ruskin, *Lectures on Art*, § 66 (*Works*, xx. 73).
[3] *Life and Letters of Sir Charles Hallé*, 10.

2. Love is the inspirer of the highest song. When our heart is enlarged we can run in the way of God's commandments. Life breaks out into music and light. The obedience which the law demands, which at first promised only to bring constraint and a gloomy darkening of life's joy, is the spring of happiness and peace. In the joy of reconcilement we are in accord with God's will for us, and are in tune with the whole universe. We know the service which is perfect freedom. The house of our pilgrimage is made glad with music. Life laughs back its radiance in the sunshine of God's smile.

¶ Fix this in your mind as the guiding principle of all right practical labour, and source of all healthful life energy, that your art is to be the praise of something that you love. It may be only the praise of a shell or a stone; it may be the praise of a hero; it may be the praise of God. Your rank, as a living creature, is determined by the height and breadth of your love; but, be you small or great, what healthy art is possible to you must be the expression of your true delight in a real thing better than the art.[1]

3. God is the giver of the song. No man can make a song in the night himself; he may attempt it, but he will find how difficult it is. It is not natural to sing in trouble, "Bless the Lord, O my soul, and all that is within me bless his holy name"; for that is a daylight song. But it was a Divine song which Habakkuk sang when in the night he said, "Although the fig-tree shall not blossom," and so on, "yet I will rejoice in the Lord, I will joy in the God of my salvation." Methinks, on the margin of the Red Sea, any man could have made a song like that of Moses, "The horse and his rider hath he thrown into the sea"; the difficulty would have been to compose a song before the Red Sea had been divided, and to sing it before Pharaoh's hosts had been drowned, while yet the darkness of doubt and fear was resting on Israel's hosts. Songs in the night come only from God: they are not in the power of man.

¶ For when God has all that He should have of thy heart, when thou art wholly given up to the obedience of the light and spirit of God within thee, to will only in His will, to love only in His love, to be wise only in His wisdom, then it is that everything

[1] Ruskin.

thou dost is as a song of praise, and the common business of thy life is a conforming to God's will on earth as angels do in heaven.[1]

¶ I never awake in the middle of the night without feeling induced to commune with God. One feels brought more into contact with Him. The whole world around us, we think, is asleep. God the Shepherd of Israel slumbers not, nor sleeps. He is awake, and so are we! We feel, in the solemn and silent night, as if alone with God. And then there is everything in the circumstances around you to lead you to pray. The past is often vividly recalled. The voices of the dead are heard, and their forms crowd around you. No sleep can bind them. The night seems the time in which they should hold spiritual commune with man. The future too throws its dark shadow over you—the night of the grave, the certain death-bed, the night in which no man can work. And then everything makes such an impression on the mind at night, when the brain is nervous and susceptible; the low sough of the wind among the trees, the roaring, or *eerie whish*, of some neighbouring stream, the bark or low howl of a dog, a general impressive silence, all tend to sober, to solemnize the mind, and to force it from the world and its vanities, which then seem asleep, to God, who alone can uphold and defend.[2]

4. And what God gives He looks to us to render to Him again. The slightest vision of God begets in our hearts the desire to praise Him. Prayer is for ourselves, praise is for God. When we pray we really contemplate ourselves, and our own needs; when we praise we are gazing at God and at God only, and it is the sense of His infinite greatness, of His majesty, of His dominion, of His power, that compels us to burst into songs of praise and gratitude. Praise suggests melody, for this simple reason—that the contemplation of the greatness, and the glory, and the majesty of God fills our hearts with thoughts which are much too deep to be uttered in words. It is useless that we should enumerate God's perfections with our lips; it is useless that we should try to express simply what we can understand, simply what we perceive. We naturally wish to express feelings which soar far beyond our power of expressing them in words. Thus it follows that the only mode of giving expression to such feelings is by music, is by the power of sound; for remember, music is at once the most intimate and the most sublime of all the arts. It

---

[1] William Law.   [2] Dr. Norman Macleod, in *Memoir* by his brother, i. 151.

has a power of expression which is peculiarly its own, and which goes beyond that of any other form of expression.

Why does man have recourse to music to express these fine thoughts of his heart? He does so because it seems to him so free and unfettered. My lips, they stumble when I speak, I catch after words and I cannot find them; but let me betake myself to song and the notes well forth, and the melody tells its own tale, and I am in a freer atmosphere, and I can soar aloft untrammelled by sordid considerations which perforce bind me down so long as I am merely trying to speak.

¶ On Saturday I had a good bout at Beethoven's Quartetts—which I used to play with poor Blanco White—and thought them more exquisite than ever—so that I was obliged to lay down the instrument and literally cry out with delight. I really think it will add to my power of working, and the length of my life. I never wrote more than when I played the fiddle. I always sleep better after music. There must be some electric current passing from the strings through the fingers into the brain and down the spinal marrow. Perhaps thought is music.[1]

¶ In almost his earliest poem, Browning wrote the wise advice:

Respect all such as sing when all alone.

Let us sing with the understanding, and then there is scarcely any experience so uplifting as to *offer* a hymn to God; to say in the soul, " My God and Father, here is my little offering of sweet and humble adoration." Public praise and secret praise are both powerful to bring the spirit into closer touch with God. On the wings of music we can soar into the vast region where

Time and sense seem all no more.

Some years ago I found a special method very profitable in private devotion. Beginning with the section of an old hymn-book that dealt with " believers praying," I set off two hymns for each day of the month. During the first month I marked the verses of special appealing power, and month after month I used to *sing* these selected verses. That, I found, was a strong method of obtaining a direct answer to the prayer, " Create in me a clean heart, O God, and renew a right spirit within me." In such singing the right spirit is renewed.[2]

[1] Cardinal Newman, in *Life* by W. Ward, ii. 76.
[2] J. A. Clapperton, *Culture of the Christian Heart*, 142.

Why should I always pray,
　　Although I always lack?
It were a better way
　　Some praise to render back:
The earth that drinks the plenteous rain
Returns the grateful cloud again.

We should not get the less
　　That we remembered more
The truth and righteousness
　　Thou keep'st for us in store:
In heaven they do not pray—they sing,
And they have wealth of every thing.

And it would be more meet
　　To compass Thee with song
Than to have at Thy feet
　　Only a begging throng
Who take Thy gifts, and then forget
Alike Thy goodness, and their debt.

So give me joyous Psalms,
　　And Hymns of grateful praise:
Instead of seeking alms,
　　A song to Thee I'll raise:
Yet still I must a beggar be,
When lauding Thy great charity.

But where shall I begin?
　　With health and daily bread?
Or cleansing of my sin?
　　Or light around me shed?
Till I would praise, I did not see
How rich Thy gifts have been to me.[1]

II.

THE SONG IN THE NIGHT.

1. It is evident that "night" is here used as a symbol of affliction and suffering; and there is a beautiful appropriateness in the symbol which commends itself at once to our minds; for

[1] Walter C. Smith, *Thoughts and Fancies for Sunday Evenings*, 1.

the shades of night, though a relief to some from toil and labour, bring to many an increase of trial and suffering. There is an untold relief in *light*. Whilst suffering and sorrow continue just the same, light seems to reanimate hope and endurance. Darkness has the opposite effect. The greatest inward conflicts take place during its long hours—sickness is doubly weary, and full of uneasiness. The unclosed eye, the unsubdued pain, the voice of sympathy hushed—all these tax often to the uttermost the patience of a Christian. These make many a man recoil from the night season. And so it must be felt at once to be a fit symbol of trial. When, then, our text speaks of God, "who giveth songs in the night," it evidently means that it belongs to Him to put songs of praise and joy into the Christian's heart in seasons of sorrow and trial. It belongs to God, and to God alone, to give such songs. A thoughtless world seeks its happiness in that which is outward—in worldly pleasure, in earthly aims, and in the creature. So long as the outward path is smooth, pleasures succeeding each other, and keeping the mind in a perpetual state of excitement—so long as success crowns those earthly aims, and either money or fame increases—so long the world has its songs. But let a change come over the scene. Let these pleasures fail, its schemes end in disappointment, and its all is gone. The world may sing in its day — its short and uncertain day. But it knows not, and can never learn, *songs in the night*. It cannot even understand them. The most it can do is to keep silence. But the Christian's noblest and most elevated songs are not those which he sings in the day, but those which rise up in the night-season of sorrow—songs sung with tearful eyes and a heaving heart.

¶ Butterflies are said to be so sensitive to want of light that they are not only stupid at night, but are also affected in the daytime by the shadow of every passing cloud. It is a common practice of butterfly-hunters to keep their eye on an insect without pursuing it, waiting till a cloud comes, when it is nearly certain to settle down and become more or less torpid. Thus is the human soul sensitive to sorrow: the shadow of every passing cloud chills it, the deeper eclipses of life paralyse it, and these morbid hours prove not rarely the tempter's opportunity.[1]

[1] W. L. Watkinson, *The Education of the Heart*, 141.

¶ Read the lives of the great souls, and you will find almost
always that their inner career begins with a period of night and
darkness. With some, as with Paul, Bunyan, Tolstoy, it is a
despair of themselves and their world. With others, it is a crash
of the creed in which they were brought up, and a dreary scepticism when all their stars go out and there seems naught left but
chaos and old night. It is singular that we have read so many
of these experiences, and perhaps have gone through them in our
turn, without asking the reason of all this. Are we not here in
contact with a psychological law; the law that, in a lower order,
we perceive in the germination of the plant, in all the vital processes? The spiritual life, like all other life, requires darkness
and the deep for its starting-point! A man must dive into his
inmost recesses in order that he may find himself.[1]

2. What we need most is certainty of God, that we may
hold fast our faith in Him. We shall still be beset by mystery,
and the world's sorrow and our own pain will still remain a
terrible problem, but we shall see enough to make us willing to
believe and wait. We shall let every experience of trial and
sorrow bring some lessons to withdraw our hearts from the love
of the material. We shall learn to look upon the whole discipline
of life as a means of sanctification, and in our highest moments
we shall see it to be a terror to be left of God, and shall pray that
the beautiful promise may be true for us: "As one whom his
mother comforteth, so will I comfort you." When we do, the
last word to us is not tribulation, but joy. Even suffering only
sets a seal on faith, like the kiss of God upon the brow. Faith
sees far enough into the meaning of tribulation to see in it the
sign of love; for it sees in it the Father's hand.

> I know Thee who hast kept my path, and made
> Light for me in the darkness, tempering sorrow,
> So that it reached me like a solemn joy.

¶ A picture of deep pathos, carrying its own tender suggestion
to the heart, appeared in the Academy of 1897. It was painted
by Byam Shaw, and entitled "The Comforter." In the interior
of a room, upon a bed, there lies a form, the face of which is not
seen, only a hand lying upon the silk counterpane with a wedding-
ring upon the finger. By the side of the bed there sits a young
man, his elbow leaning upon the bed, his head supported by his

[1] J. Brierley, *The Secret of Living*, 218.

hand, his face drawn with grief. In his loneliness he sits there while his beloved, with slow and painful breaths, sighs out her little store of life. The picture gives the impression of stillness; the heedless world is without, ignorant and uncaring, while the pitiful tragedy is working itself out within. But the young man, as he sits there in his unutterable anguish, is not alone; the Comforter has come. Seated beside him is a white figure, unseen to him but consciously near. The pierced hands hold the hand of the young man, and in that silent room of death there is another watcher.[1]

¶ Night and darkness, with their uses and abuses, are, after all, of limited area. The sunlight is so much more than they. This ebon blackness, so seeming all-enveloping, is merely a result of your position on a sloping planet. The night's dimension is a trifle compared with the light that is abroad. All around you, though you cannot see it, the pulsing beam is raying out from the centre, spreading through the immensity of the outer spaces. It is *you* who are in the night, not the solar system. It is not for lack of sunshine that you see nothing. That is an affair of your present position, your present need. And when the need is gone, the night will go. Your destiny is not the night, but the day. Your darkest hour is only its prelude. We see already the boundary of the night, for

> On the glimmering limit far withdrawn
> God makes Himself an awful rose of dawn.[2]

> These stones that make the meadow brooklet murmur
> Are keys on which it plays.
> O'er every shelving rock its touch grows firmer,
> Resounding notes to raise.

> If all the course were smooth by which it passes
> Adown the pastures fair,
> Then those who wander through its flowers and grasses
> Would hear no music there.

> These troubles sore, and griefs, and hard conditions,
> Through which I pass along,
> When going forth to keep my Lord's commissions,
> May all be turned to song.

[1] J. Burns, *Illustrations from Art* (1912), 10.
[2] J. Brierley, *The Secret of Living*, 221.

What are they but sweet harp-strings for the spirit
    Boldly to play upon?
If all the lot were pleasant I inherit,
    These harmonies were gone!

If every path o'er which my footsteps wander,
    Were smooth as ocean strand,
There were no theme for gratitude and wonder
    At God's delivering hand.

All this will plain appear when ends life's story,
    Where rivers meet the tide
That stills their murmurs in a sea of glory,
    Where peace and rest abide.[1]

III.

THE VALUE OF THE SONG IN THE NIGHT.

1. The singing of a glad song cheers and comforts the singer. Life and sunshine are native to the soul. God fashioned us as children of light, and His original thought concerning us was that we should walk in the light, move to music, and taste the sweetness of manifold felicity. We were created for glory and gladness, as certainly as the angels were. Our invincible horror of sickness, weakness, loneliness, and death tells most eloquently that we were predestinated to health, strength, fellowship, and life. We have an ineradicable genius for joy, and when plunged into gloomy spheres of trial are perplexed and dismayed. Unnatural conditions are always perilous, and the soul subjected to deep sadness is in danger of wild unbeliefs, subtle selfishness, benumbing indifference to life, profane murmuring, and defiance.

¶ It is a fine thing to go about one's work singing some hymn with praise in it, and with Jesus' name in it. And if singing may not always be allowable under all circumstances, you can *hum* a tune. And that brings up to the memory the words connected with it. I know of a woman who was much given to worrying. She made it a rule to sing the long metre doxology whenever things seemed not right. Ofttimes she could

---

[1] W. E. Winks.

hardly get her lips shaped up to begin the first words. But she would persist. And by the time the fourth line came it was ringing out, and her atmosphere had changed without and within.[1]

¶ The music in Jenny Lind was ever an inspiration, which lifted her, as the lark is carried heavenward by its song—the lark, her own chosen symbol, carved over her house-door; the lark, the winged thing that "singing ever soars," and "soaring ever sings." "What a gift is Art," she herself writes; "music above all—when we understand, not to make it an idol, but to place it at the foot of the Cross, laying all our longings, sufferings, joys and expectations in a light of a dying and risen Saviour! He alone—and surely nothing else—is the goal of all our intense longing, whether we know it or not."[2]

2. The singing of the song has a quick effect upon the listener. When the prisoners heard Paul and Silas sing in the prison at midnight, they hearkened, they sat up on the pallets, and tried to catch the strange sounds. They rose and crept to the door of the inner dungeon and bent their heads towards it, eager to catch every word. There they stood, an awe-stricken group, listening breathlessly in the darkness. They had often heard singing in the prison before. But never before had they heard in prison strains like these. There was something holy and heavenly in them, which overawed and melted them. As they listened, strange feelings and memories stirred in them.[3]

¶ There is an exquisite sketch written by the hand which penned the immortal story of *Rab and his Friends*, of a quaint old character of other days, well known to Dr. Brown, because he was his father's beadle. The sketch (entitled "Jeems the Doorkeeper") is written with the love and humour of which the author's heart was full; and among other traits of his humble friend he gives this touching one. He had been married in his youth, but after a year his wife and their one child died together; but always afterwards he kept up the practice of family worship, though quite alone, giving out the psalm and the chapter, as if his dear wife had been there. He lived in a high storey in the Canongate, and his voice, in the notes of "Martyrdom" or "Coleshill," sounded morning and evening through the thickly

---

[1] S. D. Gordon, *Quiet Talks on Service*, 206.
[2] Canon H. Scott Holland, *Personal Studies*, 28.
[3] J. Stalker, *The New Song*, 175.

tenanted "land"; and many a careless foot was arrested and many a heart touched by that strange sound.[1]

> I heard a voice in the darkness singing
> (That was a valiant soul I knew),
> And the joy of his song was a wild bird winging
> Swift to his mate through a sky of blue.

> Myself—I sang when the dawn was flinging
> Wide his guerdon of fire and dew;
> I heard a voice in the darkness singing
> (That was a valiant soul I knew).

> And his song was of love and all its bringing
> And of certain day when the night was through;
> I raised my eyes where the hope was springing,
> And I think in His heaven God smiled, too.
> I heard a voice in the darkness singing
> (That was a valiant soul I knew).

3. The midnight song is a powerful witness in favour of our religion. There are times when the heart has to fill the place of the eye. We see nothing; the sky is dark; yet we are not dismayed. There is no ray of light upon our path that we can discern, no opening in the cloud, no rent in the gloom. Yet somehow the heart sings—sings in the shadow, sings in the silence. And at these times we are to take the song as the substitute for the sun. We are to impute to the heart's singing all that is wanting to the eye's vision. The song is itself to be our revelation. "If it were not so, I would have told you," says the Lord—would not have suffered you to sing. The heart's joy demands a contradiction if it be not true. If my soul says "Yea," and God does not say "Nay," the "Yea" is to prevail. The silence of God is vocal. If hope cries, and He answers not, hope's cry is to be itself the answer, for He has sent me a wing instead of a star; He has given me a song in the night.

> Her child is crying in the darken'd room!
> The mother hears, and soon with her arms
> She clasps her darling, banishing alarms,
> Dispersing with her presence fear and gloom.

[1] J. Stalker, The New Song, 179.

And does thy Heavenly Father turn aside
  Unheeding, when thy cry to Him ascends
    From depths of night? Nay, comfort He extends,
Thy heart is strengthened and thy tears are dried.

Thy voice can reach Him, crying in the night,
  Afraid and desolate, scarce knowing why:
    Lo! thou art not forsaken, He draws nigh!
Be still, sad heart, for He will give thee light.[1]

[1] Una, *In Life's Garden*, 92.

The Treasuries of the Snow.

Literature.

Bompas (W. C.), *Northern Lights on the Bible*, 99.
Burrell (D. J.), *The Spirit of the Age*, 203.
Collyer (R.), *Nature and Life*, 43.
Gunsaulus (F. W.), *Paths to the City of God*, 136.
Hind (T.), *The Treasures of the Snow*, 11.
Jordan (D. A.), *Sunday Talks on Nature Topics*, 103.
Lambert (J. C.), *Three Fishing Boats*, 117.
Leader (G. C.), *Wanted a Boy*, 60.
McCook (H. C.), *The Gospel in Nature*, 82.
Talmage (T. De Witt), *Sermons*, v. 311.
Church of England Magazine, lxx. (1871) 285 (Thursfield).
Churchman's Pulpit : Septuagesima Sunday, lxii. 287 (Perry).
Homiletic Review, lix. 66 (Fry)

The Treasuries of the Snow.

Hast thou entered the treasuries of the snow?

Job xxxviii. 22.

1. The references to snow in Scripture are few, as might be expected in a land where snow seldom or never fell. But even though the writers may never have felt the cold touch of the snowflake on their cheek, they had in sight two mountains the tops of which were suggestive. Other kings sometimes take off their crowns, but Lebanon and Mount Hermon all the year round and through the ages never lift the coronets of crystal from their foreheads. The first time we find a deep fall of snow in the Bible is where Samuel describes a fight between Benaiah and a lion in a pit; and though the snow may have crimsoned under the wounds of both man and brute, the shaggy monster rolled over dead and the giant was victor. But the snow is not fully recognized in the Bible until God interrogates Job concerning its wonders, saying: "Hast thou entered the treasuries of the snow?"

¶ In the Psalms there is an exquisite hint of a snowfall through the perfect stillness, and a magnificent storm-piece into which the snow comes with other elements. In the Proverbs, again, there is a passage, where the writer says, "As the cold of snow in the time of harvest, so a faithful servant refreshes the soul of his master." Isaiah has a noble image of the truth falling softly on the heart, as the snow falls softly on the earth. There is not a word about the snow from the lips of the Saviour; and it is only noticed at all in the New Testament in a secondary sense,—used as a comparison, never as an experience.[1]

2. In this great poem of Job, the snow is given a place among the wonders of the world, and ranked with the morning stars and the sea and the lightnings and leviathan and death. It

[1] R. Collyer, *Nature and Life*, 46.

is one of the things over which Job is bidden to meditate in
his heart, in order to restore his shaken faith in God's greatness
and goodness and mercy. It is taken as one of the thousand
revelations that are open to all men of the Divine Power that
lives and moves through all the universe and finds nothing too
great for its mighty guidance, nothing too small for its constant care.

> Come see the north wind's masonry.
> Out of an unseen quarry evermore
> Furnished with tile, the fierce artificer
> Curves with white bastions with projected roof
> Round every windward stake, or tree, or door.
> Speeding, the myriad-handed, his wild work
> So fanciful, so savage, nought cares he
> For number or proportion. Mockingly,
> On coop or kennel he hangs Parian wreaths;
> A swan-like form invests the hidden thorn;
> Fills up the farmer's lane from wall to wall,
> Maugre the farmer's sighs; and at the gate
> A tapering turret overtops the work.
> And when his hours are numbered, and the world
> Is all his own, retiring, as he were not,
> Leaves, when the sun appears, astonished Art
> To mimic in slow structures, stone by stone,
> Built in an age, the mad wind's night-work,
> The frolic architecture of the snow.[1]

3. In the Authorized Version the translation is "the treasures
of the snow." The Hebrew word means treasuries or magazines.
Snow and hail, says A. B. Davidson, are represented as having
been created and laid up in great storehouses in the heavens or
above them, from which God draws them forth for the moral
ends of His government. But it will not be necessary to insist
upon the difference between the two words. The treasures of
the snow are in its treasuries.

We shall endeavour to enter the treasuries by considering—

 I. The Formation of Snow.
 II. The Qualities of Snow.
 III. The Use of Snow.

[1] Emerson, "The Snow-Storm."

I.

THE FORMATION OF SNOW.

1. Snow is no more than a form of water. It is simply the vapour of water in a crystallized form. Indeed, the term "crystal" found in most of the European languages is derived from the Greek word *crystallos*, meaning ice or frozen water, and was subsequently transferred to pure transparent stones cut into seals, which, as was thought, were produced only in the extreme cold of lofty passes of the Alps. The atmosphere is charged with watery vapour to an immense extent, and when the temperature is sufficiently low to freeze this moisture, snow is formed. When produced in calm air, the icy particles build themselves into beautiful stellar shapes, each star possessing six rays.

Lieutenant Maury made an estimate based upon the average annual rainfall, which is sufficient to cover the earth to the depth of five feet, that this atmospheric ocean contains an amount of water equal to a lake sixteen feet deep, three thousand miles broad, and twenty-four thousand miles long. From this reservoir of moisture mist and dew are continually precipitated, and from the same storehouse issue forth also hail, snow, and rain. The challenge made to Job, "Hast thou seen the treasuries of the hail?" was perhaps unanswerable in the days of the patriarch. In a measure it is still unanswered; but modern investigations in meteorology have enabled us to draw aside the cloud-curtain, peep into Nature's laboratory, and obtain a reasonably clear mental insight of the formation of snow.

¶ In the range of inorganic nature, I doubt if any object can be found more perfectly beautiful than a fresh, deep snowdrift, seen under warm light. Its curves are of inconceivable perfection and changefulness; its surface and transparency alike exquisite; its light and shade of inexhaustible variety and inimitable finish, the shadows sharp, pale, and of heavenly colour, the reflected lights intense and multitudinous and mingled with the sweet occurrences of transmitted light. No mortal hand can approach the majesty or loveliness of it.[1]

[1] Ruskin, *Modern Painters* (*Works*, iii. 445).

2. There is a beauty and mathematical exactness in the structure of crystals that bespeak intelligence. The whirling snowstorm, instead of being, as it seems at the first glance, a bewildering chaos, is a most wonderfully ordered cosmos. If ever anything seems a matter of mere chance it is the fluttering down of a snowflake. And yet we know it to be a fact that no flake falls save in accordance with the same eternal laws which govern the rush of suns through the vast realms of space—that not one hastens or loiters but as the steady forces guide it—that each one is poised to its resting-place as surely as if angel hands had borne it down from heaven. And that fact helps us to realize what we are learning more surely every day, that there is no such thing as chance anywhere, not even in the riot of the storm; that chance, when you come to look into it, always resolves itself into unknown depths of law, that law is only a human phrase for the working of the Divine Wisdom and Power, and that so there is oneness everywhere .from the very centre to the outmost rim of the universe ; not an atom escapes from the all-ruling hand; God is in all things, and God is one.

¶ Descartes announced that he had discovered ninety-three various forms or patterns of snowflakes. The words had scarcely fallen from his lips before another declared that he had found nine hundred. Indeed there is no limit to their diversity; it is fair to say that no two of them are precisely alike, just as no two leaves in Vallombrosa are alike, just as no two human faces are alike on all the earth. This infinite variety is also a distinguishing feature of the work of God.[1]

¶ I do not see how one can consider without a feeling of reverence and awe what Ruskin would call such " ethics of the dust "—this grand mathematical legislation of the universe carried down to and governing even invisible atoms. For we must remember that, if the atomic theory be true, the shape of each tiny crystal depends in its turn upon the obedient march and movement of millions of infinitesimal atoms. How small these are it is almost impossible to realize ; but it is estimated that, if a drop of water were swollen to the size of the earth, each constituent atom would still be less than the size of a cricket-ball. You would, therefore, get into billions and trillions, in order to take the atomic census of a snowflake. Now, each one of those individual atoms acts in accordance with regular laws,

[1] D. J. Burrell, *The Spirit of the Age*, 205.

and the beauty and symmetry of every snowflake depend upon the exact manipulation of these atoms by the Divine energy— their exact obedience to the Divine method of the universe. Surely men need not go to tales of ancient miracles to satisfy their craving for the wonderful. Why, here is a miracle that you can hold in your hand! You tread on a thousand miracles at every step you take.[1]

¶ Supposing you were to go to school during the dinner-hour, when no one was about, and saw lying on the desk an exercise book. If, on opening it, you saw on one page a blot of red ink and another of black, and turning over another leaf saw the imprint of four dirty fingers and a thumb, you would say at once, "These came by accident; and the boy who made these marks did not intend to make them." But if, turning over more leaves, you came upon a well-drawn square, and then a perfect circle, and then upon groups of figures drawn and combined, just as in your Euclid, you would say, " Ah ! that did not come by chance. The boy that drew that circle meant to do it; the boy that drew that figure has passed the 'pons asinorum,' he can do such-and-such a proposition." If another boy were to come in and look over your shoulder, and say, "Oh no, they all came by chance," you would open your eyes in amazement, or see at once that he was trying to make a fool of you. We all, by the very law of our minds, at once conclude that that which is full of intelligence and appeals to intelligence comes from intelligence. And so when I enter into "the treasuries of the snow," and see the

> tiny spherule traced with lines
> Of nature's geometric signs,

I see in it a revelation of the personality, the intelligence, the wisdom of God.[2]

¶ It may be argued, as it has been argued by the Rev. Aubrey Moore, in *Lux Mundi*, that "the counterpart of the theological belief in the unity and omnipresence of God is the scientific belief in the unity of nature and the reign of law"; that "the evolution which was at first supposed to have destroyed teleology is found to be more saturated with teleology than the view which it super-seded"; that "it is a great gain to have eliminated chance, to find science declaring that there must be a reason for everything, even when we cannot hazard a conjecture as to what the reason is"; that "it seems as if in the providence of God the mission of modern science was to bring home to our unmetaphysical ways of

---

[1] C. J. Perry.   [2] T. Hind, *The Treasures of the Snow*, 15.

thinking the great truth of the Divine immanence in creation, which is not less essential to the Christian idea of God than to the philosophical view of nature." But on the opposite side it may be represented—as, indeed, Mr. Aubrey Moore himself expressly allows—that all these deductions are valid only on the preformed supposition, or belief, " that God is, and that he is the rewarder of such as diligently seek him." [1]

3. The perfection of the snow crystals assures us that God cares for little things. The simplest creatures of the Divine Hand and the minutest details of their structures are not unworthy of infinite power. Who could have thought these crystals of the snowstorm worthy of such care ? Only a snowflake ! Is it not a waste of beauty ? What unnumbered myriads of them are floating there through the skies ! How they blanket the fields ; drift in great banks along the fences and railway tracks ; fill the ravines in the hills ; pack the gorges of the mountain ; and lie heaps on heaps upon the highest summits ! Surely, as we think of the seeming waste of beauty, we may sing over these flowers of the snow, these crystal gems of the winter storm, as Gray sang in his *Elegy* :

> Full many a gem of purest ray serene
>   The dark unfathomed caves of ocean bear,
> Full many a flower is born to blush unseen,
>   And waste its sweetness on the desert air.

Yes ! These flowers of the snow, these gems of the winter storm, God has wrought out with as careful touch as the *Victoria Regia* or the twinkling lustre of Venus, the evening star.

¶ Nothing is small or great in God's sight ; whatever He wills becomes great to us, however seemingly trifling, and if once the voice of conscience tells us that He requires anything of us, we have no right to measure its importance. [2]

> And God works in the little as the great,
>   A perfect work, and glorious over all,
> Or in the stars that choir with joy elate,
>   Or in the lichen spreading on the wall. [3]

[1] *Life and Letters of G. J. Romanes, F.R.S.*, 249.
[2] Jean Nicolaus Grau.   [3] Walter C. Smith, *Raban.*

II.

THE QUALITIES OF SNOW.

1. The first thing that strikes us about snow is its *purity*. The snow is white because the tiny crystals of which it is made reflect so much light. So much light is reflected by the snow that it often makes people snow-blind from excess of light.

¶ What is the blackest thing in all the world? Not jet, nor ebony; not the raven's plume, nor the pupil of an Ethiop's eye. The blackest thing in all the world is said to be the blight at the heart of a flower when it is just stricken with death. So the blackest thing in the moral universe is sin at the centre of a soul, spreading corruption through the whole nature of man.

What is the reddest thing in the world? Not the glow of the sunrise or of the sunset; not the heart of a ruby. The reddest thing in the world is the stream that flows from the fountain of life. Blood; "the life is in the blood." The most vivid of all tragedies is that of Calvary. In all the moral universe there is naught that so touches the heart of the race.

What is the whitest thing in the world? The whitest thing in the world is the driven snow, for this is not superficial, but whiteness through and through. In all the moral universe there is nothing so glorious as the whiteness of holiness; the fine linen, clean and white, which is the righteousness of saints.

What is the greatest thing in the world? Love! Ay. Not our love to God, but God's love to us, manifest in Jesus Christ. The love that holds the hyssop-branch of our frail faith and with it sprinkles the blood upon the soul defiled with the blackness of sin, until it becomes as white as the driven snow. This is the marvellous alchemy of grace. There is forgiveness with God.[1]

2. Snow too has a wonderful *power*. One flake is weak enough, but what can the avalanche and glacier not do? Here is God's dynamite. In this apparent weakness is the hiding of His strength. The flake that falls into the cleft of the rock, with a few more of its feeble kinsfolk, shall take hold of the roots of the everlasting mountain and tear them asunder. This is God's way of working. He builds His temple without the sound of hammer or of axe. The sunshine, the atmosphere, the fallen rain—these

[1] D. J. Burrell, *The Spirit of the Age*, 208.

are His calm potencies. You trample the snowflakes under foot, the children play with them; yet they have within them the possibility of great convulsion. Here are magazines of power. Men work amid demonstration, the shouting of ten thousand voices, the booming of heavy artillery. God's power is quiet, constant, persistent, infinite, everywhere. So ubiquitous is His omnipotence that men have sometimes taken Force to be their god. When it was desired to blow a ledge of rocks out of New York harbour there were years of preparation—digging of mines, placing of charges, laying of fuses; then the city stood listening; the explosion, the waterspout, and it was done. God rides through the universe in His chariot of Almightiness and its ponderous wheels move as silently as the waving of a butterfly's wings.

¶ A learned physicist has declared that to produce from the vapour of water a quantity of snowflakes which a child could carry would demand energy competent to gather up the shattered blocks of the largest stone avalanche of the Alps, and pitch them twice the height from which they fell. If a single baby handful require such force for its creation, what power must have been put forth to produce the thick blanketing of snow that lies upon the northland, from mountain-top to valley, during the winter season ? [1]

¶ Writing to his sister in England from Fort Vermilion, Bishop Bompas said : " In your letter I am amused at your regret that you cannot promise me snow and ice in heaven. All I can say is, let us be thankful for it here while we have it, and say, ' Praise Him, snow and vapours.' Depend on it there would be a gap in the display in the wonders of God in Nature if this country were left out. Nowhere in Nature is God's power more forcibly shown, as you will find explained in Job xxxvii. and Psalm cxlvii." [2]

Hark ! the rushing snow !
The sun-awakened avalanche ! whose mass,
Thrice sifted by the storm, had gathered there
Flake after flake, in heaven-defying minds
As thought by thought is piled, till some great truth
Is loosened, and the nations echo round,
Shaken to their roots, as do the mountains now.[3]

[1] H. C. McCook, *The Gospel in Nature*, 94.
[2] *An Apostle of the North : Memoirs of Bishop Bompas*, 77.
[3] Shelley, *Prometheus Unbound*.

3. Another thing that is worth observing in the snow is the *silence* of its falling. What should you think of a lace mill in which more than a thousand different patterns of lace were being made? Would you not say that this was a very "treasury of lace"? But if you could find such a mill you would see whirring wheels, grinding gears, humming spindles, great leathern belts, and many men and deft-fingered women at work. You would also expect to see a big, tall chimney to furnish the draught to burn large quantities of coal under the boilers to make the steam, to furnish the power, to drive the gears, belts, spindles, and wheels to make the lace. And then if you should look closely at the lace under a microscope the threads would look as rough as a clothes-line. What shall we say of the treasuries of the snow—the silent treasure-house out of which falls, without chimney or belt or wheel or spindle or noise or fuss, most beautiful crystals, which, examined under a microscope, only grow more beautiful—so many kinds that we cannot remember even the names of them all, much less their shape, and so many in number as to cover a vast tract of country a foot deep with them in twelve hours?

> The snow had begun in the gloaming,
>   And busily all the night
> Had been heaping field and highway
>   With a silence deep and white.
>
> Every pine and fir and hemlock
>   Wore ermine too dear for an earl,
> And the poorest twig on the elm-tree
>   Was ridged inch deep with pearl.
>
> From sheds new-roofed with Carrara
>   Came Chanticleer's muffled crow,
> The stiff rails softened to swan's-down,
>   And still fluttered down the snow.
>
> I stood and watched by the window
>   The noiseless work of the sky,
> And the sudden flurries of snow-birds,
>   Like brown leaves whirling by.
>
> I thought of a mound in sweet Auburn
>   Where a little headstone stood;
> How the flakes were folding it gently,
>   As did robins the babes in the wood.

Up spoke our own little Mabel,
  Saying, "Father, who makes it snow?"
And I told of the good All-father
  Who cares for us here below.

Again I looked at the snow-fall,
  And thought of the leaden sky
That arched o'er our first great sorrow,
  When that mound was heaped so high.

I remembered the gradual patience
  That fell from that cloud like snow,
Flake by flake, healing and hiding
  The scar that renewed our woe.

And again to the child I whispered,
  " The snow that husheth all,
Darling, the merciful Father
  Alone can make it fall!"

Then, with eyes that saw not, I kissed her;
  And she, kissing back, could not know
That *my* kiss was given to her sister,
  Folded close under deepening snow.[1]

III.

The Use of Snow.

1. Snow is a warm sheath for the earth. Its very colour is unfavourable to the radiation of heat. It follows that when heavy beds are laid upon the earth they act precisely as do bed-coverings or clothes to the human body. The warmth of the covered soil is kept within itself. Moreover, to some extent the rays of the sun penetrate the snow even when it is of considerable thickness. From these two facts results a third fact; viz. that the upper or surface stratum of the ground, even though it be frozen at the first fall of the snow, is soon thawed out, and does not again fall below the freezing-point during the winter, at least while the snow lasts.

[1] J. R. Lowell, *The First Snow Fall.*

From its loose texture, and from the fact that it contains several times its bulk of air, snow is a very bad conductor of heat. It is ranked with wool among the poorest of conductors, and thus it forms an admirable covering for the ground from the effects of radiation. It is relatively as warm to the earth in its thick enswathement of white packed crystals as is the softest wool to the human body. It has happened not infrequently in times of great cold that the soil is forty degrees warmer than the surface of the overlying snow. These facts will suffice to show the value of the snowy mantle which God sends to the earth during the severe frosts of winter.

¶ In Vermont, for four successive days of one winter, the temperature immediately above the snow was thirteen degrees below zero. Beneath the snow, which was four inches deep, the temperature was nineteen degrees above zero, a difference of thirty-two degrees within four or five inches. Under a drift of snow two feet deep the temperature was twenty-seven degrees above zero, thus making a difference of forty degrees, showing that the soil beneath the snow-beds was from thirty-two to forty degrees higher than the temperature of the air. The value of this fact in preserving the life and vigour of plants is at once apparent. It is for this reason that in the borders and glades of woods and forests violets and other small plants begin to vegetate as soon as the snow has thawed the soil around their roots; and they are not infrequently found in full flower under two or three feet of snow.[1]

¶ In the Lake Superior region, much colder than our own,—where the snow falls with the first frosts, and stays to the edge of summer,—many of the plants we dig up, and put into our cellars, are left in the ground with perfect safety, because " He giveth snow like wool " to preserve them under its warm fleece. In my readings, I have found many curious records of persons buried under the snow, surviving through long spans of time; but, if a hand or a foot was exposed, that was lost.[2]

> Fill soft and deep, O winter snow,
> The sweet azalea's oaken dells,
> And hide the bank where roses blow,
> And swing the azure bells!

[1] H. C. McCook, *The Gospel in Nature*, 100.
[2] R. Collyer, *Nature and Life*, 52.

O'erlay the amber violet's leaves,
    The purple aster's brookside home,
Guard all the flowers her pencil gives
    A life beyond their bloom.

And she, when spring comes round again,
    By greening slope and singing flood
Shall wander, seeking, not in vain,
    Her darlings of the wood.[1]

2. Snow is a useful fertilizer. It prepares the soil for the uses of man. Every agriculturist recognizes this. Many a sheaf of wheat is a sheaf of reaped snowstorm. Many bushels of golden grain are but snowflakes turned to life in rye and barley. The great wheat-fields must have snow or the substitute for it. It is better than the manure which seizes hold of stubborn clods and dried fields, for it wraps them with its white cloak and makes them warm for spring sowing. It refuses to conduct their heat away. It hides it in radiant silence while it wakes the earth up to its coming possibility. Nothing so relieves a field of the care of a crop, or helps it to forget the scratching of the plough or harrow, or makes it independent of the sun which exhorted it to work, as a heavy snowstorm which hides it from December until April.

The snow is falling softly o'er the plain,
    And slowly hiding 'neath a veil of white
    The fields that once with flowers were bedight
In days of summer sun and summer rain.
'Tis thus forgetfulness has healed my pain—
    By slowly hiding from my inward sight
    The dear dead joys that made the past so bright;
And therefore I am happy once again.
Yet e'en this painless peace must have an end;
    The sun will melt the snow in happy tears,
        And gild the earth with glory as of yore:
So if I meet thee once again, dear Friend,
    Thy smile will straightway melt the mists of years,
        And all the happy past be ours once more.[2]

3. Snow acts as a stimulus to mind and character. It has

---

[1] J. G. Whittier, *Flowers in Winter*.
[2] Ellen Thorneycroft Fowler, *Love's Argument and other Poems*, 123.

been noticed that as in the Tropics, land is fruitful, in snowy countries man is fruitful; as a rule the colder the climate, the more vigorous do we find intellect and character. The strong young races that from time to time have freshened the earth with men have always had a home in some winter land; and nearly all the most precious fruits in the higher departments of life and learning have ripened within the snowline. This just means—does it not?—that it is not a good thing for men that life should be made too easy for them. A certain amount of hardship to be contended with, a certain amount of opposition to be overcome, brings a man out, puts him upon his mettle and develops all his higher faculties. We see this in the matter of climate, in the actual winters and snows that the seasons bring.

¶ It is remarkable that in the thin edge of land between Cincinnati or St. Louis and Chicago there is this difference, that, in the gravest times the nation has ever known, the great ballads, whose influence for good was incalculable, — ballads like the "Battle-cry of Freedom,"—came from the city that is set farthest in the snow. I mention these instances as hints of what I mean by that better blessing in the snow than the contemplation of its starry order and noble uses as it lies on the land. What every healthy man and woman feels, when, after the disheartening rains of the last weeks in the autumn, the first powder of the white blessing falls; and then, as winter deepens, the snow comes in good earnest, and

> The whited air
> Hides hills and woods, the river and the heaven,

that is the intimation of the difference between the snow present in, and absent from, our life.[1]

¶ The eighteenth year of my ministry in Myrtle Street commences to-day. Through all these seventeen years I have not had one day's illness. Oh! my God, what a responsibility! I have had trials, severe and awful, especially the irreparable loss of my dear wife. But I think that I can say that these afflictions have been of inestimable service, this last in particular; what self-knowledge, what experience, what a power of sympathy it has produced! I now look upon an untried man as an uneducated man. Of all schools, the school of affliction is that which teaches most effectually.[2]

[1] R. Collyer, *Nature and Life*, 56.
[2] *Hugh Stowell Brown*, in *Life* by W. S. Caine, 140.

¶ Surely it is not true blessedness to be free from sorrow, while there is sorrow and sin in the world ; sorrow is then a part of love, and love does not seek to throw it off.[1]

A cold wind stirs the blackthorn
    To burgeon and to blow,
Besprinkling half-green hedges
    With flakes and sprays of snow.

Thro' coldness and thro' keenness,
    Dear hearts, take comfort so:
Somewhere or other doubtless
    These make the blackthorn blow.[2]

[1] George Eliot.   [2] Christina G. Rossetti.

Hearsay and Experience.

LITERATURE.

Clifford (J.), *Daily Strength for Daily Living*, 325.
Cook (G. A.), *The Progress of Revelation*, 75.
Dewhurst (E. M.), *The King and His Servants*, 46.
Drummond (J.), *Spiritual Religion*, 141.
Garbett (E.), *Experiences of the Inner Life*, 13.
Jellett (H.), *Sermons on Special and Festival Occasions*, 22.
King (E.), *The Love and Wisdom of God*, 242.
Maclaren (A.), *Expositions :* Esther and Job, 63.
Marshall (J. T.), *Job and his Comforters*, 130.
Moule (H. C. G.), *From Sunday to Sunday*, 72.
Neale (J. M.), *Sermons*, iii. 434.
Spurgeon (C. H.), *Metropolitan Tabernacle Pulpit*, xxxiv. (1888), No. 2009.
Vaughan (C. J.), *Voices of the Prophets*, 22.
Wagner (G.), *Sermons on the Book of Job*, 281.
Watson (R.), *The Book of Job*, 392.
Wright (D.), *The Power of an Endless Life*, 20.
Christian World Pulpit, xxxix. 181 (Ross Taylor); xli. 198 (M'Adam Muir); lxxv. 187 (Herbert).
Churchman's Pulpit : Good Friday and Easter Eve, vii. 93 (Williams).

HEARSAY AND EXPERIENCE.

I had heard of thee by the hearing of the ear;
But now mine eye seeth thee,
Wherefore I abhor myself, and repent
In dust and ashes.

Job xlii. 5, 6.

1. WHATEVER may have been the date at which this poem was written, it obviously represents a transition period in Jewish religious thought, and one of much interest and importance. Most modern scholars are agreed that, while Job himself belonged to patriarchal times, the unknown author who has so skilfully made the trials and patience of the patriarch the basis of his great poem cannot have written earlier than the time of Solomon, and probably wrote during the period of the Captivity. But whatever the date may have been, the time was one when men's minds were passing from an older and simpler faith to the fuller recognition of the facts of the Divine government. In the earlier ages of Israel's history, the national creed was this—Jehovah is righteous and His power is ever on the side of righteousness; therefore, prosperity always attends the good, and punishment follows hard on the steps of the evil-doer. The outward lot is an index to the inward character. If, for example, the people were willing and obedient, it might be confidently expected that their vineyards and fields would yield abundant harvests; whereas the ungodly should be as the chaff which the wind driveth away, a prey to the pestilence and the sword, swept off in the mid-time of their days. Such was their simple but powerful creed, true in its essence while rudimentary in its form, suited to their condition as children in both understanding and desire, while also fitted to be a stepping-stone to higher truth so soon as their hearts learned to seek a higher than earthly good.

But, according to the ways of human nature, the form became stereotyped, as though the letter rather than the spirit of the law were the abiding and essential element; and men settled down into the undoubting conviction that the measure of the Divine favour might in every case be gauged by the measure of outward prosperity. And with what result? As time went on and the horizon widened, and experience of life grew more varied, the question arose—How is this creed to be reconciled with facts? What about the prosperity of the wicked? What about the troubles and sore afflictions of the righteous? The facts were broad, staring, undeniable; what, then, about the ancient creed? Men of honest purpose could not shut their eyes to the seeming contradiction, and felt themselves like persons shipwrecked, cast out in a wide and troubled sea. Was the faith of their fathers and their own faith proved to be a baseless dream? Must they yield up their trust in Jehovah as the supreme and righteous Ruler? Must they think of God—if there be a God—as either indifferent to moral distinctions, or else powerless to give effect to His preferences? The rise of such questions marked an era of first importance in Israel's religious history. It was the emerging out of comparative childhood, an advance to a theology at once more spiritual, more true to the facts of life, and charged, moreover, with new sympathies for human sorrow and need. In the breathing, burning words of this poem we have the lasting record of this great transition, this passing of the old faith into the new.

¶ The Book of Job hovers like a meteor over the old Hebrew literature: in it, but not of it, compelling the acknowledgment of itself by its own internal majesty, yet exerting no influence over the minds of the people, never alluded to, and scarcely ever quoted, till at last the light which it heralded rose up full over the world in Christianity.[1]

¶ I call the Book of Job, apart from all theories about it, one of the grandest things ever written with pen. One feels, indeed, as if it were not Hebrew; such a noble universality, different from noble patriotism or sectarianism, reigns in it. A noble Book; all men's Book! It is our first, oldest statement of the never-ending Problem—man's destiny, and God's ways with him here in this earth. And all in such free flowing outlines; grand in its

---

[1] J. A. Froude, *Short Studies*, i. 296.

sincerity, in its simplicity, in its epic melody and repose of reconcilement.

There is the seeing eye, the mildly understanding heart. So *true*, everyway ; true eyesight and vision for all things ; material things no less than spiritual : . . . Such living likenesses were never since drawn. Sublime sorrow, sublime reconciliation ; oldest choral melody as of the heart of mankind ;—so soft, and great ; as the summer midnight, as the world with its seas and stars ! There is nothing written, I think, in the Bible or out of it, of equal literary merit.[1]

2. In its essential feature the Book of Job is thus, in the first place, the history of a great moral struggle and victory. It is the powerful poetic presentment of the ascent of a man's soul from darkness into light, from a narrow and failing creed into a bolder, broader, and truer one. Everything about the book, as it has been said, speaks of a man who had broken from the narrow littleness of the peculiar people. It is in some measure the story of a good man's life, who lived in days when good and pious men believed that sin and suffering were almost identical terms—that goodness and prosperity always went together.

¶ The nearest approach to the desolation and sublime sorrow of Job is the blasting misery and grief that falls upon the old, discrowned Lear of Shakespeare. But Lear, under the weakening of age, is the active instrument in the procurance of his troubles. Upon Job, radiant in his integrity and unfailing humaneness, the catastrophe descends as a bolt out of the blue.[2]

3. But the author has a wider practical design. He considered his new truth regarding the meaning of affliction as of national interest, and to be the truth needful for the heart of his people in their circumstances. But the teaching of the book is only half its contents. It contains a history, and this history furnishes the profoundest lesson to be learned. It exhibits deep and inexplicable affliction, a great moral conflict, and a victory. The author meant the history which he exhibits and his new truth to inspire new conduct and new faith, and to lead to a new issue in the national fortunes. In Job's sufferings, undeserved and inexplicable to him, yet capable of an explanation most consistent with

---

[1] T. Carlyle, *Heroes and Hero-Worship*, 45.
[2] J. Vickery, *Ideals of Life*, 103.

the goodness and faithfulness of God, and casting honour upon His steadfast servants; in his despair, bordering on unbelief, at last overcome; and in the happy issue of his afflictions—in all this Israel should see itself, and from the sight take courage and forecast its own history.

I.

THE HEARING OF THE EAR.

"I had heard of thee by the hearing of the ear."

1. Job does not mean to say that before his affliction he was entirely destitute of all knowledge of God. The words, " I had heard of thee by the hearing of the ear," taken by themselves, and without reference to Job's history, might mean this. It is language which one might use of days spent in entire ignorance of God, when darkness reigned in the heart. How many there are who hear of God by the hearing of the ear and nothing more! What they hear makes no impression upon their hearts. They never realize the presence and attributes of God. There is no contact between God's mind and theirs. The words which they hear are but a *sound*, conveying no ideas or thoughts. Was this the case with Job? His whole history seems to us to say most distinctly, " No." He is described in the very beginning of this book as one who " feared God "; and all the workings of his mind under his affliction show, at any rate, some real knowledge of God. What Job means to describe is his progress in the knowledge of God, which he does by comparing it to the two senses of *hearing* and *sight*. The ear, as compared with the eye, is a very imperfect medium of knowledge. When we hear the description of any-thing, it always requires some previous knowledge, as well as some imagination, to realize the picture set before us. If a person has not the previous knowledge requisite, or the imagination necessary to realize the thing or things described, the description, however beautiful and vivid, is to them mere sound. In sight, on the contrary, there is no such difficulty—no such effort of the imagination is required—and hence it is found that the only

effectual way of teaching very little children, so as to give them accurate knowledge, is to present objects to the eye.

¶ Ruskin believed the secret of life as well as of art to lie in a sort of heavenly obedience, a triumphant energy, a fiery contemplation. The reason why he clothed his message at first in terms of art is a mere question of faculty. To Ruskin the purest delight of which his spirit was capable came through the eye, through the mysteries of light and colour, of form and curve—the devices which make such a man say in a rapture of spiritual satisfaction, "Yes, it is like that !" He had both the eye for effect and the eye for detail, sight at once extended and microscopical. He wrote of himself, "I had a sensual faculty of pleasure in *sight*, as far as I know unparalleled." [1]

"I do beseech thee, God, show me thy face."
"Come up to me in Sinai on the morn!
Thou shalt behold as much as may be borne."
And on a rock stood Moses, lone in space.
From Sinai's top, the vaporous, thunderous place,
God passed in cloud, an earthly garment worn
To hide, and thus reveal. In love, not scorn,
He put him in a clift of the rock's base,
Covered him with his hand, his eyes to screen—
Passed—lifted it : his back alone appears !
Ah, Moses, had he turned, and hadst thou seen
The pale face crowned with thorns, baptized with tears,
The eyes of the true man, by men belied,
Thou hadst beheld God's face, and straightway died ! [2]

¶ A poor Chinaman came to a missionary for baptism, and when asked if he had heard the Gospel, replied that he had not heard it, but he had seen it. His neighbour had been an inveterate smoker of opium and a man of violent temper. But he had become a Christian and his whole life was altered. He gave up opium, and became loving and amiable. "So," said the man, "I have seen the Gospel."

2. In the first clause of the text we find the root of Job's perplexities. He had accepted implicitly the traditional belief of his day regarding God's providence; but, conscious of rectitude, he sees plainly that, in his own case, that belief does not square with the facts. And he is too honest and too fearless to shut his eyes

[1] A. C. Benson, *Ruskin : A Study in Personality*, 48.
[2] George MacDonald.

to the contradiction. He will neither be untrue to his own con-sciousness of integrity, nor yet will he "speak unrighteously for God." Let those trouble-bringing "comforters" press him as they may, he will not affirm the thing that is not. No; amid the wreck of all else—stripped of all his possessions, ravaged in body by hideous disease, seized by the neck and dashed to pieces by God as a guilty and hateful thing, met by his former friends, not with the sympathy he had looked for, but with cutting moralizings and angry scorn—his noble manhood refused to cringe; he would not gainsay his integrity. "There is no violence in mine hands, and my prayer is pure." Neither in his dealings with men nor in his walk with God had he done aught that could explain his overwhelming experiences. Here, then, was a distinct contradic-tion between his old religious belief—what he had heard of God by the hearing of the ear—and the facts of his personal experi-ence. Accordingly, like many a man after him, Job found him-self adrift on the surging waves of doubt.

¶ Mrs. Humphry Ward's *Robert Elsmere* is the story of a clergyman who had sadly to renounce his faith because, in the presence of enlightenment, it was no longer tenable. He is de-scribed as a man of noble character who followed truth whereso-ever it led him. And in following what he believed to be truth, he, of course, did well. But this has perhaps not been sufficiently noted: in the delineation of his character the beliefs from which he parted were really never his. He had been taught them as a child, he had received them by tradition, he had never turned them over in his mind, never sounded their depths. And so, when another aspect of truth was presented to him which he studied with earnestness, and which he found contained much that was helpful to his life, the old beliefs, which he had only fancied that he had believed, could not but fall away. The tradi-tion which we accept may be true in every detail, the authority before which we bow may be worthy of all veneration, but if, having attained to years and powers in which we are capable of making a decision for ourselves, our faith is still held on the frail and solitary tenure that, owing to the accident of our birth in a Christian country, we were taught it in our childhood, it will fail us in the time of trouble.[1]

[1] P. M'Adam Muir.

II.

THE DIRECT VISION.

"But now mine eye seeth thee."

1. It might be supposed at first that the simplest way of re-storing Job to peace would have been to reveal to him that his afflictions were not due to his sin, but were the trial of his righteousness, and in this way solve the problem that perplexed him. But the elements of blameworthiness in Job's conduct forbade this simple treatment. The disease had spread in his mind, and developed moral symptoms, which required a broader remedy. Besides, it is God who now speaks to Job; and in His teaching of men He never moves in the region of the mere under-standing, but always in that of the religious life. He may re-move perplexities regarding His providence and ways from men's minds; but He does not do so by the immediate communication of intellectual light, but by flushing all the channels of thought and life with a deeper sense of Himself. Under the flow of this fuller sense of God, perplexities disappear, just as rocks that raise an angry surf when the tide is low are covered and unknown when it is full. This is the meaning of God's manifestation to Job out of the storm. He brings Himself and His full glory near to Job, and fills his mind with such a sense of Him as he had never had before—"Now mine eye seeth thee." His former knowledge of God, though he had prided himself upon it, seems to him now only such a knowledge as one gets by hearsay, confused and defective. His present knowledge is that of eyesight, immediate and full.

¶ I quite agree with you that such things as these—God's goodness and grace in the hearts He has made—are the *true stars* we have to look to in our night, and if some of them have set sooner, they did shine for us, and are shining still. Our small horizon is not His universe, I think this is a conviction that grows on us the more we dwell on it, and how thankful we should be when God has given us in our history realities of *life* to help us to rise to the realities of *faith*! It is a way in which sight helps faith; for surely something akin to this lies in the words of Christ, " He that hath *seen* me hath *seen* the Father "—not merely that Christ is the *image* of God, but that a Divine life witnessed by us on earth is the *evidence* of a God. So that one may say, we can be as sure of God as if we had *seen* Him, and if we are sure of *Him* we are sure of *everything*.[1]

¶ How can a man, without clear vision in his heart first of all, have any clear vision in the head ? It is impossible ![2]

¶ Job has been told nothing, but he feels the terrible and tingling atmosphere of something which is too good to be told, the refusal of God to explain His design is itself a burning hint of His design. The riddles of God are more satisfying than the solutions of man.[3]

O Master of my soul,
  To whom the lives of men,
That floated once upon Thy breath,
  Shall yet return again.

Give me the eyes to see,
  Give me the ears to hear,
Give me the spiritual sense
  To feel that Thou art near.

So, when this earthly mist
  Fades in the azure sky,
My soul shall still be close to Thee,
  And in Thee cannot die.[4]

2. The revelation always comes as men are able to receive it. For ourselves—for us who have left far behind us that simple answer to the problems of life, which satisfied Job's friends, and nearly broke Job's heart—we too feel our darkness still. Life is still full of strange reverses, inexplicable wounds. Yet, as we too feel inclined to take our places by Job's side in his hour of doubt, we feel that we have light vouchsafed to us that was withheld from him. The light given in this book was dim and scanty. We see in it the dawn of one of those new and healing truths, fragments of which are flashed upon the human soul in hours of pain. But we see the dawn only. The whole revelation of the Christian life, of the life of Christ—the upward course of One who was despised, and humiliated, and scourged, and slain, who was

---

[1] *Letters of John Ker*, 84.   [2] Carlyle, *Past and Present*.
[3] G. K. Chesterton.   [4] Edwin Hatch.

"made perfect through sufferings"—has brought a new idea into the world, one whose future fulness is only indicated and fore-shadowed in this book. But it was one which the age of Job could hardly have conceived, and which centuries later the Jewish nation steadfastly rejected. It has leavened race after race with the ennobling sense that, as this great tale, as this "flower of Old Testament poetry," has its root in sorrow, so the highest, the divinest life may be compatible with sorrow, may rest on pain and self-sacrifice. To how many sufferers has the lesson come like spring airs to a frozen soil—has taught them that the truest use of pain, sometimes even of spiritual pain, and racking doubts and disturbing questions, is not to paralyse but to strengthen the soul.

¶ Are there not far worse things in the world than outward misery such as ill-health and suffering, even than bereavement and loss of those we love? Is not a heart full of selfishness a worse misery than a body full of pain? And may not the patience and power of endurance, and of forgetting self, that sorrow and trial are often seen to work out in a character, be worth the sorrow and the trial? Can you imagine a higher character than Christ's, and was not His "made perfect through sufferings"? Suffering, like all else in life, falls into its right place and finds its reason and meaning to those who believe in a Father who deals with His children in love; to those who refuse that belief it must be a dreary and meaningless business, I grant.[1]

¶ One of the thoughts which pass sometimes through our minds about the sufferings of the Cross is, What *could* be the necessity of such suffering? What *was* the use of it? How, with infinite power, could not its ends have been otherwise attained? Why need He have suffered? Why could not the Father save Him from that hour? But I suppose that, after all, the real difficulty is not about Him, but about ourselves. Why pain at all? I can only say that the very attempt to give an answer, that the very thought of an answer *by us* being conceivable, seems to me one which a reasonable being in our circumstances ought not to entertain. It seems to me one of those questions which can be expressed only by such a figure as a fly trying to get through a glass window, or a human being jumping into space; that is, it is almost impossible to express the futility of it. It is obvious that it is part of a wider subject, that it could not be answered *by itself*, that we should need to know a great many other things to have the power

[1] *Principal Story : Memoir by his Daughters*, 152.

of answering. The facts which witness to the goodness and the love of God are clear and undeniable; they are not got rid of by the presence and certainty of other facts, which seem of an opposite kind; only the co-existence of the two contraries is perplexing. And then comes the question, which shall have the decisive governing influence on wills and lives? You must, by the necessity of your existence, trust one set of appearances; which will you trust? Our Lord came among us not to clear up the perplexity, but to show us which side to take.[1]

> 'Tis peace in pain to know that pain
>   Secured us pain's eternal end;
> And that the more exceeding gain,
>   To which by grace our souls ascend,
> My great Redeemer won for me
> By more exceeding agony.
>
> 'Tis true my pain is still my pain:
>   Heavy its hand on thought and prayer!
> But while that Love to me is plain
>   It lays *its* hand upon despair:
> And soon I know this faint "How long?"
> For me may quicken into song;
>
> Beholding Thee—in what repose,
>   By what still streams of Paradise!
> Beholding memory of Thy woes
>   Still in those deep pathetic Eyes:
> Ah me! what blest exchange for pain,
> If I attain, if I attain!
>
> Am I too soon in love with death?
>   I know not if 'tis ill or well:
> If ill, then, Master, stay this breath,
>   Deny mine ear the passing bell!
> One thing I ask, since I am Thine,
> Thy Will be done, Thy Will be mine.[2]

3. There are special moments in life when the veil of the other world seems to be uplifted by the hand of the Holy Spirit, and through the "rent curtain" of the seen we perceive God so close and near that we seem to stand face to face with Him. What has been to us little more than a name, or a vast and vague

---

[1] Dean Church, *Life and Letters*, 274.
[2] S. J. Stone, *Poems and Hymns*, 116.

abstraction, becomes all at once a living Person. The occasion may widely vary. It may be an illness, an accident, an open grave, an awakening text, a word dropped from a child's lips, or a silent communing of the heart with itself at some midnight hour when everything has slept save the conscience within us. But there can be few who have not experienced such a sight of the Deity at some time or other.

¶ To learn to love, one must first learn to see. "I lived for twenty years by my sister's side," said a friend to me, one day, "and *I saw her* for the first time at the moment of our mother's death." Here, too, it had been necessary that death should violently fling open an eternal gate, so that two souls might behold each other in a ray of the primeval light.[1]

¶ I have learned much on this journey, and hope to tell things in the autumn at Oxford that will be of great use, having found a master of the religious schools at Florence, Filippo Lippi, new to me, though often seen by me, without seeing, in old times, though I had eyes even then for some sights. But this Filippo Lippi has brought me into a new world, being a complete monk, yet an entirely noble painter.[2]

¶ It was the consciousness of something eternal, within and without him, that made Green what he was. His wife once told him that he was like Sir Bors in the "Holy Grail," and the likeness holds in more senses than one. A "knight of the spirit" he assuredly was; not Galahad, "crowned king far in the spiritual city"; not Percivale, sadly resolved "to pass away into the quiet life"; not Lancelot, with "the fire of madness in his eyes"; but

Sir Bors it was
Who spake so low and sadly at our board;
And mighty reverent at our grace was he:
A square-set man and honest; and his eyes,
An out-door sign of all the warmth within,
Smiled with his lips—a smile beneath a cloud,
But heaven had meant it for a sunny one.

And if we had asked him whether he had seen the Divine vision, we can fancy that, like Sir Bors, he would have answered,

"Ask me not, for I may not speak of it;
I saw it."[3]

[1] M. Maeterlinck, *Treasure of the Humble*, 192.
[2] Ruskin, in E. T. Cook's *Life*, ii. 205.
[3] R. L. Nettleship, *Memoir of Thomas Hill Green*.

III.

THE RESULT OF THE VISION.

"Wherefore I abhor myself, and repent in dust and ashes."

1. *The vision of God reduces Job to self-humiliation.*—In seeing God he saw himself. The glory of that light streamed upon him, disclosing the recesses of his nature, permitting him with horror to behold imperfections and weaknesses which the darkness had hitherto hidden from his view. It was so different estimating himself in the light which the criticism of his friends threw around him and estimating himself in the light which searched the thoughts and intents of his heart. So long as he had brooded over his sorrow, and had listened to the attempts of his friends to explain the purpose of the Almighty in sending it, so long he could not detect any unrighteousness in himself, he could declare himself to be guiltless of the evil imputed to him as the exceptional cause of his exceptional misery. But when he looked from himself to God, when he saw the Eternal Holiness and Purity, the new sight awoke within him a knowledge of himself which all his self-inspection had been unable to produce. The greatest earthly wisdom became as foolishness, the greatest earthly virtue became as vileness by the contrast. He might exculpate himself before men, he could not exculpate himself before God; He had been uttering words which he ought not. He had been defiant where he ought to have been submissive; he had been mis-interpreting the Divine Law; he had been rushing forward where he ought to have held back. He was face to face, not with the prejudiced, partial judgment of men which he might well resent, but with the impartial righteous judgments of God from which there was no appeal; and the knowledge of that judgment removed all pride in his own integrity. All that he could now say—he the upright, he the resolute—in his own justification, was, "I abhor myself, and repent in dust and ashes."

¶ Those who ascend the Mount of Purification have learnt so to hate the corruptions of the first kingdom, that linger as scales before their eyes, preventing their vision of God, that they welcome with joy any pain, even, that shall deliver them from these hindrances. When their longing for the beatific vision, or perfect union with their true Lord and country, overmasters their personal sense of defilement and unfitness for His presence, they rise upwards to their goal, for they find no prison walls or barriers to keep them in any school of discipline.[1]

¶ There are, perhaps, twelve cases in the Bible that are very conspicuous, in which men have had a vision of God, more or less intense, more or less truly glorious. But in every case they have been prostrated, and humiliated and overwhelmed, and the more intense the vision of God, the more intense the humiliation and the more utter the prostration.[2]

2. *The vision of God awakens repentance.*—One glimpse of God with the eye of the heart does for Job more than all the harangues of his friends. They had charged him falsely, and his pride was only hardened by their unjust accusations. God had not charged him at all, but the very vision revealed at once his mistaken position. He saw his error, and sought to correct himself.

¶ When the electric light was first discovered, I was in a large hall where the gaslights were shining brightly and seemed perfect, but the moment the electric light shone, all the rest seemed as if they were put out. And so it is when God's light shines into us. It discloses the dimness of our light, the imperfection of our perfection. God would not have witnessed to the uprightness of Job if it had not been real; but this did not hinder it from appearing as nothing in the Light of God. This is the repentance of the righteous. It is not that their righteousness has been no righteousness, but God, perhaps in a moment, has shown to them greater heights, deeper depths, more earnest convictions, and so old attainments seem as if they were not.[3]

¶ All torn asunder, all annihilated, Francis cast himself on his face before God, the God who had made heaven and earth, the God who is all truth and all holiness, and before whose omnipotence nothing can stand without complete truth, complete holiness. Francis looked into the depths of his being, and he saw that on the whole earth there was not to be found a more useless creature, a greater sinner, a soul more lost and fallen to the bad than himself, and from the depths of his need he groaned before God: "Lord, be merciful to me a poor sinner!" And it came to pass that the empty cave over Poggio Bustone beheld a miracle, one that always happens when a soul in complete dis-

[1] Mrs. Russell Gurney, *Dante*.
[2] A. T. Pierson, in *The Keswick Week*, 1907, p. 27.   [3] M. F. Sadler, 75.

trust of itself calls out to its God in confidence and hope and charity—then there comes to pass the great miracle of *justification*. " I fear everything from my badness, but from Thy goodness I also hope for all," this was the innermost meaning of the prayer Francis sent up to God. And the answer came, as it always comes—" Fear not, my son, thy sins are forgiven thee ! "[1]

¶ For dramatic effectiveness Watts's picture of the " Death of Abel " is most impressive. We see Cain in the first moment of awakening from the passion which led him to do the dreadful deed, overwhelmed with remorse. His dark form stoops over his brother's prostrate figure, whose ghastly pallor is brought out by the light which casts Cain's body into shadow, and his hands cover his face in an agony of despair. Above him the clouds open, revealing the heavenly host in various attitudes, all expressive of their mournful concern for this new thing in the universe—the first death—the wonder and fear which this awful unknown fruit of human sin had produced. And following up the story of Cain, the artist has made a powerful epic poem of the world's first tragedy. He shows the first murderer coming back from his weary wanderings in search of rest, to the rude, earth-built altar on which his brother had offered up his acceptable sacrifice. His sufferings have deepened his repentance and purified his character, and haggard and worn-out he throws himself on the altar, recognizing the justice and righteousness of his doom. With true insight the artist has painted the angel of sympathy hovering over him in pity; the curse is removed, and the forgiveness of God calms his agitated spirit as the light of heaven illumines his worn-out frame.[2]

O, blest the souls that see and hear
The things of God to-day revealed,
Of old to longing saint and seer
Within the future closely sealed.

Be ours the vision, ours the will
To follow, though the faithless ban;
The love that triumphs over ill,
The trust in God and hope for man.

And Thou whose tides of purpose bear
These mortal lives that come and go,
Give us to feel through toil and prayer
Thy deep eternal underflow.[3]

[1] J. Jörgensen, *St. Francis of Assisi*, 73.
[2] Hugh Macmillan, *G. F. Watts*, 149.   [3] F. L. Hosmer.

3. Penitence is ever a mark of sainthood.—It is the special charm of Job's story that it exhibits this high-strung and strenuous integrity dwelling in the same spirit with the acutest penitence and throbbing self-loathing. We can recognize these qualities apart, and appreciate them in their singleness, but that they should blend in the same life, tenant the same spirit, and be sources of power to the same character, conflicts with our habitual thought. We expect John Bunyan, after his flagrant vices, to pass through an agony of remorse. It is the working of a just law, the fitting harvest to follow such sowing. That David should be immersed in floods of repentance after his base and cruel transgression is what we anticipate, and we are unsatisfied until we see it. We listen for the cry, "Father, I have sinned," of the prodigal son as soon as we see him in his father's embrace, receiving the fruits of his joy at his return. But when the one perfect servant of God, the exceptional man of all men, God's boasted choice, who has hated evil, striven to be true and do right, and suffered countless ills in order to succeed; when he abhors himself and repents in dust and ashes, as overcome with his grief, we are tempted to treat his language as affectation, his penitence as paralysis, and his self-loathing as disease.

And yet it is notorious that the minds of culminating power in the vast brotherhood of the world's workers and redeemers, the shepherds and kings sent of God to lead forth judgment unto victory, have not been more deeply marked by their persistent devotion to purity of thought, uncompromising fidelity to fact, and aspiration after perfection, than by their quivering sensitiveness to the smallness of their achievements, acute sense of personal fault, and prevailing consciousness, often attended by spasms of weakening pain, of absolute failure.

¶ It is Paul, the sovereign thinker of the Christian Church, the fearless antagonist of an unprogressive Judaism, potent beyond all men of his century as a man and as a missionary who is in his own esteem "less than the least of all saints, not meet to be called an apostle, a persecutor, an injurer, a blasphemer, and the chief of sinners." It is Augustine, saint and bishop, cultured and strong, with a manhood behind him of helpful toil and large success, who, as he lies dying at Hippo, his spirit bathed with serenity, though the Vandals are besieging the city, has written on the walls opposite him, "The sacrifices of God are a broken spirit; a broken and contrite heart, O God, thou wilt not despise." It is the sweet, seraphic, and holy Saint Bernard who chants the same verse as his swan song as he passes on to the calm seas of God's eternal love. It is Lady Jane Grey who repeats the cry for mercy of the penitential Psalms, as she ascends the scaffold. And Sir Thomas More solaces his spirit with the same strains as he lays his head upon the block to receive the fatal blow of the headsman's axe. It is William Carey, breathing out his life in one steadfast flame of missionary enthusiasm, who sings at life's close the self-depreciatory and Christ-trusting words:

> A guilty, weak, and helpless worm
> On Thy kind arms I fall;
> Be Thou my Strength and Righteousness,
> My Saviour, and my all.

It is the broad-minded Christian scholar and teacher, the creatoi of the "Broad Church" of our country, and the "Master" to a large and increasing host of disciples, who asks that the Fifty-first Psalm may be read to him as he enters upon the fuller life beyond :—that same song which John Rogers recited as he went to the stake, and Jeremy Taylor fashioned into a prayer. It is clear thinking and pure-minded Thomas Erskine, of Linlathen, said by his friends, and those most competent to judge, to be one of "the best and holiest" of men, "with least of the stains of earth, and most of the spirit of heaven," who repeats again and again at the close of his immensely fertile life, the words, "The blood of Jesus Christ, His Son, cleanseth from all sin; for He made Him sin for us who knew no sin, that we might become the righteousness of God in Him." So that the righteous Job in his penitence anticipates the Church of the first-born in heaven, and ascends to the rank of pioneer of the spirits of the just made perfect, as he goes through the seven-times heated furnace of sorrow for sin to his larger wisdom and sunnier prosperity. Even Don Silva feels:

> Men may well seek
> For purifying rites: even pious deeds
> Need washing.[1]

¶ Yes, all that part of Dr. Pusey's *Life* is wonderfully moving and sacred. I do not wonder that it has moved you so deeply:

[1] J. Clifford, *Daily Strength for Daily Living*, 332.

it certainly did me. But now let me try to set down the bearings of it all with regard to what you say about yourself; for I want you to think them over.

Sometimes a thing like this, which burns deeply into one's own conscience, makes all one's past professions seem almost unreal, and one's righteousness (as it is) filthy rags. Seen by such a standard, all one's confessions have been mere lip confessions, all one's communions seem almost mockeries, and all life hitherto a hideous sham. Thank God that He does send us such revelations. But then there is a danger lest we, in the excitement of the moment, forget how far the Lord hath helped us hitherto—how He is the surety that our life hitherto has not been in vain—a danger, in fact, lest we should deny the grace that we have already received. I have known devout penitent souls pull down their Christian life in the desire to undergo such a self-emptying, as they think it. You have no desire to do that, of course: but all the same it is very necessary to learn one's lessons of humiliation and penance without doing despite to what God has done in us already.[1]

4. *The way of penitence is the way of redemption.*—Christ cannot become Redeemer for those who feel no need to be redeemed, nor can they feel the need to be redeemed who have no serious estimate of sin. Nor can they have a serious estimate of sin who have no special consciousness of the holiness of God. It is all terribly logical and self-consistent. Redemption cannot appeal in the absence of the necessary presuppositions. Your idea of redemption must correspond with your idea of God. They who can enter into the spirit of the *De Profundis* and the *Miserere* are they to whom redemption will appeal. There it is, that ancient cry: "My sin is ever before me"; "Against thee, thee only, have I sinned, and done this evil in thy sight"; "If thou, Lord, shouldest mark iniquities, O Lord, who shall stand?" "Create in me a clean heart, O God; and renew a right spirit within me." Depend upon it, that the conscience which finds reality in these words possesses the data which redemption must always presuppose. They to whom such language is Oriental exaggeration will always tend to a Christianity with redemption left out. And yet it is the most sensitive consciences on earth who have identified themselves with that self-abasing estimate. One

[1] Bishop W. E. Collins, in *Life* by A. J. Mason, 58.

can only believe that they are right, and that they have arrived at this conclusion not because they strayed the farthest from God's presence, but because they saw the clearest into what God is. When the passions of the world are hushed, and the tumult of the flesh is calmed, when a man is more real, more himself, than at other times, then it is that he is disposed to say: "I had heard of thee by the hearing of the ear; but now mine eye seeth thee, wherefore I abhor myself, and repent in dust and ashes." The man who says that is the man who will cry aloud for redemption.

¶ Redemption is the raising up of a man from the evil condition in which he feels sacrifice as pain, into a condition in which it is felt as joy, a condition of true and perfect life.[1]

¶ As in its purer parts the human nature is a prototype of the Divine, so hence we may form some conception of the mode in which human repentance softens Divine justice, how it is at once accepted as the earnest of better things, as the beginning of a new life, and as being in itself the fruit and pledge of that Christian simplicity which brings us to the condition of little children. We must have conquered many worldly, many complicated, many anti-Christian feelings, before we arrive at the repentance of the prodigal son. . . . Well may it be conceived how this state of mind is more congenial to the Divine nature, has in it more softness, more faith, more love, more elevation, more purity, than the calm virtue of ninety-and-nine just persons who need no repentance.[2]

When I look back upon my life nigh spent,
    Nigh spent, although the stream as yet flows on,
I more of follies than of sins repent,
    Less for offence than Love's shortcomings moan.
    With self, O Father, leave me not alone—
Leave not with the beguiler the beguiled;
    Besmirched and ragged, Lord, take back thine own:
A fool I bring thee to be made a child.[3]

[1] J. Hinton.
[2] Bishop Stanley, in *Memoirs of Edward and Catherine Stanley*, 192.
[3] George MacDonald, "Organ Songs."

THE MAN THAT IS BLESSED.

LITERATURE.

Banks (L. A.), *David and his Friends*, 23.

Burrell (D. J.), *The Morning Cometh*, 243.

Davies (D.), *Talks with Men, Women and Children*, i. 234.

Deshon (G.), *Sermons for all the Sundays of the Ecclesiastical Year*, 322.

Foston (H. M.), *The Waiting Life*, 1.

Kingsley (C.), *Westminster Sermons*, 110.

McFadyen (J. E.), *Ten Studies in the Psalms*, 3.

Maclaren (A.), *Sermons Preached in Manchester*, iii. 225.

McLeod (M. J.), *Heavenly Harmonies for Earthly Living*, 27.

Matheson (G.), *Leaves for Quiet Hours*, 171.

Parker (J.), *The Ark of God*, 113.

    „   „   *The City Temple*, v. 289.

Pulsford (J.), *Infoldings and Unfoldings*, 1.

Simeon (C.), *Works*, v. 1.

Smellie (A.), *In the Hour of Silence*, 326.

Stall (S.), *Five Minute Object Lessons to Children*, 93.

Tholuck (A.), *Hours of Christian Devotion*, 85.

Thomas (J.), *Myrtle Street Pulpit*, iii. 172.

Walker (A. H.), *Thinking about It*, 59.

Watson (J.), *Respectable Sins*, 241.

Winter (G.), *Keep to the Right*, 59.

British Congregationalist, May 28, 1908 (Jowett).

Christian World Pulpit, xxvi. 269 (Mursell).

Expositor, 2nd Ser., i. 81 (Cox).

Preacher's Magazine, iii. (1892) 342 (Hawker) ; v. (1894) 414 (Walker) ; vi. (1895) 211 (Tubbs).

Sunday Magazine, 1883, p. 704 (Maclaren).

THE MAN THAT IS BLESSED.

Blessed is the man that walketh not in the counsel of the wicked,
Nor standeth in the way of sinners,
Nor sitteth in the seat of the scornful.—Ps. i. 1.

1. DEEP as is the interest attaching to the Psalter as the great storehouse of sacred poetry, and vast as is its importance considered as a record of spiritual life under the Old Dispensation, scarcely less interest and importance attach to it with reference to the position it has ever occupied both in the public worship of the Church and in the private life of Christians. No single book of Scripture, not even of the New Testament, has, perhaps, ever taken such hold on the *heart* of Christendom. None, if we may dare judge, unless it be the Gospels, has had so large an influence in moulding the affections, sustaining the hopes, purifying the faith of believers. With its words, rather than with their own, they have come before God. In these they have uttered their desires, their fears, their confessions, their aspirations, their sorrows, their joys, their thanksgivings. By these their devotion has been kindled and their hearts comforted. The Psalter has been, in the truest sense, the Prayer Book of both Jews and Christians.

¶ The Jewish Psalms have furnished the bridal hymns, the battle songs, the pilgrim marches, the penitential prayers, and the public praises of every nation in Christendom, since Christendom was born. They have rolled through the din of every great European battlefield; they have pealed through the scream of the storm in every ocean highway of the world. Drake's sailors sang them when they clave the virgin waters of the Pacific; Frobisher's, when they dashed against the barriers of Arctic ice and night. They floated over the waters on that day of days when England held her freedom against Pope and Spaniard, and won the naval supremacy of the world. They crossed the ocean with the *Mayflower* pilgrims; were sung round Cromwell's camp-fires, and his Ironsides charged to their music; whilst they have filled the peaceful homes of England with the voice of supplication and the breath of praise. In palace halls, by happy hearths, in squalid rooms, in pauper wards, in prison cells, in crowded sanctuaries, in lonely wilderness—everywhere they have uttered our moan of contrition and our song of triumph; our tearful complaints, and our wrestling, conquering prayer.[1]

¶ If all the greatest excellences and most choice experience of all the true saints should be gathered from the whole Church since it has existed, and should be condensed into the focus of one book; if God, I say, should permit any most spiritual and gifted man to form and concentrate such a book, such a book would be what the Book of Psalms is, or like unto it. For in the Book of Psalms we have not the life of the saints only, but we have the experience of Christ Himself, the Head of all the saints. So that you may truly call the Book of Psalms a little Bible. Be assured that the Holy Spirit Himself has written and handed down to us this Book of Psalms as a Liturgy, in the same way as a father would give a book to his children. He Himself has drawn up this Manual for His disciples; having collected together, as it were, the lives, groans, and experience of many thousands, whose hearts He alone sees and knows.[2]

There's lots of music in the Psalms, those dear sweet Psalms
    of old,
With visions bright of lands of light and shining streets of
    gold;
I hear them ringing, singing still, in memory soft and clear,
"Such pity as a father hath unto his children dear."

They seem to sing for evermore of better, sweeter days,
When the lilies of the love of God bloomed white in all the
    ways:
And still I hear the solemn strains in the quaint old meeting
    flow,
"O greatly blessed the people are the joyful sound that know."

No singing-books we needed then, for very well we knew
The tunes and words we loved so well the dear old Psalm
    Book through;
To "Coleshill" at the Sacrament we sang, as tears would fall,
"I'll of salvation take the cup, on God's name will I call."

[1] J. Baldwin Brown.   [2] Luther.

And so I love the dear old Psalms, and when my time shall
    come,
Before the light has left my eyes, and my singing lips are
    dumb,
If I can only hear them then I'll gladly soar away,—
"So pants my longing soul, O God, that come to Thee I
    may."

2. The First and Second Psalms are distinguished by having
no title or preliminary inscription. They appear to stand as an
introduction to the Psalter. They serve as an overture to the
great choral symphony which follows, giving forth the two great
themes which are to be wrought into so many forms of melody in
later Psalms. The one strikes the key-note of the blessedness of
keeping God's law; the other puts into music the hope of a coming
Messiah, and so together they anticipate almost all that is to
follow. At what stage of the collection of the Psalter they were
prefixed, or by whom, we do not know, and the knowledge would
be of no importance.

The teaching of these Psalms as to the blessedness of keeping the
law is to some extent the characteristic Old Testament teaching of
the outward prosperity of the righteous, and the transiency of the
wicked. Christianity does not altogether repeat that teaching.
The Cross has taught new lessons of the meaning of suffering and
the mystery of pain; and now that the Holy One of God has been
made perfect by suffering, the Old Testament thoughts as to the
connexion between well-doing and well-being, so far as externals
go, have been modified and deepened. But the inmost heart
of them remains true for evermore, and these Psalms declare a
universal and irreversible law, rooted in the nature of things, and
eternal as the throne of God, when they declare that obedience
is blessedness, and sin is destruction.

¶ The benediction, in the opening of the First Psalm, divides
at once the virtue which is to be strengthened, or to find voice, in
the following Psalms, into three conditions, the understanding of
which is the key to the entire law of Old Testament morality.

"Blessed is the man who" (first) "has not walked in the counsel
of the ungodly."

That is to say, who has not advanced, or educated himself, in
the "*counsel*" (either the opinions or the advice) of men who are
unconscious of the existence of God.

That is the law of our Intellectual Education.

" Nor " (secondly) " stood in the way of sinners."

That is to say, who has not adopted for the *standing*, establishing, and rule of his life, the ways, customs, or principles of the men who, whether conscious or unconscious of God's being, disobey His commands.

That is the law of our moral conduct.

" And hath not " (thirdly) " sat in the seat of the *scornful.*"

That is to say, who has not, in teaching or ruling others, permitted his own pride or egotism to make him intolerant of their creeds, impatient of their ignorance, or unkind to their failings. This throne of pride is, in the Vulgate, called the throne of *Pestilence.* I know not on what ground; but assuredly conveying this further truth, that the source of all noisome blast of heresy, " that *plaguing* strays " in the Christian Church, has been the pride and egotism of its pastors.

Here, then, are defined for us in the first words of the Psalter, the three great vices of Intellectual Progress, Moral Stature, and Cathedral Enthronement, by which all men are tempted in their learning, their doing, and their teaching; and in conquering which, they are to receive the blessing of God, and the peaceful success of their human life. These three sins are always expressed in the Greek Psalter in the same terms.

Ungodliness is *asebeia* ; Sin is *hamartia* ; Pride is *hyperēphania* ; and the tenor of every passage throughout the Psalms, occupied in the rebuke or threatening of the " wicked," is coloured by its specific direction against one or other of these forms of sin.

But, separate from all these sins, and governing them, is the monarchic " Iniquity," which consists in the *wilful* adoption of, and persistence in, these other sins, by deliberately sustained false balance of the heart and brain.

A man may become impious, by natural stupidity. He may become sinful, by natural weakness. And he may become insolent, by natural vanity. But he only becomes unjust, or unrighteous, by resolutely refusing to see the truth that makes against him; and resolutely contemplating the truth that makes for him.

Against this " iniquity," or " unrighteousness," the chief threatenings of the Psalter are directed, striking often literally and low, at direct dishonesty in commercial dealings, and rising into fiercest indignation at spiritual dishonesty in the commercial dealing and " trade " of the heart.[1]

3. The first word in the Psalter is a word expressive of

[1] Ruskin, *Rock Honeycomb* (*Works*, xxxi. 121).

emotion, being an exclamation: O the blessedness of so and so. The Hebrew word is often rendered *happy* in the A.V. (as Ps. cxxvii. 5, cxliv. 15, cxlvi. 5; Deut. xxxiii. 29; Job v. 17; Prov. iii. 13, xiv. 21, xvi. 20, xxviii. 14); and it might for distinctness be so rendered always. It occurs in the Psalter twenty-six times.

¶ How abundantly is that word " Blessed " multiplied in the Book of Psalms! The book seems to be made out of that word, and the foundation raised upon that word, for it is the first word of the book. But in all the book there is not one " Woe." [1]

¶ The Welsh translation is very expressive—" *White is that man's world* who walketh not in the counsel of the ungodly." The translator gives up all attempt at being literal, and seeks to express the central and governing thought that no spot or blemish can mar the whiteness of that man's character, experience or life. This conveys the idea of the completeness and fulness of the blessings expressed by the word " blessed." [2]

4. We all wish to know who the blessed man is. No one who values life, who cares for its enjoyments and its hopes, can be indifferent to this question, namely: Who is the vitally, the truly happy man? Here we have a distinct declaration upon the subject. The voice is loud, sweet, clear. The man who pronounces this opinion has evidently no difficulty upon the subject. His sentences are so sharp cut, so evidently spoken from the heart, that to him, at least, there is no doubt as to the happy man. Who is he then? He is described in this verse by what are called negatives. There is nothing affirmative said about him. We are told what he *does not* do. He does not walk in the counsel of the ungodly; he does not stand in the way of sinners; he does not sit in the seat of the scornful. As if goodness came by not doing things. But it so happens that we cannot understand some of the very highest things in life unless they are put to us in precisely this way.

¶ When God Himself came down from Heaven to set things in order, He took precisely the course that is taken by the writer of this verse. What did He say? He said, " Thou shalt not lie; thou shalt not kill; thou shalt not commit adultery; thou shalt not steal; thou shalt not bear false witness." As if goodness

---

[1] Donne.　　[2] D. Davies, *Talks with Men, Women and Children*, i. 235.

consisted in not doing evil; as if not to do anything were to do everything that is best. It is so in the teaching of your own children. Do you not begin by telling your little child what he *must not* do? If you were to set your child something that he must do, you would find it very difficult to accommodate yourself to his early perception. But if you tell him not to do certain things, you can more easily get at his understanding. There are more ways of saying *Thou shalt not* than there are of saying *Thou shalt*.[1]

¶ The man that walketh in the counsel of the ungodly is not a happy man. Can I teach any young life that one lesson? Do you want to go out to-night to seek a happy man? The Psalmist tells you that there is one direction in which you need not go, for he has been there before you, and the happy man cannot be found; and that is the direction of the counsel of the ungodly. Then where? The Psalmist says, "I can save you trouble in another direction; if you want to find a happy man, you will not find him in the way of sinners. I can yet save you a journey; you will not find a happy man amongst those who sit in the seat of the scornful." Then how much of the devil's territory is left for exploration? Not an inch. He has taken up the counsel of the ungodly, the way of sinners, the seat of the scornful. Take these things from the satanic empire and you have left nothing.[2]

5. This picture, then, begins with negatives. "Blessed is the man that walketh *not* in the counsel of the wicked, *nor* standeth in the way of sinners, *nor* sitteth in the seat of the scornful." It is not an accident that behind the shelter, as it were, of a forbidding wall of negatives, the fruits of holy character grow up. For in a world like this, where there is so much wickedness, and where there are so many men who do not live after the highest pattern, and from the highest motives, no good thing will ever be achieved, unless we have learned to say, "No! This did not I because of the fear of the Lord."

¶ There must be a daring determination, if need be, to be singular; not a preference for standing alone, not an abstinence from conventional signs of worldliness simply because they are conventional; but there must be first of all close-knit strength, which refuses to do what men round about us are doing. The characteristics of religious men must be, as the first thing that strikes one, that they are "a people whose laws are different

[1] Joseph Parker, *The City Temple*, v. 289.   [2] *Ibid.*, 290.

from all the people that be on the face of the earth." If you
have not learned to shelter your positive goodness behind a
barrier of negative abstinence, there will be little vitality and
little fruit in the weakling plants that are trying to blossom in
the undefended open, swept by every wind.[1]

¶ The free man is he who is *loyal* to the Laws of this Universe;
who in his heart sees and knows, across all contradictions, that
injustice *cannot* befall him here; that except by sloth and cowardly
falsity evil is not possible here. The first symptom of such a
man is not that he resists and rebels, but that he obeys. As poor
Henry Marten wrote in Chepstow Castle long ago:

> Reader, if thou an oft-told tale wilt trust,
> Thou'lt gladly do and suffer what thou must.

Gladly; he that will go gladly to his labour and his suffering, it
is to him alone that the Upper Powers are favourable and the
Field of Time will yield fruit.[2]

> How happy is he born and taught
>   That serveth not another's will;
> Whose armour is his honest thought,
>   And simple truth his utmost skill!
>
> Whose passions not his masters are;
>   Whose soul is still prepared for death,
> Untied unto the world by care
>   Of public fame or private breath;
>
> Who envies none that chance doth raise,
>   Nor vice; who never understood
> How deepest wounds are given by praise;
>   Nor rules of state, but rules of good;
>
> Who hath his life from rumours freed;
>   Whose conscience is his strong retreat;
> Whose state can neither flatterers feed,
>   Nor ruin make oppressors great;
>
> Who God doth late and early pray
>   More of His grace than gifts to lend;
> And entertains the harmless day
>   With a religious book or friend;

[1] A. Maclaren.   [2] Carlyle, *Latter-Day Pamphlets*, 213.

This man is freed from servile bands
Of hope to rise or fear to fall;
Lord of himself, though not of lands,
And having nothing, yet hath all.[1]

6. Now in this abstinence there is a certain progress. It is quite clear that there is an advance in the permanence of association with evil expressed by the three attitudes, walking, standing, sitting. It is also clear that there is an advance in the intensity of evil expressed by the progress from " counsel " to " way " ; from thought, purpose, plan, to its realization in a course of action, and that there is a further progress from " the way of sinners " to " the seat "—by which is meant, not a thing to sit upon, but an assembly seated—or the " session of the scorners."

¶ There is a perilous progress in sin.
At first I content myself with *walking in the counsel of the wicked.* It is an occasional companionship. It is a meeting only now and again. For a little while I am with them, and then some better influence calls me away—a remembrance of my mother's prayer, a sentence in a letter from a friend, a verse of the Bible shot suddenly into my mind.

But by and by I am found *standing in the way of sinners.* They have gained a greater power over me and a completer fascination. I have learned to love them too well. I linger much longer in their society, and it is hard almost to impossibility for me to tear myself from them. The poison is working; the leaven is spreading ; my condition is more fixed and more hopeless by far.

And, at last, where do you see me ? I am *sitting in the seat of the scornful.* I am at home among those who laugh at God and Christ and heaven and hell. You cannot discriminate me from them; I have joined their ranks; I am one of their number. Their resorts are mine ; their sneers and sarcasms are mine ; their seared conscience and withered heart are mine. Oh dreary ending of a dreary journey !

As I would escape that lowest depth of all, let me not look over the precipice or set my feet on the fatal slope. *Blessed is the man* who says, " I cannot; I will not," to the first allurements of sin. *Blessed is the man* who will not so much as walk in the Enchanted Ground.[2]

¶ In the great Psalm of life, we are told that everything that a man doeth shall prosper, so only that he delight in the law of

---

[1] Sir Henry Wotton, " Reliquiae."   [2] A. Smellie, *In the Hour of Silence,* 326.

his God, that he hath not walked in the counsel of the wicked, nor sat in the seat of the scornful. Is it among these leaves of the perpetual Spring,—helpful leaves for the healing of the nations,—that we mean to have our part and place, or rather among the "brown skeletons of leaves that lag, the forest brook along"? For other leaves there are, and other streams that water them,—not water of life, but water of Acheron. Autumnal leaves there are that strew the brooks, in Vallombrosa. Remember you how the name of the place was changed: "Once called 'Sweet water' (Aqua bella), now, the Shadowy Vale." Portion in one or other name we must choose, all of us,—with the living olive, by the living fountains of waters, or with the wild fig trees, whose leafage of human soul is strewed along the brooks of death, in the eternal Vallombrosa.[1]

I.

THE COUNSEL OF THE WICKED.

1. Who are these people who come before us at the first stage, and whom the Authorized Version describes as "the ungodly," and the Revised as "the wicked"? We may find a name for them that will bring them into clearer focus for us than either of these, and perhaps enable us to obtain a photograph of them which we shall more distinctly recognize in life. Following the derivation of the Hebrew word, we begin to find them appearing before us as a people who are abnormal and out of course; and this idea of them agrees very closely with their standing in the Psalm.

They stand out before us as a class of people whose aim has never taken shape through the fascination of life's nobler constraints. And perhaps we shall do well to translate their Hebrew name, for our purposes, as "the lawless." We do not need to think here always of any way of life that startles us with singularity or violence. We meet with its representative continually in business or in the street, and his look and behaviour are for the most part quite commonplace.

His sins are chiefly, so far, those of omission; the sins of commission are close behind. His indulgent mother would indignantly repudiate any suggestion of his perilous condition by

[1] Ruskin, *Proserpina* (*Works*, xxv. 247).

exclaiming, "He has never done anything wrong!" But has he done anything good, anything decided and firm? A moral negative will soon be transformed into a strong positive. Ruskin reminds us that at the judgment the verdict will not turn on the "have-nots," but on the "haves." The deciding question will not be, "How much evil have you *not* done?" but, "How much good have you done?" When the body is in a general low condition, it catches disease quickly; when the soul is in a general low condition, it easily catches sin. The ungodly youth is he who never shows indignation against sin, whose whole bearing is dull, insipid, and easy-going. The ungodly person is a moral invertebrate, a creeping thing; hence Pope's line pathetically applies to him:

We first endure, then pity, then embrace.

Our salvation consists in not enduring; to tolerate is to be lost.

Lord, with what care hast Thou begirt us round!
Parents first season us; then schoolmasters
Deliver us to laws; they send us, bound
To rules of reason, holy messengers,
Pulpits and Sundays, sorrow dogging sin,
Afflictions sorted, anguish of all sizes,
Fine nets and stratagems to catch us in,
Bibles laid open, millions of surprises;
Blessings beforehand, ties of gratefulness,
The sound of glory ringing in our ears:
Without, our shame; within, our consciences;
Angels and grace, eternal hopes and fears!
Yet all these fences and their whole array
One cunning bosom-sin blows quite away.[1]

2. We read of walking in the *counsel* of these people. But again we shall have to ask whether we can bring the meaning into a better focus. The word "counsel" was an excellent translation in its time; but the virtues of words alter so, and nowadays when we speak of any one's "counsel" we are apt to think merely of his advice to others. But for our translation of the Hebrew here, we seem to want a word broad enough to include the kind of plan and tone he is cherishing in his heart as suitable for his *own* living.

Expediency is the guide of life! Behold a master-maxim the spirit of which pervades a large amount of morally dreary human

[1] George Herbert.

thinking! It may be thinking infused with a great deal of business-like shrewdness, distinguished by moderation and *savoir faire*. It may encourage and guide you, if you adopt it, in developing ready efficiency of the kind that pays. It may help to build you up in alert self-confidence. And so far we shall call it *prudence*. But look further into its bearings. What if, while it may be putting one in the way of reaching a host of factitious little ends that awaken new greeds and ambitions in their attainment, it does not trouble to ask after any glorifying of life through a supreme aim that wins the satisfied homage of one's inmost heart? Then it is plainly a prudence of *the lawless*—of those who, with all their skill and diplomacy, neglect life's highest norm and living rule.

¶ No human actions ever were intended by the Maker of men to be guided by balances of expediency, but by balances of justice. He has therefore rendered all endeavours to determine expediency futile for evermore. No man ever knew, or can know, what will be the ultimate result to himself, or to others, of any given line of conduct. But every man may know, and most of us do know, what is a just and unjust act. And all of us may know also, that the consequences of justice will be ultimately the best possible, both to others and ourselves, though we can neither say what *is* best, or how it is likely to come to pass.[1]

¶ As soon as prudence has begun to grow up in the brain, like a dismal fungus, it finds its expression in a paralysis of generous acts.[2]

¶ A poor little worldly maxim will have no attractions for a man who has been contemplating the Divine ideal. You know the sort of maxim to which I refer, the false lights which are offered me by the treacherous world. "Look after Number One!" "The devil take the hindermost!" "In Rome do as Rome does!" "It does not do to be too particular!" "You cannot do much unless you have a bit of the devil in you!" These, I say, are the perilous lights which are born in miasma, and lead men into the sloughs of despond and the mire of wickedness. The godly man will be instinctively aloof from them. By his very diligence in the highest he will have a refined perception which will enable him to discern 'sin afar off. And he will reject its counsel as an offensive thing.[3]

[1] Ruskin, "*Unto This Last*" (*Works*, xvii. 28).
[2] R. L. Stevenson, *Aes Triplex*.
[3] J. H. Jowett, in *The British Congregationalist*, May 28, 1908.

II.

The Way of Sinners.

1. We are all sinners; it behoves every one to say, " Depart from me, for I am a sinful man, O Lord." But the class of persons here referred to are those who love sin, who roll it under the tongue as a sweet morsel, who not only have sinned, but do sin, and intend to sin, openly, unblushingly, and wittingly, when opportunity arises. These are the persons who "know a thing or two"—alas! many things they might well be ignorant of. There is a terrible fascination about a man who has seen the world, especially its seamy side; he is so jovial, so interesting, so charming—to the weak. These are the men who coined that dangerous phrase, "seeing life"—a phrase born not from above, but from below.

2. So another place that the happy man must avoid is "the way of sinners." In Isaiah's prophecy God gives it as one of the first things to do, when a man will turn from wickedness to righteousness and from sorrow to happiness, to get out of the way in which he has been going. He says, "Let the wicked forsake his way." "The way of sinners" is the way of sorrow and unhappiness. Whatever of good it promises, it is a false way. It may seem attractive, but you may be sure that the end of the way is misery.

¶ A man who is accustomed to breathe the air of the uplands cannot endure the foulness of these unclean haunts. When our soldiers came back from the South African war, where they had been sleeping on the open veldt, with the wandering air blowing about them while they slept, they could not bear the fusty mustiness of the closed bedrooms at home. There is nothing like the open air to make one recoil from the stench. Let a man leave a crowded meeting, and go for a couple of minutes into the open air, and then let him return, and his revived perception will make a discovery from which he will shrink. And so it is in the life of the spirit; once we have begun to find our delight in the will of the Lord we shall begin to wonder how we were ever able to "stand" in the ways of the world.[1]

[1] J. H. Jowett, in *The British Congregationalist*, May 28, 1908.

III.

THE SEAT OF THE SCORNFUL.

1. There is still this third place that a man, if he will be really happy, must avoid—"the seat of the scornful." We should notice this evolution in sin; this going down the three steps. The first is the listening to the counsel of the ungodly until—it may be almost unconsciously—a man begins to walk in that counsel. The next step lower is where a man begins to stand in the way of sinners, and the third and worst of all is where he sits down in the seat of the scornful. God have mercy on the man who has already taken the third step in sin; who not only walks in the counsel of the ungodly, and stands in the way of sinners, but sits in the seat of scorners! God have mercy on the boy who has gone so far that he can make a joke of his mother's religion, that he can make a sneer about his father's God, that he can scorn the voice of God's Word that calls him to repentance! The sarcasm and cynicism and scorn of a sharp wit is often very fascinating to young people, but the man who exercises it is never happy. It is a blossom which grows on a tree that is bitter at the heart.

2. Unless we set our back to the wall, and hit the scornful right from the shoulder, we are lost; a nervous concession to him is fatal,—there is nothing for it but to stand erect and fight it out. Where an innocent youth who has just left home, and come to the city to mingle in business with all sorts and conditions of men, would despise the ungodly and fear the taint of the sinner, he would probably succumb to the scornful, and surrender under the fire of ridicule. *The hardest thing in the world for a young religious person to endure is scorn.*

3. Perhaps, amongst ourselves in modern times, a characteristic symptom of the settling into this still lower condition is a perversion of the gift of humour. Humour is not here the joyous bubbling out of a wayward spring that flows to cheer and refresh. It expresses not so much brightness and delicacy of perception as a tendency—essentially commonplace at heart—to turn everything over to show its least impressive side, and to provoke one's

own meaningless sense of superiority by a sportive or satirical view of its exceeding flatness. The tone of weariness in it may not be very marked, but is yet evident to the reflective listener. You could not call it gaiety. Indeed, persistent perversion of the healthy meanings of life—and *perversion of meaning* is perhaps here the root-idea of the "scorn"—could scarcely prompt much gaiety. The tone of those who most skilfully and divertingly practise it cannot be expected to be quite that of the lark.

But perhaps we shall find no humour ; only the tone of a man who knows life well, and with a certain finality, having "lost his illusions" about it. He will not be surprised by any appearance either of practical and devoted idealism or of any baseness. He knows just how much and how little there is in either. Perhaps if your own beliefs are intense and earnest, he will listen to an expression of them quite respectfully, if he is in the mood, and even show you what seems like a certain personal sympathy. He is so grave and considerate that you think you are impressing him at last. But the real subject of his consideration is the place you are to fill in his private museum of moral curiosities. Your serious resolution is just part of this general odd fact of life to him ; and his very tolerance, exempt from all fellowship with you, is only the smooth completion of inner complacent scorn.[1]

(1) There is *religious* scorn, which has its classical illustration in the spirit of the Pharisees, and which in our time was admirably described by Hutton in his well-known essay on the "Hard Church." It is that spirit of narrow and arid intellectualism which starts either with the letter of Scripture or certain theological axioms, and then proceeds to infer and to deduct, till at last it has forged an iron chain with which to bind, first its own mind, and then the minds of other people.

¶ The delusion that our human belief is commensurate with the spiritual influences of God,—nay, is a sure pledge, and *the* pledge, of those influences,—constitutes not merely the essence of bigotry, but almost all the other far from capricious peculiarities which distinguish the inquisitorial theology of the Hard Church. This it is which makes its theologians so eager to find, in marks of bare power, some grounds for God's authority quite distinct from His character ; because, having an idolatrous regard for

[1] H. Foston, *The Waiting Life*, 22.

faith, as a sort of charm, they want to find some iron foundation for it sufficiently unspiritual to remain unshaken when God Himself is hidden from the heart. They think they have discovered that foundation; they believe it unassailable; they think that wherever God acts at all they should recognize Him by this mark; they look out for that mark; if they do not see it they scold and say, "God is not with you; on the contrary, corrupt human nature is with you; what you struggle to express is wholly opposite in nature to what I have attained; my belief is even more certain to me than any conviction I could possibly have that God has any part in your belief or no belief; you are either a liar or an idiot." [1]

(2) There is also *worldly* scorn, and this is illustrated in the case of persons who have achieved material success and lost their sense of proportion, and regard rank and riches as the final standard of manhood. While they may not say it, they have come in the background of their minds to look upon a man with slender possessions as a poor creature who has failed, to expect deference from those who are not as rich as themselves, to resent all independence on the part of any one who owes his living to them, and to treat the claims of intelligence and of culture to at least an equal place with those of worldly goods as a sentimental impertinence.

(3) There is one other scorn which may not be passed over; it is that of the *evil-liver*. When a man in his youth first breaks those commandments of virtue which are written both in his body and in his soul, he has qualms of conscience and fits of repentance. He will frankly confess that he has done wrong, and he is willing to promise amendment. By and by he comes to such a callousness that he will defend his very vices as a necessary part of nature, and an intention of the Creator, and he will ridicule the restraints and decencies of virtue. When a man old and greyheaded sets himself to corrupt youth by foul conversation, and closes his life with only one poignant regret, that he can no longer practise the sins which he loves, then one sees scorn rank and full blown, and ready for the burning, whose damnation tarrieth not.

¶ The world deifies and worships human nature and its impulses, and denies the power and the grant of grace. This is the

[1] R. H. Hutton, *Theological Essays*, 347.

source of the hatred which the world bears to the Church; it finds a whole catalogue of sins brought into light and denounced which it would fain believe to be no sins at all; it finds itself, to its indignation and impatience, surrounded with sin, morning, noon, and night; it finds that a stern law lies against it, where it believed that it was its own master and need not think of God; it finds guilt accumulating upon it hourly, which nothing can prevent, nothing remove, but a higher power, the grace of God. It finds itself in danger of being humbled to the earth as a rebel, instead of being allowed to indulge its self-dependence and self-complacency. Hence it takes its stand on nature, and denies or rejects Divine grace. Like the proud spirit in the beginning, it wishes to find its supreme good in its own self, and nothing above it; it undertakes to be sufficient for its own happiness; it has no desire for the supernatural, and therefore does not believe in it. And as nature cannot rise above nature, it will not believe that the narrow way is possible; it hates those who enter upon it as if pretenders and hypocrites, or laughs at their aspirations as romance and fanaticism, lest it should have to believe in the existence of grace.[1]

¶ I saw a wayfarer entering a city, in the region of Vanity Fair. The city lay upon a hill; and the highway through the centre thereof was steep and rough. By-streets were well paved, but the main thoroughfare was broken and stony; purposely neglected by citizens who have no liking for certain pilgrims or their king. No sooner had this wayfarer passed through the gate than he was accosted by a civil-spoken person who bade him "good morrow," and inquired of his destination. Upon hearing that he was bound for the Celestial City, the stranger deplored the abruptness of the hill, and the rudeness of the way, and begged him to turn aside:—"for though" said he, "the side streets lead farthest round and you will be longer mounting the hill, the walking will be easier, and the top will be gained at last with smaller loss of breath."

Persuaded by so plausible a counsellor, the pilgrim turned aside and found it even as was said, for this ascent was smooth and gentle. Methought, had he known that the stranger's name was "Ungodly," or remembered Evangelist's advice, "Keep thine eyes straight before thee, and let no man's counsel turn thee to the right hand or to the left," it had been otherwise.

Passing through many streets, smoothly paved, but narrow, crooked, and somewhat slippery withal, he came presently to a broad place where tables were spread bountifully, in the open,

[1] J. H. Newman, *Discourses to Mixed Congregations*, 148.

and a great company of people were making merry. He was somewhat faint; their good cheer whetted more sharply the keen edge of his appetite. Cumbered by the crowd he still essayed to press on, when he was accosted by a jovial voice, and invited without ceremony to eat and drink. He demurred, pleading the urgency of his journey. Whereupon his new acquaintance became sober of countenance, and spoke with great respect of the pilgrims and their king. He too was once a pilgrim, and still is minded to gain the Celestial City. 'Tis not far ahead. He knows a short road; and having tarried yet awhile to make merry with his friends, he hopes to arrive, after all, before the golden gate is shut. Said he, continuing—"You look white, man. Take a pull at this red wine. 'Tis of ancient vintage and much esteemed in these parts." And our pilgrim, used only to quench his thirst with water from the brook, drank, and finding the flavour good, drank to the bottom of the goblet.

The wine which greatly refreshed his tongue seemed nowise to stimulate his feet, and I observed, as the sun declined, that he still lingered conversing amicably with his new-found friend. Moreover his face was flushed, and his eyes were heavy; I disliked the manner of his speech; and though the revellers around had grown to be noisy and unseemly in their jesting, I thought he rather smiled on them, and certain is it that he did not stop his ears or turn away his face.

Then it seemed to me that many days passed ere I found myself again climbing the steep and rough street that leads through the centre of the city. Nigh half-way up the hill at the corner of a by-street there is a wine-shop much resorted to by men who say there is no God; who also make it their peculiar pleasure to taunt with bitter gibes such pilgrims as labour up the rugged way. The day was sunny; chairs and tables were set out of doors; and not a few had come together to enjoy their refreshment and their fun. I stood apart while several pilgrims passed. Some of them were sore pained by the ribaldry of the scoffers, one of whom exceeded the others in the cruel sharpness of his scorn. He seemed to know the pilgrim life full well; and his poison shafts struck between the joints of the harness. I drew near to get a clear sight of his face, and was dumb with amazement when I saw that he bore the features of that same pilgrim who had turned aside from the steep way to walk in the counsel of Ungodly, whom I had also seen standing in the way of sinners, and drinking with them from their cup. Then I groaned in spirit, for I thought that he was lost indeed.

But while I watched and wept there appeared among the

pilgrims One of majestic mien, who came nigh and looked full into the face of this scorner. Unutterable sorrow beamed from His deep eyes, and His look of patient love might have riven a heart of stone. A crown of thorns was upon His brow, and the wounds of the hands which He outstretched were fresh and bleeding.

Suddenly the voice of the scorner ceased; his face grew livid; his lips fell wide apart, and his knees smote together like the knees of Belshazzar when he saw the handwriting on the wall. Then he rose from his seat, and with faltering steps came and fell down before the Lord, and thus he said: "O Lord Christ, I have crucified Thee afresh; I have put Thee to an open shame; I have reviled my Creator; I have sinned against the Holy Ghost; there is no forgiveness for me in this world or in the world to come. Yet, O Lord, ere Thou utterest my doom, grant me this prayer: Suffer me but once to kiss Thy feet, and to tell these foolish ones how I have sinned—how Thou hast loved!"

Then the Lord Christ smiled as He answered, "Him that cometh unto Me I will in no wise cast out. Son, thy sins which are many are all forgiven; never more must thou wander from My side."

While these things happened a crowd had gathered, and at this point the crowd grew angry. The scoffers were enraged that their companion should forsake them. High words ensued. Stones and dirt began to fly. "Have at him" was the word. The onset was fierce and pitiless, and I could but note how frantic were the efforts of the re-instated pilgrim to shield with his own body his gracious Lord. His clothes were torn; his face was smeared with blood; and at last one rude fellow struck him on the head with a bludgeon, so cruel a blow that I said within myself, "Now he is slain." But even as he fell the arm of the Saviour caught him around. Then the drooping head was lifted, the marred face flashed with unearthly glory, and as he leaned upon the breast of Jesus, a radiant mist encompassed them; and as they vanished, I awoke, and behold it was a dream.[1]

[1] G. Hawker, in *The Preacher's Magazine*, 1892, p. 343.

The Four Acts of Religion.

LITERATURE.

Benson (E. W.), *Boy-Life*, 60.

Boston (T.), *Complete Works*, iv. 262.

Fairbairn (R. B.), *Sermons in St. Stephen's College*, 97.

Garbett (E.), *The Soul's Life*, 1.

Gregg (D.), *Our Best Moods*, 31.

Hiley (R. W.), *A Year's Sermons*, iii. 1.

Jowett (J. H.), *Thirsting for the Springs*, 129.

Lightfoot (J.), *Whole Works*, vi. 96.

Martineau (J.), in *The Outer and the Inner World*, 1.

Matheson (G.), *Moments on the Mount*, 213.

Moore (D.), *The Golden Lectures*, 2nd Ser., No. 3171.

Parkhurst (C. H.), *A Little Lower than the Angels*, 159.

Simeon (C.), *Works*, v. 15.

Spurgeon (C. H.), *Metropolitan Tabernacle Pulpit*, xxxiii. (1888), No. 2033.

Voysey (C.), *Sermons*, xxvii. (1904), No. 2.

Christian World Pulpit, xix. 377 (Statham); xxii. 257 (MacDonald); lxvi. 129 (Rees).

Church of England Magazine, xli. 272 (Pulcher).

Churchman's Pulpit: Ember Days, xv. 433 (Woolmer).

Clergyman's Magazine, 3rd Ser., xi. 333 (Youard).

Contemporary Pulpit, 1st Ser., x. 183 (Spurgeon).

Expositor's Library: The Psalms, i. 132 (Keble), 137 (Stracey), 140 (MacEwen), 148 (Rees).

Plain Sermons by Contributors to the "Tracts for the Times," i. 19.

Twentieth Century Pastor, xxxi. (1912) 315.

The Four Acts of Religion.

Stand in awe, and sin not:
Commune with your own heart upon your bed, and be still.
Offer the sacrifices of righteousness,
And put your trust in the Lord.—Ps. iv. 4, 5.

1. The Fourth Psalm is an evening petition, emanating from the same period in David's life as the morning petition which precedes it. Both may reasonably be referred to the occasion of Absalom's rebellion. The present Psalm is slightly different from its predecessor in tone, inasmuch as it assumes in part the form of a gentle loving expostulation with the enemies, and seeks for their conversion rather than their overthrow. A quieter tone prevails. There is less of complaint, more of joyous confidence. The difference is just that between a man rising to encounter a day of trial by faith in Jehovah and a man seeking rest in the conviction that all things work together for the good of the righteous, and that even for the most hardened sinner there is hope of repentance.

¶ This is the evening psalm of Christendom. A great body of devout and homiletic literature has gathered round this Psalm, particularly among our people, on the fourth and sixth verses. The Vulgate version of the former is, *Irascimini et nolite peccare: quae dicitis in cordibus vestris, et in cubilibus vestris compungimini.* This was explained commonly as, "Be wroth (with yourselves) and sin not (further); say in your hearts whatever you say; repent in your beds." The seventh verse is, *Signatum est super nos lumen vultus tui Domine*—"There is stamped on us the light of Thy countenance, O Lord." This verse was a text for Charlemagne in his struggle against images in churches. His *Capitulare* on the subject is almost a series of sermons, pleading against things which "dim instead of reveal the light of God's countenance."[1]

[1] C. L. Marson, *The Psalms at Work*, 9.

2. The fourth and fifth verses contain four acts, those four acts which belong to the birth of the religious life—self-awakening, self-communion, self-confession, and self-abandonment. There is, first, the awakening of self-life to the presence of another law, a moral law which says, "Stand in awe, and sin not." There is, secondly, the communing of the soul with itself, the asking of that momentous question, "Am I in harmony with this moral law?" There is, thirdly, the recognition of righteousness and the unreserved confession of sin and weakness. Lastly, there is the perception that the consciousness of merit is itself a want of harmony with law, and the soul by an act of self-forgetfulness loses its sense alike of merit and of demerit in the trust of the living God.

¶ My soul, wouldst thou reach this blessed conclusion? Wouldst thou arrive at this final haven of moral peace where thy weakness shall itself become thy strength? Thou mayest arrive at it, but it must be after a storm—a storm whose peculiarity shall be its inaudibleness to any ear but thine. Ere thou canst reach the final rest thou must enter into communion with thyself, must examine thine old nature in the stillness of solitude. Thine must be a struggle with thine own thoughts—a struggle where there is no clang of arms, but whose soreness lies in its very silence. How still is that communion which thy God requires of thee! "Commune with thine own heart"; what converse so silent as that? "Thine *own* heart"; not the heart of another. The heart of another would give more companionship, but it would give less test of truth. Thou mightest compare thy righteousness with the righteousness of thy brother, and go down to thy house rejoicing, and yet all the time thou mightest be in discord with the moral law of God. Only in thine own heart canst thou see thyself truly reflected, therefore it is with thyself that thy Father bids thee commune. "Commune upon thy bed"; not alone with thine own heart, but with thine own heart in the stillest locality—in the silence of the midnight hour, where there is no distraction, and where there is no deception. There thou shalt learn what it is to be an individual soul. In the world thou art taught to forget this; thy little life is swallowed up in the crowd, and thy moral good or ill seems an indifferent thing. But here the world's judgment is reversed. When thou art alone with God the crowd melts away, and thou art to thyself an universe. Thy very sense of sin reveals to thee the infinitude of thy being. Thy very moral struggle tells thee that in spite of thyself thou art an immortal. Commune with thine own heart, O my soul.[1]

¶ In Angelica, you have the entirely spiritual mind, wholly versed in the heavenly world, and incapable of conceiving any wickedness or vileness whatsoever.

In Salvator, you have an awakened conscience, and some spiritual power, contending with evil, but conquered by it, and brought into captivity to it.

In Dürer, you have a far purer conscience and higher spiritual power, yet, with some defect still in intellect, contending with evil, and nobly prevailing over it; yet retaining the marks of the contest, and never so entirely victorious as to conquer sadness.

In Giorgione, you have the same high spiritual power and practical sense; but now, with entirely perfect intellect, contending with evil; conquering it utterly, casting it away for ever, and rising beyond it into magnificence of rest.[2]

I.

Self-Awakening.

"Stand in awe, and sin not."

1. "Stand in awe, and sin not." This seems to be a little remote from the phraseology of modern religious life. Our vocabulary is of a different type and order. Words like awe, fear, trembling, appear to be almost obsolete. Our speech finds its emphasis in such words as happiness, joy, peace, comfort. The Psalmist throws us back to quite a different plane. "Stand in awe, and sin not!" This man has had a vision of the great white Throne. He has been contemplating the terrors of the Lord. He has listened to the awful imperatives. He has had a glimpse of the midnight of alienation. He spent his days in levity, as though God and duty were distant and irrelevant trifles. But now his eyes have come upon the whiteness of the Eternal, the unsullied sovereignty, the holiness that would not be trifled with, and his careless walk is sharply arrested. His levity is changed into trembling. His indifference is broken up in awe.

[1] G. Matheson, *Moments on the Mount*, 214.
[2] Ruskin, *Modern Painters* (*Works*, vii. 373).

We have seen the experience in miniature, even in the fellowship of man with man. One man has introduced a piece of indecent or questionable foolery in the presence of another man, and he has been immediately confronted with a face which chilled his blood and froze his levity into a stilled and wondering silence. No man's life will ever be deepened into fruitful awe if he has not seen similar features confronting him in the countenance of God. "The face of the Lord is against them that do evil." "Woe is me, for mine eyes have seen the King." We have to see the Face if we are to be checked in our frivolity, and if we are to feel our indecencies blazing within us like a destructive fire.

¶ We do not like the hymns in which the whirlwind sweeps and drives. We prefer the hymns that are just filled with honey. And so the " sweet " hymns are the favourites, and the sweeter they are the more welcome they are to our palates. We have partially dropped the hymns which harrow and alarm, and which minister to our fear. Some of us have what we sometimes call a " sweet Jesus." We know Him only as the Speaker of gentle and condescending speech, and of tender, winsome invitation. We have not a Jesus before whom we frequently " stand in awe." We glide on in the religious life heedlessly, and at no moment do we stand appalled.[1]

¶ Men do not feel the power of the Gospel when in Christ they discern nothing to fear. Many men are lost because they do not see the great white Throne. Thomas Boston said that the net of the Gospel needed to be weighted with the leads of the terrors of the law, or it would lightly float on the surface and no fish be caught. We must steadily keep in view the sterner patches of the New Testament teaching. We must contemplate the whiteness of the Eternal, and stand in awe.[2]

2. "Stand in awe, and sin not." If we do not stand in awe, we are likely to sin, and to think lightly of it. There are various interpretations that we can put upon sin. We can treat a sin as being merely a moral mistake. We can regard it as being only an irresponsible legacy from a sinful parentage. We can think of it as being nothing more than the legitimate outcropping from our animal nature, the warranted self-assertion of the material side of our complex being and therefore not exactly sinful, but rather the natural tone sounded by one of the lower vibrating strings of our

[1] J. H. Jowett, *Thirsting for the Springs*, 131.　　　[2] *Ibid.*, 133.

humanity. Or we can, without committing ourselves to any doctrine bearing upon us with uncomfortable pressure, contemplate our sin as being a violation of the conventional ideas of the more respectable element of society; or go so far even as to think of it as being a transgression of the moral law—attaching to the phrase "moral law," however, no signification over-earnest in its exactions; for a mere "law," if carelessly thought of, becomes that impersonal and visionary thing that touches no sensitive spot in our deeper nature.

¶ Christ's teaching concerning sin has been before the Church and the world for many centuries, but neither the world nor the Church has fully accepted it. The old practice of straining out gnats and swallowing camels still prevails; and, if the sins which the Jews considered great have been recognized in their extreme littleness, still, those which they regarded as too small to deserve notice are looked upon very much as the Jews looked upon them in our Saviour's day; and, on the whole, sin, according to the world and according to the Church too, is more what the Scribes and Pharisees pronounced it to be than what Jesus Christ said it was.[1]

¶ There is a pathetical story of Origen,—that when he had fallen into a foul apostasy, and, after some recovery from it, came into a congregation, and was desired to preach; he took the Bible, and opened it accidentally at the Fiftieth Psalm, and his eye fell first to read these words in the sixteenth and seventeenth verses of it:—"But unto the wicked God saith, What hast thou to do to declare my statutes, or that thou shouldest take my covenant in thy mouth? Seeing thou hatest instruction, and castest my words behind thee." Upon reading the words, he remembered his own fall; and, instead of preaching, he fell a weeping, and wept so bitterly, that he caused all the congregation to weep with him.[2]

II.

SELF-COMMUNION.

"Commune with your own heart upon your bed, and be still."

When we have gazed upon the undefiled heights, upon the holiness of God, we are then to hold a soliloquy with ourselves.

[1] *Life of Hugh Stowell Brown*, 390.   [2] J. Lightfoot, *Works*, vi. 111.

In his *Saints' Everlasting Rest*, Richard Baxter says that every good Christian is a good preacher in his own soul. The very same methods that a minister uses in his preaching to others every Christian should endeavour after in speaking to himself. Having seen the Throne, let us hold converse with our own hearts.

¶ Central Africa was to Stewart what Arabia was to Paul—a retreat in which he examined his own heart, revised his life, developed the self-reliance which is based upon the reliance of faith, and sought complete consecration to Christ and His service. In these great solitudes he had his musing times and sessions of sweet thought, and heard the voice of God more distinctly than elsewhere. " His faith in God, always strong," Dr. Wallace writes, " though not effusive, was strengthened by his experiences of the solitary life in the heart of Africa, entirely cut off from Christian fellowship. In a letter written to me, when his only companion was a native boy, he said that he had never felt so near heaven, and added that now to him, 'God, holiness and heaven are the only things worth living for.' " [1]

1. The "heart" is the seat, not only of the desires and emotions, but also of the conscience and the intellect. The Psalmist appeals, in these words, to the conscience and reason of his hearers. He would have them collect their thoughts, and " say in their heart " something like those words of Isaiah, " Come ye, and let us walk in the light of Jehovah."

There is the belief of the head and the belief of the heart. And these two blend together in one. As the heart believes, the objects of belief gradually clear and become definite to us. We no longer use words merely : we feel within us that they have a meaning ; but our inward experience becomes the rock on which we stand : it is like the consciousness of our own existence. Can I doubt that He who has taught me to serve Him from my youth upward—He who supported me in that illness, who brought me near to the gates of death and left me not alone, is none other than God Himself ? Can I doubt that He who gave me the impulse to devote myself to His work and to the good of mankind, who in some way inexplicable to me enables me to calm the violence of passion, the thought of envy, malice, impurity, to whom I go to lay open my breast and cleanse the thoughts of my heart, can be none other than the true God ? Can it be that that

[1] J. Wells, *The Life of James Stewart of Lovedale*, 93.

example which He has given me in the life of His Son is other than the truth for me and for all mankind ? Here we seem to have found the right starting-point. " Lord, I believe; help thou mine unbelief." [1]

¶ In Psalm lxxvii. 6 we read: " I commune with mine own heart; and my spirit maketh diligent search." Here David and his heart are talking together ; and see what his heart saith unto him in Psalm xvi. 7: " My reins instruct me in the night seasons." For that the heart and reins do signify the same thing, when they are taken in a spiritual sense, and that they, so taken, do signify the conscience,—is a matter so copiously evident in Scripture that I need not to use any instances to prove it. And so in John viii. 9, when our Saviour bids, " Whosoever is without sin, cast the first stone" at the woman taken in adultery, it is said of the company present, that they were " convicted of their own conscience." The word in the Greek doth properly signify "a conviction by argument": there was something within them that over-argued them, and talked and disputed them clean away. And so in Rom. ii. 15: " The consciences of the very heathen spake, as it were, within them," and gave in evidence either for them or against them, their thoughts either accusing or excusing, " inter se invicem," as the Vulgar Latin,—as in a discourse among themselves.[2]

> Commune with thine own heart !—no need
>   To wander the wide earth around ;
> If but in thine own breast thou read
>   Aright—thy God thou wilt have found ;
> Who habiteth Eternity
> There condescends to dwell with thee.
>
> Commune with thine own heart ! for there
>   The Heaven-ascending ladder lies,
> A pathway into purer air,
>   A window giving on the skies ;
> Through which thou mayest wing thy flight,
> And mingle with the Infinite. . . .
>
> Commune with thine own heart !—for there
>   The better, nobler self resides,
> That in the life Divine doth share,
>   And ever in the Presence bides ;
> The self with Deity at one,
> As with its beam the central sun.

[1] Benjamin Jowett, *College Sermons*, 21.   [2] J. Lightfoot, *Works*, vi. 101.

> There—from the world of sense aloof—
> Such insight shall be granted thee
> As shall afford thee ample proof
> Of thine august paternity;
> The Spirit witnessing with thine
> That thou art sprung from seed Divine.[1]

2. "Upon your bed."—"To commune upon one's bed" is a form of expression taken from the common practice and experience of men. We know that, during our intercourse with men in the daytime, our thoughts are distracted, and we often judge rashly, being deceived by the external appearance; whereas in solitude, we can give to any subject a closer attention; and, further, the sense of shame does not then hinder a man from thinking without disguise of his own faults. David, therefore, exhorts his enemies to withdraw from those who witnessed and judged of their actions on the public stage of life, and to be alone, that they may examine themselves more truthfully and honestly. And this exhortation has respect to us all; for there is nothing to which men are more prone than to deceive one another with empty applause, until each man enters into himself, and communes alone with his own heart. Paul, when quoting this passage in Eph. iv. 26, or, at least, when alluding to the sentiment of David, follows the Septuagint, " Be ye angry, and sin not." And yet he has skilfully and beautifully applied it to his purpose. He there teaches us that men, instead of wickedly pouring forth their anger against their neighbours, have rather just cause to be angry with themselves, in order that, by this means, they may abstain from sin. And, therefore, he commands them rather to fret inwardly, and be angry with themselves; and then to be angry not so much at the persons, as at the vices of others.[2]

¶ Whoso goeth to his bed as to his grave, may go to his grave as to his bed.[3]

3. The familiar maxim, "Know thyself," shows that self-knowledge has for ages been considered desirable. In the ethical codes of the wiser moralists of the ancient world, the duty of self-analysis was prominent. As it was recommended and practised by them, however, it was quite different from the duty

[1] William Hall, "Via Crucis."   [2] Calvin, *Psalms*, i. 44.   [3] Bishop Horne.

which is enforced here. Goethe, again, was an eager student of
his own nature, and he was incessant and triumphant in his
devotion to that study; but his one aim was to know his art, by
knowing that on which it was to tell; and, to reach it, he was
ready to sacrifice himself. Or, a man may seek acquaintance with
his own nature for the worst as well as for the best of purposes.
With a view to ends altogether unworthy of him, he may study
the habits of his soul with the utmost care.

It is with the heart in its relation to things unseen and
eternal that we are to commune. This is a duty which is strictly
specific in its relation to certain objects. These are the habits of
a man's nature in reference to God's truth, and immortality, and
to whatever else constitutes us moral and responsible beings.
What are our relations to God? What are our feelings towards
Him? In what spirit and manner do we fulfil the obligations
which He has laid on us? These are the questions which it is
our highest interest to ask, and which we can answer only when
we know our hearts and know them well. While this is our
object, it often happens that by observing our dispositions towards
what is external we are able to see most clearly into the inner
man. We cannot take a purely abstract view of our own character.
We must test ourselves by what tests us. We have to look out
at times that we may look in. When we comprehend the
influence which business and pleasure, our companions and our
pursuits, exert on our moral nature, we see also how it stands
affected towards what is higher and better. Our purpose, however,
in all this must be to judge ourselves spiritually. Our aim is
not simply to become masters of our own thoughts and feelings.
Neither is it a desire to control the minds of others. We commune
with our hearts that we may know what we are morally, and how
we stand related to things that are unseen and eternal.

> I had a treasure in my house,
>   And woke one day to find it gone;
> I mourned for it from dawn till night,
>   From night till dawn.
>
> I said, "Behold, I will arise
>   And sweep my house," and so I found
> What I had lost, and told my joy
>   To all around.

> I had a treasure in my heart,
>   And scarcely knew that it had fled,
> Until communion with my Lord
>   Grew cold and dead.
>
> "Behold," I said, "I will arise
>   And sweep my heart of self and sin;
> And so the peace that I have lost
>   May enter in."
>
> O friends, rejoice with me! Each day
>   Helps my lost treasure to restore;
> And sweet communion with my Lord
>   Is mine once more.[1]

(1) This communing must be marked by uncompromising fidelity. It were better not to take this trust in hand than to be faithless to it. Honesty and impartiality should characterize our inquiries. We must not desist from them when they become painful, because they awaken a slumbering conscience, or are at war with some dearly loved indulgence.

(2) In our self-communings Scripture should be our guide. Its aim is to lead the man who communes with himself to seek communion with Him by whom he can be transformed into the image of God. The Spirit of holiness, which alone can purify man's nature, is made known in the Word of truth. As a mere duty, the habit to which the text exhorts us would fail to do us good; but when we engage in it aright, it gives us trust and desire, bringing us into the presence of our best Friend. It first casts us down, and then raises us up. It declares to us the plague of our own hearts, that we may repair to Him who is the great and good Physician of souls.

¶ Never yet did there exist a full faith in the Divine Word which did not expand the intellect, while it purified the heart; which did not multiply and exalt the aims and objects of the understanding, while it fixed and simplified those of the desires and feelings.[2]

4. We should distinguish heart-communion from some things from which it differs. Thus we are not to identify the exercise with religious contemplation, that higher form of intellectual

---

[1] Caroline A. Mason.   [2] S. T. Coleridge.

homage which the mind, when elevated above the level of earthly things, pays to the wisdom of God. Neither is meditation to be confounded with the exercise of reading, even though it be thoughtful, prayerful, scriptural reading. This may be helpful to heart-communion, but it is not the same, and is not a substitute for it. In all reading we have a view to the acquirement of some new truth, or at all events, to more deepened impressions of truths already known, in the hope that these truths, apprehended by the understanding more perfectly, may appeal with more power to the conscience and the heart. But in meditation we are not learning truths, but applying them. We are reducing what we have acquired to practice; our business lies directly with the affections and the will, which on the admitted sufficiency of present light, and under the felt force of present convictions are urged forward to greater attainments in practical holiness, to resolutions of higher aim, and victories more prominent, sanctified, and complete over all the desires of the flesh and of the mind.

¶ It is not every "speaking in the heart" [the literal translation of the words] that the Psalmist here engageth to; for the fool speaks in heart, and saith in his heart, "There is no God": the epicure speaks in his heart, and saith, "I shall never be moved": the atheist speaks in his heart, and saith, "Tush, God hath forgotten, he will never see it." And these persons to whom David speaketh, if we hit the occasion of the Psalm aright, were ready enough to say in their heart, "We will none of David, and nothing to do with the son of Jesse": but the text enjoineth such a conference in the heart, as that the matters betwixt a man and his own heart may be debated to the very utmost,—that the heart may be so put to it in communing with it, as that it might speak its very bottom.[1]

¶ Behold, beloved, among yourselves, and regard and wonder marvellously; for I can tell you a sad story in your ears, which ye will not believe, though it be told you. I have lived these forty years, and somewhat more, and carried my heart in my bosom all this while, and yet my heart and I are as great strangers, and as utterly unacquainted, as if we had never come near one another. And is there none, in this congregation, that can say the like? He spake very good sense, and much piety in it, that complained that he had lived so many years above threescore, and had been a student in the Scripture all his time, and yet could never attain

[1] J. Lightfoot, *Works*, vi. 99.

to take out that lesson in the first verse of the nine-and-thirtieth Psalm,—" That he should not offend with his tongue." But it is to speak a thing of monstrousness and amazement, to say that a man should live so long a time as I have done,—nay, as some do, to threescore, to fourscore years,—and yet never to get into acquaintance and to communication with their own hearts! who could believe such a report? and yet, how common is this amongst men![1]

5. It is not mere worldly self-communion that the Psalmist recommends. It is not the far-seeing prudence of the man of the world, meditating upon his pleasures and his gains. It is not the self-complacency of the self-righteous, seeking out grounds for trusting in himself that he is righteous, and despising others. It is not the morbid self-contemplation of one merely gazing upon the workings of his own mind as he would watch some delicate machinery, without earnest resolves of self-amendment.

¶ "Self-anatomy" may surely be either good or evil; to be free from it altogether, as is the case with many of the noblest women, is no doubt a blessing, and suited to their nature. I much doubt whether it be the same with men; a more distinct introspection of our own motives and feelings seems natural to us, and we are likely to go wrong without it. On the other hand, it is apt to become a dangerous and "morbid trick," when its predominance makes the judgment chiefly analytical; then we come practically to look upon ourselves as a collection of wheels and springs, moved mechanically by "motives," and we are suspicious and jealous of ourselves in a way the reverse of true Christian humility and watchfulness, misinterpreting our best and noblest impulses, either by persuading ourselves that they are merely imaginary or by resolving them into corrupt wishes. We then act in the same way towards others, especially those who may be in, or may be brought into, any near relation to ourselves, mistrusting in them all that is not comprehensible. Yet I doubt not that self-anatomy is in some form needful to deliver us from carnal delusions; and wisely-tempered self-consciousness, if it has its miseries, may also bring blessings unspeakable both on ourselves and on those who have it not.[2]

(1) It is, first, the effort of the mind by grace to draw away its thoughts and its affections from earth to heaven; from the things which are seen to realities unseen except by faith. It

[1] J. Lightfoot, *Works*, vi. 111.   [2] *Life of F. J. A. Hort*, i. 166.

is surely not by mere accident that the sin which ruins souls is so often described in Scripture as the "forgetfulness of God." "The wicked shall be turned into hell, and all the nations that forget God." They cannot indeed finally and for ever banish the remembrance of God completely from their minds. They only wish they could. But they do their best. And so they set their affections on things below. They drown the remembrance of heaven and hell and death and judgment by the never-ceasing clamour of earthly cares and carnal lusts, in which they plunge themselves day by day, and all day long. He, then, that would avoid their sin and danger must have his seasons of stated religious self-communion; when he may close his eyes upon the things of time and sense, and suffer the Spirit of God to draw up his mind to thoughts of the things eternal: when he may renew his strength to "use this world, as not abusing it" by secret acts of communion with that God who "is a Spirit."

(2) Secondly, the Psalmist's self-communion is for the trial of a man's spiritual condition. "Examine yourselves whether ye be in the faith; prove your own selves." And the questions to be asked by one who sets about it are not merely concerning what he does, or what he feels, or what he fancies. The inquiry is not what he once was, or what he hopes to be, but what he is. What is the prevailing tone and bias of his mind? What does he take most pleasure in? From what motive does he act? What are his friendships, and his favourite haunts? What is he in the unrestrained intercourse of private life? For many are the self-deceits that men put upon themselves. Scarcely any danger indeed is more earnestly exposed in Scripture than the danger of thinking we are safe when we are not: the danger of fancying ourselves accepted sons of God whilst unmortified passions proclaim us children of the wicked one: the danger of speaking and thinking confidently of our religious hopes, whilst the entire or partial absence of the Spirit's fruits declares our hopes a lie. And when the Psalmist calls us to self-communion, he would have us use it to test ourselves, by sound Scripture rules, whether the Spirit of Christ have real possession of us or not.

¶ If thou canst not continually recollect thyself, yet do it sometimes, at the least once a day, namely, in the morning or at night. In the morning fix thy good purpose, and at night examine thyself what thou hast done, how thou hast behaved thyself in word, deed, and thought; for in these, perhaps, thou hast oftentimes offended against God and thy neighbour. "Examine me, O Lord, and prove me; try my reins and my heart." [1]

¶ If, after a serious retrospect of your past lives, of the objects you have pursued, and the principles which have determined your conduct, they appear to be such as will ill sustain the scrutiny of a dying hour, dare to be faithful to yourselves, and shun with horror that cruel treachery to your best interests which would impel you to sacrifice the happiness of eternity to the quiet of a moment. [2]

(3) And thus, thirdly, its proper office is to convince us of sin, and to humble us in remorse and shame for it. Humility, says one—genuine humility—is almost the last virtue man learns upon earth. All that lies around us is framed as if to teach us pride. And the only remedy is the consciousness of sin. To produce in us through grace this consciousness of sin, we are exhorted to self-communion. For genuine humility, observe, is not the mere vague self-condemnatory tone of a man merely lamenting his fallen nature. Many will confess their sinfulness who give no heed to their daily sins. Many will be heard to speak in the most exaggerated language of the depravity of their human nature who have no idea whatever of their own specific faults. They call themselves the worst of sinners, but they do not search out and confess their sins. And hence it often happens that no men slight the Church's calls to self-discipline so contemptuously as those who need them most.

¶ Although I had long known and admired Dr. McLaren in his preaching and his writings, it was only during the later years of his life that I became personally acquainted with him. My first introduction to him took place in Aberdeen in the house of my friend Sir George Reid, to whom he was sitting for his portrait. After this he was frequently under my medical care on his visits to Edinburgh, and especially during the year preceding his death. From the first of this acquaintance I was deeply impressed with his remarkable personality. While my interviews with him mainly bore reference to matters concerning his health, there soon began to grow up a feeling of something

[1] Thomas à Kempis.
[2] Robert Hall, *Funeral Sermon for the Princess Charlotte.*

more than professional relationship, namely, a true and firm friendship.

Of Dr. McLaren it might truly be said he was clothed with humility. Who could have known from anything he said of himself that this man was one of the foremost preachers and expositors of the age, whose name was a household word throughout Christendom? Yet who could be for any time in his company without feeling that his presence and his words were at once an inspiration and a benediction?[1]

(4) But, fourthly, the believer's self-communion is no mere idle and fruitless habit of morbid self-contemplation. Its use is, that it is the handmaid of real repentance. It is the healthy self-scrutiny of one earnestly desirous of amendment: whose remorse and shame are not the mere sorrow of the world, but the natural outpouring of a heart that God has touched, and awakened to a real longing to be wholly His. He communes with his own heart to see his dangers and through grace to avoid them. He marks how the infinite variety of his passions, feelings, and ideas ripened into words and actions. He breaks up the ground of his heart, to find the seeds of those habits which are ready to spring up and give the colour to his life. He watches how some trivial indulgence strengthens into a criminal necessity; how a momentary thought returns, and becomes rooted in one's bosom, and springs up a plant of iniquity; how an action, which startled him at first, steals silently and rapidly into the train of things committed without hesitation.

¶ The great work is done by men who have in them a Divine dissatisfaction; who are ever striving for something higher, who have not attained, but who press on toward the mark. The decline of this spirit is the beginning of the end. It is told of Thorwaldsen, the great Danish sculptor, that, feeling his freshness of conception decaying, he said to a friend, "My power is on the decline." Asked what he meant, he pointed to a statue of Christ. "That," said he, "is the first piece of work I have ever been satisfied with. Till now my idea has always been far beyond my power to reach it. But it is no longer so. I shall never have a great idea again." In the spiritual life there can be no self-satisfaction. "Be ye therefore perfect, even as your Father which is in heaven is perfect."

"An ingenious artist of our time," says Hazlitt, in his *Table-talk*,

[1] Sir James Affleck, in *Dr. McLaren of Manchester*, 263.

" has been heard to declare, that if ever the Devil got him into his clutches he would set him to copy his own pictures." By doing this, he would encourage a self-complacency and satisfaction with what had already been attained, which would render all further advance impossible. "Thus," says Hazlitt, "the secure, self-complacent retrospect to what is done is nothing; while the anxious, uneasy looking forward to what is to come is everything. We are afraid to dwell upon the past, lest it should retard our future progress; the indulgence of ease is fatal to excellence." [1]

(5) Once more, our self-communings should lead us up to Christ; to Him who never bends over us with such deep compassion as when we are humbled with the sense and consciousness of sin. For the duty enjoined on us in the text is not an end, but a means. It is the instrument of godliness, not godliness itself—one of the workman's tools and implements with which the goodly fabric is built up. The end of it is Christ: Christ in whom alone " the sacrifice of righteousness," which the next verse tells of, is offered up, and through whom alone the believer builds up his trust in God. The whole purpose and object of self-communion is to take away our trust in self, and place it unreservedly on Him; to make us feel our need of pardon, and to tell us where and for what we need it; to impress on us the sense of our own hearts' weakness and deceitfulness, that we may go to Him for light and strength. It is to make us, in short, better Christians, and more self-denying and self-watchful men.

¶ To be with God, there is no need to be continually in church. Of our heart we may make an Oratory, wherein to retire from time to time, and with Him hold meek, humble, loving converse. Every one can converse closely with God, some more, others less: He knows what we can do. Let us begin then; perhaps He is just waiting for one generous resolution on our part; let us be brave. So little time remains for us to live. Let us live and die with God: sufferings will be ever sweet and pleasant to us, while we abide with Him; and without Him, the greatest pleasures will be but cruel anguish. May He be blessed for all! Amen. [2]

6. "Commune with thine own heart upon thy bed, *and be still.*" This brings us to the centre of our subject. We need quiet hours. We are too much in society—much more, from the necessities of

---

[1] J. Burns, *Illustrations from Art* (1912), 88.
[2] Brother Lawrence, *The Practice of the Presence of God*, 41.

our age partly, than our fathers were. We are too gregarious. We do not listen enough for the quiet tones of truth, as it speaks directly to the soul; but we look for the responsive verdict and the answering nod of our fellow-men. In all right growth there is quietness. The flowers unobserved expand their buds, and with a like noiseless progress the cornfields whiten with the grain of autumn. It is even so in the spiritual world. The heart that communes with itself and with its God makes no display, but steadily and surely the blessed results appear, in its growing resemblance to the Man Christ Jesus.

¶ Be able to be alone. Lose not the advantage of Solitude, and the Society of thyself, nor be only content, but delight to be alone and single with Omnipresency. He who is thus prepared, the Day is not uneasy nor the Night black unto him. Darkness may bound his Eyes, not his Imagination. In his Bed he may lie, like Pompey and his Sons, in all quarters of the Earth, may speculate the Universe, and enjoy the whole World in the Hermitage of himself. Thus the old ascetick Christians found a paradise in a Desert, and with little converse on Earth held a conversation in Heaven; thus they astronomized in Caves, and, though they beheld not the Stars, had the Glory of Heaven before them.[1]

III.

SELF-CONFESSION.

"Offer the sacrifices of righteousness."

1. What are "sacrifices of righteousness"? It is probable that in this Psalm they are not sacrifices which, instead of consisting in slaughtered animals, consist in actions which are in accordance with God's will; they are sacrifices that are offered in the right disposition, in the disposition that is in conformity with the mind of God, and not in a hypocritical spirit.

2. But whatever these words may have meant to the Psalmist, they can mean only one thing for us who live in the light of the Gospel day. When a man has contemplated the dazzling holiness of God, and in self-communion has discovered his own

[1] Sir Thomas Browne.

dark appalling need, and, full of trembling, turns again to the Father, he has only one resource. He must " offer the sacrifice of righteousness." Christ Jesus is our " Righteousness." " Christ our Passover is sacrificed for us."

(1) When the Israelites brought their sacrifices, the first thing they did was to lay their hand on the victim, and *make a confession of sin.* "The sacrifices of God are a broken spirit." Let us own our shortcomings and transgressions. Let us not cloak or excuse our sins. Let us go to our chamber, and tell the Lord what we have done, pouring out our hearts before Him. Let us confess our pride and unbelief, our dishonesty, our false-hood, our disobedience to parents, our every breach of the Divine law ; whatsoever we have done amiss ; let us confess it before Him, and thus go to Him in the only way in which He can receive us, even as sinners owning our guilt.

> Out of the gulf into the glory,
>   Father, my soul cries out to be lifted.
> Dark is the woof of my dismal story,
>   Thorough thy sun-warp stormily drifted !—
> Out of the gulf into the glory,
> Lift me, and save my story.
>
> I have done many things merely shameful ;
>   I am a man ashamed, my Father !
> My life is ashamed and broken and blameful—
>   The broken and blameful, oh, cleanse and gather !
> Heartily shame me, Lord, of the shameful !
> To my judge I flee with my blameful.
>
> Saviour, at peace in Thy perfect purity,
>   Think what it is, not to be pure !
> Strong in Thy love's essential security,
>   Think upon those who are never secure.
> Full fill my soul with the light of Thy purity ;
> Fold me in love's security.
>
> O Father, O Brother, my heart is sore aching !
>   Help it to ache as much as is needful ;
> Is it you cleansing me, mending, remaking,
>   Dear potter-hands, so tender and heedful ?
> Sick of my past, of my own self-aching—
> Hurt on, dear hands, with your making.

Proud of the form Thou hadst given Thy vessel,
  Proud of myself, I forget my donor;
Down in the dust I began to nestle,
  Poured Thee no wine, and drank deep of dishonour!
Lord, Thou hast broken, Thou mendest Thy vessel!
In the dust of Thy glory I nestle.[1]

¶ Give me leave to relate unto you a story out of the Turkish history, and to apply it :—

Uladislaus, the king of Hungary, having made a league with Amurath, the great Turk, and solemnly covenanted and sealed to articles thereof in the name of Christ, was afterwards persuaded to break it, and to go to war against Amurath. Being in the heat of the fatal battle at Varna, the Turk draws the articles of the league out of his bosom, and spreads them towards the crucifix which he saw in the Christian's banner, with these words: "Now, Christ, if thou be a God, as they say thou art, revenge the wrong done unto thy name by these thy Christians, who made this league in thy name, and now have thus broken it." And, accordingly, was this wretched covenant-breach avenged with the death of Uladislaus, and almost all his army.

Should Christ spread our covenant before us, upon the same accusing terms as he spread his before Christ, what could we answer? Or, if Satan should spread our covenant before God against us, as Hezekiah did the Assyrian's letter, what could we say for ourselves in so horrid and so plain a case? If the Lord should implead us, and speak such bitter things as these against us, "You have suffered the solemnest covenant to be thus broken, that ever was sworn unto by men: the horridest heresies and errors have grown amongst you that ever did among a nation : as glorious a church as was under heaven is thus near ruined before your eyes: and the glorious gospel that shone upon earth is almost destroyed,—and you look on!" How could we answer, or hold up our faces before the Lord? but how must iniquity lay her hand upon her mouth, and not be able to speak a word![2]

(2) The main thing, however, is to bring to the Lord *the offering which He has divinely appointed and provided.* There is one sacrifice of righteousness without which we cannot be accepted. We come to God by faith in Jesus Christ, we plead the precious blood of atonement, and say, "My Lord, for His dear sake who died upon the tree, receive Thy wanderer, and now be pleased to

---

[1] George MacDonald, *Poetical Works*, ii. 358.
[2] J. Lightfoot, *Works*, vi. 123.

grant me that repentance and remission of sins which He is exalted to give."

¶ How monstrous and shameful the nature of sin is, is sufficiently apparent from that great atonement which is necessary to cleanse us from the guilt of it. Nothing less has been required to take away the guilt of our sins than the sufferings and death of the Son of God. Had He not taken our nature upon Him, our nature had been for ever separated from God, and incapable of ever appearing before Him. And is there any room for pride, or self-glory, whilst we are partakers of such a nature as this? Have our sins rendered us so abominable and odious to Him that made us, that He could not so much as receive our prayers, or admit our repentance, till the Son of God made Himself Man, and became a Suffering Advocate for our whole race; and can we in this state pretend to high thoughts of ourselves? Shall we presume to take delight in our own worth, who are not worthy so much as to ask pardon for our sins without the mediation and intercession of the Son of God?[1]

There is one only Way
From death to life for me:
It is by Thee, O Crucified!
I, also, in Thy death have died,
And, since Thou livest, live in Thee,
Who art the living Way.

There is one only Way
Of righteousness for me:
O Jesus, risen—living now—
My only righteousness art Thou!
I draw my life and strength from Thee,
Who art the living Way.[2]

IV.

SELF-ABANDONMENT.

"Put your trust in the Lord."

1. How graciously the passage closes! The awe and the trembling converge in fruitful trust! The discovery of the holy

[1] William Law, *Serious Call to a Devout and Holy Life*, 299.
[2] E. H. Divall, *A Believer's Rest*, 154.

Sovereignty, the discovery of personal defilement, the discovery of a Redeemer, are consummated in the discovery of rest. When I have found my "Righteousness" my part is now to trust. The awe, the purity of the holy Sovereignty will become mine. Trust keeps open the line of communication between the soul and God. Along that line convoys of blessedness are brought into the heart; manifold gifts of grace for the weak and defenceless spirit. When I trust I keep open the "highway of the Lord," and along that road there come to me from the Eternal my bread, my water, my instructions, my powers of defence. "I can do all things through Christ which strengtheneth me." I can "work out my own salvation with fear and trembling."

¶ It seems to me that the great difference between the Christian and the unbeliever is this: the unbeliever says that he cannot lay hold of God, and so believes in himself only. The Christian in proportion as he lays hold of God cannot believe in himself. Now the highest point of the Christian character is that in which we attain forgetfulness of self and act simply as God's creatures. Such is the temper seen in St. Paul and St. John very clearly. But this self-forgetfulness is the fruit of a long process of training in trust in God. To you and me the pain of life lies in the perpetual contrast between the aspiration of our spirit and the poor realization of our actual life. It is no wonder that people have tried at many times to simplify the problem—that they have sought a special form of life in which they might be free from ordinary temptations—the monastery, the brotherhood, the ascetic practice; but all in vain, for the difficulty lay not without, but within—not in the world, but in their own heart.[1]

¶ Looking back, I can say that the hardest battles of life are those fought with self; this is the one ever-present foe; the great crisis-fights are those which are fought within. Interpret life as we may, there are moments in which we cannot do without God; we must invoke His aid against the foe within. The victory lies in the gift of being ready to meet life's vicissitudes with calmness. Such a victory is won with the conviction of the presence and providence of the living God, in whom worldly anxieties and ambitions may be vanquished.[2]

2. How are we to put our trust in the Lord?

(1) First, we are to *trust Him as willing to receive us,* to forgive

[1] *Life and Letters of Mandell Creighton,* i. 327.
[2] Bishop Boyd Carpenter, *Some Pages of My Life,* 173.

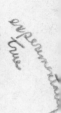

us, to accept us, and to bless us. Are we despairing? Do we say, "There is no hope"? "Put your trust in the Lord." Are we saying, "I am without strength, and, therefore, cannot be saved"? Why not? "Put your trust in the Lord." Does the evil one say that God will not receive us? "Put your trust in the Lord," who is infinitely gracious, and full of compassion. "As I live, saith the Lord God, I have no pleasure in the death of the wicked; but that the wicked turn from his way and live." Surely we may trust in Him whose mercy endureth for ever.

¶ For a long time no equivalent could be found in the language of Aniwa for "faith," and my work of Bible translation was paralysed for the want of so fundamental and oft-recurring a term. The natives apparently regarded the verb "to hear" as equivalent to "to believe." I would ask a native whether he believed a certain statement, and his reply would be, should he credit the statement, "Yes, I heard it"; but, should he disbelieve it, he would answer, "No, I did not hear it," meaning, not that his ears had failed to catch the words, but that he did not regard them as true. This definition of faith was obviously insufficient. Many passages, such as "Faith cometh by hearing," would be impossible of translation through so meagre a channel; and we prayed continually that God would supply the missing link. I spared no effort in interrogating the most intelligent native pundits, but all in vain, none caught the hidden meaning of the word.

One day I was in my room anxiously pondering. I sat on an ordinary kitchen chair, my feet resting on the floor. Just then an intelligent native woman entered the room, and the thought flashed through my mind to ask the all-absorbing question yet once again, if possible in a new light.

Was I not resting on the chair? Would that attitude lend itself to the discovery?

I said, "What am I doing now?"

"Koikae ana," "You're sitting down," the native replied.

Then I drew up my feet and placed them upon the bar of the chair just above the floor, and leaning back in an attitude of repose, asked: "What am I doing now?"

"Fakarongrongo," "You are leaning *wholly*," or, "You have lifted yourself from every other support."

"That's it!" I shouted, with an exultant cry; and a sense of holy joy awed me, as I realized that my prayer had been so fully answered.

To "lean on" Jesus wholly and only is surely the true

meaning of appropriating or saving faith. And now "Fakaron-grongo Iesu ea anea mouri" ("Leaning on Jesus unto eternal life," or "for all the things of eternal life") is the happy experience of those Christian islanders, as it is of all who cast themselves unreservedly on the Saviour of the world for salvation.[1]

(2) Especially are we to *trust in the Lord as He reveals Himself in the person of His Son Jesus Christ*. In Him we see love written out in capital letters. "Put your trust in the Lord" as having provided the one sacrifice for sin, whereby He has put away for ever all the sins of those who believe in Him. God is just, and the justifier of him that believeth. We are to believe that the precious blood can make us whiter than snow, scarlet sinners as we are. Let us come with that daring trust which ventures all upon the bare promise of a faithful God. Let us say, "I will go in unto the King, and if I perish I perish."

(3) We are to trust in the Lord, next, *that by the work of His Holy Spirit He can renew us*. The glorious Lord, who made the world out of nothing, can make something out of us yet. If we are given to anger, the Holy Spirit can make us calm and loving. If we have been defiled with impurity, He can make us pure in heart. If we have been grovelling, He can elevate us. He can put heavenly treasure in earthen vessels. He can set us at last among the heavenly choristers, that our voice, sweeter than that of angels, may be heard amongst their everlasting symphonies. He will even here put us among the children, and set us with the princes of His people. Let us believe that the Holy Ghost can create us anew, can raise us from our dead condition, and can make us perfect in every good work to do His will.

¶ A pleasing memory of early church going at Perth was that of the solemn administration of the Lord's Supper. In the procession of the elders, the child (as John Watson was then) was specially interested in an old man with very white hair and a meek, reverent face. Some time after he was walking on the road and passed a man breaking stones. The white hair caught his attention, and he looked back and recognized the elder who had carried the cup. Full of curiosity and wonder, he told his father the strange tale. His father explained to him that the reason why the old man held so high a place in the Church was that, although he was one of the poorest men in all the town, he

[1] *John G. Paton*, iii. 55.

was one of the holiest. " Remember," said his father, " the best man that ever lived upon this earth was the poorest, for our Lord had not where to lay His head "; and he added, " James breaks stones for his living, but he knows more about God than any person I have ever met." So he learned that evening, and never departed from the faith, that the greatest thing in all the world is character, and the crown of character is holiness.[1]

[1] W. Robertson Nicoll, *Ian Maclaren*, 21.

Rest after Toil.

LITERATURE.

Jerdan (C.), *For the Lambs of the Flock*, 15.
Jowett (J. H.), *Thirsting for the Springs*, 94.
Moberly (G.), *Plain Sermons Preached at Brighstone*, 34.
Power (P. B.), *The "I Wills" of the Psalms*, 1.
Price (A. C.), *Fifty Sermons*, xi. 353.
Vaughan (C. J.), *Voices of the Prophets*, 75.
    „   „   *The Family Prayer and Sermon Book*, i. 737.
Churchman's Pulpit: Good Friday and Easter Even, vii. 189 (Keble).
Expositor's Library: Psalms, i. 167 (Keble), 173 (Greenwood).
Good Words, 1866, p. 818 (Vaughan).
Plain Sermons by Contributors to the "Tracts for the Times," vi. 85 (Keble).
Sunday Magazine, 1895, pp. 494, 496, 499 (Wells).

Rest after Toil.

In peace will I both lay me down and sleep:
For thou, Lord, alone makest me dwell in safety.—Ps. iv. 8.

1. The Psalms form the most wonderful expression of human feelings that was ever penned. Those who know the Psalms only slightly do not understand this. But those who are wise enough to know them well, to learn them by heart and use them, know that there is not any state of feeling, not any condition in life, for which that wonderful book does not furnish the most exact and well-fitted expressions that can be conceived or desired. With joy and thankfulness the Psalms run over; they abound in expressions of faith, and trust, and cheerful confidence in the mercy and goodness of God. Of penitential sorrow and distress for sins, of humble confession and repentance, they are so full that they almost seem to contain nothing else. For peaceful times, for anxious times, for times of affliction and grief, for reliance on God in the morning or in the evening, awake or asleep, at midnight or at midday, in solitude or in society,—none know so well as those who know the Psalms, or some of them, by heart, what a store of heavenly expressions they furnish by which Christian hearts may pour themselves out to God in strains the most beautiful, and most exactly suitable to all their various states of feeling and condition. It has been said of Holy Scripture in general, and it is more applicable to the Psalms than to any other book in it, that its eye follows us, like the eye of a picture, ever fixed upon us, turn where we will.

> Eye of God's Word! where'er we turn
> Ever upon us! Thy keen gaze
> Can all the depths of sin discern,
> Unravel every bosom's maze:

Who that has felt thy glance of dread
   Thrill through his heart's remotest cells,
About his path, about his bed,
   Can doubt what Spirit in thee dwells?

2. There are two great and equal necessities of man's nature: work and rest. A man cannot be happy without either, without both, of these. We must have work; and we must have rest. Once the two things were one; and once again they will be one. An unfallen being finds repose in activity. In heaven there is no night. The will of God is done there, not only perfectly, but continually. Those holy spirits which behold the face of God, and are sent forth thence to minister to the heirs of salvation, could do but half, not half, of their office, if they took either night or day for rest from labour. They rest not day nor night. They rest in working. Meanwhile there is, for us, a divorce of the two things which God had joined together, work and rest. Work begins where rest ends: not until work is ended can rest begin. That is the condition of earth. Man goes forth to his work and to his labour until the evening. When night comes, no man can work.

I.

REST OF BODY AND MIND.

1. This is one of those many verses in the Bible, in the Psalms especially, which must come home to every heart of man, if read with any degree of simple faith. It sets full before us the most comfortable and refreshing picture of a devout, sober, honest person, his day's work ended, his passions kept in order, his sins repented of, and his prayers seriously said, laying himself down to his night's rest, in the full consciousness that he is neither alone nor unguarded; that as there has been a merciful Eye watching over him, a mighty Hand stretched out to guard him, through the dangers and temptations of the day, so it will be with him in the night also. His eyelids sink down with sleep; the Eye of the Lord never becomes heavy. Therefore such an one, be he young or old, rich or poor, is able to compose himself to sleep without fear.

2. This entire rest and tranquillity of God's faithful servants, when they lay them down on their bed at night, is beautifully expressed in the text by the words, "In peace will I both lay me down and sleep." "I will lay me down," says the Psalmist, "*all together*": all my powers of mind and body, agreeing as it were one with another; not torn by violent passions, by desire on the one hand and remorse on the other; not in the condition of the natural man as described by St. Paul, "The good that I would I do not, but the evil that I would not that I do"; and again, "I delight in the law of God after the inward man, but I see another law in my members, warring against the law of my mind." Not so is it with him of whom the Psalmist here speaks; rather he resembles the spiritual man, as described by the same St. Paul: "The very God of peace sanctify you wholly, and I pray God your whole spirit and soul and body be preserved blameless unto the coming of our Lord Jesus Christ."

¶ Beauty consists, says Ruskin, in certain external qualities of bodies which are typical of Divine attributes, and in the appearance of felicitous fulfilment in vital things. Every one has heard of the repose of true beauty; why is repose beautiful? Because it is "a type of Divine Permanence," and satisfies

> The universal instinct of repose,
> The longing for confirmed tranquillity,
> Inward and outward, humble and sublime—
> The life where hope and memory are one.[1]

3. The need of taking rest in sleep is a universal law of God's providence over men here in this lower world. In respect of it there is no difference between the highest and the lowest. Therefore, as death, so sleep may be truly called a great leveller. The greatest king and the meanest of his subjects, whatever difference there is between them at any given time of their waking moments, must alike forget themselves in sleep before a great many hours are over. To every one of us, one as much as another, there will then be but one chance of safety: that is, if God should be pleased to watch over us, and be with us, when we are away from ourselves. It is one of God's ways of continually reminding us all what frail, helpless beings we are, what an absolute nothing without Him.

[1] E. T. Cook, *The Life of Ruskin*, i. 199.

4. Sleep is the image of death, and the slumber of every night, rightly understood, is to a Christian a kind of sacramental token of that last long sleep. These words, therefore, may well be used, and always have been understood by devout persons, as most proper for a dying Christian also. Of a dying *Christian* : for only such an one has a warrant from Holy Scripture to regard death as no more than a quiet sleep. Observe how these expressions, " fallen asleep," " sleeping in Jesus," and the like, are always used in the New Testament. They are constantly employed to denote the death, not of all persons, but of those who die in the Lord. Thus, our Saviour, speaking of Lazarus : " Our friend Lazarus sleepeth, but I go, that I may awake him out of sleep." Again, the word is used of Stephen : when he had prayed for his murderers, " he fell asleep." So St. Paul speaks with horror of some men's notion that there was no resurrection, because in that case it must follow that those who are " fallen asleep in Christ are perished." In another place, he assures the Thessalonians that " them also which sleep in Jesus will God bring with him " when He comes to raise the dead.

¶ Sleep was one of the apostolic names for death, full of tenderness and peace, but it must not be understood to mean inaction. It is rest from the weariness and harassment of the present life; it is the entrance into the freedom and buoyancy of the life to come. In the sweetest letter of consolation ever written to a parent on the death of a child, Archbishop Leighton says : " And is he so quickly laid to rest ? Happy he ! . . . John is but gone an hour or two sooner to bed, as children used to do, and we are undressing to follow." Life is a long undressing, during which the frailties and faults of our imperfect nature are gradually slipped, and we enter unburdened into the unseen world. As the wrinkles are smoothed from the face of a sufferer by the gentle hand of death, so that the war-worn veteran returns to his youth, so the weariness departs from the soul, and it enters into the rest for which amid this struggle we often hunger and thirst.[1]

¶ Sleep is that death by which we may be literally said to die daily; a death which Adam died before his mortality; a death whereby we live a middle and moderating point between life and death; in fine, so like death, I dare not trust it without my prayers and a half adieu unto the world, and take my farewell in a colloquy with God.

[1] John Watson, *The Potter's Wheel*, 156,

The night is come, like to the day,
Depart not Thou, great God, away.
Let not my sins, black as the night,
Eclipse the lustre of Thy light:
Keep still in my horizon; for to me
The sun makes not the day, but Thee.
Thou, whose nature cannot sleep,
On my temples sentry keep;
Guard me 'gainst those watchful foes
Whose eyes are open while mine close;
Let no dreams my head infest
But such as Jacob's temples blest.
While I do rest, my soul advance;
Make my sleep a holy trance;
That I may, my rest being wrought,
Awake into some holy thought;
And with as active vigour run
My course as doth the nimble sun.
Sleep is a death: O make me try,
By sleeping, what it is to die;
And as gently lay my head
On my grave, as now my bed.
Howe'er I rest, great God, let me
Awake again at last with Thee;
And thus assur'd, behold I lie
Securely, or to awake or die.
These are my drowsy days; in vain
I do now wake to sleep again;
O come that hour, when I shall never
Sleep again, but wake for ever!

This is the dormitive I take to bedward; I need no other laudanum than this to make me sleep; after which I close mine eyes in security, content to take my leave of the Sun, and sleep unto the Resurrection.[1]

5. Often in the midst of life, often in the very spring-time of life, we are in death. But whenever it comes—the decisive, the final sickness—it brings with it one call, one trial, one necessity, one only possibility—a call to rest. Nothing can now be done but to lie still. And is that so easy? Visit a bed of death, and see whether even patience, whether even submission, much more, whether affiance, whether faith, is the grace of every man! We

[1] Sir Thomas Browne.

see then the truth of the saying, " And that not of yourselves, it is the gift of God ! "   To rest on the Lord then is just as impossible with man as it is in life to work for God.   But faith—the man of faith—can do it.   He thinks this one of the chief blessings, one of the chief evidences too, of Christ's Gospel, that it never sets a man to do anything impossible ; that its demand is always appropriate, its call exactly suitable to youth and to age, to health and to sickness, to life and to death.   To him now it says only these two words, Faith, rest !   Lie still and look upward.   What has been left undone cannot now be done : rest it upon Christ. What has been ill done cannot now be amended : rest it upon Christ.   What has been done amiss cannot now be undone : rest it upon Christ.   Lean all thy weight upon Him.   He is sufficient. He has borne all.   Trust Him, and doubt not.   He will undertake for thee.   It is enough.

¶ Two days later, with no premonitory consciousness of anything but perfect health, he fell suddenly ill, and a serious operation was deemed necessary.   He was taken at once to a hospital and the operation was performed.   It was apparently wholly successful, but strength was slow in returning, and the end began to be in doubt.   For six weeks he lingered, bearing his painful days and nights with cheerful courage and a sweet and patient self-effacement.   All his thought was centred in the effort to keep from the one dearest to him the foreboding that was becoming a certainty to him.   To a friend who sat by his side he said, " For myself, I regard death merely as the passing shadow on a flower." On 17th March he expressed a wish to be taken home, and there on 19th March, in the greyness of the deepening twilight, the end came.   He met death as he had met life, bravely and serenely, fully conscious of the loosening of the cords that held him to the earth.   With his last look and smile he said, " In spite of all, I am going to sleep; put out the lights " ; and for those who loved him darkness came.[1]

> Mysterious Night, when our first parent knew
> Thee by report Divine, and heard thy name,
> Did he not tremble for this goodly frame,
> This glorious canopy of light and blue ?
> But through a curtain of translucent dew,
> Hesperus with the host of heaven came,
> Bathed in the hues of the great setting flame,
> And lo !   Creation broadened to man's view.

[1] Ferris Greenslet, *Thomas Bailey Aldrich*, 237.

Who could have guessed such darkness lay concealed
Within thy beams, O Sun, or who divined,
When flower, and leaf, and insect lay revealed,
Thou to such countless worlds hadst made us blind?
Why should we then shun death with anxious strife
If Light could thus deceive, wherefore not Life?[1]

II.

REST OF SPIRIT.

"Come unto me, all ye that labour and are heavy laden, and I will give you rest." Faith is the apprehension of that rest; the laying hold now upon the promise, the entering at last into the fruition. Faith which works is also a faith which rests.

1. There is a resting of faith which is habitual. Faith rests while it works. This is a peculiarity of the true Gospel. No false religion could teach it. Many human forms even of the true Gospel do not teach it. Many professed disciples of Christ Himself—men to whom the name of religious persons cannot be denied—never learn it. True faith rests habitually; rests in working. It is a paradox; but a paradox full of truth, full of beauty, full of admonition.

When King Asa went out against Zerah the Ethiopian, and set the battle in array against overwhelming numbers, he "cried unto the Lord his God, and said, Lord, it is nothing with thee to help, whether with many, or with them that have no power: help us, O Lord our God; for we rest on thee, and in thy name we go against this multitude." Faith rested while it wrought. And when King Hezekiah saw the mighty host of Sennacherib coming to fight against Jerusalem, he said to his captains of war, "There be more with us than with him: with him is an arm of flesh; but with us is the Lord our God to help us, and to fight our battles. And the people," it is added, "rested themselves upon the words of Hezekiah, King of Judah." It was an example of faith resting (not after, but) in working. The Gospel of Christ lays great stress upon this point. "What shall I do," asks an awakening conscience, "to work the works of God?" Surely

[1] Blanco White.

some great feat of self-sacrifice; some "giving of my first-born for my transgression"; some deed of self-mortification and self-crucifixion, after which the world shall be dead to me and I to the world; this surely must be the life to which God calls one who, being a sinner, would be an heir of salvation? Mark the answer. "This is the work of God, that ye believe on him whom he hath sent." To work is to believe. To believe is to rest. "Say not in thine heart, Who shall go up for me into heaven? or, Who shall descend for me into the deep? The word is very nigh thee. If thou shalt confess with thy mouth the Lord Jesus, and shalt believe in thine heart that God hath raised him from the dead, thou shalt be saved." Faith is rest.

¶ It is not by retiring from active life or business, or by going down to a cottage in the country, that a man can secure peace of mind. Trifles may be as exhausting and troublesome, as worrying and irritating, as commerce or concerns of State; leisure leaves the mind open to conscience: the only real peace is in the mind; but if the mind is in a turmoil, to retreat into it is only to exchange one set of troubles for another. No man lived more in the rush and turmoil of the world than our great Prime Minister, Mr. Gladstone, and one of the secrets of his success was that when he returned home from the House of Commons he threw off his cares and left them behind him on the Treasury Bench. He used to call his library at Hawarden "the Temple of Peace." If he could do so with his immense responsibilities, surely any man might make his mind a sanctuary.[1]

> O Thou upon whose bosom lay
> Those hearts made weary by the way
>   Of life's incessant care,
> My spirit too, with toil oppressed,
> Seeking in vain an earthly rest,
> Is driven dove-like to Thy breast,
>   And bid to nestle there.
>
> It is not that I wish to lie
> Forgetful of the earth and sky,
>   And hid from human ken:
> I would not prize, I would not crave
> A rest unconscious like the grave,
> Nor seek repose that could not brave
>   The wills and wants of men.

[1] Lord Avebury, *Peace and Happiness* 346.

I seek Thy rest that I may find
A stronger impulse to the mind,
 And higher stretch of wing,
Even as the lark more freely soars
Because he hears the song he pours,
And is impelled by music's oars
 To work as well as sing.

Thou didst Thyself on earth recline
Upon Thy Father's breast divine,
 And rest on Him Thy will;
And therefore it was given to Thee
The mightiest of all souls to be,—
To walk upon the stormy sea
 And bid its waves be still.

If I am sheltered by Thy love,
I shall not hurt by heaven above
 The path of earth below;
But in my spirit's deep repose
I shall be strong against my foes,
And bear the thorn upon the rose,
 Unmurmuring as I go.

If first upon the mountain height
I see Thy radiance calm and bright
 Before I seek the plain,
With face illumined by the skies
I'll go where the demoniac lies,
And by Thy rest will soothe his cries,
 And burst his iron chain.[1]

2. There is a resting of faith which is occasional.

(1) After long confusions and conflicts within, as to the true way of salvation, at last we see and apprehend it. Christ is all. He has made peace. He has brought in an everlasting righteousness. In Him God is well pleased. In Him we have redemption through His blood, the forgiveness of sins. Can it be but that the soul, finding Him, should, for joy of that finding, rest and refresh itself, consciously, in the Lord?

(2) Sometimes doubt returns. A book which has fallen in our way, the conversation of an unbeliever, something less

[1] G. Matheson, *Sacred Songs*, 134.

palpable—a thought of unbelief, springing we know not whence within—has caused us new perplexity, new searchings of heart. What are we to think of Christ? Art Thou He that should come? or must we still look out, as of old, for some one who shall come—or perhaps never come—to be the Saviour of sinners and the Light of the world? At last the clouds disperse, and we see above the brightness of the firmament a form like that of the Son of God in heaven. The clear shining after rain has been vouchsafed to us and faith has rest and is edified.

(3) So it is sometimes after great labour. We have undertaken some work which is all for God. Ashamed of the idleness and self-indulgence which has so long bound and debased us; feeling the wickedness of such a return for the self-forgetting, self-sacrificing love of Christ; seeing the days passing away, and nothing done, nothing even attempted, to bring Him one life, one soul, for His travail even unto death for us; we did at last arouse ourselves by the help of prayer, and calling Him in went forth into the vineyard to bear something of the burden and heat of the day. The toil was at first difficult; flesh and blood rebelled, Satan opposed, conscience misgave me; but I persevered; persevered unto weariness; came back at late evening, faint and hungry; but faith strengthened and brightened within me as I stood before the Lord to report to Him of my poor endeavours: I found Him nearer to me when I thus began to treat Him as a Person, as One who had work for me and would receive my reckoning; that night I was able to say, as never before, "In peace will I both lay me down and sleep: For thou, Lord, alone makest me dwell in safety."

(4) It would be ungrateful if we did not add one more to these occasional restings of faith, one which depends not upon any circumstance, inward or outward, of human life, but is provided everywhere, of God's goodness, in that blessed communion and fellowship which is the Church and body of Christ. When faith droops, under the pressure of things temporal, whether adverse or prosperous, how often does it draw newness of vigour from obeying the call, "Let us go unto the house of the Lord," or the charge, "Do this in remembrance of me!" It is only presumption—it is not faith—that can dispense with these things. Christ judged better for us, as men not of the world yet in it, when He

bade us not to forsake the assembling of ourselves together, promised to be with even two or three thus gathered, and affixed a peculiar grace to the petition in which two should agree. If faith would know what is meant by her resting, she must frequent, with earnestness and large expectation, the table provided in the wilderness, the feast of which it is written, that, when Jesus took bread and blessed it, and gave it to them, "their eyes were opened, and they knew him." Faith, struggling elsewhere, rests here. "Handle me, and see."

¶ On the next day Francis clothed Divini in the grey clothes of the Order and girded his loins with the cord, and gave him the name "Pacificus," because he had left the world's tumult for the peace of God. Thus, too, a century later, another much greater poet was to seek for peace among the children of St. Francis. One evening he, already grey and bowed down, stood before a lonely cloister in the Apennines and knocked at the door. And to the porter's question as to what he sought there, the great Florentine (Dante) gave only the one all-including answer, "*Pace!*" ("Peace!")[1]

III.

THE GIVER OF REST.

The giver of rest is God—"thou, Lord, alone makest me dwell in safety." God is here revealed to us as exercising personal care in the still chamber. And there is something here which should be inexpressibly sweet to the believer; for this shows the minuteness of God's care, the individuality of His love; how it condescends, and stoops, and acts, not only in great, but also in little spheres; not only where glory might be procured from great results, but where nought is to be had save the gratitude and love of a poor feeble creature, whose life has been protected and preserved, in a period of helplessness and sleep. There is something inexpressibly touching in this "lay me down" of the Psalmist. In thus lying down, he voluntarily gave up any guardianship of himself; he resigned himself into the hands of another; he did so completely, for, in the absence of all care, he slept; there was here a perfect trust.

[1] J. Jörgensen, *St. Francis of Assisi*, 155.

My barque is wafted to the strand
 By breath Divine,
And on the helm there rests a Hand
 Other than mine.

One who has known in storms to sail
 I have on board ;
Above the raging of the gale
 I have my Lord.

He holds me when the billows smite,
 I shall not fall.
If sharp, 'tis short; if long, 'tis light;
 He tempers all.

Safe to the land! Safe to the land!
 The end is this ;
And then with Him go hand in hand
 Far into bliss.[1]

¶ There is no peace like the peace of the man who loves to
lie down at night with the thought of God possessing his mind
and heart. Happy the man who delights to recall the thought
of God before he sinks into slumber !

Be my last thought how sweet to rest
For ever on my Saviour's breast.

There is no peace like the peace of a man who, when he
awakes in the morning, gives first welcome to the thought of God.

Fairer than the morning, lovelier than the daylight,
Dawns the sweet consciousness, I am with Thee.

The man who finds in God his shield, who seeks in Him his
glory, and who makes in Him his boast, will have mornings of
joy, and evening times of light.[2]

¶ Let us learn as Luther did, who, looking out of his window
one summer evening, saw, on a tree at hand, a little bird making
his brief and easy dispositions for a night's rest. "Look," he said,
"how that little fellow preaches faith to us all. He takes hold
of his twig, tucks his head under his wing, and goes to sleep,
leaving God to think for him !"[3]

[1] Dean Alford.   [2] J. H. Jowett, *Thirsting for the Springs*, 99.
[3] P. B. Power, *The "I Wills" of the Psalms*, 19.

In *The Sunday Magazine* for 1877 the following hymn, written by a young Brahmin lady, was published:—

I lay me down in peace
Beneath Thy wing,
And safely sleep.
Thy watch can never cease,
For Thou, O King,
My soul wilt keep!

My sins are all forgiven,
So now I see
Thy Presence bright.
A day's march nearer heaven
And nearer Thee
I am this night.

For all the tenderness
Which Thou hast shown
To me this day,
For strength in feebleness,
To Thee alone
My thanks I pay.

Thy holy angels stand
As guards above
My lowly bed;
And Thine own gracious hand,
Thy hand of love,
Is 'neath my head.

What if, before the morn,
Thou bid'st me rise
And come to Thee?
Then homeward swiftly borne,
Beyond the skies,
My soul shall be.

Or if it be Thy will
That I should see
Another day,
O let Thy presence still
Remain with me,
And be my stay![1]

[1] Ellen Lakshmi Goreh.

The Greatness of Man.

LITERATURE.

Alexander (J. A.), *The Gospel of Jesus Christ*, 512.

Ballard (F.), *Does it Matter what a Man Believes?* 154.

Barton (G. A.), *The Roots of Christian Teaching*, 45.

Bersier (E.), *Sermons*, vi. 203.

Davies (J. Ll.), *The Gospel and Modern Life*, 88.

Hodge (C.), *Princeton Sermons*, 64.

Hutton (W. H.), *The Lives and Legends of the English Saints*, 1.

Kingsley (C.), *Sermons for the Times*, 129.

Lorimer (G. C.), in *Marylebone Presbyterian Pulpit*, ii. No. 6.

Maclaren (A.), *Expositions of Holy Scripture* : 1 Timothy to Hebrews, 212.

Maurice (F. D.), *Sermons in Country Churches*, 148.

Melvill (H.), *The Golden Lectures*, 321.

Meyer (F. B.), *The Way into the Holiest*, 34.

Muir (P. M.), *Modern Substitutes for Christianity*, 91.

Perin (G. L.), *The Sunny Side of Life*, 255.

Smellie (A.), *In the Hour of Silence*, 189.

Sowter (G. A.), *Trial and Triumph*, 199.

Vaughan (J.), *Sermons* (Brighton Pulpit), xvii. No. 1094.

Wilkinson (J. B.), *Mission Sermons*, ii. 81.

Christian World Pulpit, xl. 241 (Clifford) ; lxxii. 73 (Clayton) ; lxxvi. 324 (Morris).

Expositor, 3rd Ser., x. 81 (Cheyne).

Homiletic Review, xxi. 167 (Dobbs) ; lx. 142 (Vance).

THE GREATNESS OF MAN.

For thou hast made him but little lower than God, and crownest him with glory and honour.—Ps. viii. 5.

1. This Eighth Psalm seems to belong to the time when David had charge of his father's flocks, rather than to any other period of his life. We may agree with Delitzsch and others that probably none of the Davidic Psalms in the Psalter were composed until after he was anointed king, and became "the sweet psalmist of Israel" (2 Sam. xxiii. 1, R.V.). But that does not forbid our finding here a vivid reminiscence of some brilliant night on the hills of Bethlehem, when the shepherd youth lifted up his soul to God, praising Him for the glory of the heavens, and, even more, for the honour He has bestowed upon man. It is probable that many of the Psalms were written in the tranquil old age of the royal singer, recalling the most remarkable events of his earlier life, and reproducing the thoughts and emotions that had then stirred mightily within him, and to some extent the very words in which they had found expression.

It is an evening song, the carol of the nightingale rejoicing in the sheen of the moon and the stars. Yet we may be sure that the soul of the singer was flooded with the sunlight of Divine grace and favour. It is a lyrical episode to the grand lyric of the creation, touching it at the story of the fourth and sixth of the creative days. There are several kindred songs, celebrating the wonders of nature as exhibiting the perfections of God. But not one of them combines so marvellously the highest poetic beauty with inspiring suggestiveness. It touches the extreme points of God's self-attestation to man, uniting the glory of the beginning with the greater glory of the close, the light that flashed out when there was yet no human eye to behold it, with the light of the city of the redeemed.

2. The culminating point of the Psalm is the glory originally

bestowed upon man in investing him with the sovereignty over all creatures upon the earth, alluding to the Divine ordinance in Gen. i. 28. The Divine work on the fourth day of creation, and the crowning work of the sixth, are brought vividly into the present, and in sharp contrast. The glory of the visible heavens with their flaming orbs seems to entitle them to higher estimation than any possible product of almighty power. But upon man, in his insignificance and feebleness, even a greater glory was bestowed, and he is invested with the highest dignity. Under God, and yet but a little lower, he is made lord over all the earth. Every tenant of land, and air, and sea, is subjected to his power.

3. Is this glorious Psalm *prospective*, as well as *retrospective* ? By any legitimate interpretation, does it include within its sweep of space, and time, and power, God's redemptive as well as His creative work ? Does it contain any hint of a greater glory and a higher dignity in the future ?

We think that it does most assuredly. If not distinctly in the thought of the sacred poet, it lay in the thought and purpose of God, as clearly as if already accomplished, that whenever the full glory of fellowship with God should be realized, whenever the germinal and immature living principle that he received by the Divine breath—his higher Divine nature—should attain its most perfect beauty and strength, he would indeed be *lord over all* in a loftier sphere. He was not made in the image of God that he might for ever be a keeper of sheep and driver of oxen, or that he might subjugate the lion, and harpoon the whale. This " dominion over the beasts of the field, the birds of the air, and the fish of the sea " is a parable for the future, when more absolutely, " all things shall be put under his feet." His rule over the brute creation was a fact in the then present, in accordance with his capacity in the first period of his existence. It comprehends a prophecy and pledge that, whatever position he shall hereafter occupy, when the glory of his nature reaches its fullest development, and he attains fitness for higher dignity and rule, he shall be lord paramount, none above him save God only.

The purpose of Jehovah seemed to be defeated when sin entered into the world, and the indispensable conditions of spiritual growth and pre-eminence ceased to exist, but it has never been abandoned. It is realized through Christ, as Head of a new humanity, who, by uniting them to Himself, as partakers of His own life, restores to men all they had lost, whether actual or possible. They become associated with Him in the highest glory and honour.

In the light of these comments we can understand the effective use which the author of the Epistle to the Hebrews makes of the 8th Psalm in chap. ii. 5–10. The splendid significance which he attributes to it is quite within its legitimate scope and meaning, in its historic connexion with the account in Genesis.

4. It is to be noticed that the familiar words of the fifth verse, "For thou hast made him a little lower than the angels," are changed by the Revisers into, "For thou hast made him but little lower than God." No alteration can possibly be more significant. Seeing that its accuracy is indisputable, one may truthfully assert that this single correction is sufficient in itself to justify the replacement of the older version by the newer, wherever the Bible is read in public. Old association is nothing in comparison with truth. Nor can any truth be of greater importance than the difference between angels and God, as related to humanity. If it be asked why the writer of Hebrews in the second chapter refers to man as being "a little lower than the angels," the answer is very simple. He was evidently quoting from memory, and his remembrance was not of the Hebrew Scriptures, but of their translation into Greek in the Septuagint. This was a version made some two centuries before Christ by a number of Jewish scholars, for the benefit of their fellow-countrymen in North Africa who had lost the use of their mother-tongue. They were probably deterred by reasons of reverence from adopting what they knew to be the exact translation, and so fell back upon a secondary meaning of the word "Elohim." But timidity has no more right than rashness to rob us of that which is true. In matters of such vast import we need not only the truth, but the whole truth, and nothing but the truth. There is little significance or inspiration for us in the suggestion of our kinship to angels; but the whole meaning of our life, as well as all our hope beyond death, turns upon the question whether or not we are related to God. As the worth of every coin in this realm depends

upon the impress of the royal image, not that of any statesman, so does the intrinsic value of human nature, together with its present duty and eternal hope, depend, not upon kinship with angels, but upon the reality of that relationship to the Divine which is so graphically set forth in the first chapter of Genesis.[1]

¶ The race started high. At the beginning of his career man's moral and spiritual plane was but little lower than that of the Deity. Humanity is Jehovah's finest product. God's greatest work is not a planet, a shining sun, an ether sea, a potent law, a celestial city; it is not singing angels and shining seraphim, but man. At the summit of creation God made man but little lower than God, stamped him with the Divine image, crowned him, and gave him dominion over all creatures. This is the Bible doctrine of the origin of man, and it takes us to the heights. To be a member of the human race, the Psalmist declares, is to come of a great line. It is to have Jehovah for an hereditary ancestor. It is to trace one's descent from altitudes but little lower than the lofty peaks whose dizzy heights lose themselves in the clouds of the infinite, where Divine Being has its explanation. To have the blood of man in your veins is to be dowered with a heritage of being past the price of all worlds and the glory of all angels.

One may be a very lowly, a very humble and obscure and unworthy member of this human race; he may be some unfortunate defective or cripple; he may be a vagabond on the streets, a waif without a home, a criminal in a dungeon, the victim of his own vices; but upon him there lingers the tracery of the skies and about him is the livery, though in rags, of the life that is but little lower than God. He belongs to the first family of the realm. He possesses a dignity unequalled by all material things. He has a soul; and Jesus was speaking calmly and without exaggeration when He said: "What shall it profit a man, if he shall gain the whole world, and lose his own soul?"[2]

> Hark! the Eden trees are stirring,
> Slow and solemn to your hearing!
> Plane and cedar, palm and fir,
> Tamarisk and juniper,
> Each is throbbing in vibration
> Since that crowning of creation,
> When the God-breath spake abroad,
> Pealing down the depths of Godhead,

---

[1] F. Ballard, *Does it Matter what a Man Believes?* 154.
[2] J. I. Vance, *Tendency*, 31.

Let us make man like to God.
And the pine stood quivering
In the Eden-gorges wooded,
As the awful word went by;
Like a vibrant chorded string
Stretched from mountain-peak to sky!
And the cypress did expand,
Slow and gradual, branch and head;
And the cedar's strong black shade
Fluttered brokenly and grand!—
Grove and forest bowed aslant
In emotion jubilant.[1]

5. There are evidently two thoughts struggling together in the mind of the Psalmist—the littleness and the greatness of man. In a mind apt to pensive reflections, alive to moral truths, and responsive to the impressions of God's great universe, the unscientific contemplation of any of the grander forms of nature produces that double effect. And certainly the grandest of them all, which is spread over our heads, forces both these thoughts upon us. They seem so far above us, they swim into their stations night after night, and look down with cold, unchanging beauty on sorrow, and hot strife, and shrieks, and groans, and death. They are so calm, so pure, so remote, so eternal. Thus David felt man's littleness. And yet—and yet, bigness is not greatness, and duration is not life, and the creature that knows God is highest. So the consciousness of man's separation from and superiority to these silent stars springs up strong and victorious over the other thought.

¶ We are shown that no suffering, no self-examination, however honest, however stern, no searching-out of the heart by its own bitterness, is enough to convince man of his nothingness before God; but that the sight of God's creation will do it.[2]

I.

MAN AND NATURE.

1. Our knowledge of God, and our interest in God's works and ways, should begin, not with the beginning of the Creation, or

[1] E. B. Browning, *Drama of Exile.*   [2] Ruskin.

with the phenomena of the external world, but with the present relations of God to our own spirits, to ourselves personally and to mankind. What is God to us, and what are we to God? These are the questions which concern us most closely. If we can attain to a clear and firm faith on these points, we may be content to remain in some ignorance as to the *mode* of God's working in nature. The trust and love which are based upon our own spiritual relations with God will not depend upon our settling how the laws of nature are made to serve the will of God, but will overflow, as it were, upon the outward world, will be ready to accommodate themselves thankfully to whatever science may disclose to us.

Take the case of the Israelites themselves, whose sacred books the ancient Scriptures were. In what character was God first and chiefly known to them? As Jehovah, the God of the Covenant, the God of Abraham, Isaac, and Jacob. The young Israelite was taught, as soon as he was able to learn, that he was the subject of a righteous King, whose laws he was bound to obey. By this righteous King his race had been called out and claimed. Jehovah had been the Friend and Guide of his fathers, and by a series of mighty acts had delivered the people of Israel, and made a nation of them. The absolute allegiance of every Israelite was due to a Lord who was not to be confounded with any outward or visible thing. Worship of outward and visible things was a crime against the invisible Lord. Jehovah was the Lord of visible things, and He desired the children of the chosen seed to be also spiritually masters of visible things. He bade them serve Him and be true to Him apart from any relations with outward things; and He then promised to reward with outward things those who in spirit were loyal to Him.

¶ The books of the New Testament are the books of a spiritual Kingdom, a Kingdom revealed in Christ, and having for its sphere the spiritual natures of men. Jesus Christ, the Son of God, manifests and declares the Father. By His death and resurrection He founds a Kingdom in which men are brought near to their Father in heaven. The Apostles go forth to proclaim this Kingdom, and their Master the Lord of it, and to invite men to enter into it and be thereby saved. The high spiritual and human importance of the Gospel would naturally make all questions relating to the physical world comparatively

insignificant to those who were charged with the first pro-
mulgation of the Gospel. Accordingly, in the New Testament
we find scarcely a single allusion to the earliest history of the
world or of mankind. If then we are to follow such guidance
all difficulties and problems about the laws of nature and the
antiquity of the world and of the human race are insignificant
compared with the great truths of our relation to Christ and to
the Father in the Spirit.[1]

¶ There is nowhere for a moment any doubt in Christ as to
what the true life of man is. He is here and now, a creature of
Nature, like other creatures; but his true life is not natural, like
that of the fowls of the air, or the lilies of the field. He is
essentially a moral being, with relations beyond nature, and
wants, and aspirations, and duties which connect him with a
Divine or supernatural order. From first to last this spiritual
conception underlies the Gospels, and makes itself felt in them.
There is no argument, because there is no hesitation. " Is not
the life more than meat, and the body than raiment ? " The
possibility of a negative answer is not supposed. The claims of
the natural order, some have even thought, are unduly depressed.
The spiritual life seems to overshadow and displace them. But
this is only by way of emphasis, and in order to rouse men from
the dreams of a mere sensual existence. " After all these things
do the Gentiles seek "—those who know no better, to whom the
meaning of the spiritual and Divine order has not come. But
" seek ye first the kingdom of God, and his righteousness; and all
these things shall be added unto you." The spiritual must be
held in its true place as primary; after this the natural has also
its place, and to be recognized in addition.[2]

2. Now there never has been a time when it was more
necessary to keep in mind the truth that, in virtue of his relation
to God, man is great above all that we call nature. For, apart
altogether from the ubiquitous blight of unbelief, the rush and
crush of a civilization which is essentially selfish tends to dis-
hearten myriads, if not drive them to despair. The ever-
increasing pressure of modern life tends to divide mankind more
and more sharply into two classes, those who think too much of
themselves and those who think too little. It were hard to say
which of these classes is the more numerous, but it is not difficult
to discern which is the more to be pitied. We hear often and

---

[1] J. Ll. Davies, *The Gospel and Modern Life*, 97, 101.
[2] Principal John Tulloch.

rightly about the curse of pride. Yet there is a kind of pride
which is not only holy but the very starting-point of nobility.
We quote Scripture freely as to the beauty of humility, and it
were doubtless unmeasured gain if all who bear the Christian
name herein displayed the Christian spirit. Still there is a false
as well as a true humility. There is an estimate of oneself so poor
and small as to become a dangerous slope ushering down to a
bottomless gulf of despair. Self-conceit is no doubt ugly enough
to merit the protests it calls forth. But the opposite extreme is
far worse. Self-conceit may be objectionable, but self-contempt
is ruinous. The former is quite compatible with a lofty hope
and a vivid sense of duty. The latter leads straight away to
depression, despair, and suicide.

¶ It is a pitiful, nay, even a tragic fact, that more men and
women are found. to-day than ever heretofore, echoing, whether
with coarse speech or in highly intellectual reviews, the old wail
of Omar Khayyám—

> Ah Love! could thou and I with Fate conspire
> To grasp this sorry scheme of things entire,
>   Would not we shatter it to bits—and then
> Remould it nearer to the Heart's Desire!

It is verily a real gospel for to-day that can answer such doleful
quatrains with an emphatic No![1]

¶ Oh, my Father! keep me humble. Help me to have respect
towards my fellow-men—to recognize their several gifts as from
Thee. Deliver me from the diabolical sins of malice, envy, or
jealousy, and give me hearty joy in my brother's good, in his
work, in his gifts and talents; and may I be truly glad in his
superiority to myself, if Thou art glorified! Root out all weak
vanity, all devilish pride, all that is abhorrent to the mind of
Christ. God, hear my prayer! Grant me the wondrous joy of
humility, which is seeing Thee as All in All.[2]

II.

THE NOBILITY OF MAN.

1. What are the chief difficulties in the way of an encourag-
ing belief in man's nobility?

---

[1] F. Ballard, *Does it Matter what a Man Believes?* 158.
[2] *Memoir of Norman MacLeod*, ii. 318.

(1) First, there is the absurdity, as it seems to not a few, of the Almighty caring for such a race, and therefore the possibility of the Incarnation. "Which," asks Mr. Frederic Harrison, "is the more deliriously extravagant, the disproportionate condescension of the Infinite Creator, or the self-complacent arrogance with which the created mite accepts, or rather dreams of, such an inconceivable prerogative? His planet is one of the least of all the myriad units in a boundless Infinity; in the countless aeons of time he is one of the latest and the briefest; of the whole living world on the planet, since the ages of the primitive protozoon, man is but an infinitesimal fraction. In all this enormous array of life, in all these aeons, was there never anything living which specially interested the Creator, nothing that the Redeemer could care for, or die for? If so, what a waste creation must have been! . . . Why was all this tremendous tragedy, great enough to convulse the Universe, confined to the minutest speck of it, for the benefit of one puny and very late-born race?"

But is it not the fact that along with the discovery of Man's utter insignificance, there has come the discovery of powers and faculties unknown and unsuspected, so that more than ever all things are in subjection to him, his dominion has become wider, his throne more firmly established? Is it not the fact that the whole realm of Nature is explored by him, is compelled to minister to his wants, or to unfold its treasures of knowledge? Is it not the fact that more than ever it can be said—

> The lightning is his slave; heaven's utmost deep
> Gives up her stars, and like a flock of sheep
> They pass before his eye, are numbered, and roll on!
> The tempest is his steed, he strides the air;
> And the abyss shouts from her depth laid bare,
> "Heaven, hast thou secrets? Man unveils me; I have none."

¶ Not the production of any higher creature, but the perfecting of humanity is to be the glorious consummation of Nature's long and tedious work. Man seems now, much more clearly than ever, the chief among God's creatures. The whole creation has been groaning and travailing together in order to bring forth that last consummate specimen of God's handiwork, the Human Soul.[1]

[1] J. Fiske, *Man's Destiny*, 31.

This earth too small
For Love Divine! Is God not Infinite?
If so, His Love is infinite. Too small!
One famished babe meets pity oft from man
More than an army slain! Too small for Love!
Was Earth too small to be of God created?
Why then too small to be redeemed?[1]

(2) How is the man who knows himself to be but commonplace, and is daily driven to take his chance in the crushing crowd of the unprivileged and unknown, to find hope and inspiration? This, it must ever be remembered, is the type of doubt which most of all prevails. It is well for the "aristocracy," in body or mind or position, to descant upon the "pleasures of life," and extol its delightful opportunities. Unfortunately, under present social conditions, the rank and file of humanity scarcely know what these mean. Surely it is one of the most monstrous and cruel anomalies of civilization that the vast majority of our fellows should be toiling through hard, drab, dreary lives, in order that a minority may have chances of sipping life's nectar which are inevitably denied to themselves. Who would not feel inspired if, with Ruskin, we could travel luxuriously through all Europe's fascinations of nature and art? Would not myriads of poor, overworked men and women be invigorated if they could winter at Davos Platz, or escape the cutting winds of spring by a sojourn in the Riviera, or flee from the depressions of a wet summer to the sunny South of France? But these reliefs and enjoyments, we know, are for the favoured few. If amongst such, ennui and depression oft prevail, and globe-trotting millionaires find a disposition to suicide, how are the struggling many to keep heart amidst their wearing and wearying monotonies?

Yet the humblest hind or the poorest struggler in the slums may, if he will, herein congratulate himself that he is "crowned with glory and honour." And if parsons are not pleasing to him, he may receive his crown from the hands of so competent a witness as Professor Huxley, who thus estimates "that great Alps and Andes of the living world—Man": "Our reverence for the nobility of manhood will not be lessened by the knowledge that Man is in substance and in structure one with the brutes; for he

[1] Aubrey de Vere.

alone possesses the marvellous endowment of intelligible and rational speech . . . so that now he stands raised upon his accumulated experience as upon a mountain-top, far above the level of his humble fellows, and transfigured from his grosser nature by reflecting here and there a ray from the infinite source of truth."[1] More than that. The lowliest pauper may not only say with Descartes, " I think, therefore I am," but may quote the Psalmist in addition—I am " but little lower than God." For, accepting the testimony of latest science as just quoted, we know of no thinker in the universe save God and ourselves. Our power to think, compared with His, is truly both infinitesimal and derived, but it is real, and it is the medium of a kinship as valid and inspiring as is the dawning consciousness of a baby prince that his father is the king supreme in the land. How then can the man who appreciates such relationship to the Divine be driven even by modern cynicism into self-contempt? In his possession of mind he is, in very deed, the son of the King of kings.

There is, however, by all acknowledgment, something higher than mind. Intellectual power is one thing; moral character is another. To-day, happily, no one dare say, in respectable society, that so long as a man is clever it does not matter whether he is good. The folly which openly declares that " there are no good and there are no bad "[2] needs no disproof. For it not only contradicts itself,[3] but in putting an end to the possibility of morality it makes itself as contemptible as degrading. F. W. Robertson was immeasurably more true and worthy of regard when he wrote in his diary, " I resolve to believe in myself, and in the powers which God has given me." Such a resolve, no less humble than potent, is based not upon " promises," but upon facts equally undeniable and immeasurable. Besides God, so far as our knowledge extends, no other than man can say " I will." That he can and does so determine, is beyond controversy, for it is hourly consciousness. But such moral freedom marks man out from all the known universe as " but little less than Divine."[4]

¶ No human life is perfect, not one is without its limitation, but David Hill so followed Christ that he was known as His. In

---

[1] Huxley, *Man's Place in Nature*, 76.

[2] Editor's reply in *The Clarion* to Rev. C. Noel.

[3] *Not Guilty*, 260.   [4] F. Ballard, *Does it Matter what a Man Believes?* 174.

China the life he lived was recognized by the Chinese as corresponding to the Life he preached, and they called him "The little Jesus." A few days after the news of his death was cabled to this country, a relative of his, herself the daughter of a Fijian missionary, met the writer, and we spoke together of our dear friend. Suddenly, looking at me with tearful eyes, she challenged me. "You knew him," she said, "well; was he not like Jesus Christ?" The question was unexpected, but like a flash came the perception that only one answer was possible—"Yes, he *was* like Jesus Christ."[1]

(3) But the chief difficulty is sin and the fruits of it. What then? Are we to abandon in despair our hopes for our fellows, and to smile with quiet incredulity at the rhapsodies of sanguine theorists like David? If we are to confine our view to earth—yes. But there is more to see than the sad sights around us. All these men—these imperfect, degraded, half-brutified men—have their share in our Psalm. They have gone out and wasted their substance in riotous living; but from the swine-trough and the rags they may come to the best robe and the feast in the father's house. The veriest barbarian, with scarcely a spark of reason or a flickering beam of conscience, sunken in animal delights, and vibrating between animal hopes and animal fears—to him may belong the wondrous attributes; to be visited by God, crowned with glory and honour, higher than all stars, and lord of all creatures.

¶ I see *Jesus*; and my most vexing questions are answered, my most grievous misgivings dispelled.

I contrast my littleness and weakness with the vastness of the material world round about me, and with the inexorable action of natural law, and I am sorely disquieted; what am I among these constellations and systems and irresistible forces? But He redeems me at a tremendous cost, and I know that I must be a thing of price.

I look at my solitude in the midst of the millions who people the universe; and again I am filled with perplexity and foreboding. But He loves me and gives Himself for me; He sanctifies and keeps and chastens and cleanses me—me apart from all others. So I am comforted, for I understand that I am not forgotten.

I think of my guiltiness and sin in the presence of the holy

[1] J. E. Hellier, *Life of David Hill*, 74.

law; and this thought begets still keener doubts and worse
alarms. But His Cross assures me that there are remembrance
and forgiveness and welcome for guilty men. It justifies me
altogether. It solves my every difficulty, victoriously, touchingly, divinely.

I am saddened by the shortness and transitoriness of my life;
once more trouble is born within my soul. But then there rises
in front of me the sight of Him who has conquered death as my
Representative and Forerunner, leaving behind Him a rifled and
empty grave. Here is the very consolation for which I yearn.

The vision of Jesus is indeed the medicine for all my dis-
tresses. It never fails to effect a cure. It ends my every sickness, solves my every riddle, peoples my every desolation, defeats
my every dread.[1]

2. Two facts are to be taken into account. And when both
are reckoned with then we know that man is indeed and in truth
" but little lower than God."

(1) *The first fact is Creation.*—Turn to that noble archaic
record, Gen. i. 26–28, which transcends the imaginings of modern
science as far as it does those legends of creation which make the
heathen literature with which they are incorporated incredible.
Its simplicity, its sublimity, its fitness attest its origin and
authority to be Divine. "God created man in his own image"
(Gen. i. 27). There we have the Divine likeness. Our mental
and moral nature is made on the same plan as God's: the Divine
in miniature. Truth, love, and purity, like the principles of
mathematics, are the same in us as in Him. If it were not so, we
could not know or understand Him. But since it is so, it has
been possible for Him to take on Himself our nature—possible
also that we shall be one day transformed to the perfect image of
His beauty.

But we must notice that it is in relation to God, because of
the Divine likeness, not in himself, that man is great. One of the
ablest attempts to supersede Christianity is that which goes by
the name of Positivism or the Religion of Humanity, which sets
Man on the throne of the universe, and makes of him the sole
object of worship. "A helper of men outside Humanity," said
the late Professor Clifford, "the Truth will not allow us to see.
The dim and shadowy outlines of the Superhuman Deity fade

---

[1] A. Smellie, *In the Hour of Silence*, 189.

slowly away from before us, and, as the mist of His Presence floats aside, we perceive with greater and greater clearness the shape of a yet grander and nobler figure, of Him who made all gods and shall unmake them. From the dim dawn of history, and from the inmost depths of every soul, the face of our Father *Man* looks out upon us with the fire of eternal youth in His eyes, and says, ' Before Jehovah was, I am.' "

¶ The Great Being, Humanity, is only an abstraction. "There is no such thing in reality," Principal Caird reminds us, " as an animal which is no particular animal, a plant which is no particular plant, a man or humanity which is no individual man. It is only a fiction of the observer's mind." There is logical force as well as humorous illustration in the contention of Dean Page Roberts, that " there is no more a humanity apart from individual men and women than there is a great being apart from all individual dogs, which we may call Caninity, or a transcendent Durham ox, apart from individual oxen, which may be named Bovinity." Nor does the geniality of Mr. Chesterton render his argument the less telling : " It is evidently impossible to worship Humanity, just as it is impossible to worship the Savile Club : both are excellent institutions, to which we may happen to belong. But we perceive clearly that the Savile Club did not make the stars and does not fill the universe. And it is surely unreasonable to attack the doctrine of the Trinity as a piece of bewildering mysticism, and then to ask men to worship a being who is ninety million persons in one God, neither confounding the persons nor dividing the substance." [1]

(2) *The second fact is Redemption.*—Man looks not at the face of the stars, but into the faces of his fellow-men. He looks down into his own guilty heart and darkened mind. He looks at fallen, sinful human nature. He sees man imbruted, besotted, his face written over with the ruin of God's law, and his powers eaten out with lust, and he says : " It cannot be. The song is false. Man is too vile to claim the care of the holy God," and the old doubt breaks forth afresh.

> What is man, that thou art mindful of him ?
> And the son of man, that thou visitest him ?

Jesus is the triumphant vindication of the high origin of man. He came to reveal God, to tear aside the veil human fear had

[1] P. M'Adam Muir, *Modern Substitutes for Christianity*, 112.

woven across the face of Deity. He succeeded, and said, " He that hath seen me hath seen the Father." But He came also to reveal man, to tear away the disguises sin had woven around the human, to show the higher, the finer, the Divine possibilities there are for every soul in Him. He has succeeded here also. "Whoso-ever believeth that Jesus is the Christ is born of God." We see the world's vastness and man's littleness, and say, "What is man that thou art mindful of him ? " We see God's holiness and man's sinfulness, and say, "What is man that thou art mindful of him ? " Then we see Jesus. We see how low Divine love can stoop and how high it can lift ; and once more the ancient song arises without a broken note—

"Thou hast made him but little lower than God !"

Thou hast, O Lord, a wondrous plan,
 To build a tower to reach the skies ;
Its base is earth, its progress man,
 Its summit sacrifice.

'Tis only for the summit's sake
 Thou layest the foundation-stone ;
The mornings of creation break
 For sacrifice alone.

Thou wouldst not have prepared one star
 To float upon the azure main,
Hadst Thou not witnessed from afar
 The Lamb that should be slain.

Thou wouldst not have infused Thy life
 Into the insect of an hour,
Hadst Thou not seen 'neath nature's strife
 Thy sacrificial flower.

To Him that wears the cross of pain
 Thou leadest all Thine ages on ;
Through cloud and storm, through wind and rain,
 Through sense of glories gone. . . .

Thou wilt not let me live alone ;
 Thou wilt not let me keep my rest ;
Thy blast on every tree has blown
 To throw me on Thy breast.

Thou madest me for Him whose love
From dawn to eve made His will Thine,
And all my ages only move
Within that light to shine.[1]

¶ The creation was the work of a word. The redemption was
the work of a life—of a life of self-denial, of a death on the Cross.
The creation cost God nothing. The redemption cost the death
of His Son, and all that that death implied. Measure the
distance between the words "Let there be light" and the words
"Eloi, Eloi, lama sabachthani," and that will show the interval
which separates the value of the created universe from the value
of man. Christians can ask no other measure of the greatness
of the human soul. Christians can ask no further proof of the
infinite importance of human life and human action. The self-
conquests that seem so small, the resistance to temptation, the
triumphs over besetting sin, the keeping of the temper, the sacrifice
of self, the adherence to truth—measure them by their share in
the Cross of Christ, and see who can call them little things. And
in this, too, as in so much else, revelation does but proclaim what
is ever whispered in the inmost shrine of the spirit given to man.
The creation that we see is vast, and its forces are mighty, but
vaster far and mightier far out of all comparison are those eternal
differences between right and wrong on which rest for ever the
feet of the throne of God.[2]

[1] G. Matheson, *Sacred Songs*, 13.   [2] Archbishop Temple.

KNOWING AND TRUSTING.

LITERATURE.

Bonar (H.), *Light and Truth* : Old Testament, 188.
Cook (F. C.), *Church Doctrine*, 215.
Hutton (R. E.), *The Crown of Christ*, 187.
Leach (C.), *Sermons for Working Men*, 112.
Maclaren (A.), *Expositions of Holy Scripture* : Psalms i.–xlix., 16.
Pierson (A. T.), *The Making of a Sermon*, 41.
Simeon (C.), *Works*, v. 32.
Spurgeon (C. H.), *New Park Street Pulpit*, vi. (1860) 10.
Voysey, *Sermons*, vi. (1883) No. 7.
Webb-Peploe (H. W.), *The Titles of Jehovah*, 1.
Homiletic Review, New Ser., xxxviii. 414 (Behrends).
Literary Churchman, xxxv. (1889) 260 (Hardman).

KNOWING AND TRUSTING.

And they that know thy name will put their trust in thee ; for thou, Lord,
hast not forsaken them that seek thee.—Ps. ix. 10.

THIS Psalm is the foundation of many ancient Collects. Dante
quotes it to St. James in Paradise. He says hope had first come
to him

> From him who sang
> The songs of the Supreme, himself supreme
> Among his tuneful brethren. "Let all hope
> In Thee," so spake his anthem, "who have known
> Thy name."[1]

I.

KNOWLEDGE OF THE NAME OF GOD.

The name of God stands for His Person, His character. A man's
name is often the exact opposite of himself, but God's names are
revelations of God. The early patriarchs knew Him by the name
Elohim. They knew Him so far, and adored Him with deep
awe and absolute trust in His power, righteousness, and good-
will. That name raised them out of earthly and debasing
associations, delivered them from the fetishism of idolatry, and
brought them into near contact with the spiritual world; they
trusted in Him according to the measure of their knowledge, and
were saved by their faith. A further disclosure of the Divine
goodness and love was made by the revelation of the name
Jehovah, when the Lord made all His goodness pass before Moses,
and proclaimed, "Jehovah, Jehovah Elohim, merciful and gracious,
long-suffering, and abundant in goodness and truth." With that
revelation was associated an entire system of typical institutions,

[1] *Paradiso*, Canto xxv. 11. 71-5.

preparing the way for a still more perfect discovery, at once quickening the conscience, making it sensible of the extent of human sinfulness, and indicating the conditions and principles of a future atonement. The forms of the living Word and of the living Spirit gradually disclosed themselves to the prophetic vision, never fully revealed, yet ever approaching nearer to a personal manifestation; but the Name itself in its highest sense was first suggested, then declared, by the voices which heralded the Incarnation and by the utterances of the Incarnate Word.

1. God is, of course, the embodiment of almighty power. But we learn that He uses His power for beneficent ends. It was His almighty power that shaped a world into being. At His voice chaos became order, darkness fled, and light and life came. It is by His power that He moves every atom of the globe, expands and beautifies every leaf, erects every blade of grass, builds up every tree, and paints every flower in the garden. His Almightiness flashes in the lightning, rolls in the thunder, guides the light, roars in the volcano, wings the angels, and feeds the sparrows. It is His almighty hand that seizes the curtain of darkness, and swings it across the chambers of the sky every night, and puts tired man to rest, and covers him with His feathers. It is His power that sends the sun every morning to wake us to duty and pleasure.

> I sing the almighty power of God,
>   Which made the mountains rise;
> Which spread the flowing seas abroad,
>   And built the lofty skies.

Does this not help me? Yes. If God is almighty, then He is able to help and keep me. If He is possessed of all power I may put my soul and body and all my concerns into His hands, assured that none shall be able to pluck me out. "Help is laid upon one that is mighty," so I may trust and not be afraid. I am poor and feeble; He is strong. In my pilgrimage I often come into danger, and may fall, but underneath is the omnipotent arm of God.

¶ When we have got into our blood for ever the conception of God which crowns Him the King, Holy and Almighty, we are prepared upon a sound moral basis to receive Him as the loving and merciful Father. One therefore anticipates that the new doctrine will be based on the conception of the Divine Fatherhood —not the Fatherhood that throws away the Judgeship and the Righteousness of God, but the Fatherhood that gathers these up into a nobler and final unity; and that the Incarnation of our Lord Jesus Christ, as the revelation of the Father and the Head of the human race, will yield more blessed and practical fruit in the life of the race from year to year.[1]

2. God is also the embodiment of perfect justice; but we must complement this truth by saying that He is the Everlasting Father. We cannot trust an impersonal force, who neither loves nor hates and who hears no prayer. Such a God is only a God in name. He does not care for me; He does not know what care is, and how then can I care for Him; how can I bring myself to trust in Him? It were a blessing if I could only be like Him— unconscious and careless—like the insect of a summer's day, or the flower by the wayside, or the fish that sport in the sea. My reason, my conscience—these are my curse! The birds of the air are my superiors. For, with such a God, all that you count best in me is stifled and is a monstrous blunder. The heavens are brass, the earth is iron, and no one is to be pitied as am I, who cry but receive no answer. I can only hate the system which gave me birth, and to talk of trust is to mock me, to add insult to injury.

> Truly there is no law but truth; there is
>   No judge but justice. They who use the sword
>   Shall perish by the sword, for no reward
>   Is there but virtue, nor shall evil miss
> The strict revenge of its calamities,
>   Since in and of ourselves, perforce, are scored
>   Exact effects for every deed and word,—
>   Nor life, nor death forego the least of this!
> Nothing effects our destinies save we:
>   Ours is the seed we sow, the fruit we reap—
>   Yea, and the heart's one flame of ecstasy,
> And the soul's vigil we are sworn to keep,
>   And life's low average of strife and sleep,
>   And, O, the best we are and dare not be![2]

---

[1] John Watson, *The Cure of Souls.*
[2] George C. Lodge, *Poems and Dramas*, ii. 141.

¶ There is no power to generate trust in any philosophy that identifies God with the order of the universe.   There is no pity for the weak and the wicked.   Tennyson does not put it too strongly when he represents Nature as not only careless of the single life, but as crying, from scarped cliff and quarried stone—

> A thousand types are gone;
> I care for nothing, all shall go.

And philosophical theism, deifying reason and moral law, can rise no higher than the moan—

> Oh yet we trust that somehow good
> Will be the final goal of ill,
> To pangs of nature, sins of will,
> Defects of doubt, and taints of blood.

Even so much as that no classic poetry or philosophy had ventured to utter.   It had no such dream.   And whence Tennyson brought it becomes clear when Christmas bells are ringing—

> Ring out the darkness of the land,
> Ring in the Christ that is to be![1]

¶ In his *Jungle Books*, Kipling gives us his view of the order in which we have our place, and it is all summed up in this stanza with which he closes his description of the Jungle—

> Now these are the laws of the jungle,
> and many and mighty are they;
> But the head and the hoof of the law,
> and the haunch and the hump, is—Obey!

3. The supreme name of God is Love—not love merely as good-will, but love as active, seeking the lost until they are found, seeking all until they are found.   That converts the poet's dream into a blessed certainty, and the faintness of his trust into solid assurance.   The omnipotence of God does not make Him attractive to me.   The omniscience of God sounds the death-knell of my hope.   The justice of God thrusts me into the dungeon of despair.   In such an atmosphere there cannot be the first breath of faith.   But when you make it clear to me that this omnipotent, omniscient, holy God is also infinite in His tenderness, that He loves me and wants me, that He is my Father, and that in Christ His Fatherhood has become incarnate, so that when I

[1] A. J. F. Behrends.

see Him I see the Father, my faith is kindled and my trust knows no misgiving. Here, in God's love for me, sealed by manger, cross, and open grave, is the Ariadne thread which leads me out of the cave of darkness, despair, and death.

¶ When David Gray, the young poet of Kirkintilloch, lay dying in his cottage home by the banks of the Luggie, about which he had sung so sweetly, his last words, whispered in the ear of his mother, were, "God has love, and I have faith." With this sweet utterance upon his lips, and this blessed confidence in his heart, he "fell asleep."

¶ Another instance of the effect of his preaching is given in the story of how, during a confirmation which he was holding in an East-end church, a poor hawker of infidel literature strolled into the church, and listening to the Bishop's address was struck by his assertion of the Fatherhood of God. At the close of the service the man asked a church-worker at the door, with much earnestness, "Is what the Bishop says true? Is God indeed the Father of men?" "Of course it is true," said the lady. "Then," said he, "my occupation is gone; I have been teaching the reverse of this for years, but I can do so no more."[1]

II.

TRUST IN GOD.

1. In its literal force the term used by the Psalmist means "to flee to a refuge." Elsewhere we read, "Be merciful unto me, O God, be merciful unto me; for my soul trusteth in thee: yea, in the shadow of thy wings will I make my refuge." The words recall the time when David betook himself to the cave of Adullam for shelter from his persecutors. In imagination we can see the rough sides of the cavern that sheltered him arching over the fugitive, like the wings of some great bird, and just as he has fled thither with eager feet and is safely hidden from his pursuers there, so he has betaken himself to the everlasting Rock, in the cleft of which he is at rest and secure. To trust in God is neither more nor less than to flee to Him for refuge, and there to be at peace. The same presence of the original metaphor, colouring the same religious thought, is found in the beautiful words with

[1] *Life of Bishop Walsham How*, 170.

which Boaz welcomes Ruth, when he prays for her that the God of Israel may reward her, "under whose wings thou art come to trust."

Such a figure as that is worth tomes of theological lectures about the true nature of faith, telling us, as it does, by means of a picture which says a great deal more than many a treatise, that faith is something very different from a cold-blooded act of believing in the truth of certain propositions; that it is the flight of the soul—knowing itself to be in peril, and naked, and un-armed—into the strong Fortress.

What is it that keeps a man safe when he thus has around him the walls of some citadel? Is it himself, is it the act by which he took refuge, or is it the battlements behind which he crouches? So in faith—which is more than a process of a man's understanding, and is not merely the saying, "Yes, I believe all that is in the Bible is true; at any rate, it is not for me to con-tradict it," but is the running of the man, when he knows himself to be in danger, into the very arms of God—it is not the running that makes him safe, but it is the arms to which he runs.

¶ The man that stands with his back against an oak-tree is held firm, not because of his own strength, but because of that on which he leans. There is a beautiful story of a heathen convert who said to a missionary's wife, who had felt faint and asked that she might lean for a space on her stronger arm, "If you love me, lean hard." That is what God says to us, "If you love Me, lean hard." And if you do, because He is at your right hand, you will not be moved. It is not insanity; it is not arrogance; it is simple faith, to look our enemies in the eyes, and to feel sure that they cannot touch us. "Trust in Jehovah; so shall ye be established." Rest on the Lord, and ye shall rest indeed.[1]

¶ Dr. Cochran became the great character of Urumia and of western Persia. A Moslem lady of high rank in the town once remarked, as he was starting away, "We always feel that the city is perfectly safe when Dr. Cochran is here." In 1887 Mrs. Cochran wrote: "It is wonderful what confidence these people have in us, and even in our people. The Governor gave Joe (Dr. Cochran) his gold watch to send to Europe to be repaired. Joe told him there was no chance to send it unless by some of our Nestorians as far as Constantinople, and there would be several changes of hands, and perhaps it would not be safe. 'Oh yes,' said he, 'the hands of all your people are good.'"[2]

[1] A. Maclaren.   [2] R. E. Speer, *The Foreign Doctor*, 298.

There is no unbelief!
Whoever plants a seed beneath a sod,
And waits to see it push away the clod,
He trusts in God.

Whoever says, when clouds are in the sky—
"Be patient, heart: light breaketh by-and-bye,"
Trusts the Most High.

Whoever sees, 'neath winter's field of snow,
The silent harvest of the future grow,
God's power must know.

Whoever lies down on his couch to sleep,
Content to lock each sense in slumber deep,
Knows God will keep.

There is no unbelief!
And day by day, and night, unconsciously,
The heart lives by that faith the lips deny—
God knoweth why.[1]

2. The more fully we know God, the more implicitly shall we trust Him. He will draw out our affection and confidence if we really know and understand Him. Trust is from the same root as truth—true, truer, truest—trust. It is repose upon God's truth. Faith rests on His faithfulness. Hence the more we know of His truth and faithfulness the more perfectly do we rest and repose upon them. Trust is the response to His attraction, but we need to come within the range of that attraction. His Word He has magnified above all His name as the grand mirror of Himself. Having the written and living Word together, we have no reason to ask, "Show us the Father." In the Scriptures and in the Lord Jesus Christ we have a complete exhibition of God's Being.

¶ Man, whilst ignorant of God, is always leaning on an arm of flesh. See God's ancient people, how continually were even they, notwithstanding all their advantages, trusting in the creature, rather than in God. To Egypt or Assyria they looked in their troubles, rather than to their heavenly Protector. Indeed, there was not any thing on which they would not rely

[1] Lytton.

rather than on God. But, when they were made sensible of their folly, and had discovered the real character of God, they instantly renounced all these false confidences, saying, "Asshur shall not save us; we will not ride upon horses; neither will we say any more to the work of our hands, Ye are our gods: for in thee the fatherless findeth mercy." The same proneness to creature-confidence is found amongst ourselves. Who does not, at first, rely on his own wisdom to guide him, his own strength to support him, and his own goodness to procure for him acceptance with God? But in conversion we learn where alone our hope is to be placed, even in "God, who worketh all our works in us," and "in Christ, who of God is made unto us wisdom, and righteousness, and sanctification, and redemption." This was the effect of conversion in St. Paul, who accounted all his former attainments to be but "loss for Christ, and desired to be found in Christ, not having his own righteousness, which was of the law, but the righteousness which was of God by faith in Christ." And the same effect invariably follows from a discovery of God as reconciled to us in Christ Jesus.[1]

3. Trust gradually deepens into love. The three letters G O D mean nothing, and there is no power in them to stir a man's heart. It must be the knowledge of the acts of God that brings men to love Him. And there is no way of getting that knowledge but through the faith which must precede love. For faith realizes the fact that God loves. "We have known and believed the love that God hath to us." The first step is to grasp the great truth of the loving God, and through that truth to grasp the God that loves. And then, and not till then, does there spring up in a man's heart love towards Him. But it is only the faith that is set on Him who hath declared the Father unto us that gives us for our very own the grasp of the facts, which facts are the only possible fuel that can kindle love in a human heart. "We love him because he first loved us," and we shall never know that He loves us unless we come to the knowledge through the road of faith. So John himself tells us when he says, "We have known and believed." He puts the foundation last, "We have known," because "we have believed" "the love that God hath to us."

¶ Students of acoustics tell us that if you have two stringed instruments in adjacent apartments, tuned to the same pitch, a

[1] C. Simeon, *Works*, v. 34.

note sounded on one of them will be feebly vibrated upon the other as soon as the waves of sound have reached the sensitive string. In like manner a man's heart gives off a faint, but musical, little tinkle of answering love to God when the deep note of God's love to him, struck on the chords of heaven up yonder, reaches his poor heart.[1]

¶ There is a Man whose tomb is guarded by love; there is a Man whose sepulchre is not only glorious, as a prophet declared, but whose sepulchre is loved. There is a Man whose ashes, after eighteen centuries, have not grown cold; who daily lives again in the thoughts of an innumerable multitude of men; who is visited in His cradle by shepherds and by kings who vie with each other in bringing to Him gold and frankincense and myrrh. There is a Man whose steps are unweariedly retrodden by a large portion of mankind, and who, although no longer present, is followed by that throng in all the scenes of His bygone pilgrimage, upon the knees of His Mother, by the borders of the lakes, to the tops of the mountains, in the byways of the valleys, under the shade of the olive trees, in the still solitude of the deserts. There is a Man, dead and buried, whose sleep and whose awaking have ever eager watchers, whose every word still vibrates and produces more than love, produces virtues fructifying in love. There is a Man who, eighteen centuries ago, was nailed to a gibbet, and whom millions of adorers daily detach from this throne of His suffering, and kneeling before Him, prostrating themselves as low as they can without shame; there, upon the earth, they kiss His bleeding feet with unspeakable ardour. There is a Man who was scourged, killed, crucified, whom an ineffable passion raises from death and infamy, and exalts to the glory of love unfailing, which finds in Him peace, honour, joy, and even ecstasy. There is a Man pursued in His sufferings and in His tomb by undying hatred, who, demanding apostles and martyrs from all posterity, finds apostles and martyrs in all generations. There is a Man, in fine, and One only, who has founded His love upon earth, and that Man is Thyself, O Jesus, who hast been pleased to baptize me, to anoint me, to consecrate me in Thy love, and whose Name alone now opens my very heart, and draws from it those accents which overpower me and raise me above myself.

But among great men, who are loved? Among warriors? Is it Alexander? Cæsar? Charlemagne? Among sages? Aristotle or Plato? Who is loved among great men? Who? Name me even one; name me a single man who has died and left love upon his tomb. Mahomet is venerated by Muslims; he is not loved.

[1] A. Maclaren.

No feeling of love has ever touched the heart of a Muslim repeating his maxim: "God is God, and Mahomet is His prophet." One Man alone has gathered from all ages a love which never fails. Jesus Christ is the sovereign Lord of hearts as He is of minds.[1]

O Power of Love, O wondrous mystery!
How is my dark illumined by the light,
That maketh morning of my gloomy night,
Setting my soul from Sorrow's bondage free
With swift-sent revelation! yea, I see
Beyond the limitation of my sight
And senses, comprehending now, aright
To-day's proportion to Eternity.
Through thee my faith in God is made more sure,
My searching eyes have pierced the misty veil;
The pain and anguish which stern Sorrow brings
Through thee become more easy to endure.
Love-strong I mount, and Heaven's high summit scale;
Through thee, my soul has spread her folded wings.[2]

III.

EXPERIENCE OF GOD.

1. The Psalmist is content to ground his deepest trust on experience. "They that know thy name" means "They that know thy fame." Faith is not credulity. It is built, says the Psalmist, on the law of averages—on a study of the census, "Thou hast not forsaken them that seek thee." We shall never get a living faith until we get back that view. We rest our faith on the command of God; we should rest it on the name of God— on the fame of God. "They that know thy name shall put their trust in thee"—it is experience interpreted by faith.

¶ There are two suggestions contained in Watts's picture of "Faith" which we do well to recall. First, in his figure there is nothing languishing, mediæval, or sacerdotal. The conventional type is that of a languishing woman gazing upward, with sentimental pose of head and expression of countenance. Instead of this he has represented her as a powerful and resolute figure

---

[1] Père Lacordaire, O.P., *The Foundation of the Reign of Jesus Christ.*
[2] Katrina Trask.

belonging to our common humanity, not to the cloister or the Church. And by this he reminds us that faith is the conquering principle in all walks of life. It is not merely in order to possess the things above, but also to conquer the things beneath, that faith is essential. In all the ranks of life it is ordainèd that we must walk by faith and not by sight. The second thought is that faith is a heroic, not a passive virtue. The characteristic act of faith is to lift up the eyes toward Heaven, but also to fight the evil things of earth. So Watts has represented her as holding the sword in her lap, and while she lets the waters wash her feet they wash away the blood of conflict. To gain faith we must fight, not meditate, not languish, and to make faith victorious we must make it the active principle of our lives.[1]

> At midnight, when yon azure fields on high
>   Sparkle and glow without one cloudy bar,
>   The radiance of some "bright particular star"
> Attracts, perchance, and holds my watching eye.
>
> That star may long have vanish'd from the sky;
>   Yet still its unspent rays, borne from afar,
>   Come darting downwards in their golden car—
> Proof it once glitter'd in the galaxy.
>
> So in my heart I feel a healing ray
>   Sweetly transmitted from a Star divine,
>   Which once illumed the coasts of Palestine:
> And though its beauty beams not there to-day,
>   I know that Star of old did truly shine,
>   Because its cheering radiance now is mine.[2]

2. **Our fathers proved the worth of their religion.** One of the healthiest facts of human nature, and of human life, has ever been that spirit of reverence for the past which links generation to generation, and practically makes the race one. Perhaps this was most strongly developed among the Jews. For noble precedent, for inspiring motive, for reassurance, for guidance and strength, the Jew always appealed to his fathers. In battle he invoked "the God of his fathers"; in exile he sighed for the "land of his fathers"; in travel he carried with him "the bones of his fathers"; and in death he spoke of being "gathered to his fathers." The destruction of that veneration for the past which

[1] J. Burns, *Illustrations from Art* (1912), 124.   [2] R. Wilton.

binds the generations together, is equalled in point of misfortune only by that somewhat ruthless spirit which questions the testimony borne by honest men who have preceded us. What is that testimony? It is that the religion of Jesus is a grand reality and not a human dream; that the Bible contains a Divine and all-satisfying revelation of God; that it is not a fabrication or an imposture; that the heart of man is weary till it find rest in Christ; that there is such rest in Christ; that in the cross of the Crucified One there is hope for all, comfort for all, heaven for all. Some of the best literature we are familiar with to-day comes from the days of "our fathers." What are we to say then to the testimony they bore? They have gone—they went all too soon—like the advance-guard of an army, across the bridge which spans the gulf. They shout back to us that the bridge is safe. What are we to say? Oh, not because they were religious will we be religious too; but surely we will go long before we speak ill of the bridge which bore them over![1]

¶ We call Him the "God of our fathers"; and we feel that there is some stability at the centre, while we can tell our cares to One listening at our right hand, by whom theirs are remembered and were removed; who yesterday took pity on their quaint perplexities, and smiles to-day on ours, not wiser yet, but just as bitter and as real; and who accepts their strains of happy and emancipated love, while putting into our hearts the song of exile and the plaint of aspiration.[2]

¶ Yesterday I preached at Kiel (one of the parish churches of Morven). It was a strange thing to preach there. As I went to the church hardly a stone or knoll but spoke of "something which was gone," and past days crowded upon me like the ghosts of Ossian, and seemed, like them, to ride even on the passing wind and along the mountain-tops. And then to preach in the same pulpit where once stood a revered grandfather and father! What a marvellous, mysterious world is this, that I, in this pulpit, the third generation, should now, by the grace of God, be keeping the truth alive on the earth, and telling how faithful has been the God of our fathers! How few faces around me did I recognize! In that seat once sat familiar faces—the faces of a happy family; they are all now, a few paces off, in a quiet grave. How soon shall their ever having existed be unknown? And it shall be so with myself![3]

[1] J. Thew.   [2] James Martineau.   [3] *Memoir of Norman MacLeod*, i. 111.

3. If we have had experience of God's goodness for ourselves, and if we really believe that He will not forsake us, we shall not forsake Him; we shall trust Him at all times. When the day is bright, and we live in the sunshine, it is easy enough to trust then. But wait until the sun is hid, the child is sick, work scarce, and we walk through the valley of pain and weariness. How do we act then? When the light goes out in our home, and those fingers whose touch was once our joy are cold and stiff, and that voice, once our inspiration, is silent, never more to be heard, save in those dreams of other days which will come to us, do we trust then? Yes, even then the child of God who knows his Father's name, and has learned to spell the word "Saviour," can and does trust. When the way is dark, and we cannot see, we shall put our hand in His, and with the poet say—

> Thy way, not mine, O Lord,
>   However dark it be!
> Lead me by Thine own hand;
>   Choose out the path for me.
>
> Smooth let it be or rough,
>   It will be still the best;
> Winding or straight, it leads
>   Right onward to Thy rest.

¶ I saw a picture in Birmingham which interested me a good deal. It represented a house through the window of which a beautiful figure was departing. At the other side of the picture the door was open, and a poor dejected, ragged figure was entering. There was a strong cold wind outside the door, which blew in the dead leaves, and straws, and rubbish. The picture was intended to illustrate the somewhat pithy saying—"Love flies out of the window when Adversity comes in at the door." But I pick up the old Bible, and it tells me that "God has not forsaken any that trust Him." Hear this sweet word: "When my father and my mother forsake me, then the Lord will take me up."[1]

¶ Dr. MacDonald of North Leith told some of us lately of a man who went to a distant part of the country to see a woman who was known as "the woman of great faith." He found her in a humble cottage, and on asking if she was the woman of great faith, she replied, "No, I am the woman of little faith in a great Saviour."[2]

---

[1] C. Leach, *Sermons to Working Men*, 123.
[2] J. Wells, *Life of James Hood Wilson*, 105.

A Goodly Heritage.

LITERATURE.

Bruce (W. S.), *Our Heritage*, 143.
Duff (R. S.), *Pleasant Places*, 11.
Durward (P. C.), *Our Protestant Heritage*, 1.
Maclaren (A.), *A Year's Ministry*, 1st Ser., 205.
Mayor (J. E. B.), *Sermons*, 201.
Price (A. C.), *Fifty Sermons*, iv. 193.
Skrine (J. H.), *A Goodly Heritage*, 2.
Voysey (C.), *Sermons*, v. (1882) No. 32.
Christian World Pulpit, v. 289 (Baldwin Brown) ; xxv. 180 (Statham).
Church of England Magazine, xiv. (1843) 80 (Newnham).
Expositor's Library : The Psalms, i. 433.

A GOODLY HERITAGE.

The Lord is the portion of mine inheritance and of my cup:
Thou maintainest my lot.
The lines are fallen to me in pleasant places;
Yea, I have a goodly heritage.—Ps. xvi. 5, 6.

WRITTEN in time of urgent need, this Psalm opens in the form of a prayer, which is, however, shortly changed into a pious meditation. The Psalmist declares that he has vowed allegiance to God, fellowship with the holy, self-severance from idolaters (2–4). Jehovah is his possession, and with such an inheritance he is all contentment (5, 6). Jehovah inspires him with wisdom, more especially with moral discrimination; and Jehovah is before him and about him, so that he may confidently expect to show an unswerving front to fortune (7, 8). And therefore his heart and soul rejoice; and therefore, too, in spite of present dangers, his whole man has confidence that he shall not be numbered with the inhabitants of Sheol, but shall experience life and happiness, the happiness which God continually showers with liberal hand on those He loves (9–11).

¶ Here is a Psalm well worthy to be called, as the margin of King James's Bible translates the Jewish heading, a "golden" Psalm. Golden indeed it is; it belongs to that Bible within the Bible which the Christian instinct teaches all of us to rediscover for ourselves, and in which the New Testament writers took such keen delight. In childlike faith these holy men of old found their Saviour in the 16th Psalm; and so may we, on the single condition that we do not disregard those laws of the human mind which God Himself made. Childlike faith must in us be coupled with manly reasonableness. The first believers practically re-wrote the Psalter for edification, without thinking of its original meaning; they took every one of the 150 Psalms into the shrine of Gospel utterances. We who come after them cannot give this particular proof of our belief in the divinity of the Old Testament revelation. In adapting the Psalms to the needs of edification, we who desire to consecrate our intellect to Christ must seek counsel of a criticism and an exegesis which are nothing if they are not psychological; that is, if they are not in full accordance with the laws of the human mind.[1]

¶ This Psalm was the last Scripture read by Hugh M'Kail the evening before his execution in the Grassmarket of Edinburgh. After reading it, he said to his father, and those about him, "If there were anything in this world sadly and unwillingly to be left, it were the reading of the Scriptures. I said, 'I shall not see the Lord, even the Lord, in the land of the living.' But this need not make us sad, for where we go, the Lamb is the Book of Scripture, and the light of that city; and where He is, there is life, even the river of the water of life, and living springs."

I.

A WEALTHY ESTATE.

" The Lord is the portion of mine inheritance and of my cup."

1. The two words which are translated in our version " portion " and "inheritance" are substantially synonymous. The latter of them is used continually in reference to the share of each individual, or family, or tribe in the partition of the land of Canaan. There is a distinct allusion, therefore, to that partition in the language of our text; and the two expressions, part or "portion," and "inheritance," are substantially identical, and really mean just the same as if the single expression had stood: "The Lord is my portion."

¶ The "portion of my cup" is a somewhat strange expression. It is found in one of the other Psalms, with the meaning " fortune," or "destiny," or "sum of circumstances which make up a man's life." There may be, of course, an allusion to the metaphor of a feast here, and God may be set forth as "the portion of my cup," in the sense of being the refreshment and sustenance of a man's soul. But more probably there is merely a prolongation of the earlier metaphor, and the same thought as is contained in the figure of the "inheritance" is expressed here (as in common con-

[1] T. K. Cheyne, in *The Expositor*, 3rd Ser., x. 210.

versation it is often expressed) by the word "cup"—namely, that which makes up a man's portion in this life. It is used with such a meaning in the well-known words: "My cup runneth over," and in another shape in, "The cup which my Father hath given me, shall I not drink it?" It is the sum of circumstances which make up a man's "fortune." So the double metaphor presents the one thought of God as the true possession of the devout soul.[1]

2. Each family in Israel by the command of God received its portion by the casting of the lot. The result was not regarded as fortuitous, but as disposed and determined by God Himself. In each case the portion was accepted as a direct. Divine gift. It was to be held in inalienable possession through all time. A creditor might establish a claim to temporary possession, but in the fiftieth year it must go back to the original owner. No title, therefore, could be stronger, no claim more sure and permanent, than that which was thus acquired. In the case of the Psalmist the property acquired and possessed as an inalienable gift was not a fair estate on the productive Israelitish territory, but the great God Himself, to be his own God for ever.

¶ Palestine is the England of the East. I think that it is Miss Martineau who says that nothing which she had seen about the world so reminded her of the rolling Yorkshire and Northumberland moors, as the approach to Palestine by Hebron. Certainly it was a remarkable dispensation of the hand of Providence that planted the people whom God meant to be His psalmists for all time, who were to touch that true keynote of the relation of man to man, to nature, and to God, which was to ring through history, in a country singularly fair, glad, fertile, and homelike; where men could pass from under the shadow of the terror of nature, could lie in her lap, and bask in her smile. Consider for a moment the physical condition of the home where God established His sons. "For the Lord thy God bringeth thee into a good land, a land of brooks of water, of fountains and depths that spring out of valleys and hills; a land of wheat, and barley, and vines, and fig trees, and pomegranates; a land of oil olive, and honey; a land wherein thou shalt eat bread without scarceness, thou shalt not lack any thing in it; a land whose stones are iron, and out of whose hills thou mayest dig brass." "For the land, whither thou goest in to possess it, is not as the land of Egypt, from whence ye came

[1] A. Maclaren, *A Year's Ministry*, 1st Ser., 207.

out, where thou sowedest thy seed, and wateredest it with thy foot, as a garden of herbs: but the land, whither ye go to possess it, is a land of hills and valleys, and drinketh water of the rain of heaven: a land which the Lord thy God careth for; the eyes of the Lord thy God are always upon it, from the beginning of the year even unto the end of the year."

The country was small, compact, infinitely broken and varied in outline, full of features, crowded with nooks of beauty, where a man might easily learn to nestle as in a home, and which he might come to love with a passion which would make him a patriot of the Greek, Roman, or German type; in striking contrast to the prevalent tone of Asiatic political life. His home by the spring with the terebinth grown to shadow it, the rich grass in the hollow where the brook was purling by, and gleaned through the verdure; the hills sweeping up behind in a wide amphitheatre of beauty, terraced with vineyards, whose grapes glowed ruddy in the westering sun; broad belts of yellow corn-land on the slopes, and the barns bursting with the garnered spoils of the year; such a home, I say—and there were myriads of such in Palestine in its palmy days—would make the land seem fair and lovely as it seemed to Moses when he surveyed it from the borders of the waste; a land to love, to fight for, to die for, before it should be pressed by the footsteps of the insolent foe.

It was a land, too, of noble agriculture, tasking men's loftier faculties and powers. Moses speaks with a kind of contempt of the agriculture of Egypt, where the land was watered with the foot, " as the garden of herbs." The thing to be chiefly desired in Egypt was that the land should become one vast plain of fertile mud. The country, as it were, tilled itself. The Nile manured it; the husbandman had but to drop his seed into the ooze and was sure of his fruit. But Palestine demanded strenuous labour, test of brain as well as hand, patience, courage, faith. Like the Rhineland or Switzerland, it was matter of constant care and toil to till it; it strained all the faculties, but it repaid the culture with glorious fruit. But the chief point, after all, was the fulness of feature, of points of beauty and interest to which the heart could turn and the memory could cling. It was a land of rich, prodigal variety, of forms around which imagination could play. To live in it, as compared with Egypt or Babylonia, was an education; of all the lands of the East incomparably the fittest to be the home and the training school of a race of hardy, brave, free, and cultivated men. " *Out* of Egypt have I called my son." Palestine, not Egypt, was their goodly home.[1]

[1] J. Baldwin Brown.

3. In the division of the Land of Canaan among the tribes, no part was assigned to the tribe of Levi, because, as was expressly declared, Jehovah would be their portion or share (Num. xviii. 20, the same word which occurs here), and the gifts consecrated to Jehovah the provision for their support (Deut. x. 9, xviii. 1, etc.). That which was true nationally of Levi, was true in its deepest spiritual import of every believing Israelite. "What must not he possess," says Savonarola, "who possesses the possessor of all?" In the words of St. Paul, "All things are yours, for ye are Christ's, and Christ is God's."

¶ To have a portion in God is to possess that which includes in itself all created good. The man who is in possession of some great masterpiece in painting or sculpture need not envy others who have only casts or copies of it. The original plate or stereotype is more valuable than any impressions or engravings thrown off from it; and he who owns the former owns that which includes, is capable of producing, all the latter. So, if it be given to any human spirit to know and enjoy God, to be admitted to the fellowship, and have a portion in the very being of the Infinite, then is that spirit possessor of that whereof "Paul, Apollos, Cephas, or 'the World'"—all material and all mental excellence—is but the faint copy, the weak and blurred transcript. Surveying the wonders of creation, or even with the Word of inspiration in his hand, the Christian can say, "Glorious though these things be, to me belongs that which is more glorious far. The streams are precious, but I have the Fountain; the vesture is beautiful, but the Wearer is mine; the portrait in its every lineament is lovely, but that Great Original whose beauty it but feebly depicts is my own. 'God is my portion, the Lord is mine inheritance.' To me belongs all actual and all possible good, all created and uncreated beauty, all that eye hath seen or imagination conceived; and more than that, for 'eye hath not seen, nor ear heard, nor hath it entered into the heart of man to conceive what God hath prepared for them that love him'—all things and beings, all that life reveals or death conceals, everything within the boundless possibilities of creating wisdom and power, is mine; for God, the Creator and Fountain of all, is mine." [1]

¶ When I lived in the woods of Indiana, I used to hear a great deal of talk about the inflorescence of the prairies in spring. I tried to imagine what it was. I had never seen a prairie, and

[1] John Caird, *Aspects of Truth*, 211.

I was filled with curiosity to see one, especially at that season of the year when the flowers were in bloom, of which I had heard such glowing descriptions. I had to make up some sort of notion respecting them, and I did the best I could. I put my garden alongside of another, and I added several others to these; and then I thought of all the flowers they would contain; but it was a comparatively limited idea that I had in my mind. And I remember very well the morning when I first rode out upon a real rolling prairie. After passing through a piece of woods I struck it. The sun was shining aslant—for it was about nine o'clock; the dew was on the grass and on the flowers; and very soon I was out at sea —or the effect was the same as if I had been. I could see no timber in any direction. It looked as though the prairie went to a point where the sky touched it, in front, on the right, and on the left. The flowers covered every little swell and hillside. It seemed as if all the flowers in creation had been collected there.

Instead of little bits of flower-beds here and there, there were vast stretches of flowers. Here was a patch of pansies a mile long; there was a patch of tulips two or three miles long; and here was a patch of phlox five or six miles long. Here were great quantities of one sort of flowers, and there were great quantities of another sort. Further than the eye could reach the ground was covered with flowers. It looked as though the sun had dropped down upon the earth and stained everything with its colours. And it was easy to conceive that if I should go on, and on, and on, if I should travel all day, and to-morrow, and the next day, and next week, I should still find flowers. And oh, what was my garden-conception of a prairie compared with what I took in when I saw one?

You build up your idea of God from the household, from the best persons you know, and from the highest experiences that you have had. You gather together on earth all those conceptions which to you make a heroic, noble, resplendent being, and the sum of these you call God. But how different is the idea which you have of Him now from that which you will have of Him when you see Him as He is![1]

> Lord, what remains?
> When I would count my gains,
> I find that Thou hast torn them all away;
> And under summer suns I shrink with cold,
> Shiver, and faint with hunger, yet behold
> My brethren strong and satisfied and gay.

[1] H. W. Beecher.

I had a friend
Whose love no time could end:
That friend didst Thou to Thine own bosom take;
For this my loss I see no reparation:
The earth was once my home: a habitation
Of sorrow hast Thou made it for his sake.

I had a dream
Bright as a noontide beam:
I sought for wisdom. Thou didst make its taste
(Which was as spice and honey from the south)
Ashes and gall and wormwood in my mouth.
Was this the fruit I sought with so much haste?

I had a love
(This bitterest did prove);
A mystic light of joy on earth and sky;
Strange fears and hopes; a rainbow tear and smile,
A transient splendour for a little while,
Then—sudden darkness: Lord, Thou knowest why.

What have I left?
Of friend, aim, love, bereft;
Stripped bare of everything I counted dear.
What friend have I like that I lost! what call
To action? nay, what love?
Lord, I have all
And more beside, if only Thou art near.[1]

4. How can we possess God? We possess things in one
fashion and persons in another. The lowest and most imperfect
form of possession is that by which a man simply keeps other
people off material good, and asserts the right of disposal of it as
he thinks proper. A blind man may have the finest picture that
ever was painted; he may call it his, that is to say, nobody else
can sell it, but what good is it to him? Does the man who draws
the rents of a mountain-side, or the poet or painter, to whom its
cliffs and heather speak far-reaching thoughts, most truly possess
it? The highest form of possession, even of things, is when they
minister to our thought, to our emotion, to our moral and intellectual growth. Even them we possess really, only according as
we know them and hold communion with them.

But when we get up into the region of persons, we possess

[1] Adeline Sergeant.

them in the measure in which we understand them, and sympathize with them, and love them. Knowledge, intercourse, sympathy, affection—these are the ways by which men can possess men, and spirits, spirits. A man who gets the thoughts of a great teacher into his mind, and has his whole being saturated by them, may be said to have made the teacher his own. A friend or a lover owns the heart that he or she loves, and which loves back again; and not otherwise do we possess God. We have God for ours first in the measure in which our minds are actively occupied with thoughts of Him. We have no merely mystical or emotional possession of God to preach. There is a real, adequate knowledge of Him in Jesus Christ. We know God, His character, His heart, His relations to us, His thoughts of good concerning us, sufficiently for all intellectual and for all practical purposes.

¶ There is no other way by which a spirit can possess a spirit, that is not cognizable by sense, except only by the way of thinking about Him, to begin with. All else follows that. That is how you hold your dear ones when they go to the other side of the world. When your husband, or your wife, or your child goes away from home for a week, you do not forget them. Do you have them in any sense if they never dwell in the "study of your imagination," and never fill your thoughts with sweetness and with light?[1]

¶ The love of Christ which burns in one Christian's breast does not become enfeebled if other hearts catch the flame from his, but rather, by contact of congenial elements, glows in each separate heart with a fervour all the more intense. The peace of God may be diffused through the spirits of a multitude which no man can number, and yet each redeemed soul may say of it, "It is all my own"—nay, better than if all or exclusively his own; for it is a peace, a joy, a happiness, which, by the electric flash of sympathy passing from heart to heart, becomes, by reason of the multitudes who share it, redoubled, multiplied, boundlessly increased to each. Let no man, therefore, in spiritual things, glory in his own or envy another's good; for to every individual member of Christ's Church it may be said, "Whatever others have obtained, still the whole, the illimitable all of Truth and Love and Joy is left for you."[2]

[1] A. Maclaren, *A Year's Ministry*, 1st Ser., 209.
[2] John Caird, *Aspects of Truth*, 207.

¶ God places Himself at the disposal of every one, and it is for us to appropriate Him. The reason why the sun produces in one place geraniums, camellias, azaleas, all forms of exquisite flowers, and does not produce them in another place, is not in the sun. The cause of the difference is in the use to which you put the sun. It shines on the south side of my barn; and what does it produce there? A warm spot, where chickens and cows gather. It shines on the south side of my neighbour's barn; and what does it produce there? Flowers and grapes. What is the reason of the difference? Does the sun change? No; but it is put to different uses. It is just the same sun, with just the same vivific power to all; but its effects are different when it is differently employed.[1]

5. God can become our portion only when we seek Him as the highest good. Like the Levites we must make Him our all, and renounce all that would compete with Him. There cannot be two supreme, any more than there can be two pole-stars, one in the north, and the other in the south to both of which a man can be steering. You cannot stand with

> One foot on land, and one on sea,
> To one thing constant never.

If you are going to have God as your supreme good, you must empty your heart of earth and worldly things, or your possession of Him will be all words, and imagination, and hypocrisy. There must be a fixed, deliberate, intelligent conviction lying at the foundation of my life that God is best, and that He and He only is my true delight and desire. Then there must be built upon that intelligent conviction that God is best the deliberate turning away of the heart from these material treasures. And then there must be the willingness to abandon the outward possession of them if they come in between us and Him.

¶ Just as when a chemist collects oxygen in a vessel filled with water, as it passes into the jar it drives out the water before it; so the love of God, if it come into a man's heart in any real sense, in the measure in which it comes, will deliver him from the love of the world.[2]

> O love that casts out fear,
> O love that casts out sin,
> Tarry no more without,
> But come and dwell within.

[1] H. W. Beecher.   [2] A. Maclaren, *A Year's Ministry*, 1st Ser., 210.

True sunlight of the soul,
　　Surround me as I go;
So shall my way be safe,
　　My feet no straying know.

Great love of God, come in,
　　Well-spring of heavenly peace,
Thou Living Water, come,
　　Spring up, and never cease.

Love of the living God,
　　Of Father and of Son,
Love of the Holy Ghost,
　　Fill Thou each needy one.[1]

II.

A Secure Tenure.

"Thou maintainest my lot."

God Himself is the guardian of the estate. The land, the partition of which amongst the tribes lies at the bottom of the allusive metaphor of the text, was given to them under the sanction of a supernatural defence; and the law of their continuance in it was that they should trust and serve the unseen King. It was He, according to the theocratic theory of the Old Testament, and not chariots and horses, their own arm and their own sword, that kept them safe, though the enemies on the north and the enemies on the south were big enough to swallow up the little kingdom at a mouthful. And so, says the Psalmist allusively, in a similar manner, the Divine Power surrounds the man who chooses God for his heritage, and nothing shall take that heritage from him.

1. Our possession is secure, because it enters into the fibre of our being, and becomes part of ourselves. The lower forms of possession, by which men are called the owners of material goods are imperfect, because they are all precarious and temporary. Nothing really belongs to a man if it can be taken from him. What we may lose we can scarcely be said to have. They *are*

[1] Horatius Bonar.

mine, they *were* yours, they *will be* some other person's to-morrow. Whilst we have them we do not have them in any deep sense; we cannot retain them, they are not really ours at all. The only thing that is worth calling ours is something that so passes into and saturates the very substance of our soul that, like a piece of cloth dyed in the grain, as long as two threads hold together the tint will be there. That is how God gives us Himself, and nothing can take Him out of a man's soul. He, in the sweetness of His grace, bestows Himself upon man, and guards His own gift, in the heart, which is Himself. He who dwells in God and God in him lives as in the inmost keep and citadel. The noise of battle may roar around the walls, but deep silence and peace are within. The storm may rage upon the coasts, but he who has God for his portion dwells in a quiet inland valley where the tempests never come. No outer changes can touch our possession of God. They belong to another region altogether. Other goods may go, but this is held by a different tenure. The life of a Christian is lived in two regions; in the one his life has its roots, and its branches extend to the other. In the one there may be whirling storms and branches may toss and snap, whilst in the other, to which the roots go down, may be peace.

¶ Often we do not learn the depth and riches of God's love and the sweetness of His presence till other joys vanish out of our hands and other loved presences fade away out of sight. The loss of temporal things seems ofttimes to be necessary to empty our hearts, that they may receive the things that are unseen and eternal. The door is never opened to Him until the soul's dead joys are borne out; then, while it stands open, He enters bearing into it joys immortal. How often is it true that the sweeping away of our earthly hopes reveals the glory of our heart's refuge in God! Some one has beautifully said, "Our refuges are like the nests of birds: in summer they are hidden among the green leaves, but in winter they are seen among the naked branches." Worldly losses but strip off the foliage and disclose to us our heart's warm nest in the bosom of God.[1]

2. God will fortify our hearts, so that we may not weakly barter away our possession. None can dispossess us against our wills, but the offers of the world are persistent and alluring, and

[1] J. R. Miller, *The Shining Life.*

we need a special defence. This God provides for all who trust Him. He sets up within us an impregnable defence, even His own presence. He is near unto all them that put their trust in Him; no harm shall come to them. We have at once the joy of possession and in the possession safety.

¶ Transfiguration is wrought in human life by the indwelling of Christ. In what measure Christ enters into us, and fills us, and abides in us, depends upon the measure of our surrender to Him. He is ready to fill us and live in us. A perfumer bought an earthenware vase and filled it with attar of roses. The rich perfume entered into the material of the vase, and completely permeated it. Long after it ceased to be used, it still carried the fragrance. Even when it was old and broken, its shattered and worthless fragments retained the sweetness. So it is when the love of God has been shed abroad in a human heart by the Divine Spirit, and the earthly life has been struck through with the life of Christ. It is all Christ; self dies. Christ lives in the soul, and His beauty shines out in the life.[1]

3. The life which the Psalmist knows to be undying is the continual energy of loving fellowship with God. The death to which this life can never yield is the silence of the land of forgetfulness, where there is no revelation and no praise of God. These two ideas are embodied for the Psalmist under the form of life in this world on the one hand and death and Sheol on the other. Now the religious consciousness can never be satisfied by asserting a noumenal transcendental truth without applying it to actual phenomenal experience. The indissolubleness of the life in God is to the Psalmist a present reality. As such it must approve itself true under the present forms and conditions of his existence, that is, in physical life as contrasted with physical death. In no other way can he conceive the great truth as present and practical. It would be ridiculous for the inspired singer, who possesses an ideal truth in ideal certainty, to pause in the fulness of his faith, and reflect on the empirical fact that, after all, no man escapes death. He knows that he cannot yield to death in the only form in which he fears it, namely, as separation from God; and he conceives this immunity in the only form in which he has any means of conceiving it, namely, as continued physical life. It is true that this persuasion

[1] J. R. Miller, *The Shining Life.*

is a paradox. It is true that so high a confidence, so unconditionally expressed, can reign to the exclusion of all doubt and fear only in a moment of highest elevation, and that the same singer, under a sense of sin and weakness, of failing strength and of God's displeasure, must soon have passed through bitter experiences such as we read of in other Psalms—experiences far removed from the joyful confidence and energy of the words before us. But so long as the strong sense of full loving communion with God which our Psalm expresses remains undimmed, no doubt can receive entrance. What we call physical impossibilities never had any existence for the faith of the Old Testament, which viewed every physical condition as implicitly obedient to Jehovah's law of righteousness. So long, then, as the Psalmist stands in unfailing fellowship with God he must live, and cannot cease to live. It is only when the sense of sin arises as the consciousness of impeded fellowship with God that there can arise at the same time a sense of uncertainty and limitation in the hope of life.[1]

¶ When a river is dry and shallow in the summer-time, you see the rocks that rise within its bed. And they obstruct the stream, and make it chafe, and fret it as it journeys to the ocean. But when the rains have come, and the river is in flood, it covers up the rocks in its great volume, and in the silence of a mighty tide, flows to its last home within the sea. It is not longer than it was before. It is only deeper than it was before. Measure it by miles, it is unchanged. Measure it by volume and how different! So with the life that is the gift of Jesus. It is not longer than God's immortality. It is only that same river deepened gloriously, till death itself is hidden in the deeps. Knowledge is perfected in open vision; love is crowned in an unbroken fellowship; service at least shall be a thing of beauty, fired by the vision of the God we serve. That is eternal life, and that alone. That is its difference from immortality. That is the gift of the Lord Jesus Christ to the immortal spirit of mankind.[2]

¶ One lovely summer evening some years ago I received a message that an elder in the church I used to serve was taken suddenly ill. He was a man looked up to and loved by the whole community, but modest and retiring, making no parade of the religion that in reality coloured all his life. When I arrived

[1] W. Robertson Smith.   [2] G. H. Morrison, *The Afterglow of God*, 219.

at his home I found that the hand of death was upon him, and he knew it. Falteringly, and in broken words, for I loved him, I tried to talk to him, and to speak some comforting word. "I am glad to see you," he said, "and it was good of you to come"; and then looking at me with a look of calm resignation on his face, he said, "I am not going to live, but I am not afraid to die. No one can do anything for me now. This is a matter between my own soul and God, and I settled it long ago." Then briefly he gave me an outline of his religious life. Every day he contrived, no matter how busy, to spend, in addition to the usual family devotions, a portion of time alone with God. Sometimes this was done in the fields of his farm, at other times in the loft of one of the out-houses, just wherever he happened to be employed, and his own family or servants never knew it. As I said, he made no parade of his religion, and never, as far as I knew, prayed in public; but he lived his religion. He was a hard-working, industrious man all his life, and had not the opportunity of getting much education in his youth. One thing, however, he knew; he knew Christ and lived in daily communion with Him. I left him that night promising to see him again in the morning, but before the morning came he had gone to be with Christ whom he loved and served.[1]

¶ "Open the door and let in more of that music," the dying man said to his weeping son. Behmen was already hearing the harpers harping with their harps. He was already taking his part in the song they sing in Heaven to Him who loved them and washed them from their sins in His own blood. And now said the blessed Behmen, "I go to-day to be with my Redeemer and my King in Paradise," and so died.[2]

When He appoints to meet thee, go thou forth;
    It matters not
If south or north,
    Bleak waste or sunny plot.
Nor think, if haply He thou seek'st be late,
    He does thee wrong;
To stile or gate
    Lean thou thy head, and long!
It may be that to spy thee He is mounting
    Upon a tower,
Or in thy counting
    Thou hast mista'en the hour.

[1] H. W. Morrow, *Questions Asked and Answered by our Lord*, 129.
[2] Alexander Whyte, *Jacob Behmen: an Appreciation*.

But, if He come not, neither do thou go
   Till Vesper chime;
Belike thou then shalt know
   He hath been with thee all the time.[1]

III.

A Satisfied Ambition.

"The lines are fallen in pleasant places; yea, I have a goodly heritage."

The man who finds his treasure in God, declares that he is satisfied. The happiness of this mysterious nature of ours is never to be found merely in the possession of God's gifts, the works of His hand, or the bounties of His providence. The soul can find its true satisfaction only in rising beyond the gifts, and claiming the Giver as its own. When you covet the friendship or love of a fellowman, it does not satisfy you that he bestows upon you only outward gifts—his money, his property, his books —what cares a loving, longing heart for these? Unless the man gives you something more than these, gives you *himself*, and becomes yours by the bond of deepest sympathy and affection, the rest are but worthless boons. So is it in the soul's relations with God. That after which, as by a mysterious and inborn affinity, every devout spirit yearns, is not God's gifts and bounties, but Himself. The wealth of worlds would be, to the heart longing after Deity, a miserable substitute for one look of love from the Great Father's eye. "My soul thirsteth for God" is the language in which Scripture gives expression to this deep want of our nature, and points to the ineffable satisfaction provided for it,— "My soul thirsteth for God, for the living God."—"As the hart panteth after the water-brooks, so panteth my soul after thee, O God!"—"If a man love me, my Father will love him, and we will come unto him, and make our abode with him."—"I in them, and thou in me, that they may be made perfect in one."

1. Animal enjoyment may be pure of its kind, may be part of the constitution of things, but it is brief, exhaustive! But those pleasures which are filled with the spirit, the mind, the heart, are

[1] T. E. Brown, *Old John and other Poems*, 244.

fresh. And what is true of the mind is truer still of the soul.
We have a tripartite nature—Body, Soul, and Spirit. We may
not be able to break it up, and divide it by exact analysis, but
there is that which answers to Paul's definition; there is body,
soul, and spirit. We feel it. And in the soul there is a region
infinite—it can have the very pleasures of God Himself. It
can share His nature; it can share His thoughts; it can share
His purposes; it can share His purity. It can come away from
that which is bounded, intellectually, by earth's horizon, and it
can enter into the region where, in fellowship with God, it shall
realize the infinite vision and true rapture of the soul. And this
is inexhaustible, because the soul is immortal. The love of
Christ is an ever-progressive thing—" to know the love of Christ
which passeth knowledge." "That we may be filled with all the
fulness of God."

¶ All the happiness of this life is but trying to quench thirst
out of golden empty cups.[1]

> Filled with a grateful, calm content,
> My soul sits happy, and she sings;
> While all the many, many things
> That men call good, and think them so,
> That are not mine, and may not be,—
> My Father doth not give them me—
> I am content to let them go.
>
> Pass by, gay world, yes, pass thee by,
> Nor too much vex me with thy care;
> O, restless world, thou art so fair!
> See, I have learned this thing of thee;
> Thou look'st so little in the light
> Which pours upon my inner sight,
> And shines from great eternity!

2. In harmony with the great Centre, we will be in harmony
with all things in His universe. Nature will serve him who
serves her God; and all her varied powers and agencies will
rejoice to obey the behests and minister to the welfare of one
who is the loved and loving child of their great Master and Lord.
The earth will be fulfilling its proper function in yielding us

[1] William Law.

bread, and the heavens in shedding their sweet influences on our path. For us the morning will dawn and the evening descend. For us "the winds will blow, earth rest, heavens move, and fountains flow." We shall be able to claim a peculiar property in the works of our Father's hand, and the bounties of our Father's providence.

¶ The love of nature, wherever it has existed, has been a faithful and sacred element of human feeling; that is to say, supposing all circumstances otherwise the same with respect to two individuals, the one who loves nature most will be always found to have more faith in God than the other. It is intensely difficult, owing to the confusion and counter influences which always mingle in the data of the problem, to make this abstraction fairly; but so far as we can do it, so far, I boldly assert, the result is constantly the same: the nature-worship will be found to bring with it such a sense of the presence and power of a Great Spirit as no mere reasoning can either induce or controvert; and where that nature-worship is innocently pursued,—*i.e.*, with due respect to other claims on time, feeling, and exertion, and associated with the higher principles of religion,—it becomes the channel of certain sacred truths, which by no other means can be conveyed.[1]

3. We enter into fellowship with God through Jesus Christ. He is the true Joshua, who puts us in possession of the inheritance. He brings God to us—to our knowledge, to our love, to our will. He brings us to God, making it possible for our poor sinful souls to enter His presence by His blood; and for our spirits to possess that Divine Guest. "He that hath the Son, hath the Father;" and if we trust our souls to Him that died for us, and cling to Him as our delight and our joy, we will find that both the Father and the Son come to us and make Their home in us. Through Christ the Son, we will receive power to become sons of God, and if children, then heirs, heirs of God, because joint-heirs with Christ.

¶ During the great Durbar at the time of the late King's coronation, the Maharajah of Nabha did a beautiful action, which illustrates this truth. As he went away after the celebration he paid a great sum into the Treasury, in order that the land on which his encampment had been spread might be free of taxation

[1] Ruskin, *Modern Painters* (*Works*, v. 378).

for ever, for he said: "I, the king, have rested here, therefore the land shall be free from burdens for ever." And so to-day the King unfolds before us a wondrous inheritance, a priceless possession, the power that gives us new hope, and sets before us possibilities where we have hitherto found closed doors; and as He offers gifts, for the price paid was beyond man's calculation, He says: "The King has lived down here on earth, knowing our temptations, weaknesses, and sorrows; therefore, man's daily, earthly life shall be free from the oppression of the burden for evermore if he will have it."[1]

> O Christ our All in each, our All in all!
> Others have this or that, a love, a friend,
> A trusted teacher, a long worked for end:
> But what to me were Peter or were Paul
> Without Thee? fame or friend if such might be?
> Thee wholly will I love, Thee wholly seek,
> Follow Thy foot-track, hearken for Thy call.
> O Christ mine All in all, my flesh is weak,
> A trembling fawning tyrant unto me:
> Turn, look upon me, let me hear Thee speak:
> Tho' bitter billows of Thine utmost sea
> Swathe me, and darkness build around its wall,
> Yet will I rise, Thou lifting when I fall,
> And if Thou hold me fast, yet cleave to Thee.[2]

[1] Harrington C. Lees.　　　　　[2] Christina G. Rossetti.

THE VISION OF GOD HERE AND HEREAFTER.

LITERATURE.

Adams (J.), *Sermons in Syntax*, 148.

Banks (L. A.), *The Great Promises of the Bible*, 234.

Cottam (S. E.), *New Sermons for a New Century*, 61.

Jupp (W. J.), in *Sermons by Unitarian Ministers*, 1st Ser., 77.

Kuegele (F.), *Country Sermons*, New Ser., i. 298.

Maclaren (A.), *Sermons*, ii. 1.

    „   „   *Expositions :* Psalms i.–xlix., 52.

Matheson (G.), *Moments on the Mount*, 39.

Molyneux (C.), in *Penny Pulpit*, New Ser., ii. 129.

Park (E. A.), *Discourses*, 356.

Price (A. C.), *Fifty Sermons*, iii. 161 ; v. 369.

Purves (P. C.), *The Divine Cure for Heart Trouble*, 310.

Raleigh (A.), *The Little Sanctuary*, 257.

Simeon (C.), *Works*, v. 82.

Smellie (A.), *In the Secret Place*, 208.

Snell (H. H.), *Through Study Windows*, 42.

Spurgeon (C. H.), *New Park Street Pulpit*, i. (1855) No. 25.

Stanford (C.), *Symbols of Christ*, 323.

Trumbull (H. C.), *Our Misunderstood Bible*, 268.

Vaughan (J.), *Sermons* (Brighton Pulpit) iv. (1865) No. 490 ; xi. (1874) No. 835.

Voysey (C.), *Sermons*, vi. (1883) No. 13.

Christian World Pulpit, i. 120 (Binney); xli. 371 (Hocking); lvi. 75 (Dawson) ; lviii. 40 (Sheldon), 65 (Pearse) ; lxvi. 360 (Horne).

Church of England Magazine, xxviii. 210 (Pearson) ; lxvii. 256 (Harding).

The Vision of God Here and Hereafter.

As for me, I shall behold thy face in righteousness :
I shall be satisfied, when I awake, with thy likeness.

Ps. xvii. 15.

1. THE investigations as to the authorship and the date of this
Psalm yield the usual conflicting results. Davidic, says one
school; undoubedly post-exilic, says another, without venturing
on closer definition; late in the Persian period, says Cheyne.
Perhaps we may content ourselves with the judgment of Baethgen :
" The date of composition cannot be decided by internal indications." The background is the familiar one of causeless foes round
an innocent sufferer, who flings himself into God's arms for safety,
and in prayer enters into peace and hope. The psalm is called a
" prayer," a title given to only four other psalms, none of which
is in the First Book. It has three movements, marked by the
repetition of the name of God, which does not appear elsewhere,
except in the doubtful verse 14. These three are vv. 1–5, in
which the cry for help is founded on a strong profession of
innocence; vv. 6–12, in which it is based on a vivid description
of the enemies ; and vv. 13–15, in which it soars into the pure
air of mystic devotion, and thence looks down on the transient
prosperity of the foe and upwards, in a rapture of hope, to the
face of God.[1]

2. "As for me, in righteousness let me behold Thy face:
Let me be satisfied, when I awake, with Thy likeness." With
the low desires of worldly men the Psalmist contrasts his own
spiritual aspirations. He does not complain of their prosperity ;
it does not present itself to him as a trial of patience and a
moral enigma, as it does to the authors of Ps. xxxvii. and lxxiii.
Their blessings are not for an instant to be compared with his.

[1] A. Maclaren.

283

"To behold Jehovah's face" is to enjoy communion with Him and all the blessings that flow from it; it is the inward reality which corresponds to "appearing before Him" in the sanctuary. "Righteousness" is the condition of that "beholding"; for it is sin that separates from God. He concludes with a yet bolder prayer, that he may be admitted to that highest degree of privilege which Moses enjoyed, and *be satisfied with the likeness or form of Jehovah.* Worldly men are satisfied if they see themselves reflected in their sons: nothing less than the sight of the form of God will satisfy the Psalmist.

¶ Likeness to God is not a far-off hope, a light that gleams upon us through the mists of time, a prize to be won only when revolving years have passed. It is a present and immediate experience, or rather it is a thing which does not belong to the sphere of time and cannot be spoken of in forms of expression that belong to it. In religion the spirit passes out of the realm of time, rises above the passing shows of things, the vain fears and vainer hopes that pertain to the things seen and temporal. The outward life may be still in some measure a life of effort, struggle, conflict; but in that inner sphere in which the true life lies, the strife is over, the victory already achieved; hope has passed into fruition, struggle into conquest, restless effort and endeavour into perfect peace—"the peace of God which passeth all understanding." [1]

3. What is meant by "when I awake"? Not "when the night of calamity is at an end"—a sense which the word will not bear. What the writer desires is the *daily* renewal of this communion; and, as the passage in Exodus suggests, a *waking sight* of God, as distinguished from a dream or vision. These words are commonly explained of awaking from the sleep of death to behold the face of God in the world beyond, and to be transfigured into His likeness. Here, however, this reference is excluded by the context. The Psalmist does not anticipate death, but prays to be delivered from it. The contrast present to his mind is not between "this world" and "another world," the "present life" and the "future life," but between the false life and the true life in this present world, between "the flesh" and "the spirit," between the "natural man" with his sensuous desires, and the "spiritual man" with his Godward desires.

[1] John Caird.

Here, as in xvi. 9–11, death fades from the Psalmist's view. He is absorbed with the thought of the blessedness of fellowship with God. But the doctrine of life eternal is implicitly contained in the words. For it is inconceivable that communion with God, thus begun and daily renewed, should be abruptly terminated by death. It is possible that the Psalmist and those for whom he sang may have had some glimmering of this larger hope, though how or when it was to be realized was not yet revealed. But whether they drew the inference must remain doubtful. In the economy of revelation, "heaven is first a temper and then a place."[1]

> Our heaven must be within ourselves,
>   Our home and heaven the work of faith
> All thro' this race of life which shelves
>   Downward to death.
>
> So faith shall build the boundary wall,
>   And hope shall plant the secret bower,
> That both may show magnifical
>   With gem and flower.
>
> While over all a dome must spread,
>   And love shall be that dome above;
> And deep foundations must be laid,
>   And these are love.[2]

¶ We see here into the inmost nature of the Old Testament belief. All the blessedness and glory of the future life which the New Testament unfolds is for the Old Testament faith contained in Jehovah. Jehovah is its highest good; in the possession of Him it is raised above heaven and earth, life and death; to surrender itself blindly to Him, without any explicit knowledge of a future life of blessedness, to be satisfied with Him, to rest in Him, to take refuge in Him in view of death, is characteristic of the Old Testament faith.[3]

¶ The impotence of death on the relation of the devout soul to God is a postulate of faith, whether formulated as an article of faith or not. Probably the Psalmist had no clear conception of a future life; but certainly he had a distinct assurance of it, because he felt that the very "sweetness" of present fellowship with God "yielded proof that it was born for immortality."[4]

[1] A. F. Kirkpatrick.   [2] Christina G. Rossetti.
[3] Delitzsch.   [4] A. Maclaren.

I.

The Immediate Earthly Experience.

The soul's desire for a vision of God is satisfied by spiritual communion here and now.

1. The opening phrase of this verse is expressive of a noble singularity. "As for me." The man who says that isolates himself in an attitude of moral grandeur from all that is base, carnal, and worldly. It is the utterance of moral manhood, of a soul that has the heroism to separate itself from the majority, and stand majestically aloof and alone in its superior choice. "As for me." This is the motto of a spiritual aristocracy. *Noblesse oblige.* The man who utters it ranks himself with the world's moral minorities. "As for me." That is the language of true soul-nobility. And there are times when we too must dare to utter it, if we would be true to our higher nature and count for anything in the world.

This man has a consciousness of a religious, Divine life in him. He describes the wicked, the worldly, the men that have their portion in this life, who believe in nothing but appetite, what they can grasp and handle, the men who never call on God, who do not serve Him. But, he says, "I believe in God; I pray to God; I have communion with God. As for me, I stand separate from these men. I am not living simply for the senses, the appetites, the passions, gaining all I can get, and keeping all I gain, or spending it upon my lusts. I am not doing that; I am conscious that I am not. And I am conscious that I have within me a Divine faith; I have a communion with God; I can bare my heart to God, and say, Thou hast tried me, and hast found nothing—no insincerity." This is not the language of the Pharisee, "God, I thank thee that I am not as other men; I pay tithes; I fast twice in the week." It is not that. It is not a persuasion founded upon mere ritualism and externalism. It is a humble, thankful, moral, spiritual consciousness that this man, believing in God, loves Him, has communion with Him, and, under the influence of that Divine faith, keeps himself from the path of the destroyer, from the works and the society of the wicked.

¶ It cannot be supposed that the bodily shape of man resembles, or resembled, any bodily shape in Deity. The likeness must therefore be, or have been, in the soul. Had it wholly passed away, and the Divine soul been altered into a soul brutal or diabolic, I suppose we should have been told of the change. But we are told nothing of the kind. The verse (Gen. i. 26—God created man in his own image) still stands as if for our use and trust. It was only death which was to be our punishment. Not *change*. So far as we live, the image is still there; defiled, if you will; broken, if you will; all but defaced, if you will, by death and the shadow of it. But not changed. We are not made now in any other image than God's. There are, indeed, the two states of this image—the earthly and heavenly, but both Adamite, both human, both the same likeness; only one defiled, and one pure. So that the soul of man is still a mirror, wherein may be seen, darkly, the image of the mind of God.[1]

¶ We become like those with whom we associate. A man's ideals mould him. Living with Jesus makes us look like Himself. We are familiar with the work that has been done in restoring old fine paintings. A painting by one of the rare old master painters is found covered with the dust of decades. Time has faded out much of the fine colouring and clearly marked outlines. With great patience and skill it is worked over and over. And something of the original beauty, coming to view again, fully repays the workman for all his pains. The original image in which we were made has been badly obscured and has faded out. But if we give our great Master a chance He will restore it through our eyes. It will take much patience and skill nothing less than Divine. But the original will surely come out more and more till we shall again be like the original, for we shall *see* Him as He is.[2]

¶ Thoreau's regard for Emerson and Mrs. Emerson was very deep and affectionate, and it was natural that a young man, even when possessed of Thoreau's strength of character, should be lastingly influenced by so distinctive and commanding a personality as Emerson's. In has been remarked by several of those who knew both men, that Thoreau unconsciously caught certain of the traits of Emerson's voice and expression—that he deliberately imitated Emerson is declared on the best authority to be an "idle and untenable" assertion. The following account of Thoreau's

---

[1] Ruskin, *Modern Painters* (*Works*, v. 259).
[2] S. D. Gordon, *Quiet Talks on Service*, 19.

receptivity in this respect is given by one of his college class-mates, Rev. D. G. Haskins :—

"I happened to meet Thoreau in Mr. Emerson's study at Concord—the first time we had come together after leaving college. I was quite startled by the transformation that had taken place in him. His short figure and general cast of countenance were of course unchanged; but in his manners, in the tones of his voice, in his modes of expression, even in the hesitations and pauses of his speech, he had become the counterpart of Mr. Emerson. Thoreau's college voice bore no resemblance to Mr. Emerson's, and was so familiar to my ear that I could have readily identified him by it in the dark. I was so much struck by the change that I took the opportunity, as they sat near together talking, of listening with closed eyes, and I was unable to determine with certainty which was speaking. I do not know to what subtle influences to ascribe it, but after conversing with Mr. Emerson for even a brief time, I always found myself able and inclined to adopt his voice and manner of speaking."

The change noticed in Thoreau was not due only to the stimulating influence of Emerson's personality, though that doubt-less was the immediate means of effecting his awakening. Underneath the sluggish and torpid demeanour of his life at the University there had been developing, as his schoolmates after-wards recognized, the strong, stern qualities which were destined to make his character remarkable, and these had now been called into full play both by the natural growth of his mind, and by the opportunities afforded in the brilliant circle of which he was a member. "In later years," says John Weiss, who knew him well at Harvard, "his chin and mouth grew firmer, as his resolute and audacious opinions developed, the eyes twinkled with the latent humour of his criticisms of society." It was a veritable trans-formation—an awakening of the dormant intellectual fire—and it has been ingeniously suggested that the "transformation" of Donatello in Hawthorne's novel may have been founded in the first place on this fact in the life of Thoreau.[1]

2. What does spiritual communion imply?

(1) It implies *spiritual nearness.*—To see a face you must be near a person. Very near, to faith's apprehension, is the Divine presence. "He is not far from each one of us." That is the teaching of Scripture. If He seem far, it is not because He is far, but because our perceptions are impaired. Miles do not make distance. Distance is disparity. It is moral discrepancy, and not

[1] H. S. Salt, *Henry David Thoreau,* 56.

local separation. You may *be* very near, and *feel* very near to one
from whom oceans sunder you. But where there is no moral
sympathy, you may be very close to a person and yet very far
apart. Distance is in incapacity rather than in measurement.
Incapacity to perceive, and to understand, and to reciprocate.
" God is a spirit," and in proportion as our natures are spiritual is
the sense of God vivid and near. To the soulless man the whole
universe seems destitute of God. But to the man of spiritual
sensibilities, His glance is in every sunbeam, His reflexion is in
every stream, His face in every flower. To such, the face of
Nature is as the face of God.

¶ By spiritual insight, protected and cherished, not by dulness
and formality, but by continual moral sensitiveness, is man enabled
to look at life, and all whereby God reveals Himself, with that
discrimination which alone is vision.[1]

(2) It implies *intimacy of fellowship.*—But there must be something more than mere vicinity. There must be intimacy of
fellowship, familiar interchange of thought and affection. The
porter who stands at the gate, the servant who waits in the hall,
knows little of the master's mind and purpose. But to the inner
circle of friends who " behold his face " he reveals himself. *They*
know him. The sight of the face implies constant and affectionate
intercourse.

(3) It implies *propitiousness.*—The showing of the face in
Scripture is always the token of goodwill, favour, and well-
pleasedness. To see the face of God is to have the strongest
evidence that God loves the soul so privileged. It is to drink in
without stint all that is in His heart of grace.

3. The suggestion of the true sight of God coming to us
through sympathy with the Divine purpose and nature is
emphasized in the expression, " I shall behold thy face *in
righteousness.*" This is the medium through which the character
and disposition of God become manifest to us. It is only the
heart which is one with God that attains the vision of God.
A righteous God can be seen only in an atmosphere of righteousness. Sin distorts the medium, so that we can have no perfect
vision. Moral alienation from God paralyses the optic nerve of

[1] Professor Oman.

the soul. Or change the figure. You have looked upon the calm surface of a mountain tarn, lying like a lustrous jewel in its rocky hollow, and you have seen the sun and clouds reflected from that surface as though there were another firmament at your feet; or, when you have stood upon its margin you have even seen given back, feature for feature, your own face. But suddenly a breeze has swept across its bosom and ruffled its glassy smoothness, and then of the sun and heavens you could see nothing but broken lights and scattered images, and of your own face nought that was recognizable. Just so the gusts of passion sweep over the soul, and the image of God that was mirrored there becomes blurred and broken. The vision of the Face is no more seen. Only the righteous heart can see the Righteous God. It is only the heart which is at peace with Him that can have the true revelation of God. So long as we are selfish and sinful, " we see through a glass darkly"; but, once we have grown Christlike, "then face to face." "Blessed are the pure in heart; for they shall see God." [1]

4. That which satisfies us must be suited to our nature. You might as well try to fill a chest with wisdom as a soul with wealth. That which satisfies us must be large as our capacity; earthly good comes drop by drop, a little at most, and a little at a time; but we need a good that shall furnish for an ever-enlarging capacity an ever-enlarging supply. That which satisfies us must satisfy the hunger of every faculty; some things meet one faculty and some another; not one meets all, and, in the fullest sense, not one meets one. "The eye is never satisfied with seeing, nor the ear with hearing." That which satisfies us must be holy; for, sooner or later, men find that the sin to which they have looked for their earthly heaven is the very element of hell. That which satisfies us must be immortal as our being. That which satisfies us must have infinite power to engage and delight our highest love; for " desire is love in motion, delight is love in rest."

¶ "Oh, blessed vision!" was the apostrophe of an ancient confessor; " oh, blessed vision! to which all others are penal and despicable! Let me go into the mint house and see heaps of gold, and I am never the richer; let me go to the pictures and see

[1] J. Halsey.

goodly faces, I am never the fairer; let me go to the court, where I see state and magnificence, and I am never the greater; but, oh, Saviour! I cannot see Thee and not be blessed. I can see Thee here through symbols: if the eye of my faith be dim, yet it is sure. Oh, let me be unquiet till I shall see Thee as I am seen!"[1]

¶ There comes a time in the life of every one who follows the truth with full sincerity when God reveals to the *sensitive* soul the fact that He and He alone can satisfy those longings, the satisfaction of which she has hitherto been tempted to seek elsewhere. Then follows a series of experiences which constitute the "sure mercies of David." . . . The sensitive nature is, from day to day, refreshed with a sweetness that makes the flesh-pots of Egypt insipid; and the soul cries, "Cor meum et caro mea exultaverunt in Deum vivum."[2]

¶ One class-night, John Smalley, the chapel-keeper, was Mr. Harrison's substitute as leader. He was an original thinker, plain and somewhat dogmatic, but thoroughly good. When he spoke to me, he said something of this sort: "Thomas, the Bible says, 'Ye shall find me, when ye seek me with your whole heart.'" It was a hard saying, but it did me good, for it made me pray more than ever. Gradually, however, the truth came to me. Very slowly I saw that my sins had been punished, but so gradually did the darkness pass I never could say exactly when I found peace. It might have been said that it was like a train coming out of a tunnel, very slowly; so much so that one could not tell when it began to be light; but the light came, and there has been no tunnel in my experience ever since! It was twilight for some weeks, though not the twilight of evening, but of the morning! One day it came into my mind that I would go and see John M'Lean, the young local preacher who took me to class, and who tried to help me many a time. It was in my heart to ask him if he thought I might rejoice a bit, as the darkness was not so great. When I reached his house he saw me coming, and when we met he said, "Tom, you need not tell me what you have come for! You have found peace, for I see it in your face!"[3]

> My heart is yearning:
> Behold my yearning heart,
>   And lean low to satisfy
>   Its lonely beseeching cry,
> For Thou its fulness art.

[1] C. Stanford, *Symbols of Christ*, 344.   [2] Coventry Patmore.
[3] *The Life-Story of Thomas Champness*, 29.

Turn, as once turning
  Thou didst behold Thy Saint
    In deadly extremity;
    Didst look, and win back to Thee
His will frighted and faint.

Kindle my burning
  From Thine unkindled Fire;
    Fill me with gifts and with grace
    That I may behold Thy face,
For Thee I desire.

My heart is yearning,
  Yearning and thrilling thro'
    For Thy Love mine own of old,
    For Thy Love unknown, untold,
Ever old, ever new.[1]

II.

THE HIGHER HEAVENLY EXPERIENCE.

The soul's desire for a vision of God will be satisfied by a full revelation hereafter.

1. *Death is not a sleep but an awaking.*—The representation of death most widely diffused among all nations is that it is a sleep. The reasons for that emblem are easily found. We always try to veil the terror and deformity of the ugly thing by the thin robe of language. As with reverential awe, so with fear and disgust, the tendency is to wrap their objects in the folds of metaphor. Men prefer not to name plainly their god or their dread, but find round-about phrases for the one, and coaxing, flattering titles for the other. The furies and the fates of heathenism, the supernatural beings of modern superstition, must not be spoken of by their own appellations. The recoil of men's hearts from the thing is testified by the aversion of their languages to the bald name— death. And the employment of this special euphemism of sleep is a wonderful witness to our weariness of life, and to its endless

[1] Christina G. Rossetti.

toil and trouble. Everywhere that has seemed to be a comforting and almost an attractive name, which has promised full rest from all the agitations of this changeful scene. The prosperous and the wretched alike have owned the fatigue of living, and been conscious of a soothing expectance which became almost a hope, as they thought of lying still at last with folded hands and shut eyes. The wearied workers have bent over their dead, and felt that they are blessed in this at all events, that they rest from their labours; and, as they saw them absolved from all their tasks, have sought to propitiate the Power that had made this ease for them, as well as to express their sense of its merciful aspect, by calling it not death, but sleep. But that emblem, true and sweet as it is, is but half the truth.

We shall sleep. Yes; but we shall wake too. We shall wake just because we sleep. For flesh and all its weakness, and all its disturbing strength, and craving importunities—for the outer world, and all its dissipating, garish shows, and all its sullen resistance to our hand—for weariness, and fevered activity and toil against the grain of our tastes, too great for our strength, disappointing in its results, the end is blessed sleep. And precisely because it is so, therefore for our true selves, for heart and mind, for powers that lie dormant in the lowest and are not stirred into full action in the highest, for all that universe of realities which encompass us undisclosed, and known only by faint murmurs which pierce through the opiate sleep of life, the end shall be an awaking. The spirit, because emancipated from the body, shall spring into greater intensity of action, shall put forth powers that have been held down here, and shall come into contact with an order of things which here it has but indirectly known. To our true selves and to God we shall awake.

¶ Heaven will not be pure stagnation, not idleness, not any mere luxurious dreaming over the spiritual repose that has been safely and for ever won; but active, tireless, earnest work; fresh, live enthusiasm for the high labours which eternity will offer. These vivid inspirations will play through our deep repose, and make it more mighty in the service of God than any feverish and unsatisfied toil of earth has ever been. The sea of glass will be mingled with fire.[1]

[1] Phillips Brooks.

Oft have I wakened ere the spring of day,
And from my window looking forth have found
All dim and strange the long-familiar ground;
But soon I saw the mist glide slow away,
And leave the hills in wonted green array,
While from the stream-sides and the fields around
Rose many a pensive day-entreating sound,
And the deep-breasted woodlands seemed to pray.

Will it be even so when first we wake
Beyond the Night in which are merged all nights,—
The soul sleep-heavy and forlorn will ache,
Deeming herself mid alien sounds and sights?
Then will the gradual Day with comfort break
Along the old deeps of being, the old heights?[1]

2. *Death is the revealer of the great reality.*—"I shall be satisfied, when I awake, with thy likeness." "Likeness" is properly "form," and is the same word as is employed in reference to Moses, who saw "the similitude of the Lord." If there be, as is most probable, an allusion to that ancient vision in these words, then the "likeness" is not that conformity to the Divine character which it is the goal of our hopes to possess, but the beholding of His self-manifestation. The parallelism of the verse also points to such an interpretation. If so, then we have here the blessed confidence that, when all the baseless fabric of the dream of life has faded from our opening eyes, we shall see the face of our ever-loving God. Here the distracting whirl of earthly things obscures Him from even the devoutest souls, and His own mighty works which reveal do also conceal. In them is the hiding as well as the showing of His power. But there the veil which draped the perfect likeness, and gave but dim hints through its heavy swathings of the outline of immortal beauty that lay beneath, shall fall away. No longer befooled by shadows, we shall possess the true substance; no longer bedazzled by shows, we shall behold the reality.

¶ Holman Hunt wrote an affectionate letter begging Shields not to grieve at the death of their great and good old friend, Madox Brown:—

"He had done his work, and done it nobly and well, and it

[1] Edith M. Thomas.

was evident that he could not have made much of further life in his art, and from his nature I think it is pretty clear that he had made up his mind about other matters, and would learn no more here, while elsewhere he may, with his singular honesty and consistency, rise to the highest pinnacle of wisdom. Death is a very little change, seen from the other side, and yet it must be a great clearer away of mists." [1]

3. *The fulness of that future satisfaction.*—Seeing God we shall be satisfied. With all lesser joys the eye is not satisfied with seeing, but to look on Him will be enough. Enough for mind and heart, wearied and perplexed with partial knowledge and imperfect love; enough for eager desires, which thirst, after all draughts from other streams; enough for will, chafing against lower lords and yet longing for authoritative control; enough for all my being—to see God. Here we can rest after all wanderings, and say, " I travel no further; here will I dwell for ever."

> When I awake I shall have done with tears,
> And the rough retinue of cares and fears;
> No memory of shadows shall remain
> That haunted all these heavy hours of pain—
>
> Shadows of lingering doubt and old distrust,
> The heritage and burden of our dust;
> They shall depart as visions of the night
> Are conquered by the floods of morning light.
>
> When I awake the soul's deep, yearning quest
> Shall find in perfect love eternal rest.
> Then I shall see Him, even as He is,
> Who, while I wandered, knew and named me His.
>
> When I awaken in the better land,
> Divine Redeemer, like Thee I shall stand.
> Not long the slumber and the dream abide—
> When I awake I shall be satisfied.

[1] *Life and Letters of Frederic Shields*, 321.

GOD'S GENTLENESS AND MAN'S GREATNESS.

LITERATURE.

Allon (H.), *The Indwelling Christ*, 233.

Batchelor (H.), *The Incarnation of God*, 53.

Brooks (P.), *The Spiritual Man*, 301.

Bushnell (H.), *Christ and His Salvation*, 18.

Dods (M.), *Christ and Man*, 129.

Grimley (H. N.), *The Temple of Humanity*, 24.

Hoare (E.), *Strength in Quietness*, 40.

Irons (D. E.), *A Faithful Ministry*, 182.

Johnston (J. B.), *The Ministry of Reconciliation*, 196.

Leach (C.), *Sunday Afternoons with Working Men*, 241.

Mackennal (A.), *The Life of Christian Consecration*, 67.

Moody (A.), *The Message of Salvation*, 69.

Moore (A. L.), *From Advent to Advent*, 50.

Newton (J.), *The Problem of Personality*, 157.

Palmer (J. R.), *Burden-Bearing*, 265.

Pearce (J.), *Life on the Heights*, 36.

Pearse (M. G.), *The Gospel of the Day*, 44.

Spurgeon (C. H.), *Metropolitan Tabernacle Pulpit*, xii. (1866) No. 683.

Taylor (W. M.), *The Limitations of Life*, 344.

Trench (R. C.), *Sermons Preached in Westminster Abbey*, 339.

Vaughan (J.), *Sermons* (Brighton Pulpit), iv. (1865) No. 512.

Woodford (J. R.), *Sermons :* O. T. Ser., 105.

Christian World Pulpit, iv. 232 (Leach).

GOD'S GENTLENESS AND MAN'S GREATNESS.

Thy gentleness hath made me great.—Ps. xviii. 35.

1. THIS Psalm is a hymn of praise after deliverance from deadly perils. It is also found with slight verbal alterations in 2 Sam. xxii., in connexion with that part of David's history which is mentioned in the title. The writer of the Book of Samuel found it already in existence as a song of David. Its composition probably belongs to the Psalmist's later life. It is evidently a thankful retrospect of God's wonderful dealings with him, referring especially to the time when his life was most beset with dangers,—his bitter and protracted persecution by Saul, his expulsion from his throne and kingdom by Absalom, and the fierce foreign wars that distracted him for a long time thereafter. But from all these he had been graciously delivered, and from a peaceful old age he now looks back with wonder and gratitude. He combines the whole of that stormy past in one idealized and glowing picture. In the imminent peril described, he gives us the concentration of many perils, and in his description of a gracious interposition, the concentration of repeated interpositions, brought to a common focus at which they are seen as one, with corresponding intensity. In the poet's imagination it is a Theophany, a visible exhibition of the presence and power of the great Jehovah on behalf of His servant, in such extremity that nothing less than this could have saved him. His style is majestic, his conceptions vivid, and his language graphic. It has been well said that this wonderful composition bears the marks of the classic age of Hebrew poetry. With the exception of the matchless 68th Psalm, it has no rival in this whole collection.

2. In this setting we find the jewel of our text. Who has not often dwelt in thought on this precious saying? As, after

we have heard a sweet strain of music, we keep going over and over again to ourselves some especially pleasing portion of it; or as, when we have gazed a while on a gorgeous landscape, our eyes rest at length on some object of surpassing loveliness within it; so, after we have perused this Psalm, we return again and again to the words of the text. They fall on the ear like the soft breathing of an æolian harp, and they linger there with a permanence that earthly music knows not. Many gems flash out upon us from this book of praise, but there are few with a radiance so bright as that which comes from this one, "Thy gentleness hath made me great."

I.

GOD'S GENTLENESS.

1. The term rendered "gentleness" seems to have puzzled the early translators. Luther translated the text, "When thou humblest me thou dost make me great," and the older English version, which survives in the Prayer Book, conveys something of the same meaning. "Thy loving correction shall make me great." But recent scholarship confirms the rendering of our Authorized Version—"thy gentleness"—or "thy condescension," as the Revisers' marginal reading has it. And, after all, is not this more in accord with what we know of God's dealings with man? He does indeed bring down the high looks of the proud; but with those whom He is leading from lowliness to greatness He deals differently. He does not humble them, but Himself. He empties Himself that He may make them full. And David, looking back over God's dealing with him, seizes a great truth—*the* great truth of God's dealing with man, that truth which we Christians contemplate in all its fulness as we bow before the Mystery of the Incarnation—God is love.

¶ This life, broken off from its immortal whole, has no meaning—like a fragment broken off from a statue—like a few bars cut out of the best piece of music. For the anthem, in its movement through the earthly bars, is full of minor passages and discords imperfectly resolved; but to him who hears it further on, these shall only bring in, with a richer harmony of all chords on the original key, the chorus and refrain of " God is love." And well for him that can seize on that governing key and keep it in sight and recognize its presence, though unheard, all through the music, through the most shattering discords and departures out of it. He has found that which gives it all a unity and meaning and interprets to his heart (if it should not be to his understanding, in technical terms of sharps and flats) what seems to others mere chaos and confusion of noise; and if he too lose it for a little while, though never altogether, shall not this only bring it back more grandly, more sonorously, when it returns—when the golden morning breaks with a chorus of all voices singing, " God is love ! " [1]

2. The gentleness of God, like that of one of ourselves, is not a single but a complex attribute. Its base is that quality of nature which we call goodness. The aspects and operations of gentleness are manifold. It will appear in fellow-feeling towards the suffering and the sorrowing. Gentle natures are always sympathetic. It will beget consideration for men in their mistakes, follies, and sins. Gentleness is incapable of wholesale and indiscriminate condemnation. It remembers the weaknesses and temptations of even the evil-doer. Gentleness will be patient with the dull learner, and with the feeble in limb who would fain walk uprightly. It will not grow sick and tired of the slow and the infirm, and will not cast them off in disgust and turn away with loathing. A soul of gentleness will be forbearing with men, even in their waywardness, their wilfulness, and their wrongdoing. Behind the perverse and evil demeanour there is often the beginning of a better mind. The effect must be waited for. To wax hot and consume the delinquent, is to annihilate all hopeful possibilities. The gentle are generous. Their interpretations of conduct are not heated and rash, and always lean to charity and virtue. Gentle natures are calm, because neither easily provoked nor harsh in their resentments. Gentleness is tender towards all men—abounding in sympathy for the tempted, compassionate towards the suffering, and filled with grief by the sins and the sorrows of the polluted and the guilty. The gentleness of God is substantially the same as the gentleness of man, varied only by the difference between the imperfect and sinful creature and the all-holy and ever-blessed Creator.

[1] *Life of W. B. Robertson of Irvine* (by Dr. James Brown), 252.

¶ What it cost Archbishop Benson to conquer his masterfulness of temper comes out in a touching note to his wife (July 14, 1878): "So this is my birthday. . . . I think the most grave and altogether best lesson which I have learned in nine-and-forty years is the incalculable and infinite superiority of gentleness to every other force, and the imperious necessity of humility as a foundation to every other virtue. Without this it appears to me the best characters and noblest have to be taken to pieces and built up again with the new concrete underlaid—and without gentleness things may be done, but oh, at what needless cost of tears and blood too!"[1]

> Let no man predicate
> That aught the name of gentleness should have,
>   Even in a king's estate,
> Except the heart there be a gentle man's.
>   The star-beam lights the wave,—
> Heaven holds the star and the star's radiance.[2]

3. Gentleness is not a quality which men have commonly ascribed to God. It certainly has not occupied a prominent place in the thoughts of human beings, and has by no means dwelt in their reflexions. The religions of men, which are the sum of their ideas of God, are not only silent as to the Divine gentleness, but irreconcilable with it. Power and anger represent the chief characteristics of the Deity in the minds of all nations. The tumultuous forces of creation have commonly brought the might and the wrath of God into contact with the sensibilities of men. Nature in her gentler aspects and in her more restful moods has not exerted so effective an influence over religious thought and feeling. The vast conflagration; the overwhelming flood; the raging and resistless sea; the sweep of the wild hurricane; the blinding glare of lightnings and the crash and roll of thunder; the earthquake which sends its shock to the very foundations of the globe, which makes every inch of ground feel insecure, for the time, annihilates faith in the stability of nature, and summons terror to every face;—these things constrain human impotence to tremble before almighty power.

¶ I have never seen hard mountain summits but soft slopes were there, where hung the raindrop and the snow, where the

---

[1] Canon Scott Holland, *Personal Studies*, 99.
[2] Guido Guincelli, trans. by D. G. Rossetti.

cloud loved to nestle, and the insect could find a home. The
tenderest flowers grow on the hardest, steepest crags; cliffs that
defy the foot of man to scale them, and laugh the thunderbolt
to scorn, are garlanded with the daintiest mosses, and tenanted
by the most timid creatures. The down on the breast of the
eagle is as warm and soft a nestling-place as that on the breast
of the dove. God must be gentle, or He would not have formed
feeble creatures. God must be gentle, or the world would be
hard and stern. God must be gentle, or He would not have made
the mother's heart. God must be gentle, or inexperience would
not be suffered to run its little hour, and childhood and youth
would suffer swift eclipse, and all the vanities of time would meet
a sudden end. Where has man learned gentleness? Who inspired the saying, "Blessed are the meek: for they shall inherit
the earth"? Who has put in the hearts of all the thoughtful
the certainty that patience shall conquer at the end? Nay;
were God not gentle, how could man live upon the earth? For
we presume upon His patience; we venture to be thoughtless;
we delay our penitence; and, when we have made a resolution
of amendment, take a long, long time to work it out. We are
not afraid to be pitiful to others; we are not ashamed to pity
ourselves; because deep in our heart there is the feeling that
"like as a father pitieth his children, so the Lord pitieth them
that fear him. For he knoweth our frame; he remembereth that
we are dust." [1]

4. Gentleness does not exclude severity. Doubtless small
natures are commonly petulant and irritable. Great souls are
constitutionally forbearing and gentle. But the noblest men,
when occasion demands, can veil their gentleness and frown in
severity, or quench their severity and shed only smiles of gentleness. The God of creation hurls the thunderbolt and distils the
dews, pours flaming lava over field and vineyard, and fringes with
crimson and gold the minutest stems that spring upon the waste,
musters the tempests and blackens the sky, and enkindles the
tender dyes which span the retreating storm. The Bible is full
of the wrath of God, and fuller of the love of God. It declares
"law" as well as "grace." It is written of the one Jehovah,
"The Lord said, I will destroy man whom I have created";
"Like as a father pitieth his children, so the Lord pitieth." The
same attributes were incarnate in Jesus Christ. The most terrible

[1] A. Mackennal, *The Life of Christian Consecration*, 74.

words that ever fell from human lips, and the most gentle, proceeded from the Lord Jesus. Both of the attributes which the utterances of Christ present are abundantly revealed in Holy Scripture; both are consistent, though we may not always be able to harmonize their operations; and both are essential to the moral perfection of the Deity.

¶ Not long since, I saw a range of crags, beetling over the sea—an expressive emblem, it seemed to me, of Divine gentleness and severity. On their fronts the south-western gales poured all their fury. The breakers rushed with headlong violence at their base, and were hurled back again in impotent foam and with huge uproar. Above, from the water's edge up to the sky-line, there were innumerable myriads of yellow primroses, wild hyacinths, and violets—a living heaven with living stars gleaming from the seaward slopes. The careering winds and the long rolling waves were repulsed by strength; but the fragile blossoms were nourished and sheltered in their retreats with maternal tenderness. The cliff beat back the flood with iron arms, but seemed to enclose a heart of tenderness beneath its rocky bosom.[1]

5. The Divine gentleness finds its perfect illustration in Jesus Christ. When God Himself appeared on earth in the Person of Jesus Christ, gentleness was so conspicuous that men could not understand it; they had not depth enough of soul to understand the strength that works by patience and love. They could not understand a God waiting upon men, a God suffering contradiction, a God baffled and thwarted, a God without the thunderbolts and chariots of fire, a God pleading and beseeching, weeping and moaning in the anguish of ineffectual love, a God doing nothing by violence, who neither strove nor cried, whose voice was not heard in the streets. How little have men ever known what is most Divine! They looked for one shod with blazing brass, trampling under foot all that is unworthy and hostile; and He came not breaking the bruised reed nor quenching the smoking flax. This lightness of step was unintelligible to them; this considerateness of all that was weak made them presume instead of worshipping. They did not see that the love which could uphold this infinite patience and prompt to this quiet, compassing gentleness was *the* proof of Divinity, was a greater thing and more

[1] H. Batchelor, *The Incarnation of God*, 60.

impossible to every one besides than the might that called worlds into being, was the last evidence that could be given that God is God—the source of all good, the strength of all His creatures, in whom there ever remains capacity to repair all moral disaster, love enough to overcome all hatred in His creatures, an all-enduring, untemptable gentleness which will not be provoked, will not retaliate, will not give up hoping and loving.

¶ He who hath seen Christ, hath seen the Father—the Father, in whose Name He worked, whose word He spake. That last and uttermost pledge of unfaltering love, the death on the Cross, was no plan, no thought of His own. It was the Father that prompted it, the Father, without whom He could do nothing: it was the Father who moved Him to the task: this commandment He had received of the Father, to lay down His life for the sheep. That tender, gracious, devoted, patient, forgiving gentleness, that warm, overflowing sympathy, that invincible passion of sacrificial love, that sweet human-hearted compassion, that lovely persuasiveness, which flows down to us from the Cross of Jesus—all this, then, is not only a revelation of the motives, and spirit, and affection of God the Son, but more than this, all of it is an outcome, an expression, of the character (if we may be allowed the word) of God the Father. His heart it is which the Passion of Christ makes manifest, His heart which it is given us to understand in the infinite piety, and beauty, and grace, and comfort, and goodness, and meekness of Jesus. These are all the signs, the sacraments, the interpretation, the outflow, of His Father's presence; for He and the Father are one. The winning tenderness, the wonderful humility, which look at us out of the eyes of the dear Lord, are the clearest and closest knowledge we ever here shall attain of what we mean when we name the Father, of what we shall behold when we see God.[1]

> The Man who was lord of fate,
>   Born in an ox's stall,
> Was great because He was much too great
>   To care about greatness at all.
>
> Ever and only He sought
>   The will of His Father good;
> Never of what was high He thought
>   But of what His Father would.

[1] Canon H. Scott Holland:

You long to be great; you try;
    You feel yourself smaller still:
In the name of God let ambition die;
    Let Him make you what He will.

Who does the truth, is one
    With the living Truth above:
Be God's obedient little son,
    Let ambition die in love.[1]

II.

MAN'S GREATNESS.

1. What is true greatness? Scarcely two individuals have
the same idea of greatness. All, indeed, will agree that it denotes
pre-eminence, but each will have his own preference as to the
department in which that is to be manifested. Some associate
it with the deeds of the warrior on the battlefield, and others with
the triumphs of the orator in the senate; some identify it with
the achievements of the artist, and others with the creations of
the poet. Some restrict it to the department of science or
philosophy; while, in the view of others, it is connected mainly
with the acquisition of wealth, or the attainment of rank and
power. But the greatness which God's gentleness produces is
a different thing from any of these. It may co-exist, indeed,
with many of them, but it is distinct from them all. It is
excellence in that for which especially man was originally created.
Now, as we learn from Scripture that man was made in the image
of God, it follows that men are great in the proportion in which they
are like Him. But wherein consists the greatness of God? Ask
those who are nearest Him and know Him best, and they will reply,
while they continue their song, "Holy! Holy! Holy! Lord, God
Almighty." The greatness of manhood, therefore, is greatness
in holiness. It is a moral thing; for the truest manliness and the
highest godlikeness are convertible terms.

¶ True greatness consists in being the best and doing the best
that our nature is capable of. It is making the most of ourselves.

[1] George MacDonald, *Poetical Works*, ii. 178.

This definition will bring many within the ranks of the great whom the world knows not as such; and it will cut off many who think themselves great, or are so esteemed among men. One characteristic of true greatness is that there is nothing partial or one-sided about it; it is the full, complete development of all our powers; whereas we, in our false estimate of life, often think that striking and powerful things are truly great.[1]

¶ Go out into the streets of London to-day, and ask your fellow-men what is their best work. One will tell you he can make the canvas speak with the likeness of the human form; another, that he can lend to the dead marble grace and beauty almost lifelike; another, that he has conquered England's enemies, or enchanted men with sweet music, or amassed a colossal fortune; but amidst them all comes one voice, the voice of Him at whose feet blindness and palsy, weakness and leprosy, the tossing wave and the blustering wind crouched submissive, and His claim to greatness is, as He has told us Himself, that He " came to seek and save the lost." Will your life and mine be deemed great in God's sight, judged by this standard ? I think many a humble ragged-school teacher in London will tower above poet and statesman when the day comes for the Master to reckon up His jewels.[2]

¶ Was Napoleon a great man ? If by "great" be intended the combination of moral qualities with those of intellect, great he certainly was not. But that he was great in the sense of being extraordinary and supreme we can have no doubt. If greatness stands for natural power, for predominance, for something human beyond humanity, then Napoleon was assuredly great. Besides that indefinable spark which we call genius, he represents a combination of intellect and energy which has never perhaps been equalled, never, certainly, surpassed. He carried human faculty to the farthest point of which we have accurate knowledge. . . . No name represents so completely and conspicuously dominion, splendour, and catastrophe. He raised himself by the use, and ruined himself by the abuse, of superhuman faculties. He was wrecked by the extravagance of his own genius. No less powers than those which had effected his rise could have achieved his fall.[3]

2. God's design for man is that he should be morally and spiritually great. And the aim of the moral activity of God in

---

[1] Phillips Brooks, *The Spiritual Man*, 301.   [2] *Quintin Hogg*, 398.
[3] Lord Rosebery, *Napoleon, The Last Phase*, 251.

this planet is to ensure the true greatness of man. This is the scene which He has chosen, furnished, and adorned for conducting our education. Every object of beauty, greatness, might, and splendour, and all symbols of truth, purity, beneficence, and Godhead, are the diagrams created by infinite Wisdom, Power, and Goodness for the great school of the human and Christian life. What is the design of every parent worthy of the name? Is it not to provide his children with all the means of intelligence, self-control, success, nobility, and honour? First, and above all other things, will he not train them in the knowledge and love of their Creator and Redeemer? Is it not an honest pride to him, of which he will never feel ashamed, and a delight of heart which he will never need to disguise, to see the members of his family living in the practice of every Christian virtue and in the respect and goodwill of all their fellow-men? Is not God our Father? It is a joy to Him to guide His children to glory, honour, and immortality.

(1) When God makes men great, He makes them *kingly*. Milton says, "He who reigns within himself and rules passions, desires, fears, is more than a king"—and when God handles a man He sets his feet on a throne, a crown on his head, a sceptre in his hand. He is not carried away by impulse, caprice, desire, passion, but is swayed by reason and righteousness. Nor does he rule himself alone, for he influences others, and moulds and makes the society in which he moves. He puts out evil's fires; he kindles the fires of goodness.

¶ Who is the strong man? Is he the man who passes through society with the battle-axe of Richard Cœur de Lion? The child sees a man lift a great weight with his teeth, and at once he exclaims, What a strong man! Is the child right? He would have been right had he said, "What a strong animal!" Such poor power wastes itself day by day; the man's teeth perish, where is the giant then? Here are two men under circumstances of equal provocation: the one man instantly resents the insult which has been inflicted upon him; in a moment he is in a paroxysm of rage, asserting his dignity, and smiting his opponent; men who are standing by admire the fire of his character, they say, "What a strong man!" The other man shows no sign of rage, holds himself in the severest self-control; instead of resisting evil, he answers not again, and persons who look only on the surface of things declare him a coward. Solomon would have declared him a strong man, and so would Jesus Christ. The strength of manhood is to be judged not by the fury of occasional explosions, but by the depth and solidity of moral foundations. The smallest natures are, of course, most easily excited to self-defence. Impudence is infinitely quicker than dignity. True strength is calm; incomplete power is fussy. " He that ruleth his own spirit is greater than he that taketh a city." [1]

(2) When God makes men great, He makes them *useful*. The life which is God-saved, God-built, God-blessed, is wonderfully beneficent. " I will bless thee and thou shalt be a blessing."

¶ The legend tells that the visits of a goddess to an ancient city were always known, although no eye sighted her. She paused before a lightning-blasted tree, and lo! the woodbine sprang up and covered the tree's nakedness. She lingered by the stagnant pool—the pool became a flowing stream. She rested upon a decaying log, and lo! it became a fruitful tree. She crossed a brook, and lo! wherever she put down her foot the flowers came to birth. It is even so with the life nourished and cherished by God. It leaves its mark—a gracious mark— wherever it goes. "The wilderness and the solitary places are made glad." [2]

3. The proof of a man's true greatness is found in his humility. True moral greatness is a flower which seeks the shade ; and, like the other works of God, it has to be sought out by them who take pleasure therein. There is a lid for the vessels of the temple. Humility is one of the crowning graces, and it keeps the truly great man from making long prayers at the corners of the streets, from sounding a trumpet when he gives alms, from making broad his phylacteries, or covering his face with the marks of fasting.

¶ Humility is the special virtue of Christ, the virtue proper to Him, the virtue most dear to Him, the virtue that brought Him, moved by infinite charity, from the splendour of the eternal glories, into the extremes of poverty and humiliation, so that there is nothing more illustrious in His life and death than this Divine virtue of humility, whereby He redeemed the world, and with which He prepared the medicine that healeth all our infirmities, and bringeth us from all our sin and misery to rest in Him. Here we also learn from Him that that which pleases Him in souls is humility. And if He speaks of meekness as well,

---

[1] Joseph Parker.   [2] J. Pearce, *Life on the Heights*, 46.

it is because meekness is the most exquisite and delightful fruit of humility, exhibiting the interior strength and fortitude of patience in a gentle sweetness.[1]

¶ There is little doubt that any one who knew Dr. McLaren well would agree with the statement that the most marked feature in his character was his entire freedom from anything approaching to egotism. His deep vein of shyness, as well as refined taste, made egotism, in the way of speaking of his own doings, an impossibility to him. But his want of egotism had a deeper source. It was the result of genuine deep-rooted humility. He knew that in many directions unusual powers had been given him, but that conviction led to no undue elation. Gifts brought responsibility, and conscience told of failure as to their use. . . . He never perhaps took part in a meeting in the Manchester Free Trade Hall when the large building was not filled to its utmost capacity, and for years before the close of his career, almost invariably the immense audience rose to receive him and cheered enthusiastically. Once, driving home from one of these meetings, his companion ventured to ask him if he could recall what his thoughts were as he stood waiting till the applause had ceased—a far-away, almost pained expression had been noticed. "Yes," he said, " perfectly; I all but heard the words, ' It is a very small thing that I should be judged of you, or of man's judgment; he that judgeth me is the Lord.'"[2]

> One's chiefest duty here below
> Is not the seeming great to do,
> That the vain world may pause to see;
> But in steadfast humility
> To walk the common walk, and bear
> The thousand things, the trifling care,
> In love with wisdom patiently.
> Thus each one in his narrow groove
> The great world nearer God may move.[3]

III.

GOD'S GENTLENESS AND MAN'S GREATNESS.

In the moral development and perfection of men the gentleness of God discharges the highest function. The strong hand

---

[1] Bishop Ullathorne.
[2] E. T. McLaren, *Dr. McLaren of Manchester*, 207.
[3] M. Hunt.

restrains; the hand of gentleness elicits and fosters. Authority moulds from without; love inspires from within. The strength of a thing that grows is its life, not the external force which only sways it hither and thither. The essential, the inward, the living energy which animates and perfects the moral and spiritual characters of men is the gentleness of God.

1. Two of the prime elements of personal greatness—nobility of purpose and purity of motive—are directly stimulated by the gentleness of God. Their great enemy is craven fear, perpetual anxious self-consideration; no man can be great who is always thinking of himself. When we have once apprehended that God is gentle, terrors about ourselves are effectually banished: "perfect love casteth out fear"; and in its stead there comes a sense of the infinite worthiness of God, the desire to please and "glorify" Him; there is a sense of security in Him and in His dealings with us, nay more, an absolute satisfaction with Him and with His ways, before which all ungracious feeling disappears.

2. It is in gentleness that God wins back to Himself those who have rebelled against Him and revolted from Him, subdues our waywardness, teaches and perfects us. He does not coerce us by His power; He constrains us by His love. He does not launch His thunderbolt to destroy us; He solicits penitence and obedience, waits patiently, deals gently with our passion and petulance, our ignorance and unbelief; gives us time for reflexion and experiment, for the cooling of passion, the growth of wisdom, the rectifying of mistakes. He "waits to be gracious." Not of Himself and of His insulted majesty does He think, so as to assert His greatness, but of us and of our suicidal alienation from Him, and how He may make us great.

¶ Did you ever know a man converted by the Ten Commandments, or by the Athanasian Creed? Is it not rather some word of ineffable love, some manifestation of "him whom we have pierced," some yearning of great sorrow, that, filling our heart, has subdued it to penitence or constrained it to prayer? Some calamity has befallen, some sickness nigh unto death, some bereavement of wife, or child, when God has comforted us, or pointed us to "the Lamb of God, which taketh away the sin of the world."[1]

[1] H. Allon, *The Indwelling Christ*, 243.

¶ If for every rebuke that we utter of men's vices, we put forth a claim upon their hearts ; if for every assertion of God's demands from them, we could substitute a display of His kindness to them ; if side by side with every warning of death, we could exhibit proofs and promises of immortality ; if, in fine, instead of assuming the being of an awful Deity, which men, though they cannot and dare not deny, are always unwilling, sometimes unable to conceive, we were to show them a near, visible, inevitable, but all beneficent Deity, whose presence makes the earth itself a heaven, I think there would be fewer deaf children sitting in the market-place.[1]

3. God carries on His educative processes by gentle methods. Of course it were an easy thing for God to shield us from all danger, so that we should know nothing of toil and suffering. He might flood our minds from day to day with the light of truth, so that doubt and ignorance should never darken them. He might give us strength so much beyond our needs that we should never feel the assaults of temptation, and so we should never sin. He might so appal us by the terrors of the law that we should be compelled to do His will without any vision of its beauty or approval of its goodness. But all this, pleasant though it might seem to little children, were to do violence to religion, conscience, and will, to dishonour our true manhood and to render for ever impossible our growth in the knowledge, love, and true obedience of His blessed law. No. God has begotten us : we are His children. In fatherly wisdom, in motherly gentleness, He bends to our weakness that He may educate and perfect us. By daily need, and the thirst which springs from need, the mind of man is quickened into activity and led to seek for truth that it may grow thereby. The moral nature even from childhood has free play : good and evil are ever presenting themselves in infinitely varied forms ; he is called to make a real choice between right and wrong, to set his affections upon the things that are good and fair, and with a regal will to follow in the paths of virtue. God will have us grow in the only possible way—by our own free effort. He will have us pass, with His help, through an endless series of new births, in all of which He so hides Himself that we are unconscious of His quickening power, from strength to strength, from grace to grace, till at last we appear in glory.

[1] Ruskin.

¶ There is a gentleman still living in Birmingham, who was once Mayor, of whom a pleasant little story is told. One day, when he was Mayor of the town, he had to pass up the Bull Ring, as the open space near the great Market Hall is called. A little donkey, with a big load behind it, was struggling its hardest to drag the load up the hill. A big brute on two legs was beating the poor beast that walked on four. The Mayor, the chief magistrate of the place, saw what he was doing. He might have called a policeman to lock up the fellow who used the stick on the patient, dumb creature. But instead, he went up to him and said: "Hold on, man, be merciful as well as powerful, and come behind and put your shoulder to the cart." The Mayor put his shoulder against the cart, and soon the difficulty was passed. Gentleness as well as greatness were surely there.[1]

¶ I have recalled gratefully again and again a word that my drawing-master gave me when I was a little lad, blundering at my first lesson. I had set the copy before me and was trying very hard to reproduce it—but, alas! what crooked lines. How impossible it was for anything to be like my picture;—and yet how impossible it seemed to make my picture what it should be. Smudged and messed by many rubbings out and many failures, trying only made the matter worse. Then came the master and took the pencil, and in the twinkling of an eye the thing was done, every stroke firm, straight, exact. Then my despair was completed—I had tried so hard and failed so utterly, and he had done it without trying at all! I laid down the pencil with a sigh, and said, "I shall never draw."

"Nonsense," said the master cheerily, patting me on the shoulder. "*You can draw as well as I could when I was your age!*"

What! was there a time when he bungled and blundered? I looked up in amazement.

"I mean it," he said, amused at my look.

I was an artist then—if never since. He had come down and back to me and was himself again the little awkward beginner, and I was lifted up and linked on to him. That was gentleness, and it made me great. Is not that the very Gospel of God? God hath made Himself one with us that He may make us one with Himself. He has come down to be little and weak and beset with our hindrances, that He may lift us up and set us on high amongst His heroes and conquerors.[2]

[1] Charles Leach, *Sunday Afternoons with Working Men*, 244.
[2] M. G. Pearse, *The Gospel for the Day*, 51.

4. When God corrects His children, He does so only that they
may be stimulated to grow in grace; and there is usually, in the
concomitants of their trial, something to remind them of His love.
" He stayeth his rough wind in the day of the east wind:" and, if
the thorn of trial may not be extracted, there comes the precious
assurance, " My grace is sufficient for thee; for my strength is
made perfect in weakness." How often have we had such experiences! Even when we have been most sorely smitten, there has
come to us some view of His character or some promise of His
Word which has made us feel that He had not forgotten us. And
when, under His chastening dispensation, we have turned to Him,
how full of love was His reception of us. Thus, all through our
lives, His gentleness is the background of all our discipline; and
when earth is exchanged for heaven, and we stand perfected in
holiness before the throne, looking back upon the way by which
He led us, and marking the infinite love which called us out of
the world at the first, the unwearied patience which bore with all
our follies and transgressions, the tenderness which cherished us
in every emergency, and the grace which supported us through
death, we shall be able to understand all that is implied in this
beautiful text, and we shall sing, as we could never sing on earth,
" Thy gentleness hath made me great." [1]

¶ As the eye of the cunning lapidary detects in the rugged
pebble, just digged from the mine, the polished diamond that
shall sparkle on the diadem of a king; or as the sculptor in the
rough block of marble, newly hewn from the quarry, beholds the
statue of perfect grace and beauty which is latent there, and
waiting but the touch of his hand,—so He who sees all, and the
end from the beginning, sees oftentimes greater wonders than
these. He sees the saint in the sinner, the saint that shall be in
the sinner that is; the wheat in the tare; the shepherd feeding
the sheep in the wolf tearing the sheep; Paul the preacher of the
faith in Saul the persecutor of the faith; Israel a prince with
God in Jacob the trickster and the supplanter; Matthew the
Apostle in Levi the publican; a woman that should love much in
the woman that was sinning much; and in some vine of the earth
bringing forth wild grapes and grapes of gall, a tree which shall
yet bring forth good fruit, and wine to make glad the heart; so
that when some, like those over-zealous servants in the parable,
would have Him to pluck it up, and to cast it without more ado into

[1] W. M. Taylor, *The Limitations of Life*, 354.

the wine-press of the wrath of Almighty God, He exclaims rather, " Destroy it not, for a blessing is in it," and is well content to await the end.[1]

5. By His gentleness God appeals to our whole personality, on its best and noblest side.

(1) The mind is gently disciplined and developed into maturity. God regulates His revelations to the requirements of individual reason. The sun shines mechanically and is unconscious of the influences which it emits. God is omniscient love, and never works automatically. The rays of the Supreme Intelligence are lovingly and wisely reined. Our earth is but the millionth part of the sun, yet it affects the gravitating power of that gigantic orb. The mind of man is but a spark, yet it modifies the effulgence of the Divine splendour. The beams of God's love warm and revive the latent capacities of the brain. The discordant strings of the reason are gently tuned into harmony with the Infinite. The extension of our mental horizon is graduated by unerring beneficence. Under God's wise and delicate treatment, man's mental mechanism becomes increasingly sensitive, and able to " think God's thoughts after Him."

¶ There are many states of mind which are amenable only to gentleness. You cannot *scold* a man out of his grief; if you wish a man to love you, you do not use violent language and insist on his loving you; if you wish to bring a man over to your way of thinking, you deal gently with him and are careful not to offend his prejudices or ride roughshod over his feelings. Instinct tells us that in many cases nothing but gentleness will win.[2]

(2) The will is wooed and won by the unspeakable tenderness of Jehovah. There is a very wide chasm between the animal appetites of the sinner and the self-conscious resolves of the saint. "Not my will, but thine, be done " are words which represent the acme of spiritual volition. But before this height is reached, there are delicate moral fibres to be straightened and strengthened, and selfish inclinations to be reversed. This is to be achieved, not by the compulsion of might, but by the touches and attractions of Divine benignity. We cannot be terrorized into intelligent and

[1] R. C. Trench, *Sermons Preached in Westminster Abbey*, 342.
[2] Marcus Dods, *Christ and Man*, 130.

whole-hearted submission to the will of heaven; it is under the softening influences of love that our stubborn wills are subdued, and made to flow into the harmony and rhythm of the Divine intent. This love will gradually rectify our declinations from truth and righteousness, and restore us to perfect accord with the will of the Supreme.

¶ The will itself is governed by that love which rules it and shapes it. Now the Love of God is supreme above all other loves, and that so entirely, that unless it holds sovereign sway it must perish altogether.[1]

¶ The Almighty will never come in His omnipotence to *break our will*. What is the good of a moral creature with a broken will? You might as well break a child's leg to teach it to walk, as break a child's will to teach it to obey. The heavenly Father bends the will, but never breaks it, and that only by patient love and gracious promptings; by the discipline of life, its fears and sorrows, and above all, by the shame and sorrow of the Cross, He softens the will that He may bend it. Our God loves and respects us too much ever to keep us at home with Himself as slaves or servants. Rather will He suffer us to go away into the far country until the hunger and loneliness do make the heart cry out in its sorrow. Then at last is shaped the purpose, "I will arise and go to my Father," and lo! He runs and falls upon the neck and kisses us. He stands upon no stately etiquette and makes no terms. Then it is that, arrayed in the best robes, with the ring on the finger, seated at the Father's table, full of the gladness of that joyous welcome, amazed at His infinite goodness, so patient, so eager to bless us—then it is that we learn the deep meaning of the words—"Thy gentleness hath made me great."[2]

(3) The conscience is pacified, purged, and perfected by the gentle ministrations of infinite love. Greatness, in the Divine sense, is impossible to man apart from a restful, rectified, refined conscience. The smile of the Supreme soothes, stimulates, sanctifies this delicate organism. Love alone can rehabilitate this "receiver," and make it ever vibrate with communications from the eternal rectitude. Under the ministries of God's grace, this deranged and stultified faculty becomes an unerring discriminator between good and evil, and an infallible reporter of messages from the supreme equity. In the atmosphere of God's gentle love,

[1] St. Francis de Sales.   [2] M. G. Pearse, *The Gospel for the Day*, 58.

this Divine power becomes imperturbably graceful and healthily active. A conscience "void of offence toward God and toward men" is the grand result of the beneficence of the Supreme.

¶ When a man can endure his sins no longer, and must go to some one for relief, to what sort of person will he repair? Will he feel strongly drawn towards some severely upright man—cold, hard, and unsparing towards all transgressors? No; he will keep out of his way. He would be as likely to pour forth his confessions and griefs into the bosom of a November cloud from which the sleet was falling, or into the chills of a cavern of icicles. When a boy has got into trouble and is sorry for it,—for a good boy will sometimes be ensnared by temptation, and is sure to regret it with all sincerity,—and does not know what to do, where will he go first for counsel and succour? Will it be to his father or his mother? Mostly to his mother. There are men womanly in tenderness; and there are women, though very rare, unwomanly and without sympathies; but commonly there is more gentleness in the mother; and to his mother the boy is sure to turn in his extremity. I know where I should have gone, and I dare say you do too. The mother's gentleness is a sun that never pales nor wanes, down to her life's end; and in the hour of its setting has resigned none of its warmth and splendour.

The gentleness of God performs precisely the same office to sinning and sorrowing men. Penitent sinners cannot have too vivid an idea of the gentleness of God. They will never attain to an apprehension of it too large and bright for the reality, or in excess of their own need. Their moral helplessness will require it all. There is wrath in God, and there ought to be; but not wrath only. God is a Judge; but if He were nothing but a Judge, then for a sin-stricken soul there would be nothing but despair. But the gentleness of God is a firm and unfailing hope.[1]

(4) The heart is soothed and comforted. Love alone can find its way into the innermost shrine of personality. In the atmosphere of beneficence our pores are opened, and subtle heavenly influences percolate into the soul.

¶ Harsh and heartless criticism almost fatally wounded the imaginative genius of Turner. The precocious poet Keats was mortally grieved by the cruel ridicule and savage scorn of the Press. But in the atmosphere of Supreme Love, the flickering spark of spiritual genius is revived into an aspiring flame, and the absorbent system of the soul is developed and perfected. The

[1] H. Batchelor, *The Incarnation of God*, 65.

influences with which God is surcharged are so wisely regulated
that the frailest spiritual organism can imbibe them.[1]

> And gently, by a thousand things
>   Which o'er our spirits pass,
> Like breezes o'er the harp's fine strings
>   Or vapours o'er a glass,
> Leaving their token strange and new
>   Of music or of shade,
> The summons to the right and true
>   And merciful is made.[2]

[1] J. Newton, *The Problem of Personality*, 163.   [2] Whittier.

THE PERFECT LAW.

LITERATURE.

Fox (W. J.), *Collected Works*, iii. 175.

Gibson (E. C. S.), *The Old Testament and its Messages*, 128.

Hanna (H.), *The Church on the Sea*, 384.

Irving (E.), *Collected Writings*, iii. 383.

Lee (R.), *Sermons*, 325.

Morrison (J.), *Sheaves of Ministry*, 13.

Peabody (A. P.), *King's Chapel Sermons*, 95.

Pierson (A. T.), *The Hopes of the Gospel*, 3.

Spencer (J. S.), *Sermons*, ii. 7.

Spurgeon (C. H.), *Metropolitan Tabernacle Pulpit*, l. (1904) No. 2870.

Christian World Pulpit, xlvii. 24 (Scott Holland).

Church of England Magazine, viii. (1840) 112 (Dixon).

Expositor, 1st Ser., xii. 89 (Matheson).

Homiletic Review, New Ser., xix. 566.

THE PERFECT LAW.

The law of the Lord is perfect, restoring the soul :
The testimony of the Lord is sure, making wise the simple.
The precepts of the Lord are right, rejoicing the heart :
The commandment of the Lord is pure, enlightening the eyes.
The fear of the Lord is clean, enduring for ever :
The judgements of the Lord are true, and righteous altogether.

Ps. xix. 7-9.

1. THIS Psalm consists of two parts—so distinct that some have held that their union was an afterthought, and that they must originally have belonged to different hymns. The supposition is scarcely necessary, for surely the transition is not an unnatural or a violent one—from the thought of God in nature to that of God in revelation. And very instructive is it to note how the Psalmist suggests a contrast between the two by the different names for God which he employs in the two parts of the Psalm. The Hebrew tongue has many names for God, but there are two principal ones, and it is often interesting to see which is employed. There is first the ordinary name for God, "Elohim," or "El," a name which simply speaks of the Supreme Being, the Maker and Creator of all things visible and invisible, but tells us nothing of His nature and character. But there is also the name by which God specially revealed Himself as entering into covenant with man, which spoke of His personal relations to His own people, His manifestation to them, and His unchanging love for them. This is what we might reverently call the "proper name" of God. It is sometimes represented in our Bibles as Jehovah, more often simply as the LORD, the translators having followed Jewish custom, which shrank, from motives of reverence, from pronouncing the word Jehovah because of its sacredness, and ordinarily substituted for it another word meaning Lord. Now when we turn to the Psalm before us, what do we find? In the

first part, consisting of verses 1 to 6, of which the subject is
Nature, we are told that the heavens declare the glory of God.
It is God—El, the strong, the mighty—whom the world around
reveals. Of God as Power you can learn from Nature. Would
you know Him as Love, as entering into personal relations with
man—for this, the Psalmist seems to say, you must go to Revelation. And therefore, in the second part of the Psalm, from verse 7
onwards, where he describes the glory of the revealed law, the
name of Him who gives it is changed. He no longer speaks of
Him simply as God. It is the law of the Lord that is perfect.
The Lord—that is, Jehovah, the covenant name under which the
Almighty revealed Himself to Moses at the bush, the name which
spoke to every Jew of One who had set His love upon man, who
was mindful of him, and entered into closest personal relations
with him.[1]

2. The Psalm may perhaps have been written in the first
flush of an Eastern sunrise, when the sun was seen "as a bridegroom coming out of his chamber, and rejoicing as a strong man
to run his course." The song breathes all the life and freshness,
all the gladness and glory of the morning. The devout singer
looks out, first, on the works of God's fingers, and sees all creation
bearing its constant though silent testimony to its Maker; and
then he turns himself with a feeling of deep satisfaction to that
yet clearer and better witness concerning Him to be found in the
moral law. Thus he begins the day; thus he prepares himself for
the duties that await him, for the temptations that may assail, and
the sorrows that may gather as a cloud about him. He has made
trial of the preciousness of that word. He knows its deep,
hallowing, soul-sustaining power. He knows that it is full of life
and healing. But he knows also that it is a word that searches
and tries the heart, that reveals the holiness of God, and the
sinfulness of man; and therefore he bows himself in prayer,
saying, "As for errors,—who can understand them? Cleanse
thou me from secret faults."[2]

¶ The twofold subject of this Psalm is one which in all ages
has served (with variations according to the nature of the religion

[1] E. C. S. Gibson, *The Old Testament and its Messages*, 128.
[2] J. J. Stewart Perowne, *The Psalms*, i. 86.

of the thinker) as the theme of pious meditation. Those eternal
" Lieder ohne Worte," the music of the spheres, have ever sung
to the thoughtful heart the glory of the Creator. Plato declares
that the wondrous order of the heavens is a proof of God's
existence. Hafiz enlarges on the same topic, telling us how even
the sweet scent and beauteous hue of the tiniest floweret that
decks the field is but an efflux of the perfections of the Divinity.
St. Paul shows how the heathen were not left without a witness
of God, either in the external world or in their own conscience.
Kant is said to have remarked that the two things which most
forcibly impressed him with a feeling of the sublime were the
starry heavens above him and the moral sense within him. And
Lord Bacon, in the very spirit of this Psalm, writes, " I have
delighted in the brightness of Thy temple. Thy creatures have
been my books; but Thy Scriptures much more. I have sought
Thee in the courts, fields, and gardens; I have found Thee in
Thy temples." [1]

I.

THE SCOPE OF GOD'S LAW.

1. The Psalmist opens his eyes and sees in all nature the
manifestation of law, of regularity, of reason. His eyesight,
turning its native simplicity upon the scene before him, is quite
enough to reveal to him this rude secret which it is the whole
duty of science to elucidate, this august rhythm, so firm and so
tireless, in which the endless succession of day and night proceeds.
This it is that overpowers him, " Day unto day uttereth speech,
and night unto night sheweth knowledge "—each arrives at its
turn without disorder, without accident, or chance, or perplexity.
There is about it all, as the mighty drama discloses itself, the
calmness, the majesty, of rational knowledge. As far as imagination can go, still the same reasonable law holds good, still those
ordained successions proceed, still all move along allotted path-
ways, still the evidence of conscious thought meets the searching
gaze, still it is as if the round earth everywhere were trembling
on the verge of speech. This language of theirs which is heard
in the silence reaches unto the very ends of the world. And so,
too, with this leaping sun, this bridegroom, which travels with
such steady precision, with such unfaltering certainty, along the

[1] Jennings and Lowe, *The Psalms*, 76.

course set before him. He also never comes to the close of his mission, he also is universal in his range. His going forth is from the uttermost part of the heaven, and his circuit unto the ends of it, and there is nothing hid from the heat thereof—universal law acting in silence, with absolute security of rhythm.

That is the vision which overawes the Psalmist; and is not that the very essence of our scientific presentation of Nature? Law acting in silence, that is Nature as science discloses it. Silently, in dumb show, world within world of intricate law work out their allotted transformations. We look upon the strange and busy process, as in and out, with sure accuracy, all ply their business. Most amazing! But it is dumb, some say, as they gaze; it tells nothing, it works, works in a silence that is as death; there is no voice, neither any to answer; it offers no interpretation of itself, it suggests no language and responds to no thought; it is dumb mechanism beating out an aimless task. No, we cry with the Psalmist, silent it may be, but this perfect law, this undeviating order, this calm precision, this infinite regularity of succession, this steady certainty of movement, this unbroken universality, these disciplined forces, this rhythmic harmony, this balance, this precaution, this response of day to day and night to night, that is intelligence, that is reason, that is consciousness, that is speech! No one can face it in its wholeness, part answering to part, and each to all, without becoming aware of its mystic eloquence. It all speaks, speaks as it works, speaks without a language, speaks without a sound. Reason answers to reason as deep to deep. There may be no speech or language in these dumb motions, but for all that, voices are heard among them, their sound goes out unto all the lands, and their words unto the ends of the world.

¶ It is noticeable that the very period in which science has given such astounding development to our astronomical knowledge should also have been marked by a poetical development which, through the genius of Wordsworth, restored to us that primitive vision of nature with a purity, an austerity, and a vitality which has never been paralleled since the Psalms were written. Through him we see again the earth and sky as the Psalmist saw them. We see them not as under the conceits of a rhetorical emotion which can afford to disregard science only because its purpose is so superficial and trifling. That is precisely the conception of poetry which Wordsworth overthrew. He renewed its seriousness; he stripped it of poetic fiction; he made us see nature as men who are being disciplined for eternity, who can allow themselves no idle dreams, being far too much in earnest to take the beauty of nature as the plaything of a passing hour—men who abhor shows and outward vanities, and who press through by strenuous patience into the deep heart of things. It was no rhetorician, no emotional sentimentalist, who found, in that primeval outlook over the things of the earth, the solidity of a revelation. It was in the service, in the solemn service, of modern duty that he sang in words that breathed the innermost spirit of the text—

Thou dost preserve the stars from wrong!
And the most ancient heavens, through Thee, are fresh and
    strong.[1]

¶ I remember well my first visit to Chamounix. I had read of it, I had heard about it, and I had imagined it; and now I can only say to you, that no vigour of imagination can paint in your mind a scene which is ineffably glorious, and which can be believed only by being seen. But before I got to Chamounix the sun went down, night came, and the shadows went stealing up the mountains till they drove the sun's golden feet from where they lingered on the highest peak. And then we came to the place, and we heard the wind moaning among the hills, and the sounds of mighty torrents that made one shudder. Here and there a feeble light in the darkness only made the scene more desolate and awful. You threaded your way at last into the hotel, and then with a sigh you said, "What did I come here for? It was a much better place at home." And seven hours passed by, and there came from heaven the glorious light, and the vapours and darkness vanished, and before me God's mighty and manifold works stood in all their beauty. The eyes saw what tongue cannot tell, and what the soul can never forget. The light revealed it all, it did not create it. God's great work was there, and the light had revealed it to me; so that my experience was that of the pilgrim at Bethel, Surely "this is none other but the house of God, and this is the gate of heaven." [2]

¶ I asked the earth, and it answered me, "I am not He"; and all the things that are in it confessed the same. I asked the sea and the depths, and the moving creatures, and they answered, "We are not thy God; seek above us." I asked the air, and the whole air, with the inhabitants thereof, answered, "Anaximenes

[1] H. Scott Holland.   [2] C. Vince, *The Unchanging Saviour*, 168.

was wrong; I am not thy God." I asked the heavens, sun, moon, and stars. "Nor," say they, "are we the God whom thou seekest." And I replied unto all the things around, "Ye have told me of my God, that ye are not He: tell me something of Him." And they cried out with a loud voice, "He made us."[1]

> Not only in the Book
> Is found God's word,
> But in the song of every brook
> And every bird.
>
> In sun and moon and star
> His message shines!
> The flowers that fleck the green fields are
> His fragrant lines.
>
> His whisper in the breeze,
> And His the voice
> That bids the leaves upon the trees
> Sing and rejoice.
>
> Go forth, O soul! nor fear
> Nor doubt, for He
> Shall make the ears of faith to hear—
> The eyes to see.[2]

2. But the Psalmist turns his eyes in upon himself, and he finds another world—a world, too, of law, of certainty, of regularity, of order, no less than the world of Nature. Still here, too, the same harmonies hold good, the same successions move in appointed sequence; part answers to part, and every part to the whole. Here, too, all is sane, rational, secure, quiet, and sure, as the silent stars in the night; this great work proceeds according to allotted precautions, by rule and measure and mind, punctual and precise as the sun moving out of his chamber in the morning. This higher order of life moves along the course set before it, and its laws never flag or fail; no chance confuses it, and no unruly accident disturbs it. Man can count on these laws with the same absolute validity as that with which he counts on sunrise or on sunset. And what is this wonderful world that spreads away on every side to this ancient watcher of the skies? What are these

---

[1] Augustine, *Confessions*, x. 9.   [2] F. D. Sherman.

undeviating laws which lay themselves alongside of those unbroken uniformities which govern the stars in their courses ?   We
know it is the world of consciousness, the world of the moral
law, the world of the religious spirit, the world of the fear of the
Lord.

¶ As fire burns, as water runs, so the fear of the Lord holds
on its way with undeviating certitude.   Look up at the strong sun
moving through its unalterable successions !   It cometh, we say, from
the uttermost part of the earth, and runneth about unto the ends
of the world, and there is nothing hid from the heat thereof.   It is
the very type of necessity.   "Sure as the sun in the heavens,
sure as the sun will rise to-morrow"—so we say.   Just such is
the law of the Lord, the law of the moral life.   It works with the
same relentless accuracy, with the same clearness, with the same
persistence: nothing can hold it back or turn it aside, or hide it,
or deny it, or escape it, or defy it.   There|is nothing hid from the
heat thereof.   On and on it bears down upon us, and its light
pierces, and embraces, and searches, and reveals !   We must stand
in it !   The soul is laid bare under it, wrapped round by that
dread heat which burns its way in !   Nothing can be hid !   Oh,
the severity of such a searching fire !   Who can relieve the
strain ?   Who can soften the flame ?   What may not we be
proved to have done under such a scrutiny ![1]

¶ We call it the law of God.   It is so in the sense in which
it is your law and mine.   It is greater than God's throne, nay,
His throne rests upon it.   He obeys it, rules by it,—else He might
be Zeus, or Jupiter, the fickle, wayward, unrighteous tyrant of
classic mythology, but not the Father of our Lord Jesus Christ
and our Father.   The law is inherent in its subject-matter, in
the very nature of things, and omnipotence can no more set it
aside than it can make two and two five, or a circle equal to the
polygon that incloses it.   A Zeus might ignore the law; but
though he held in his grasp all created beings and things, he could
not make the wrong right, or the right wrong.[2]

3. The Psalmist is first attracted by the external glory.   He
opens his eyes upon the world of Nature, and beholds it with a
gaze of childlike joy.   To him it is, at a first glance, the personification of gladness.   All things are messengers of the Divine glory.
The heavens are telling the glory of the Lord ; day communicates
the message to day, and night to night.   The sun is like a bride-

[1] H. Scott Holland.   [2] A. P. Peabody, *King's Chapel Sermons,* 95.

groom coming out of his chamber, and rejoicing as a strong man rejoices to run his course. The message of joy is widespread and catholic, presenting a striking contrast to the limited scope of Judaism; its voice has gone forth unto all the earth, and its words unto the end of the world. And yet, with all its catholicity and with all its widespread power, the eloquence of Nature is a silent eloquence: "There is no speech, nor language; their voice cannot be heard." The aspect of the outer universe, as it appears to the eye of the Psalmist, is that of an all-pervading, joyous, yet silently working power, uniting the lives of men in a common brotherhood; and, as we read his opening expressions of enthusiasm, we are fully prepared to find the keynote of his strain prolonged through the entire meditation.

But suddenly there is a hiatus in the song. The Singer seems to interrupt himself in the midst of his enthusiastic melody, as if a string of the harp were broken. At the very moment when he seems lost in the admiration of the world of Nature, he all at once breaks out into a strain which sounds like a revolt from the external: "The law of the Lord is perfect, restoring the soul; the testimony of the Lord is sure, making wise the simple. The precepts of the Lord are right, rejoicing the heart; the command-ment of the Lord is pure, enlightening the eyes. The fear of the Lord is clean, enduring for ever; the judgements of the Lord are true and righteous altogether." Can we account for this seeming break in the harmony? Can we explain the apparent abruptness in the transition of thought, and restore unity to the Psalmist's theme? If we call in the aid of something more than the canons of criticism, if we fall back upon the standpoint of intellectual sympathy, we shall find no difficulty in seeing that the unity has never been broken. For is it not evident that the seeming abruptness of the transition is in reality the result of a close continuity of thought? The Psalmist has been expatiating on the wonders of Nature; he has been revelling in the declaration of God's visible glory and in the traces of His creative power. Yet in the very midst of his exultation he feels that his mind is not filled. This calm beautiful Nature, where is "no speech nor language," is too silent to satisfy his soul. He feels somehow that its voice is not for him, that its sympathy is not for him, that he is receiving no answer to the communings of his heart. In the momentary reaction he turns his eye inward, and there opens to his sight a new world—the world of Conscience. He finds himself in the presence of another glory of God, another manifestation of the Infinite. All at once there breaks upon his mind the conviction that the second glory is strong just where the first glory seemed weak; that the world of Conscience supplies to a human soul the very elements which it lacks in the world of Nature, and that in supplying these elements it becomes the other side of the Divine revelation, the second half of the twofold Majesty.

¶ The day closed with heavy showers. The plants in my garden were beaten down before the pelting storm, and I saw one flower that I had admired for its beauty and loved for its fragrance exposed to the pitiless storm. The flower fell, shut up its petals, drooped its head, and I saw that all its glory was gone. " I must wait till next year," I said, " before I see that beautiful thing again." And the night passed, and morning came, and the sun shone again, and the morning brought strength to the flower. The light looked at it, and the flower looked at the light. There was contact and communion, and power passed into the flower. It held up its head, opened its petals, regained its glory, and seemed fairer than before. I wonder how it took place—this feeble thing coming into contact with the strong thing, and gaining strength!

By devout communion and contact a soul gains strength from Christ. I cannot tell *how* it is that I should be able to receive into my being a power to do and to bear by this communion, but I know that it is a fact.[1]

II.

THE CHARACTER OF GOD'S LAW.

The Law is characterized by six names and nine epithets and by nine effects. The names are law, testimony, statutes, commandments, fear, judgments. To it are applied nine epithets, namely, perfect, sure, right, pure, holy, true, righteous, desirable, sweet. To it are ascribed nine effects, namely, it converts the soul, makes wise the simple, rejoices the heart, enlightens the eyes, endures for ever, enriches like gold, satisfies like honey, warns against sin, rewards the obedient.

[1] C. Vince, *The Unchanging Saviour*, 173.

¶ The six names here given to the word of God are the same six names that are spread through the 119th Psalm. These six names are law, testimony, statutes, commandment, fear (what produces fear), and judgments. Studied more closely, it suggests that law and testimony have a close relation, as also have statutes and commandments, and fear and judgments. There is here even a deeper and profounder suggestion than possibly has ever struck many a reader—namely, that as law has three main features or departments, first, *common law*,—principles or precepts upon which all specific statutes are based,—next *statute law*, or the commandments and precepts themselves, built up on the basis of common law,—and then *legal sanctions*, of reward and penalty, which sustain both common and statute law, giving the law authority, certainty of execution, and glory in the eyes of men, so these three things are distinctly referred to in this inspired poem. Law and testimony concern the *common* law. Law is the one word of the six, most general and covering the largest meaning. Testimony is another name very wide in its application, for it is God's witness to men concerning His will and His character. *Statutes*, however, represent specific precepts; and so do commandments. But, when we come to consider that which in the law produces *fear* in the subject, and overawes by its judgments or irreversible decisions, we at once think of the sanctions which sustain the whole fabric of law and rule, as we have already been reminded of common law and statute law.[1]

¶ God needs for the manifold illustration of His perfect law, and man needs for example and encouragement in keeping it, that it show its resplendent beauty and reveal its transcending loveliness alike on the throne and on the cross, in prosperous and in adverse fortunes, in buoyant strength and vigour, and in infirmity, illness, and suffering, with the praise and under the frowns of men, in honour and beneath scorn and contempt. I have never forgotten what was said many years ago by a clerical friend of mine on his death-bed, "My words are few and feeble; but the pulpit from which I utter them must give them weight and power." Have we not, all of us, witnessed in the patience, resignation, and trust of those most severely afflicted such demonstration as no words could convey of the peace which God gives to those who love and keep His law? Thus the faithful law-keepers have numbered in their ranks equally those for whom the world has done its best, and those who have endured its severest privations and trials.[2]

[1] A. T. Pierson, *The Hopes of the Gospel*, 10.
[2] A. P. Peabody, *King's Chapel Sermons*, 100.

1. "The law of the Lord is perfect, restoring the soul." In the world of Nature there is no provision for the restoration of the soul. It neither praises nor blames; it neither weeps nor laughs; it neither applauds nor condemns the acts of struggling humanity; and, amidst all the speech which day utters unto day and night to night, there is no evidence that one word is spoken of interest in a fallen spirit.

But when the Psalmist turns his eye inward, he finds in the revelation of Conscience that which in Nature he sought in vain: "The law of the Lord is perfect, restoring the soul." The perfection which he sees is the adaptation to a world of imperfection. He hears a voice speaking to his humility, to his nothingness, to his abasement. He is in communion with a revelation which recognizes him in his ruin, which speaks to him in his fallen majesty. True it is a rough voice uttering a stern command, speaking in an accent of strong rebuke; but it is precisely this that endears it to his soul. It is not the placid tone of the indifferent universe, which seems to pass him by on the other side; it is the stern speech of a wounded parent who, in the depth of offended love, cannot pass him by.

¶ If the mountain would have come to Mahomet, Mahomet would not have gone to the mountain. If we could twist and bend the law at pleasure, we could convert it, instead of its converting us. In our sins, great or small, we virtually try to evade the law, to get round it, to violate it and shirk its penalty, to make for ourselves a law independent of it—but in vain. When we will not keep the law, the law executes itself upon and in us, body, mind, and soul, all three, it may be. To find this true is our unspeakable blessedness; for when we learn that we cannot escape the law, we embrace it, take it to our hearts, incarnate it in our lives; and then it becomes our light and our joy, and we experience the full meaning of those good words of the early time, " Great peace have they who love thy law." It becomes, too, not our restraint, but our freedom; for when the finite range of things forbidden by it is cut off for us, we emerge into unbounded liberty of choice in the infinite scope of things excellent, Divine, eternal.[1]

2. "The testimony of the Lord is sure, making wise the simple." It is a definite voice, a voice addressed to the child in the man,

[1] A. P. Peabody, *King's Chapel Sermons*, 96.

and therefore capable of being understood by all men. It speaks
to the conscience in the prohibitory form in which law speaks to
the child: "Thou shalt; thou shalt not." It gives no reason for
its command beyond the fact that it has commanded; it is what
Kant grandly calls "the categorical imperative"; it speaks as
the ultimate authority from which there can be no appeal. It is
this that makes its testimony so sure, and that renders it so
powerful in "making wise the simple." It realizes the fine
image of the poet Cowper when he says that the words "Believe
and live" are legible only by the light which radiates from them.
The child-life is not perplexed by an effort to find the reason of
the thing; this thing is itself the reason; it shines by its own
light.

¶ A well-informed writer in the *Kilmarnock Standard* states
that Thomas Carlyle, not long before his death, was in conversation with the late Dr. John Brown, and expressed himself to the
following effect: "I am now an old man, and done with the
world. Looking around me, before and behind, and weighing all
as wisely as I can, it seems to me there is nothing solid to rest
on but the faith which I learned in my old home, and from my
mother's lips."[1]

> Sometime when all life's lessons have been learned,
>   And sun and stars for evermore have set;
> The things which our weak judgment here has spurned,
>   The things o'er which we grieved with lashes wet,
> Will flash before us out of life's dark night,
>   As stars shine most in deeper tints of blue;
> And we shall see how all God's plans were right,
>   And how what seemed reproof was love most true.

3. "The precepts of the Lord are right, rejoicing the heart."
Nature is a revelation of many things which are very nearly
allied to morality: it is a revelation of the beautiful; it is a
revelation of the useful; it is, in some sense, a revelation of the
true. But while beauty, utility, and truth are all included in
the conception of the moral consciousness, neither any of them
singly nor all of them united would suffice to give that consciousness. A moral action is more than beautiful, more than useful,
more than intellectually true; it is *right*. The difference

[1] *The Treasury of Religious Thought*, Oct. 1903, p. 487.

between right and wrong is fundamentally distinct from the difference between beauty and deformity, expediency and inexpediency, intellectual truth and intellectual error. It cannot be ascribed to any other sense than the moral consciousness, just as light cannot be ascribed to any other sense than the eye. The physical universe cannot implant the moral idea in one who is not already in possession of that idea. Therefore it is that, according to the implication of the Psalmist, the physical universe cannot "rejoice the heart." If a heart is already joyful it can minister to that joy; but it cannot put joy into a sad heart; it has no power to *make* glad. And it has no power for this reason, that it cannot say to the soul of its own sadness, "It is right"; it cannot tell a man in the season of his calamity that his calamity is a moral ordinance designed to make him spiritually strong. It can tell him that the calamities of life are forces of Nature; it may even promise him that they will be found to be in harmony with the symmetry of the universe: but it cannot say to him the one thing which alone can give him peace, that they are the will of God for his salvation.

In Conscience he finds that personal comfort in calamity which he lacked in the voice of Nature—something which tells him to be still and know that the Judge of all the earth does right. It is not the mere testimony to a future symmetry of all things; it is not the mere prophecy of a completed harmony which shall vindicate the minor chords of the universe: such testimonies speak beautifully in favour of the universe, but they say little in favour of man. If my individual life is to be begun, continued, and ended in sorrow, it is small comfort to me that the completed harmony of creation will make use of my discord. But when in the hour of my calamity I hear a voice saying, "This is right for *you*: this is good for you as an individual man," I hear something which can *rejoice the heart*. I am no longer forced to come out of my private sorrow to contemplate the eternal harmonies to which my groans are an unconscious and an unwilling contribution. I am allowed to look into my private sorrow itself and to see in it a Divine statute given to my soul, a species of sacramental bread administered to my spiritual being which is bitter in its appropriation, but certain in its promise of nourishment; and I am able with some appreciation to echo the

Psalmist's words, "The statutes of the Lord are right, rejoicing the heart."

¶ To the growing soul, there are, with maturing life, deeps of joy and an ever-increasing capacity for delight. Ever grander are the chords of happiness struck by experience—provided we keep near the Author and Giver of all, who has more yet to bestow. "Experience worketh hope." It is simple fact, absolute truth, verifiable science, that delighting oneself in the Lord means constant joy. As surely as Huyghens demonstrated the wave-theory, of which Marconi's wireless was but practical proof, so have the prophets, martyrs and common saints shown in their lives the truth of the psalm of delights. They have fulfilled the joy of Jesus. Even the Son of God in humanity did not disdain the motive of happiness. He "for the joy that was set before him, endured the cross, despising the shame." Surely, this is a challenge to us to do the same. So ought we to learn that the daily cultivation of joy is both a duty and the best strengthener for life's burdens. It prepares us for whatever mortal existence may, and the eternities certainly will, bring us. Life is short, and affliction light. Joy is for ever. He who is "made after the power of an endless life" teaches this.[1]

4. "The commandment of the Lord is pure, enlightening the eyes." The metaphor is perhaps that of pure water, in whose uninterrupted medium a man can see himself reflected. It suggests that the revealing medium of Nature is not uninterrupted. Nature does not convey the impression of an unmixed revelation of love. It has its storms as well as its calms, its clouds as well as its sunshine, its thunders and earthquakes and fires as well as its still small voices. To-day it is all gentle, serene, placid; to-morrow its brow may be furrowed with wrath and its accents hoarse with anger. The Psalmist cannot see in Nature a pure reflexion of his human wants. It adapts itself to his wants chiefly in those points in which he is allied to the beast of the field; meets him rather as a creature than as a human creature; fails to supply his needs the moment his needs rise above the level of the irrational creation. But when he enters the secret places of his own soul, he looks upon a pure water of life in which he sees himself reflected at full length. It is true there are storms here also; indeed, we are not sure that Schenkel is not right

[1] W. Elliot Griffis, *The Call of Jesus to Joy*, 9.

when he says that the very idea of Conscience implies a disturbance in the moral nature. But here lies the difference between the storms of Nature and the storms of Conscience: in the former my destiny is obscured, in the latter it is made manifest. In the moral tempest of the heart I see myself more clearly. I recognize in the very sense of struggle an adaptation to my deepest wants as a human being; for I find in the sense of struggle the prophetic intimation that this is not my rest, and I hear the ever-repeated command which was heard by the ancient patriarch, "Get thee out of thy country, and from thy kindred." The struggles of Conscience are the soul's premonitions of an unfulfilled destiny; and the human portraiture bulks larger when reflected through the troubled waters. "The commandment of the Lord is pure, enlightening the eyes."

¶ Another abstract theme which Watts has impersonated is "Conscience," or the Dweller in the Innermost. A female figure with stern gesture and eyes like a flame of fire, is seen in the centre of a luminous mist that ripples round it to the edge. There is a radiant star in the middle of her forehead, and on either side are doves with soft plumage and half-outstretched wings. The breast is covered with a downy, loosely-fitting mantle, out of which at regular intervals protrude large dark feathers, which form a strange kind of halo around the face and neck. One arm is laid across her bosom, and the other supports her head in an attitude of meditation. In her lap are the arrows with which she pricks the hearts of men into conviction, and the trumpet which shall ultimately summon to the judgment-seat all mankind, there to be tried for the deeds done in the body, whether good or bad. The star on the brow may mean the eternal light of truth, of which conscience is the presentment; the doves that surround the head, the innocence and purity that characterize all her thoughts and ways; and the feathers in the mantle may remind us of the rapid flight and the keen vision of birds, with which the quick decisions, and the all-discerning, all-penetrating insight of conscience may be suitably compared. Conscience is thus light, is winged, dwells in the heart of life, is armed with avenging weapons, and looks into the unseen. We ask ourselves when gazing upon that mysterious Being with the fiery eyes and the sharp arrows and the trumpet of judgment, why it is that the Dweller in the Innermost has not a more complete control of our lives. Why is it that it enables us to see what is right, and yet we care little for it when we have seen it;

that it gives us the knowledge of what is wrong, and yet we are
not pained in doing that wrong? As conscience is constituted,
it is never what it ought to be in the best of men, and it is never
without some witnessing power in the worst.[1]

> I was ashamed, I dared not lift my eyes,
> I could not bear to look upon the skies;
> What I had done! sure, everybody knew!
> From everywhere hands pointed where I stood,
> And scornful eyes were piercing through and through
> The moody armour of my hardihood.
>
> I heard their voices too, each word an asp
> That buzz'd and stung me sudden as a flame:
> And all the world was jolting on my name,
> And now and then there came a wicked rasp
> Of laughter, jarring me to deeper shame.
>
> And then I looked, but there was no one nigh,
> No eyes that stabbed like swords or glinted sly,
> No laughter creaking on the silent air:
> And then I found that I was all alone
> Facing my soul, and next I was aware
> That this mad mockery was all my own.[2]

5. "The fear of the Lord is clean, enduring for ever." The
metaphor here is probably that of the unblemished offering.
Nothing which was unclean was allowed to have part in the life
of the nation; nothing which had a blemish in it was suffered to
ascend in sacrifice to the Fountain of Life. The unblemished
sacrifice, whatever else it symbolized, was a symbol of immortality; it marked the transition of the soul into a higher life;
and it implied that such a transition could be made only by
a soul emancipated from its uncleanness. What, then, is the
bearing of this metaphor on the Psalmist's meditation? What
does he mean by the implication that the revelation of God in
physical Nature is a less *clean* manifestation than the revelation
of God in Conscience? He clearly means to suggest that the
revelation of Nature does not convey to the mind the notion of
immortality. It is not that the eye, as it looks upon the face
of Nature, is impressed with its frailty and its perishableness; its

---

[1] H. Macmillan, *Life Work of G. F. Watts*, 187.
[2] James Stephens, *The Hill of Vision*, 65.

silence on the subject of immortality would be equally profound although we knew, as a matter of fact, that Nature would endure for ever. For the silence lies here: even if the universe were everlasting, it would still be a contingent universe; it does not convey the impression of something which *must* be. It would always be felt that its eternity lay in some force external to its own.

What the spirit of man wants is something whose death is inconceivable, which not only *will* be, but *must* be, which cannot even in thought be associated with the idea of annihilation. It seeks what the Egyptians are supposed to have sought when they built those colossal pyramids—a sign of immortality, an emblem of eternity, an image of life that cannot die. This is what the Egyptians failed to find in the pyramids; this is what the Psalmist failed to find in Nature. Nature did not convey to him the idea of *cleanness*, did not suggest to him the thought of a necessary existence, of a life whose very essence was incorruptible, of a world which must live in the very nature of things; he missed in it the sign of immortality. But when he turned his eye inward, he was once more arrested by the very thing he wanted. In the commandment of Conscience he was confronted by the sign of immortality, and found that which even in thought he could not imagine not to be.

¶ The great German philosopher, at the distance of three millenniums, has not been ashamed to reproduce the same experience. We can, as we have said, imagine a time when other systems shall circle other suns, and other physical forces shall obey other laws. But we can never imagine a time, go where this spirit may, when the forces of the moral universe shall cease to be what they are. We can never conceive a period when right shall be anything but right, or wrong anything but wrong. We can never figure to ourselves a world where "malice and hatred and envy and all uncharitableness" shall be other than loathsome and repulsive, where integrity, uprightness, purity of heart, benevolence, "the love of love, the scorn of scorn, and the hate of hate" shall be other than things of beauty and joys for ever. In this world of Conscience the Psalmist finds the sign of immortality; for he meets with that whose negation is inconceivable. Heaven and earth *might* pass away; their existence hung upon a thread of contingency; there was no reason in the nature of things why they should not cease to be: but this Divine word of Conscience, this word spoken in the inner chamber of the soul, could not pass away; once spoken, it must reverberate through all time.[1]

6. "The judgements of the Lord are true, and righteous altogether." Law and love are not opposed to one another. One of the sure tokens of God's Fatherhood is the inflexibility of His moral administration, by which alone we are turned to the right and kept in the right. The retributions of the world to come are the merciful discipline of Him who wills not that any should perish.

The Psalmist perceived that in Nature the retribution and the payment take no account of moral character; they are given simply for the special work omitted, and for the special work accomplished. The missionary may be the most pious of men, but if he goes to sea in a bad ship he will probably go to the bottom. The judgment is righteous so far as it goes; Nature exacts respect to its laws of cohesion, and if a man disregards these, she punishes him. But what of the missionary zeal, what of the fervent piety, what of the enthusiasm for humanity, which has prompted the enterprise? Has the judgment of Nature been in congruity with that? We feel instinctively that it has not; we feel that the judgment is only physically true, that the violated elements in avenging their infringement have failed to appreciate the moral grandeur of the man's character. As long as we fix our eye exclusively on the physical universe, we are perpetually confronted by the same experience: "He maketh his sun to rise on the evil and on the good." Nature is morally impartial. No special sunbeam follows the upright; no special cloud tracks the course of the ungodly. The lightning does not dart from the sky to paralyse the hand of the murderer, nor does the thunder roll displeasure on the deed of crime.

But in his own conscience a man is confronted by a direct judgment upon its right and wrong—a judgment which speaks to it only as a moral being, and refuses to deal with any other sphere than that of actions. It is a judgment invisible to every eye save that of him for whom it is intended, a sentence inaudible to every ear save that of him to whom it speaks. A man basking in the

[1] G. Matheson.

outward sunshine may be under its cloud; a man wrapt in the
outward cloud may be under its illumination.   But however silent
and however invisible is its operation, its force to him who
experiences it is terribly real.   The judgment of Conscience upon
goodness is the gift bequeathed by the Divine Founder of
Christianity : " Peace I leave with you ; my peace I give unto
you."   Christianity has brought into the world a joy which the
world knows not, a peace which, like its illustrious Giver, shines
in an uncomprehending darkness.   Into this invisible joy, into
this uncomprehended peace, the pure soul enters and finds repose.
He passes noiselessly into the paradise of God, and receives in the
midst of the world that crown of which the world is unconscious.
He obtains from the silent testimony of a reconciled Conscience
that recognition of moral purity which the many voices of Nature
fail to yield ; and in that recognition he reaches the supply of the
last remaining want in the physical revelation : " The judgements
of the Lord are true, and righteous altogether."

> The years
> Roll back; and through a mist of tears
> I see a child turn from her play,
> And seek, with eager feet, the way
> That led her to her father's knee.
>
> " If God is wise and kind," said she,
> " Why did He let my roses die ? "
> A moment's pause, a smile, a sigh,
> And then, " I do not know, my dear,
> Some questions are not answered here."
>
> " But is it wrong to ask ? "   " Not so,
> My child.   That we should seek to know
> Proves *right* to know, beyond a doubt;
> And some day we shall yet find out
> Why roses die."
>
> And then I wait,
> Sure of my answer, soon or late ;
> Secure that love doth hold for me
> The key to life's great mystery ;
> And oh ! so glad to leave it there !
> Though my dead roses were so fair.

III.

The Joy of Obedience.

1. Law is the expression of highest love, and can be fulfilled only by love. The perfectness of this law-keeping life we have in Jesus, and of all the praises which the worship of these nineteen centuries has heaped upon His name, the superlative ground of reverence, love, loyal discipleship, thankful commemoration of Him on earth till we fall at His feet in heaven, is that in Him alone we have the living law—the law of the Lord which is perfect, incarnate in a life no less perfect.

¶ The Psalmist saw a great deal more than most people of God's loving spirit, as embodied in the law. By his aspirations and by his prayers, the law had become greater and dearer to him than to most men : and when in moments of deep devotion he asked God for greater delight in His law, he cried not out, " Give me more law," but he cried, " Give me light," " Open mine eyes that I may behold wondrous things out of thy law." And the answer to his devout prayer has been given to us through Jesus.[1]

2. When love is the motive, obedience becomes not only a privilege, but a delight. The moments when for duty, for righteousness' sake, in the service of God, and of man as the child of God, we have made strenuous effort or costly sacrifice, have been the great moments of our lives,—they have given us immeasurably more than happiness,—we would have incurred what we call unhappiness in order to secure them. When, too, our lives have flowed on in an even course of faithful duty, with no breaks of supineness, negligence, waywardness, discontent, or unkindness, with no intervals on a lower plane than the table-land on which we can walk at equal pace with God and with man, it has been for us an experience immeasurably more blessed than we have derived from any fulness of enjoyment beside. Even if at such periods there has been disappointment, loss, or grief, the current of a more than earthly joy has flowed on, pure and transparent, through the turbid stream of the lower life, if sometimes beneath, much oftener above, the surface of the troubled waters. If we would only thus live always, though it were under

[1] C. Vince, *The Unchanging Saviour*, 170.

the heaviest pressure of calamity, and with not a ray of hope as to things earthly, there would still be that in our souls which would give a most indignant negative to Satan's question about Job, "Does he serve God for nought?"[1]

¶ If we see law not as something external, an obligation imposed on us from without, a despotism against which we cannot rebel, and to which we can only sullenly submit; if we see law as the law of our own life, the fruit of the tenderest and highest love, the commandments are seen not to be grievous, and obedience becomes sweet and natural. We know the difference between obedience dictated by fear and obedience dictated by love. When we are brought into a personal relation to God and enter into fellowship with Him, we realize that even in the making of our own moral life, in the creating of our own character, we are fellow-workers with God. We desire the same end as He does, and it is the best end.[2]

¶ If people would but read the text of their Bible with heartier purpose of understanding it, instead of superstitiously, they would see that throughout the parts which they are intended to make most personally their own (the Psalms) it is always the law which is spoken of with chief joy. The Psalms respecting mercy are often sorrowful as in thought of what it cost; but those respecting the law are always full of delight. David cannot contain himself for joy in thinking of it—he is never weary of its praise: "How love I Thy law! it is my meditation all the day. Thy testimonies are my delight and my counsellors; sweeter also than honey and the honeycomb."[3]

¶ There is a beautiful little sentence in the works of Charles Lamb concerning one who had been afflicted: "He gave his heart to the Purifier, and his will to the Sovereign Will of the Universe." But there is a speech in the third canto of the *Paradiso* of Dante, spoken by a certain Piccarda, which is a rare gem. I will only quote this one line: *In la sua volontade è nostra pace* (In His will is our peace). The words are few and simple, and yet they appear to me to have an inexpressible majesty of truth about them, to be almost as if they were spoken from the very mouth of God. It so happened that (unless my memory much deceives me) I first read that speech on a morning early in the year 1836, which was one of trial. I was profoundly impressed and powerfully sustained, almost absorbed, by these words. They cannot

---

[1] A. P. Peabody, *King's Chapel Sermons*, 101.

[2] H. Black, *Edinburgh Sermons*, 75.

[3] Ruskin, *Modern Painters* (*Works*, vii. 192).

be too deeply graven upon the heart.   In short, what we all want is that they should not come to us as an admonition from without, but as an instinct from within.   They should not be adopted by effort or upon a process of proof, but they should be simply the translation into speech of the habitual tone to which all tempers, affections, emotions, are set.   In the Christian mood, which ought never to be intermitted, the sense of this conviction should recur spontaneously; it should be the foundation of all mental thoughts and acts, and the measure to which the whole experience of life, inward and outward, is referred.   The final state which we are to contemplate with hope, and to seek by discipline, is that in which our will shall be *one* with the will of God; not merely shall submit to it, not merely shall follow after it, but shall live and move with it, even as the pulse of the blood in the extremities acts with the central movement of the heart.   And this is to be obtained through a double process; the first, that of checking, repressing, quelling the inclination of the will to act with reference to self as a centre; this is to mortify it.   The second, to cherish, exercise, and expand its new and heavenly power of acting according to the will of God, first, perhaps, by painful effort in great feebleness and with many inconsistencies, but with continually augmenting regularity and force, until obedience become a necessity of second nature.[1]

Time was, I shrank from what was right
    From fear of what was wrong;
I would not brave the sacred fight,
    Because the foe was strong.

But now I cast that finer sense
    And sorer shame aside;
Such dread of sin was indolence,
    Such aim at Heaven was pride.

So, when my Saviour calls, I rise,
    And calmly do my best;
Leaving to Him, with silent eyes
    Of hope and fear, the rest.

I step, I mount where He has led;
    Men count my haltings o'er;—
I know them; yet, though self I dread,
    I love His precept more.[2]

[1] W. E. Gladstone in *Life*, by John Morley, i. 215.
[2] Cardinal Newman, *Verses on Various Occasions*, 83.

HIDDEN FAULTS.

LITERATURE.

Barrett (G. S.), *Musings for Quiet Hours*, 23.
Binnie (W.), *Sermons*, 187.
Caird (J.), *Aspects of Life*, 33.
Halsey (J.), *The Spirit of Truth*, 276.
Hodge (C.), *Princeton Sermons*, 110.
Keble (J.), *Sermons for the Christian Year :* Lent to Passion-tide, 95.
King (E.), *The Love and Wisdom of God*, 97.
Maclaren (A.), *The God of the Amen*, 77.
Newman (J. H.), *Parochial and Plain Sermons*, i. 41.
Selby (T. G.), *The Imperfect Angel*, 136.
Spurgeon (C. H.), *New Park Street Pulpit*, iii. (1857) No. 116.
Strong (A. H.), *Miscellanies*, ii. 359.
Thew (J.), *Broken Ideals*, 106.
Thorold (A. W.), *Questions of Faith and Duty*, 55.
Trench (R. C.), *Westminster and other Sermons*, 249.
Voysey (C.), *Sermons*, xiv. No. 20 ; xvi. No. 39 ; xxvii. No. 9 ; xxx.
    No. 43.
Watkinson (W. L.), *The Fatal Barter*, 127.
      ,,   ,,   *Studies in Christian Character*, i. 21.
Wilson (J. M.), *Sermons Preached in Clifton College Chapel*, 60.
Christian World Pulpit, lxiv. 146 (Ossian Davies).
Churchman's Pulpit : The Lenten Season, v. 54 (Jackson), 181 (Stokoe).
Literary Churchman, 1885, p. 96 (Hardy).

Hidden Faults.

Who can discern his errors?
Clear thou me from hidden faults.

Ps. xix. 12.

1. THE Nineteenth Psalm is one of those which are called Psalms of Nature. The thoughts, at any rate in part, belong apparently to the early shepherd life of him who was promoted by God from the sheep-folds to feed Jacob His people and Israel His inheritance. In his wanderings on the hills and in the valleys around Bethlehem the bold, romantic, thoughtful youth had ample leisure to meditate upon the wonders of the natural world, and in this contemplation his mind rises from the everlasting order to the God who is there revealed; and is inspired with a sense of that unseen Presence which guides and directs the whole. As he sees the sun break forth in the morning from his couch of cloud, "as a bridegroom coming out of his chamber," until his radiance spreads over the whole clear sky, and "there is nothing hid from the heat thereof," he beholds in this a figure of the pure, and enlightening, and cheering law of Jehovah; and the desire comes for that sinlessness which can bear the full light of this Sun of Righteousness, and the words well up from his heart, "Who can discern his errors? Clear thou me from hidden faults. Keep back thy servant also from presumptuous sins; let them not have dominion over me: then shall I be perfect, and I shall be clear from great transgression. Let the words of my mouth and the meditation of my heart be acceptable in thy sight, O Lord, my rock, and my redeemer."

2. The Psalmist stands perplexed before the mystery of his own being; he is at once ignorant of himself and yet mistrustful of himself; he does not know himself, yet knows himself sufficiently well to suspect himself; therefore he appeals to the Spirit

345

who searcheth all things. How true it is that we are mainly unknown to ourselves; that within us are unexplored regions; that our heart is substantially undiscovered! Schopenhauer one day strayed into the Royal Gardens of Berlin; and when an officer inquired of him, "Who are you, sir?" the philosopher responded, "I don't know; I shall be glad if you can tell me." The officer reported him for a lunatic; but he was far from that—he was one who had deeply pondered the mystery of personality, and was accordingly puzzled by it.

¶ The exclamation of the Psalmist hits off a universal fact. "Who *can* discern his errors?" It is the cry of a man who almost despairs of ever coming to know and understand his actual inner condition, of ever coming to see himself as God sees him. There is a touch of pensive surprise in the words, as if he had just had an unwonted revelation of himself, as if he had just made discovery of faults and sins hitherto hidden from him. The sight fills him with astonishment and alarm. He had no idea there was so much lingering mischief within. He is not quite sure that he has seen the worst yet. "If there be this, there may be more." "Who *can* discern his errors?"[1]

¶ Bishop Perowne renders the text, "As for errors—who can perceive" (them)? The word "error" here is analogous to the Greek word for "sin," which gives the notion of missing the mark. It means straying, wandering from the path. There are sins of ignorance and of infirmity unconsciously, unintentionally done through lack of self-knowledge, or of jealous vigilance against the deceits of the world and the snares of Satan. There are also sins of presumption, done with deliberateness and hardened pride, and a sort of insolence against God. There are also sins which do not usually come earliest in the moral history, but which are the inevitable result and penalty of sins of carelessness and infirmity; and which imply, nay, sooner or later create, that awful insensibility which is the sure symptom of spiritual death, and for which no forgiveness, because no repentance, is possible.[2]

¶ Nothing is more common than the confession, on the part of eminently holy men, that every day of their lives gives them some new understanding of the sinfulness of their own hearts; that the guilt which once seemed slight and easily covered now rises before them in such mountainous proportions that nothing but infinite power and infinite love can remove it. These confessions

[1] J. Thew, *Broken Ideals*, 110.
[2] A. W. Thorold, *Questions of Faith and Duty*, 56.

of sin recur continually in the hymnology of the Church and constitute no small part even of the sacred Word. Is it not one of the greatest of wonders, while the holiest men esteem themselves so great sinners, while progress in goodness is marked most clearly by an increasing knowledge and abhorrence of personal sin—is it not, I say, one of the greatest of wonders that those who make no pretensions to religion, and have no aspirations after holiness, are scarcely conscious that they are sinners at all, and the greatest transgressors are least troubled by the accusations of conscience? It was the humble consciousness of his own sinfulness that gave such power to the preaching of Robert M'Cheyne, whom God took to Himself in the fulness of his youth and promise. With incomparable modesty he said one day: "The reason, I think, why so many of the worst sinners of Dundee come to hear me is that they discover so much likeness between their hearts and mine." And this is the secret of the Psalmist's power over us; this is the reason why we can hear from his lips such sad descriptions of human nature and yet, instead of cherishing an instinctive feeling of repulsion toward them, can yield our assent and make our penitent confession of their truth.[1]

I.

Our Hidden Faults.

1. What is the meaning of these words of the Poet-King, when he prays to be cleared from his hidden faults? It might seem at first to be simple and clear, to be an entreaty that he may be preserved from those sins which we commonly speak of as secret, because they are unknown to our fellow-men; as distinguished from the open and presumptuous offences which are a shameless and notorious breach of the Divine law. We are all conscious of much in that inner life, known only to ourselves and to God, that is inconsistent with our outward profession of morality and religion, in direct antagonism to His revealed will. But this very consciousness excludes all such offences from the list of those of which David is speaking. There is a further and more subtle analysis of character here implied than that which contrasts itself with an exhaustive division of sins into those which are openly exhibited, and those which are secretly indulged. There

---

[1] A. H. Strong, *Miscellanies*, ii. 360.

is a more awful truth to be learned here than that of an inner life of falsehood and impurity and unbelief, which we shrink from disclosing to our fellows. There are sins which are unknown to ourselves, there are evil influences in our hearts of which we are absolutely unconscious, until they have become stereotyped into habits, or suddenly startle us by breaking forth in unmistakable wickedness. There are offences which we cannot confess, or repent of, because we are ignorant of their existence; which we may vaguely include in our conception of a heart that is deceitful above all things and desperately wicked, in our general petitions for a clean heart and a right spirit; but which we cannot recognize or discriminate, so as to keep a special guard against them or resolve on a detailed renunciation of them. "Who," says the Psalmist, "can understand, or who can mark his errors?" It is a condition of our finite power of apprehension, that we cannot thoroughly comprehend even our own nature, or penetrate the mysteries of our own sinfulness. From wilful blindness or want of spiritual perception, or the superficial analysis of conduct, which declines to probe down to the intent and motive, or the casuistry which seeks to reconcile things which are irreconcilable, none can reckon how oft he offendeth.

¶ We are all a supreme mystery to ourselves; the mystery of creation in general, profound as it is, is as nothing to the mystery of our own existence and personality. Is there anything we know less about than the entity that says "I" whenever we speak? The chemist can take up a piece of ore, or a glass of water, and tell you what is in it to its ultimate atoms of oxygen and hydrogen. But he cannot get behind his own consciousness. He experiences states of feeling and perceives successions of ideas, but of the percipient soul he knows nothing. A man may *lose* his soul; but, even though he be a philosopher, he cannot *find* it.[1]

¶ It is with our characters as with our faces. Few of us are familiar with our own appearance, and most of us, if we have looked at our portraits, have felt a little shock of surprise, and been ready to say to ourselves, "Well! I did not know that I looked like that!" And the bulk even of good men are almost as much strangers to their inward physiognomy as to their outward. They see themselves in their looking-glasses every morning, although they "go away and forget what manner of men" they

[1] J. Halsey, *The Spirit of Truth*, 278.

were. But they do not see their true selves in the same fashion in any other mirror.[1]

¶ The ancient precept, "Man, know thyself!" was recognized as so wise and good that it was thought to be of Divine origin. The best of the ancients regarded self-knowledge as the very beginning of wisdom, just as they regarded self-mastery as the very beginning of practical virtue. It is said that Socrates, on one occasion, excused himself from giving attention to some important questions, on the ground that he could not possibly come to know such things, as he had not yet been able to know himself. There, the grand old heathen felt, was the true starting-place of all true knowledge. Wisdom, like charity, began at home. And he could not bring himself to admire those who carried on their researches at the ends of the earth, ignorant of what was proceeding in their own domains.[2]

2. Though we may be unconscious of it, sin is always sin. The principle of evil is the same whether it be hand-murder or heart-murder. Sin is not confined to the outward act; it lies also in the thoughts and motives behind the act. "The thought of the foolish is sin." The desire to injure your neighbour is sin, though it may never result in outward action. The plan to sin is sinful whether you carry it out or not. Human judges have nothing to do with inward desires, for all these are beyond their reach; but the Divine Judge reads the reins and hearts of men. The heart makes the man, and if the heart is wrong, all is wrong.

¶ In the Book of Leviticus different sacrifices are required for the sin of ignorance in the priest, the ruler of the people, and the private individual and proselyte. The priest stood at the head of the chosen people, and, in virtue of his exceptional position, might justly be expected to possess superior knowledge and a more than average sense of the authority and penetrating power of the Divine law. For a sin of inadvertence in the priest, the sacrifice of a bullock, the most costly offering known to the Levitical law, was required. The inadvertence was scarcely excusable in one living in the heart of the daily sanctities. The light of the holy place was about the man's footsteps, and in this case a sin of ignorance crept up almost to the margin of conscious sin. It demanded a costlier atonement than in others. Again, when the ruler of the people had committed a sin of ignorance, he was required to offer a he-goat. His position was

---

[1] A. Maclaren, *The God of the Amen*, 78. [2] J. Thew, *Broken Ideals*, 107.

not quite so sacred as that of the priest, nor were his religious opportunities so rich and inspiring. But still his life was devoted to high tasks of moral discrimination. He occupied a representative position, and ought to stand out from the rank and file of the congregation in quick perception and sensitive religious tone. When the private individual or proselyte had unwittingly sinned, a she-goat only, a still less costly form of sacrifice, was required. The lowliest were members of the elect congregation and worshippers of Jehovah, and could not be quite absolved from all responsibility, although the opportunities of others might be higher.[1]

3. Hidden sin is a great peril, and if unchecked will manifest itself in overt deed. Every man has two lives—the inward and the outward. Christianity directs its chief attention to the inner man, and the " inwardness " of its teachings renders it unique. Of old, murder was a thing of the hand—an outward act; but Christ speaks of murder as a thing of the heart—an inward thought or feeling. You may commit murder without shedding one drop of blood, for a man who is " angry with his brother without a cause " is a murderer. In the Sermon on the Mount there are two voices —the one an ancient voice dealing with the outward, and the other a new Voice from heaven dealing with the inner empire of the spirit. Christianity is not a painted paganism, but a condition of soul. Its great question is this, " How is it with thine heart? What is the state of thy spirit? What of the man within the man ? " The Bible is the heart-book, *par excellence*. The human race is suffering, not from skin-disease, but from heart-disease; and if man is to be lifted up he must be lifted up from the very root of his being. It is the glory of the Gospel that its masterpurpose is to subject every thought to the obedience of Christ.

¶ These secret faults are like a fungus that has grown in a wine-cask, whose presence nobody suspected. It sucks up all the generous liquor to feed its own filthiness, and when the staves are broken, there is no wine left, nothing but the foul growth. Many a Christian man and woman has the whole Christian life arrested, and all but annihilated, by the unsuspected influence of a secret sin. I do not believe it would be exaggeration to say that, for one man who has made shipwreck of his faith and lost his peace by reason of some gross transgression, there are twenty who have

[1] T. G. Selby, *The Imperfect Angel*, 144.

fallen into the same condition by reason of the multitude of small ones. "He that despiseth little things shall fall by little and little "; and whilst the deeds which the Ten Commandments rebuke are damning to a Christian character, still more perilous, because unseen, and permitted to grow without check or restraint, are these unconscious sins. "Happy is he that condemneth not himself in that thing which he alloweth."[1]

¶ A large oak-tree was cut down in a grove, and near the heart of it was found a small nail surrounded by twenty-nine concentric circles of wood, the growth of as many years. And did that little nail injure the oak? Alas! it did, for the sap carried with it the oxide from the metal, until a space of three or four feet in length and four or five inches in diameter was completely blackened. The hidden nail in the heart proved injurious to the mighty oak. And the secret sin in your heart, my brother, will injure your manhood. Even when it does not develop into an act, it will blacken the noblest part of your nature. It will convert your soul into a macadamized road for the foulest of satyrs. Your moral perception will be obscured, your moral sensibility will be blunted, your moral appetite will be vitiated, your conscience will be impaired, and all the vitalities of your soul will be brought low.[2]

4. The influence of our hidden sins reaches out to our fellow-men. What injury unknown to ourselves we may have inflicted on others! Like the widening circles on the surface of the water when the child throws the pebble into the pool, so the sins of our childhood and of other days have spread we know not whither. It is possible (we must remember) to lead others into sins which we have never committed ourselves. Arguments for mere love of amusement or display of skill may raise doubts in the mind of another which we have never felt and cannot answer. An expenditure which to us may not be worse than waste may lead another into embarrassments which will destroy the peace of years and break the hearts of those who denied themselves to provide what should have been more than enough. Our thoughtlessness may lead another to break a heart which we have never known—but it is through our fault that this heart is broken.

¶ A sanitary officer noticed how a young woman who had come up to London from the country, and was living in some

[1] A. Maclaren, *The God of the Amen*, 81.   [2] J. Ossian Davies.

miserable court or alley, made for a time great efforts to keep that court or alley clean. But gradually, day by day, the efforts of that poor woman were less and less vigorous, until in a few weeks she became accustomed to, and contented with, the state of filth which surrounded her, and made no further efforts to remove it. The atmosphere she lived in was too strong for her.[1]

¶ A light-hearted lad passes through a wood, and thoughtlessly strikes a young oak sapling. The scar heals over, but when that tree is cut down a thousand years afterwards, that blow is written on its heart. As heedlessly he puts the first thought of impurity into the soul of another, innocent up to that moment; and, owing to that thought perhaps, that soul is lost. "I've seen pretty clearly," says Adam Bede in George Eliot's story, "ever since I could cast up a sum, that you can never do what is wrong without breeding sin and trouble, more than you can ever see. It's like a bit of bad workmanship; you never see the end of the mischief it will do."[2]

II.

THEIR CAUSE.

1. One hidden and mysterious source may be found in *heredity*. Over and above the animal nature that we all possess, and that too often possesses us, are acquired tendencies to certain forms of evil which we have inherited from our ancestors. No man knows what hereditary predispositions are flowing in his veins. Peculiar appetites and sensibilities are transmitted from generation to generation; and here is the secret explanation of many a man's lapse into evil courses. The taint is in his blood. Many a man is a very powder magazine of violent passions stored up within him from forgotten progenitors. And when he goes where sparks are flying there is a sudden and fearful explosion, and everybody wonders!

¶ You may carry in your system the germs of certain diseases for years without suspecting the fact. The germs lie dormant until conditions favourable to their vitalization and development arise, and then comes the outbreak. So there are latent in many men's blood susceptibilities to the power of drink and lust which no one suspects, and which they themselves suspect least of any.

[1] E. J. Hardy.　　　　　[2] *Ibid.*

But when they are thrown into certain society, or placed under certain conditions, the fever that was in their veins breaks out and runs its course, and the end is collapse and death. It is sad to reflect that the drunkard or the libertine may transmit to his children and his children's children his passions, but that he cannot transmit his *remorse*.[1]

2. Another cause of hidden sin is *a blunt conscience*. Secret sins arise from inadequate religious knowledge, and neglect of religious thought and instruction not infrequently explains this defect of knowledge. Secret sins arise from the fact that passions which are antagonistic to keen intellectual and religious susceptibility are cherished, and passion is always more or less under the control of the will. Secret sins arise through association with men whose common frailties blind us to our own; and it is at our own choice that we enter into these associations, or, at least, that we suffer ourselves to be so completely absorbed by them.

¶ The Arctic fox, it is said, assumes a white fur in the winter months, so that it may pass undetected over the snows. When the spring comes, and the brown earth reappears, it sheds these white hairs and assumes a fur the colour of the earth over which it moves. Many fishes have markings that resemble the sand or gravel above which they make their haunts. You may watch for hours, and till they move you are unable to recognize their presence. The bird that broods on an exposed nest is never gaily coloured. However bright the plumage of its mate, it is always attired in feathers that match its surroundings, if it has to fulfil these dangerous domestic duties. Large numbers of insects are so tinted as to be scarcely distinguishable from the leaves and flowers amidst which they live. One insect has the power of assuming the appearance of a dried twig. And is there not something very much like this in the sphere of human conduct? Our sins blend with the idiosyncrasies of the age and disguise themselves. Of course we do not sin in loud, flashing colours, if we make any pretension to piety at least. Our sins always perfectly compose with the background of our surroundings. As a rule, they are sins into which we fall in common with men we esteem, men who have established a hold upon our affections, men whose sagacity we trust, and who by their excellence in some things lead us to think very lightly of the moral errors they illustrate in other things.[2]

[1] J. Halsey, *The Spirit of Truth*, 288.
[2] T. G. Selby, *The Imperfect Angel*, 150.

3. Still more, *self-love* too often conceals from conscience the sins it ought to judge and to condemn. Conscience is a judicial and not an inquisitorial faculty, and it pronounces judgment only on what it sees and knows. If we choose deliberately to cover over or to disguise the real state of our hearts, conscience will certainly fail to judge us as we ought to be judged.

¶ It is said that Catherine of Russia, when journeying through some of the most desolate and miserable parts of her dominion, ordered painted villages to be erected on certain points of the road in which she was travelling, so that the country might not look so cheerless and deserted. And just in like manner self-love deludes us by hiding the reality from us, so that we seem to be better than we really are. It will call sin by another name, so that it no longer seems to be sin. The saddest imperfections often masquerade in stolen garments, so as to disguise their own evil nature. Avarice, for example, ceases to be regarded as a sin when self-love declares it is thrift.[1]

4. Sin is hidden, because *the restraints of society hold it in check*. Anger, pride, malice, selfishness, deceit of our hearts are checked in their manifestations by the influences of society and of early habit. Therefore we do not estimate them in their true light.

¶ The traveller in the White Mountains remarks that the valley at the foot of Mount Washington is strewn with enormous boulders of granite, which have been loosened from year to year from the great overhanging cliff, and, carrying destruction in their course, have tumbled to the very spot where they now lie. If you inquire what force has separated these immense masses from the parent rock you find that behind the green fringe of foliage which waves so luxuriantly in summer, and hidden in the crevices of the mountain, are pools of water which the winter frosts change to ice. Expanding as they freeze, these little pools of limpid water have power to tear the solid rock asunder, and hurl its gigantic fragments down the mountain-side. So there are destructive powers lurking in the soul—powers which are latent during the short summer of life, but which are competent, when all restraint upon them is removed, to make the fairest seeming nature a shattered wreck. The real destructive power of sin is in great part hidden now, but it will be *felt* when the sunshine of God's grace comes to an end, and eternal winter settles down upon the soul.[2]

[1] G. S. Barrett, *Musings for Quiet Hours*, 25.
[2] A. H. Strong, *Miscellanies*, ii. 366.

III.

THEIR CURE.

1. *We must realize that God sees the things to which we are blind.*—All our latent defects are open to the eye of the Searcher of hearts. The awful beam from His presence strikes across our self-purified and self-sifted life, and detects thoughts and solicitations and unwholesome sympathies that are the hidden and deeply-folded cells in which sin conceives itself. Divine law is sent forth to enlighten all who are docile to its monitions, to search into the deep places of action, and to create a perfect inward as well as outward righteousness. Its "going forth," like that of the sun, with which the Psalmist links it in his comparison, "is from the end of the heaven," and its "circuit unto the ends of it: and there is nothing hid from the heat thereof." And as this clear and ever-growing light from God is projected across our souls, we come to feel that we are full of secret corruptions,— corruptions fraught with peril both to ourselves and to others; corruptions which, unless cleansed by continuous and immeasurable grace from God, must prevail at last over the things that are lovely and of good report. Under this widening horizon of penetrating light, we come to suspect that there may yet be undisclosed corruptions within us, and we are constrained to cry that the purifying power of God may go deeper than our own knowledge,—deep as God's knowledge, deep as a beam of that mysterious light which, unapproachable itself, yet approaches and enters into the soul of all things. "Thou hast set our iniquities before thee, our secret sins in the light of thy countenance."

> My smile is bright, my glance is free,
>   My voice is calm and clear;
> Dear friend, I seem a type to thee
>   Of holy love and fear.
>
> But I am scann'd by eyes unseen,
>   And these no saint surround;
> They mete what is by what has been,
>   And joy the lost is found.

Erst my good Angel shrank to see
My thoughts and ways of ill;
And now he scarce dare gaze on me,
Scar-seam'd and crippled still.[1]

¶ When in 1896 the engineers were planning the foundations
for the Williamsburg Bridge, New York, the deepest of their
twenty-two borings was a hundred and twelve feet below high
water. Steel drills had indicated bed-rock from twelve to twenty
feet higher than was the actual case; the diamond drill, however,
showed the supposed bed-rock to be merely a deposit of boulders.
So the diamond drill of God pierces our self-delusions, detects the
fallacy of our assumptions, proves what we thought sterling to
be only stones of emptiness, discloses the very truth of things
far down the secret places of the soul.[2]

¶ So rapidly can the human body be radiographed that
snapshots can be taken with the rays, and Dr. Rosenthal, of
Munich, has photographed the heart of a living person in one-
tenth of a second. Now, this lightning picture of a human heart
fairly represents those flashes of insight we occasionally get into
our essential self, of which the physical organ is a metaphor. At
the back of our reasonings, feelings, and volitions is a world
unknown, except as it is revealed by glimpses and expressed in
guesses. But He who made us in the lowest parts of the earth
comprehends us and knows us altogether. "For thou, even thou
only, knowest the hearts of all the children of men." As the
whole physical universe is known to the Almighty Spirit, as He
calls every star by name, and inhabits every province; so the
rational universe is displayed to the Divine gaze, and there is
no mystery of body, brain, or spirit to Him. "There is no
creature that is not manifest in his sight: but all things are
naked and laid open before the eyes of him with whom we have
to do."[3]

2. *We must welcome the light of His presence.*—The spaces
between the windows of one of the rooms of a famous palace are
hung with mirrors, and by this device the walls are made just as
luminous as the windows through which the sunshine streams.
Every square inch of surface seems to reflect the light. Let our
natures be like that, no point of darkness anywhere, the whole

[1] Cardinal Newman, *Verses on Various Occasions*, 68.
[2] W. L. Watkinson, *The Fatal Barter*, 103.
[3] *Ibid.* 98.

realm of the inward life an unchequered blaze of moral illumination.

¶ It is said that all organic germs found in the atmosphere cease a few miles out at sea. Air taken from the streets or the warehouses of the city yields large numbers of these germs. The air circulating through the ship in dock is charged with them. After the shore has been left behind, the air taken from the deck is pure, but they are still found in air taken from the hold. After a few days at sea the air on deck and in the hold alike yields no trace of these microscopic spores that are closely connected with disease. Let us be ever breathing the spirit of God's love. Let us get away from the din and dust and turmoil of life, out upon that infinite sea of love that is without length or breadth or depth, and our secret faults will vanish away, and we shall by and by stand without offence in the presence of God's glory.[1]

3. *We must educate the conscience.*—One of the surest ways of making conscience more sensitive is always to consult it and always to obey it. If you neglect it, and let it prophesy to the wind, it will stop speaking before long. Herod could not get a word out of Christ when he " asked him many questions " because for years he had not cared to hear His voice. And conscience, like the Lord of conscience, will hold its peace after men have neglected its speech. You can pull the clapper out of the bell upon the rock, and then, though the waves may dash, there will not be a sound, and the vessel will drive straight on to the black teeth that are waiting for it. Educate your conscience by obeying it, and by getting into the habit of bringing everything to its bar.

¶ Within recent times we have heard of the elaboration of instruments that may reveal new worlds of sound to us, as marvellous as the worlds of form revealed by the microscope. It is said that no man ever knows what his own voice is like till he hears it in Mr. Edison's phonograph. We are told of another instrument by which the breathings of insects are made audible. The medical expert may yet be able to detect the faintest murmur of abnormal sound in the system that indicates the approach of disease. Ingenious appliances will register for us variations of temperature that are too fine for our dull senses to perceive. We have stepped from time to time into new realms of interest and knowledge and sensation, and undiscovered realms yet lie before

[1] T. G. Selby, *The Imperfect Angel*, 157.

us. To the eye and to the ear of the Maker all these worlds have been open from the beginning. They are just coming into our horizon with the development of science. And in the same way there must be the growth within us of a fine moral science, that will bring home to our apprehension the most obscure of our secret faults.[1]

¶ A lady missionary in Algiers heard this prayer from a little Arab girl one day, " O God, take away all the ugly weeds from my heart, and plant lovely flowers there, that it may be always a garden green and beautiful for Jesus." This is just what we all want—the weeds of evil uprooted, and the flowers of good adorning the soul.[2]

4. *We must practise vigilance.*—"What I say unto you, I say unto all, Watch." Let us guard well the ingoings and outgoings of life. Let us "keep our hearts with all diligence," and double-sentry the "door of our lips." Let us turn our fear into a prayer, and our prayer into a purpose. "Search me, O God, and know my heart, try me and know my thoughts, and see if there be any wicked way in me, and lead me in the way everlasting." Let us indite our 19th Psalm, that we may never have to write our 51st. That we may avoid error, let us learn to discriminate error; and that we may discriminate error—for to discern our faults is half the battle in correcting them—let us cultivate conscience and set before us the most perfect ideals; ever considering Him who, bearing our nature, yet "did no sin, neither was guile found in his mouth."[3]

Great were his fate who on the earth should linger,
    Sleep for an age and stir himself again,
Watching thy terrible and fiery finger
    Shrivel the falsehood from the souls of men.

Oh that thy steps among the stars would quicken!
    Oh that thine ears would hear when we are dumb!
Many the hearts from which the hope shall sicken,
    Many shall faint before thy kingdom come.

Lo for the dawn, (and wherefore wouldst thou screen it?)
    Lo with what eyes, how eager and alone,
Seers for the sight have spent themselves, nor seen it,
    Kings for the knowledge, and they have not known.

[1] T. G. Selby, *The Imperfect Angel*, 141.   [2] J. Ossian Davies.
[3] J. Halsey, *The Spirit of Truth*, 290.

Times of that ignorance with eyes that slumbered
　　Seeing he saw not, till the days that are,
Now, many multitudes whom none had numbered,
　　Seek him and find him, for he is not far.[1]

¶ *Slight Ailments* is the title of a work by a distinguished
physician. Its design is to describe the symptoms of incipient
maladies, to show how serious ailments arise out of slight ones,
and to direct the treatment that these ominous signs demand.
It is unnecessary to say that this work is popular; that it has
gone through many editions. If we have the slightest reason
to suspect ourselves of being unsound, if we discover any tendency
in our constitution toward one or another malady, we at once
take the matter in hand, whatever may be the cost or incon-
venience. "Despise no new accident to your body, but take
opinion of it," writes Lord Bacon. How readily we accept his
advice! We do not delay until the disturbing symptoms give
place to decided maladies like cancer or consumption. We are
admonished by the novel weakness, the unusual pain, the nebulous
sign, and satisfy ourselves as to what the "accident" signifies,
and how it may best be dealt with. Did we not act thus, we
should before long bitterly reflect upon ourselves. Ought we not
to follow the same course touching the appearance of sinister signs
in our spiritual and moral life? to note any new accident of the
soul, and ask opinion of it?[2]

5. *We must ask God to cleanse us.*—"*Clear* thou me from
secret faults." And there is present in that word, if not exclusively, at least predominantly, the idea of a judicial acquittal,
so that the thought of the first clause of this verse seems rather
to be that of pronouncing guiltless, or forgiving, than that of
delivering from the power of. But both, no doubt, are included
in the idea, as both, in fact, come from the same source and in
response to the same cry. And so we may be sure that, though
our eye does not go down into the dark depths, God's eye goes,
and that where He looks He looks to pardon, if we come to Him
through Jesus Christ our Lord.

The Psalmist's sense of the fact that there could be no indiscriminate salvation through Church or human organization or
external and vicarious service was just as clear as that of St. Paul

---

[1] F. W. H. Myers, *Saint Paul*.
[2] W. L. Watkinson, *The Fatal Barter*, 131.

himself. He felt that he could not be effectually cleansed by his relation to the theocracy, or the national sacrifices, or the visible system and service of religion, in connexion with which he was perhaps already a leading figure. The ceremonial offering did not necessarily bring the purification of the spirit. He must be cleansed by a virtue coming down from God and through God's unknown sacrifice, and not by a power going up from himself and through his own trespass-offering. The law, with its frequent and curiously graded sacrifices, had been but a remembrancer of certain selected sins, and had led him to see that all corruption, in its wider ravage and more insidious penetration, must be purged by a Divine process.

¶ The only way for us to be delivered from the dominion of our unconscious faults is to increase the depth and closeness and constancy of our communion with Jesus Christ; and then they will drop away from us. Mosquitoes and malaria, the one unseen in their minuteness, and the other, "the pestilence that walketh in darkness," haunt the swamps. Go up on the hill-top, and neither of them is found. So if we live more and more on the high levels, in communion with our Master, there will be fewer and fewer of these unconscious sins buzzing and stinging and poisoning our lives, and more and more will His grace conquer and cleanse.[1]

¶ The consummate ability of Stas, the Belgian chemist, is celebrated because he "eliminated from his chemicals every trace of that pervasive element, sodium, so thoroughly that even its spectroscopic detection was impossible." But such is the efficacy of Divine grace that it can eliminate so thoroughly every trace of that pervasive and persistent element known as sin that we may be presented before the throne holy and unreprovable and without blemish. That the sincere may attain this purification, they are prepared to pass through the hot fires of bitter and manifold discipline.[2]

[1] A. Maclaren, *The God of the Amen*, 84.
[2] W. L. Watkinson, *The Fatal Barter*, 105.

THE MINISTRY OF SURPRISE.

LITERATURE.

Black (H.), *Christ's Service of Love*, 209.
Martin (A.), *Winning the Soul*, 199.
Morrison (G. H.), *Flood-Tide*, 252.
,,   ,, *The Return of the Angels*, 143.
Philip (A.), *The Father's Hand*, 157.

The Ministry of Surprise.

Thou preventest him with the blessings of goodness.—Ps. xxi. 3.

1. This is a companion Psalm to the one that goes before it. They both deal with the same general situation, the outbreak of national war, but differ in this respect, that while the first is a Psalm of prayer before the people go forth to the battle, the second is a Psalm of thanksgiving after they have returned victorious. In the former we are to conceive them gathered in the Temple, the king at their head, to entreat the aid of their fathers' God, that in the hour of danger He may send them help out of the sanctuary and strength from His holy hill. But in the latter the danger is past. The king's arms have been successful. His enemies have been scattered. He has re-entered the city gates with his exultant army, and made his triumphal way through the streets, and now once more, as is most meet, stands before the Lord, who has given him the victory, while priests and people make the sacred courts ring again with their shouts of thanksgiving and joy. "The king shall joy in thy strength, O Lord; and in thy salvation how greatly shall he rejoice! Thou hast given him his heart's desire, and hast not withholden the request of his lips. . . . For the king trusteth in the Lord, and through the mercy of the most High he shall not be moved. Be thou exalted, Lord, in thine own strength: so will we sing and praise thy power."

2. The gist of the text is that God's wise grace can outstrip the present stage of our experience, can pass on into the future, and be busy on our behalf before we arrive there. He not only attends us with the blessings of His goodness, He "prevents" us with them as well—goes on before and sows the days to come with mercy, so that we find it waiting us when we arrive, and

reap—or may reap—nothing but goodness as we go. It is a profound, most comfortable truth for us to rest our minds on.

¶ There is in theology a term, still used, " prevenient grace," meaning the grace which acts on a sinner *before* repentance inducing him to repent, the grace by which he attains faith and receives power to will the good. Milton, when describing the repentance of Adam and Eve in *Paradise Lost*, when they confessed their sin and prayed for forgiveness, puts it :

> Thus they in lowliest plight repentant stood
> Praying, for from the Mercy-seat above
> Prevenient Grace descending had remov'd
> The stony from their hearts, and made new flesh
> Regenerate grow instead.

But we must not limit God's prevenient grace to the act of repentance, to the steps which lead up to the consciousness of sonship with God.[1]

I.

A Prepared World.

1. When we come upon the stage of existence we find that the world has been prepared for us. "Thou hast formed the world to be inhabited" is one of the deep sayings of the prophets. For whatever ends the world has been created, it has been fashioned upon the lines of man. It has been decked in beauty for the human eye; covered with sustenance for the human frame; stored with energies that would have slept unused but for the large intelligence of man. Does the newborn child need to be clothed? Sheep have been pasturing upon the hills. Does the newborn child need to be fed? Mysterious changes have been preparing food. And does the newborn child need to be warmed? Why then, unnumbered centuries ago, the leaves were falling with the sunshine in them, that to-day we might have summer on the hearth. Not into an unprepared world is the little infant flung. Nature never calls, "I am not ready, nor can I support this gift of a new life." Nature has been getting ready for millenniums, since she awoke from the primeval chaos; and in her depths, and on her hills of pasturage, has been preparing for this very hour.

[1] H. Black, *Christ's Service of Love*, 210.

¶ We are rising to the conviction that we are a part of nature, and so a part of God ; that the whole creation—the One and the Many and All-One—is travailing together toward some great end ; and that now, after ages of development, we have at length become conscious portions of the great scheme, and can co-operate in it with knowledge and with joy. We are no aliens in a stranger universe governed by an outside God ; we are parts of a developing whole, all enfolded in an embracing and inter-penetrating love, of which we too, each to other, sometimes experience the joy too deep for words.[1]

¶ There are inhospitable regions, in which the oak cannot flourish, in which the hardy pine cannot live, and in which the mountain heather finds no place, but yet some variety of corn can be made to grow, if man can live there at all. If you were to ascend from the sea-level to the sides of the high mountains, or to proceed from the swamps of China to the prairies of America, or from the burning plains of India to the Arctic regions, you would find at the different levels, or in the different latitudes, entirely different kinds of plants, with one exception ; the corn plant you would find everywhere. In the tropical regions you would find rice ; in the bleak north, oats and rye ; in parts of the western world not congenial to wheat, you would find maize, while similar parts of Europe produce barley. So carefully has God provided for the needs of man.

2. These bounties of God come to us at a great cost. Take a single grain of corn, and remember that it cost the Creator thousands of years of forethought and labour. We know how useless it is to sow wheat on hard clay or solid rock. Soil needs first to be made, so God sets in motion the forces of rain, frost, and rivers. He sets the great glaciers grinding over the granite, sandstone, and limestone. And that took thousands of years. If God had not laboured for ages, not even the tiniest grain of corn could have existed to-day. But, further, the God who made the soil sends thousands of rays of sunshine to ripen the corn. And for every ray that we see, there are ten invisible heat rays. Now before these rays can begin their work, they have a journey to make of more than ninety millions of miles. And God keeps these messengers continually flying through the sky. He spares no labour and counts no cost to provide royally for His children.

[1] Sir Oliver Lodge.

II.

A Prepared Home.

1. Home is the child's whole world.   Within the family circle lie his earth and heaven, and through the medium of its life and fortunes the larger provision accumulated out of doors is gradually interpreted and conveyed to him.   To have first drawn breath, then, in a truly Christian home is to have been born to an inheritance which not all the world's wealth could buy.   To have been received into this world by one whose first feeling was that of trembling thankfulness to God, mingled with fear lest she should be unworthy of the trust of bringing up a child for Him; to have grown up within walls where He from whom every fatherhood in heaven and earth is named, was ever acknowledged supreme and reverently loved and served; to have been led to His footstool early, and to have had His word printed on the mind; to have been taught to rest on the day of rest, and to "love the habitation of God's house"; to have been trained in early impressionable years, for the most part unconsciously, under the influence of those around, as well as of the men and women that come about a good man's fireside and the books that lie on a good man's table, —in all this what splendid provision for all who are fortunate enough to fall heirs to it.   Truly God "prevented us with blessings of goodness."   Our lot was stored with them beforehand. We were cradled in spiritual profusion which a Loving Care had been long preparing, as a mother's choicest appointments will be ready for her babe long before it is put into her hands.

¶ Sometimes there comes a visitor to see us of whose coming we had no anticipation.   He has been long abroad, and for years we have not seen him, until one day he is standing at our door. But it is not thus that into Christian homes there come the joy and mystery of childhood.   The child is born in a prepared place, and love has been very busy with its welcome.   And prayers go heavenward with a new intensity, and some now pray who never prayed before; and fountains of tenderness are opened up, and feelings that were scarce suspected once; and God is nearer and His hand is more wonderful, and all the future has a different music, and that is why home is as a type of heaven; it is a prepared place for a prepared people. Thou goest before us with the blessings of goodness.[1]

> O'er a new joy this day we bend,
> Soft power from heaven our souls to lift;
> A wondering wonder Thou dost lend
> With loan outpassing gift—
>
> A little child. She sees the sun—
> Once more incarnates thy old law:
> One born of two, two born in one,
> Shall into one three draw.
>
> But is there no day creeping on
> Which I should tremble to renew?
> I thank Thee, Lord, for what is gone—
> Thine is the future too!
>
> And are we not at home in Thee,
> And all this world a visioned show,
> That, knowing what Abroad is, we
> What Home is too may know?[2]

¶ Mr. Moody could never speak of those early days of want and adversity without the most tender references to that brave mother whose self-sacrifice and devotion had sacredly guarded the home entrusted to her care. When, at the age of ninety, her life-voyage ended, she entered the Haven of Rest, her children, her children's children, and an entire community rose up to call her blessed. And well she deserved the praise they gave her, for she had wisely and discreetly discharged the duties God had placed upon her, and, entering the presence of her Master, could render a faithful account of the stewardship of motherhood. To rule a household of seven sturdy boys and two girls, the eldest twelve years old, required no ordinary tact and sound judgment, but so discreet was this loyal mother that to the very end she made "home" the most loved place on earth to her family, and so trained her children as to make them a blessing to society.

"For nearly fifty years I have been coming back to North-field," said Mr. Moody, long after that little circle had been broken up, "and I have always been glad to get back. When I get within fifty miles of home I grow restless and walk up and down

---

[1] G. H. Morrison, *The Return of the Angels*, 146.
[2] George MacDonald, *Organ Songs*.

the car. It seems as if the train will never get to Northfield. When I come back after dark I always look to see the light in mother's window." [1]

¶ The purest-minded of all pagans and all Emperors devotes the whole of the first book of his *Meditations* to a grateful consideration of all that he owed to others in his youth. Such humble gratitude is the mark of a great soul. He goes over the list of all who helped him by counsel or example. "The example of my grandfather, Verus, gave me a good disposition, not prone to anger. By the recollection of my father's character, I learned to be both modest and manly. My mother taught me to have regard for religion, to be generous and open-handed. The philosopher Sextus recommended good-humour to me. Alexander the Grammarian taught me not to be finically critical about words. I learned from Catulus not to slight a friend for making a remonstrance." And so on through a long list of benefits which his sweet humble mind acknowledged, finishing up with : "I have to thank the gods that my grandfathers, parents, sister, preceptors, relations, friends, and domestics were almost all of them persons of probity." [2]

2. We are ushered also into a society that was prepared. A child's education is a great deal more than a matter of lesson books and a few years' schooling. The use he is able to make of books and schooling depends on the nature he brings to them and on the surroundings among which he is born; and these again depend largely on what manner of persons those were who went before him. Education is the development of manhood, and this is determined always, on the one hand, by the stock the man springs from, and, on the other, by the intellectual and moral atmosphere he grows up in. So that in literal truth it may be said about each of us that Providence began our education not one but many hundreds of years since. All down the generations the lot we should in due time stand in has been growing more goodly and favourable, until at this particular stage in the history of the race and in our own greatly privileged land, what amelioration of manners, what elevation of morals, what enrichment of social relationships, what increase of knowledge, in a word, what multiplied spiritual wealth, opportunity, and stimulus, do we not

[1] W. R. Moody, *Life of Dwight L. Moody*, 26.
[2] H. Black, *Christ's Service of Love*, 213.

inherit! We are the heirs of the ages, and are born rich indeed. We reap where we had not strawed. Why, the very language in which we speak to one another—the medium of communion between man and man—is a legacy of the past to us, and in our earliest broken syllables we unconsciously acknowledge our indebtedness to it.

¶ The holy Andrewes before he comes to give thanks for salvation begins with what is more fundamental still. "I thank Thee," he writes, "that I was born a living soul, and not senseless matter; a man and not a brute; civilized not savage; free not a slave; liberally educated, and endowed with gifts of nature and worldly good."[1]

3. It cannot be that God is absent from the most untoward environment. There are children born into the world for whom you would say little preparation had been made by any one. Nobody seems to want them here. It is scanty care they receive from any one. They are left to grow as they may; and live, one hardly knows how; and are reared with squalor before their eyes, and coarseness in their ears, and evil everywhere. Is God beforehand with them with the blessings of goodness? Surely He is; for, after all, the world is His, nor can man's uttermost labour in evil altogether obliterate or quench His everywhere present and active loving-kindness. One thing is certain; that He has the strangest ways of blending His mercy even with the most untoward environment.

¶ I have seen little children exposed to early influences which you would have thought must inevitably have proved fatal to any seeds of goodness they brought with them into the world; and these things—drunkenness, vileness, murderous brutality, and all the unspeakable horrors that make up the daily round in a drunkard's home—were only blessed to them. There is no limit to the power of Him who overrules all things, and whose face the angels of little children do always behold, out of evil to bring good. "In him the fatherless find mercy." Let us admit that He deals with many—or allows them to be dealt with by circumstances—very strangely, very sorely. Nevertheless, these circumstances too are under His Hand. Who shall say that they are ever sufficient to blind any soul born into God's world outright to its inheritance or quite to put it beyond His reach?[2]

---

[1] A. Martin, *Winning the Soul*, 204.   [2] *Ibid.* 202.

¶ In his ballad "The Three Graves" Coleridge puts this story into the mouth of an old sexton. A young farmer, paying his addresses to the daughter of a widow, finds that the widow herself desires to marry him. When he asks in due time that the day of the marriage may be fixed, the mother maliciously depreciates the character of her daughter, and confesses her own passion. Finding herself thrust aside, she kneels down and solemnly prays for a curse upon her daughter and the lover she had accepted. A cloud hangs over the wedding, and bride and bridegroom find themselves strangely chilled and depressed. On Ash-Wednesday the widow goes to church, and takes her place by the side of her daughter's friend, who has helped forward the marriage, and curses her together with the others. Under the haunting influence of that curse the three people fade away, and, within a few short months, fill graves side by side in the country churchyard. The essence of the ballad story is expressed in the lines :

> Beneath the foulest mother's curse
> No child could ever thrive.

That conception fits a pagan condition of society in which, for both temporal and spiritual things, the power of the parent is absolute. But it makes into an almighty fiat the cry of the blood of Abel, and is untrue to the spirit of the gospel. None can curse child or neighbour into hopeless distress in either this or the coming life. He who opens and shuts the gates of blessedness has not surrendered the keys into unworthy hands.[1]

III.

A Prepared Inheritance.

1. What have we that we have not received? Behind us lie the labours and sufferings and sacrifices of the noblest, and we have entered into their labours. We have a rich inheritance, which can be described only as the blessings of goodness. The tree of our life has its roots deep in the soil and the subsoil of history. We are not only the heirs of all the ages, but the heirs of God's grace through all the ages. God's providence is only another name for God's grace, and His providence did not begin

[1] T. G. Selby, *The Divine Craftsman*, 90.

to us merely at the hour of birth. Every prophet, and every man of faith, has felt in some degree at some time of intense insight that he has been under a foreordaining, a loving purpose before birth, before history, from the very foundation of the world. God's grace began with him long before he was born, and prepared his place for him, and went before him with the blessings of goodness. Time would fail for any of us to tell all that we owe to the past, all the debt in which we stand to preceding generations, not only for temporal mercies, but even for the very intellectual and spiritual atmosphere into which we have been born, and in which we have been reared. We have a spiritual climate, as well as a geographical; and in it we have had our place prepared for us. The blessings of God's goodness have gone before us, and can in many lines be clearly seen by every enlightened mind and conscience and heart. The liberty we enjoy politically and religiously has been bought and paid for by others. The knowledge which we hold so cheap was dearly acquired by the race. Every advance in social organiza- tion which is to us now as our birthright was attained at great cost.

As a man deepens so his longings deepen, till they reach to the Infinite and the Eternal. And the strange thing is, that as these cravings alter, and rise from the transient to the enduring, so God is ever there before us, with His prepared answer to our quest. We crave for light, and the sun and moon are there, and they have been shining for unnumbered ages. We crave for love, and love is not of yesterday. It is as ancient as the heart-beat of humanity. We come to crave for pardon and for peace and for unbroken fellowship with God; and all that, in Jesus Christ our Lord, has been made ready for us long ago.

2. God's prevenient goodness is very conspicuous in the privileges of the Gospel. Our spiritual needs are all anticipated by an ample provision. And that is signified by our baptism. God's goodness came to a point there, so to speak, and was set forth with gracious impressiveness. For baptism is the seal of our lineage and signifies that we come of the elect stock. It is the Christian circumcision, and denotes that we belong to the community of the faithful, whose life is sustained by the living

Lord, and have our right and portion among them in all the goodness He has introduced into human life.

¶ To me one of the surest proofs that the Bible is indeed the Word of God is the way in which it goes before us through all the changing experience of life. Other books we leave behind. They were before us once; they are behind us now. We have outgrown them. We have reached an hour when they were powerless to cheer and guide. But always as we battle through the years, and break through the thicket into another glade, a little ahead of us, with eyes of love, we descry the figure of the Word of God. It is before us in the day of triumph. It is before us in the hour of fall. In every new temptation it is there; in every joy, in every bitterness. We move into the shadow and the heartbreak, or into the sunshine with the play of waters, and yet the Bible understands it all, and is there to meet us when we come. We are not above it when we scale the heavens, nor beneath it when we make our bed in hell. It is always a little higher than our highest. It is always a little deeper than our deepest. And that to me is an argument unanswerable that God is in Scripture as in no other book. It is not so much that *I* find *Him* there. It is rather that there *He* finds *me*.[1]

¶ Geologists find the presence of tropical species in latitudes now subjected to the rigours of a cold climate, and arctic forms in regions at present belonging to the temperate zone. In endeavouring to explain these anomalies of climate, scientists in past days went in search of vast cosmic changes, such as an alteration in the position of the terrestrial axis, a diminution in the amount of solar heat, or a gradual cooling of the earth's crust; but modern scientists are satisfied to explain these climatic conditions as the result of a familiar agency close at hand, of which we have daily experience. A genial current of water or air deflected toward our coast is, in their opinion, sufficiently powerful to create the difference of temperature which rescues us from the rigours of Lapland and fills our island with summer's pageantry and autumn's pride. So to give the nations of the earth a sweet summer for the long dark winter of their discontent God makes the stream of His grace to flow through our sanctuaries, schools, and homes, silently blessing and enriching human life.[2]

[1] G. H. Morrison, *The Return of the Angels*, 150.
[2] W. L. Watkinson, *The Fatal Barter*, 37.

IV.

A God who is always Beforehand.

1. God is before at every stage of this life. Whatever good we have gained to ourselves, there is a better still before us. The best is always in store. We go from strength to strength. And if we have an eye for the working of His Hand at all, we need never fail to find the traces of God's power marking out beforehand the path in which we go.

(1) *God is before us to enrich and to purify our joys.*—Indeed those joys are of God's own making. They arrive we know not whence or how. They come as a surprise. We had not looked for them, or learned perhaps to desire them. And then they befell us, and woke our nature into music, and made all life new. Is it not so for the most part that our great joys have come to us? the choice gifts of Providence? the signal blessings of grace? And what does this mean but just that the Divine loving-kindness had prepared for us such mercy, and then at the fitting moment laid it bare? He who has planned our path is in ambush for us, and oftenest it is at some unexpected turn of the way that His goodness stands disclosed. We stumble upon His bounty ere we know, and find to our surprise how long it had been stored for us. Does not the greatest of all gifts, the Gift Unspeakable, at times arrive upon us in this way, hiding Himself in some unlooked-for experience, then striding into our life suddenly? And of other gifts also, the arrival is, as a rule, as unexpected, and betokens a preparation we had not thought of. Our path has been sown with goodness beforehand, and we reap the harvest of it as we go.

¶ I am filled with shame and confusion when I reflect, on one hand, upon the great favours which God has bestowed and is still unceasingly bestowing upon me; and, on the other, upon the ill use I have made of them, and my small advancement in the way of perfection. Since, by His mercy, He gives us still a little time, let us begin in earnest, let us redeem the time that is lost, let us return with a whole-hearted trust to this Father of Mercies, who is always ready to receive us into His loving arms. Let us renounce, and renounce generously, with single heart, for the love of Him, all that is not His; He deserves infinitely more. Let us think of Him unceasingly; in Him let us put all our confidence. I doubt not but that we shall soon experience the effects of it in receiving the abundance of His grace, with which we can do all things, and without which we can do nought but sin.[1]

¶ Dr. John Brown ("Rab") had a favourite expression, which he was constantly using—"Unexpectedness." There is much of that in life. It plays a large part in our training. Kindness comes from unexpected quarters. So does unkindness. "It was *thou*, a man mine equal, my guide and mine acquaintance." It is, as we say, the unexpected that happens. The seemingly impossible comes to pass. Often what we plan fails, and what we expect deceives, while what we neither plan nor expect occurs. The forces that work for us and against us do more than we anticipate. If some men disappoint us painfully, others do so agreeably. The timid Nicodemus was one of the foremost at Jesus' tomb. There are flowers in the desert. The beauty of holiness blooms in unexpected places. What we lean upon breaks, what seems broken stands. Ananias was a failure, Saul became Paul. How often our fears are disappointed, our hopes surpassed, our difficulties removed. The whole of life is a succession of surprises breaking its monotony. It is like a winding road, where every turn discloses something new that beguiles and draws us on. There are many of what Faber sings of—"novelties of love." You think, sometimes, that everything has been exhausted, and then God surprises you with a fresh gladness.[2]

¶ A critic of the oratorio "Elijah" has pointed out how, after apparently exhausting every combination of sound, Mendelssohn has given one more proof of his resource, by the weird effect of a single, long-sustained note. But what is a marvel in this consummate artist is only a suggestion of the fertility of God in every life. Amiel has been described as the master of the unexpected. It is God who is its true Master. It is He who is the true Giver of surprises. No two days are alike. Our life is like a series of dissolving views. Its fashion is ever changing. God, in providence, appeals to the strange and the varied. What every child of God feels about His kindnesses is that they are new every morning, and is it not quite as true that they are fresh every evening? Is there a day that we are not constrained to say, "Thou surprisest me with the blessings of goodness"?[3]

---

[1] Brother Lawrence, *The Practice of the Presence of God*, 48.
[2] A. Philip, *The Father's Hand*, 161.   [3] *Ibid.* 162.

¶ As I look back, and recall what is past—struggles which I have not chronicled here; doubts and inward conflicts which may not be written; hours of fierce anguish of spirit; moments in hell too awful and too sacred to be recorded; joys which, though brief, are yet joys for ever; tearful times of sowing which have yielded happy harvests; kindly teachings, both tender and severe, which experience has brought—I see life as education, wonderful and changeful, but full of a Divine purpose; replete with interest, and slowly revealing that Love is its origin and Love its end. Oh, brother man, to whom life seems dark and its purpose undecipherable, hold fast to the Loving Spirit! It will guide you into the heart of things. It will so fashion you after its own likeness that, when you awake to life's true significance, you will be satisfied.[1]

(2) *God is in front to assuage our sorrow.*—There are trials and sorrows which come to all in course of nature, and in regard to which, unless men and women are very rebellious, it is possible perhaps to see no little mercy and goodness assuaging their bitterness all through. But those which come athwart the course of nature, as it were; which no one could have foreseen, and nothing appears to justify; which only darken the world to men, and confound their judgment, and tempt their unbelief—what are we to say of these sorrows? They are, alas! not uncommon, and growing experience of life furnishes always fresh evidence of the forms they may take. Where men and women lie prostrate under them—their hearth perhaps left bare, the light of youthful promise perhaps quenched, perhaps worse sorrows still befalling them—what are you to expect them to feel and say in circumstances like these? Even if they believe, is it to be thought of that they are to look up to God and say, "These things too are good. Thou comest to meet me in them with the blessings of goodness"? Yet I have known one whose worldly all was, in a quite unlooked-for hour, swept away from her, and who, after a single moment's pause, said: "The Lord gave, the Lord hath taken away! Blessed be the name of the Lord!" I have known another whose home was suddenly left desolate, and the cherished hopes of years, and the early blossom of their fulfilment strewed in ruins, and all he said was, "I needed this." And just the other day I heard of one struck down at the outset of a most promising

[1] Bishop Boyd Carpenter, *Some Pages of My Life*, 332.

career and rendered helpless for the remainder of his days, yet who was able, almost at once, to accept his Father's will and to be content with it. Had not such humble trusting sufferers found the "blessings of goodness" in those dark providences that suddenly darkened round them and seemed to others to wreck their lives ?[1]

¶ Do we complain of the sorrows of life, classing them among the insoluble problems of existence ? We owe much of life's purest and happiest experiences to these sorrows. They can reveal unexpected good qualities ; they can draw human lives into sympathy with one another ; they can bridge over chasms which seemed to decree separation between soul and soul ; they can soften, refine, and elevate. Certainly, if I may speak from my own experience, hours of sorrow serve to show what an unsuspected wealth of kindness there is in the world. Here is a box, full of letters ! No, I am not going to open it, or drag forth the letters to view. Let them lie where they are, in sacred seclusion ; but they are witnesses to the width and depth of human sympathy. They are letters, written to me, by people of all classes, in one supreme, sorrowful hour of my life. Indeed, as I go about my room, and turn from one treasury of old letters to another, I realize that the sweetest and best of them are the offspring of sorrow in some form or another. Dear letters—some written by hands now cold—you still carry your message to my heart ! You are the constant witnesses that our capacities of heart could hardly have found scope to work, or space to grow, had not sorrow opened the door of opportunity.[2]

(3) *God is in front to strengthen us in temptation.*—Temptation is the constant element in our lives that every now and then gathers itself up into some "sore hour" which tries and shakes our fidelity to the roots. The temptation to unbelief, the temptation to self-indulgence, the temptation to be untrue to some heavy charge of which we would fain be quit—temptations such as these, and others like them, are no doubt dangerous, since we may give way in our weakness and fall ignobly. But with the temptation there is always a strength available for the bearing of it, of which, if we seize and are not overborne by it, nothing but good is the issue. Blessed is the man that endureth temptation. It strengthens the thews of the spirit. It toughens faith. It

---

[1] A. Martin, *Winning the Soul*, 209.
[2] Bishop Boyd Carpenter, *Some Pages of My Life*, 331.

teaches to pray. Temptation, if met and dealt with fairly, brings blessing into our life,—and nothing else.

¶ I would especially recommend you, as far as possible, to keep your mind fixed on our Blessed Lord's love, sympathy, and presence with you—not on the temptation. Put the temptation altogether aside. Don't think of it. Don't pray about it. Don't entangle yourself with it. But keep close to God, and feel sure that "He who is in us is greater than he that is in the world," and ask of our Blessed Lord that He would encompass you with His blessed angels, and so drive far away the evil spirit. Nothing is impossible with Him. Make proof of His power and love, and resolve, though you have failed before, now henceforth to fail no more. Let it encourage you to feel that every temptation overcome makes you stronger than you were before.[1]

> It was my Time. The old hour struck,
>   The ancient self without my leave—
> The old impatience came to pluck,
>   How briskly at my sleeve !
>
> And one stood crying within my heart—
>   (It was not I)—"The strait is sore.
> Thy strength is small. So yield. Thy part
>   Requires of thee no more."
>
> Then to the god we do not know,
>   Whose perfect name lies not within
> Our speech, all speechless in her woe
>   My spirit fled, crying—"This is sin.
>
> Against his coming many times
>   Thou gavest a secret, golden power."
> Then sudden as the lark that climbs,
>   I sang, and in that dolorous hour
>
> I stood with an immortal strength,
>   Looked out upon the dangerous way,
> And singing trod its bitter length,
>   Scatheless, as even a mortal may.[2]

(4) *God is beforehand to soften trouble.*—With our cares, anxieties, daily duty—whatever is commonest, whatever is most

---

[1] J. P. F. Davidson, *Letters of Spiritual Counsel*, 65.
[2] Mildred McNeal-Sweeney, *Men of No Land*, 56.

exceptional — God is before us to make them bearable, and profitable. All our experiences whatsoever bring good to us, if we will have it. Life is a constant discovery of light and help and blessing of every kind, which are waiting us beforehand. It is not by chance that these things come there. They have all the marks of a provision made by One who knows what things we have need of. Let us be sure of it and fear nothing. Faith should recognize a friend even when sense fears a foe. And of everything that comes to meet us our hearts should be greatly able to say: "This also cometh forth from the Lord, who is wonderful in counsel and excellent in working."

¶ As Washington Irving was passing a print window in Broadway, New York, one day, his eye rested on the beautiful engraving of *Christus Consolator*. He stopped and looked at it intently for some minutes, evidently much affected by the genuine inspiration of the artist in this remarkable representation of the Saviour as the consoler of sorrow-stricken humanity. His tears fell freely. "Pray get me that print," said he; "I must have it framed for my sitting-room." When he examined it more closely and found the artist's name, "It's by my old friend Ary Scheffer!" said he, remarking, further, that he had known Scheffer intimately, and knew him to be a true artist, but had not expected from him anything so excellent as this. I afterwards sent him the companion, *Christus Remunerator*; and the pair remained his daily companions till the day of his death. To me, the picture of Irving, amid the noise and bustle of noon in Broadway, shedding tears as he studied that little print, so feelingly picturing human sorrow and the Source of its alleviation, has always remained associated with the artist and his works. If Irving could enjoy wit and humour, and give that enjoyment to others, no other writer of books had a heart more tenderly sensitive than his to the sufferings and ills to which flesh is heir.[1]

2. God may be trusted to prepare our everlasting portion. "I go to prepare a place for you," said Christ. Whatever hell be, it is not man's environment. It was prepared for the devil and his angels. Whatever heaven be, it is man's native place, prepared for him from the foundation of the world. And then within that kingdom, all made ready, there is to be the individual touch—"I go to prepare a *place* for you." Of what kind that

[1] *George Palmer Putnam*, 268.

preparation is, eye hath not seen and ear hath never heard. All we know is that we shall be at home, and shall be welcomed by familiar hands. And if here the preparation is so wonderful that waits for the little child when it is born, how much more wonderful shall it all be when dying we are born into the glory. If love has been busy making ready here, shall love not also be making ready there? It is all our Father's house of many rooms, and we but pass from one into the other.

¶ Robertson took an active part in the work of the revival movement of 1859, sometimes holding services in the open air, in the neighbouring mining village of Dreghorn, and in the opposite direction, near the Eglinton furnaces. Mr. Andrew James Symington describes one of these outdoor services. "When we arrived at the manse," he says, "we found that Robertson had gone to address a meeting of miners in the open air at their works, about a mile off. We followed, and got among the crowd of listeners. The sermon was a remarkable one, as simple in its telling illustrations as it was powerful in the enforcement of truth. Rarely have I heard such an earnest flow of impassioned eloquence—one could have heard a pin fall—and the begrimed audience, spellbound, hung on his every word. The theme was 'mansions prepared,' and the subject was approached and opened up by an allusion to the coming November 'term' time—to those who were going to 'flit'—and he asked them if they had yet looked out other houses to which they would go. Then, as to our abode on earth, he said, we were all tenants-at-will. But our heavenly Father had prepared, not cabins or houses, but mansions for us. These were freely offered, and why should we anxiously look before us to the habitations of a few short years, and yet think so little of the heavenly mansions, prepared from before the foundation of the world for all who love Him, for Christ's sake, by Him who made these glorious stars, twinkling overhead in the blue? Then he pressed home the gospel offer, and, as an ambassador for heaven, invited all to come and receive their inheritance."[1]

> Can the bonds that make us here
>   Know ourselves immortal,
> Drop away, like foliage sear,
>   At life's inner portal?
> What is holiest below
> Must for ever live and grow.

[1] A. Guthrie, *Robertson of Irvine*, 156.

I shall love the angels well,
  After I have found them
In the mansions where they dwell,
  With the glory round them:
But at first, without surprise,
Let me look in human eyes.

Step by step our feet must go
  Up the holy mountain;
Drop by drop within us flow
  Life's unfailing fountain.
Angels sing with crowns that burn:
We shall have our song to learn.

He who on our earthly path
  Bids us help each other—
Who His Well-beloved hath
  Made our Elder Brother—
Will but clasp the chain of love
Closer, when we meet above.

Therefore dread I not to go
  O'er the Silent River.
Death, thy hastening oar I know;
  Bear me, Thou Life-giver,
Through the waters, to the shore,
Where mine own have gone before![1]

¶ As you ascend the Stelvio Pass from the Italian side, you travel through wild, majestic scenery. One moment you are lost in admiration of the engineering skill that carried the zigzag road along the mountain-side; another, lingering by a waterfall, or caught by the vista of some retreating valley, the ruin of an avalanche, or the dazzling sheen of the encircling snow. But the road is nothing to the top of the pass; it hides the secret that awaits you. It is impossible to forget the thrill of emotion when we touched the summit of the pass, and the glorious secret stood disclosed. It had taken hours to ascend, and then, in a moment, in the twinkling of an eye, a marvellous panorama of mountain and glacier burst on the eye, and Austria lay in the abyss at our feet.

This present life is like crossing the Stelvio. We are going towards the glorious secret, but meantime the way hides it. The more we think of the land within the veil, the more we must look

[1] Lucy Larcom.

forward to the top of the pass, when we shall see the secret for ourselves. It is ready, as Peter writes, to be revealed. When we behold it, shall we not adore the loving-kindness of Him who hid that He might reveal, in whose light it is ours now to see light clearly? [1]

¶ A famous city in the East has triple walls. Within the huge, strong gates of the first wall the trading and mercantile populations dwell; within the gates of the second wall the space is reserved for tribesmen who are akin to the reigning house; and within the gates of the innermost wall nestle palace and park and imperial pleasure-grounds. The first gate to which Christ holds the key looks forth into infinite vistas. The gospel opportunity gives access into a new standing-ground of privilege, and through the new standing-ground passes a highway into the favoured and sacred sphere, where dwell members of a royal and priestly race, and through this sphere approach is at last made to the blessed and glorious realms beyond the angel-guarded gates.[2]

[1] A. Philip, *The Father's Hand*, 91.
[2] T. G. Selby, *The Divine Craftsman*, 80.

A Personal Providence.

LITERATURE.

Brooks (P.), *The Spiritual Man*, 281.
Burns (J. D.), *Memoir and Remains*, 293.
Clarke (G.), *From the Cross to the Crown*, 1.
Cooke (G. A.), *The Progress of Revelation*, 105.
Culross (J.), *God's Shepherd Care*, 1.
Fairbairn (A. M.), *Christ in the Centuries*, 69, 83.
Freeman (J. D.), *Life on the Uplands*, 1.
Gray (W. H.), *Our Divine Shepherd*, 1.
Howard (H.), *The Shepherd Psalm*, 1.
Jones (J. M.), *The Cup of Cold Water*, 17.
McFadyen (J. E.), *The City with Foundations*, 201.
Maclaren (A.), *Sermons Preached in Manchester*, i. 307.
Parker (J.), *The City Temple Pulpit*, vii. 270.
Smith (G. A.), *Four Psalms*, 1.
Spurgeon (C. H.), *The Treasury of David*, 398.
Stalker (J.), *The Good Shepherd*, 17.
Stoughton (J.), *The Song of Christ's Flock*, 1.
Christian World Pulpit, lxv. 232 (Parker).
Expository Times, xxii. 302.

A Personal Providence.

The Lord is my shepherd; I shall not want.—Ps. xxiii. 1.

Perhaps no single lay in the Psalter has taken such a hold of the imagination and the heart of believers as the 23rd Psalm. None can estimate its influence on the Church of God throughout the past, whether on her spiritual life generally or in the case of particular individuals. The sorrowful have been cheered by it; the troubled have been led into peace; the prisoner has sung it in his dungeon and felt himself a captive no more; the pilgrim has been gladdened by it as he wandered in the wilderness, in a solitary way, and found no city to dwell in; the fainting soul has been refreshed by it, and enabled to mount up as on eagles' wings; doubts and fears and questionings of Providence, and forebodings of ill, and all the black brood of unbelief, have been chased away by it, like the shades of night by the day-star; it has been God's balm to the wounded spirit; it has strengthened God's people to bear the cross, and to suffer their lives to be guided by His will; it has been whispered by dying lips, as the last earthly utterance of faith and gratitude and hope, the prelude of the New Song in which there is no note of sorrow.

¶ Probably few Psalms are oftener read, or with stronger feeling, by careless readers than the twenty-third, singing of God's grace to the humble, and the twenty-fourth, singing of God's grace to the noble; and there are probably no other two whose real force is so little thought of. Which of us, even the most attentive, is prepared at once to tell, or has often enough considered, what the " Valley of the Shadow of Death " means, in the one, or the "Hill of the Lord," in the other? [1]

¶ Spurgeon says of this matchless Psalm: " It is David's Heavenly Pastoral; a surpassing ode, which none of the daughters

[1] Ruskin, *Rock Honeycomb* (*Works*, xxxi. 203).

of music can excel. The clarion of war here gives place to the pipe of peace, and he who so lately bewailed the woes of the Shepherd, tunefully rehearses the joys of the flock. We picture David singing this unrivalled pastoral with a heart as full of gladness as it can hold. This is the pearl of Psalms, whose soft, pure radiance delights every eye; a pearl of which Helicon need not be ashamed, though Jordan claims it." Some one else has said: "What the nightingale is among the birds, that is this Divine ode among the Psalms, for it has rung sweetly in the ear of many a mourner in his night of weeping, and has bidden him hope for a morning of joy." I will venture to compare it also to the lark, which sings as it mounts, and mounts as it sings, until it is out of sight, and then not out of hearing. The whole Psalm is more fitted for the eternal mansions than for these dwelling-places below the clouds. The truths which are found in every sentence are almost too wondrous for mere mortal to grasp, and the heights of experience we are invited to ascend are almost too high for human climbing.[1]

¶ In January 1681, two "honest, worthy lasses," as Peden calls them, Isabel Alison and Marion Harvie, were hanged at Edinburgh. On the scaffold they sang together, to the tune of "Martyrs," Psalm lxxxiv. "Marion," said Bishop Paterson, "you would never hear a curate; now you shall hear one," and he called upon one of his clergy to pray. "Come, Isabel," was the girl's answer—she was but twenty years of age—"let us sing the 23rd Psalm," and thus they drowned the voice of the curate. No execution of the time was more universally condemned than that of these two women. A roughly-drawn picture of the scene, with the title "Women hanged," is prefixed to the first edition of *The Hind Let Loose* (1687). By its side is another engraving, which represents "The Wigtown Martyrs, drowned at stakes at sea."[2]

I.

JEHOVAH.

1. "The Lord." It is the name Jehovah. Now this name does not of itself express God's moral character, but rather His absolute, necessary, and eternal being, as the sole fount of existence, "who only hath immortality, dwelling in the light

[1] G. Clarke, *From the Cross to the Crown*, 2.
[2] R. E. Prothero, *The Psalms in Human Life*, 286.

which no man can approach unto, whom no man hath seen, nor can see." While the generations of creaturely life pass on in ceaseless flow, while "our ages waste," while the heavens themselves grow old, *He* stands up amidst His works the one, eternal, immutable "I am."

2. This great Jehovah—what is He in His relation to us? The Psalm says He is a shepherd. The figure occurs very frequently in the Old Testament to indicate His relation to the covenant people and to every faithful member thereof. It is the word of Jacob, "God who *shepherded me* all my life long"; it is the word of the seed of Jacob, "We are his people, and the sheep of his pasture." It tells of care, guidance, knowledge, defence, tenderness, love, on the part of God. Even to us, who seldom see a flock of sheep, except it may be passing through our dusty streets or scattered on the hillsides, the figure tells very much; but still more would it tell to the people of Israel.

¶ Our English version misses something of the beauty of Jacob's words (in blessing the sons of Joseph). The translation, God "who hath fed me," is too meagre. We need to say, "who hath shepherded me." The same word is the keynote of the finest of all the Psalms: "The Lord is my shepherd." It is a beautiful metaphor, which comes with an exquisite pathos and a profound significance from the lips of a dying shepherd. The poets of a later age could only echo his words: "Give ear, O Shepherd of Israel, thou that leadest Joseph like a flock." All the tender grace of the Old Testament religion is found in this lovely conception. It was not one man or two, but a whole nation, that learned to believe in God as a Shepherd: "We are his people, the sheep of his pasture." No other ancient nation ever expected from God such loving care and unerring guidance, no other nation ever promised such meek submission and faithful following. And while the Hebrew temple and sacrifice and priesthood have passed away as the shadows of better things, the Hebrew thought of a Shepherd-God will live for ever.[1]

3. "The Lord is my shepherd." Mark the fulness, the expansiveness of this idea. On the one side "the Lord," the infinite, unchangeable, and everlasting God, all that is glorious, and holy, and wise, and self-sufficient, and much to be admired; on the other

[1] J. Strachan, *Hebrew Ideals*, ii. 147.

"the Shepherd," all that is tender, compassionate, and self-sacrificing, and much to be loved. These two characters—the one, all that is lofty in its magnificence; the other, all that is lowly in its condescension; the one, all glorious; the other, all gracious—are united. They are included and concentrated in the same large and loving heart, whose every pulsation sends the tide of life through the veins of His vast universe, but at the same time does not disdain to throb with strong and unwearied regardfulness for me.

¶ You have seen a map or a plan on which these words are written: "Scale, 1 inch to a mile." Now, that is the meaning of the text; it is one inch to a mile, one inch to a universe, one inch to infinity. Do you ask me what is the meaning of that peculiar writing upon the plan? I will tell you; give me the compasses. How far is it from A to B? Stretch out compasses —"Ten inches." What does that mean? It means ten miles. Ten inches on the paper, but the ten inches stand for ten miles. That is just the text. "Shepherd" stands for Ineffable, Eternal, Infinite, Unthinkable; God on a small scale; God minimized that we may touch the shadow of His garment.[1]

II.

JEHOVAH MINE.

1. "The Lord is *my* shepherd." Here is the link that connects our hearts with the living God. It is a grand thing to consider how far out His shepherd-care extends. Man never yet lighted upon an unblest spot where no token of it could be seen. It meets us everywhere, and every hour. "The Lord is good to all; and his tender mercies are over all his works." The lilies of the field, the birds of the air, the young lions in the tawny wild, all tribes of living and sentient creatures that people this earth, all the isles of light that shine in the blue immensity of heaven—the Lord careth for them all. We are astonished, overwhelmed, lost, when we think of the boundless extent of the fields into which His care reaches forth. But here our minds are called back from wandering out into His wide dominions,

[1] Joseph Parker.

and we are directed to repose our own personal confidence in this great and unsearchable God, and to say, He is *my* Shepherd; mine, because He has given Himself to me; mine, for my heart trusts Him and clings to Him; my Shepherd, caring for *me*, loving *me*, keeping *me*.

¶ We enter the Christian life by an act of simple appropriating faith. In a sense, all faith is "appropriating." Mere intellectual faith is the act of the mind by which it lays hold on a truth and makes it *its own*. But the highest reach of this faculty of faith is when we face God's largest lessons, and lay them to heart as true for *us*. Then, not only intellect, but will and desire make these truths *ours*. Perhaps the practical meaning of this appropriating faith has never been more clearly explained than in the early history of the eminent American preacher, W. M. Taylor. When he was a boy he heard a sermon in which the preacher dwelt much on the appropriating act of faith. He asked his father what it meant. Strange to say, that father had asked much the same question when he was a child, and now he repeated his mother's answer for his own boy's guidance: "Take your Bible, and underscore all the 'my's,' and 'mine's,' and the 'me's' you come upon, and you will discover what 'appropriation' means." We wish we could induce every reader of these words to spend ten minutes in this simple exercise now. Take the Psalms. "The Lord is *my* shepherd." Is that true? True now? "He restoreth *my* soul." Do you believe it? Now? Assuredly, if Christians would exercise this direct personal trust in the loving promises of God, it would mean a marvellous access of spiritual confidence, and power, and conquest.[1]

> Happy me! O happy sheep!
> Whom my God vouchsafes to keep,
> Ev'n my God, ev'n He it is
> That points me to these paths of bliss;
> On whose pastures cheerful Spring,
> All the year doth sit and sing,
> And rejoicing, smiles to see
> Their green backs wear His livery:
> Pleasure sings my soul to rest,
> Plenty wears me at her breast,
> Whose sweet temper teaches me
> Not wanton, nor in want to be.
> At my feet the blubbering mountain
> Weeping, melts into a fountain,

[1] J. A. Clapperton, *Culture of the Christian Heart*, 37.

Whose soft silver-sweating streams
Make high-noon forget his beams:
When my wayward breath is flying,
He calls home my soul from dying,
Strokes and tames my rabid grief,
And does woo me into life:
When my simple weakness strays
(Tangled in forbidden ways),
He (my Shepherd) is my guide;
He's before me, on my side;
And behind me, He beguiles
Craft in all her knotty wiles;
He expounds the weary wonder
Of my giddy steps, and under
Spreads a path as clear as the day
Where no churlish rub says nay
To my joy-conducted feet,
Whilst they gladly go to meet
Grace and Peace, to learn new lays
Tuned to my great Shepherd's praise.[1]

¶ "My Shepherd"—as if this individual Psalmist had appro-
priated the Deity. Yet it is quite in accord with the deepest
experience and the most ideal observation. Of the sun in the
heavens every little child might say, as he bathes his little
fingers in the great flame, "The sun is my sun"; and yet it is
everybody's sun, and the little child's sun all the more truly
because it is everybody's light. He does not take God away
from others; he makes others feel how tender and how near God
may be, though we have been searching for Him with lamps
and candles and lanterns, whilst He was blazing upon us from
every star that gleamed in the under heavens which we call
the sky.[2]

¶ When preaching to children from home, Dr. Wilson often
related Lady Boyd's story of "Jamie, the Shepherd Boy," because
he found that it "told" better than any of his other stories. It
runs thus: A minister was visiting an ignorant shepherd boy on
his death-bed. He gave the boy the text, "The Lord is my
shepherd." He bade him notice that the text had five words as
his left hand had five knuckles. He repeated the text slowly,
appropriating a word for each knuckle, and getting the boy to
fold in a knuckle as he repeated each word. The minister told
him that the fourth knuckle represented the most important

[1] Richard Crashaw.   [2] J. Parker, *City Temple Pulpit*, vii. 271.

word for him, the word "my," and explained personal faith in a personal Saviour. The boy grew interested, and the light dawned upon him. One day Jamie's mother met the minister at her door, and said, "Oh, come in, my Jamie is dead, and you will find his fourth knuckle folded in, and his forefinger resting upon it."[1]

2. "The Lord is *my* Shepherd" is the language, not of nature but of grace; and it is not until by faith we have recognized Him, not in creation, not in providence, but in redemption, and that a redemption which was wrought out for and which has taken decisive effect on us, that we can look up with a glance of child-like confidence to God, and say, "My Maker is my Father, my God is my Shepherd; He who sitteth in the circle of the heavens has made for Himself a habitation in my heart, and the upholder of all the worlds is my best and nearest Friend."

Ask yourself, if since it was first put upon your lips you have ever used it with anything more than the lips; if you have any right to use it; if you have ever taken any steps towards winning the right to use it. To claim God for our own, to have and enjoy Him as ours, means, as Christ our Master said over and over again, that we give ourselves to Him, and take Him to our hearts. Sheep do not choose their shepherd, but man has to choose—else the peace and the fulness of life which are here figured remain a dream and become no experience for him.

¶ Some years ago I tried to get one of my children to commit the Twenty-third Psalm to memory; and, as she was too young to read for herself, I had to repeat it to her until she got hold of the words. I said, "Now, repeat after me, 'The Lord is my shepherd.'" She said, "The Lord is *your* shepherd." "No, I did not say that, and I want you to say to me the words I say to you. Now then, 'The Lord is *my* shepherd.'" Again she said, "The Lord is *your* shepherd." It was only after much effort I could get her to repeat the exact words. The child's mistake was in some sense natural, but many of riper years have made the same blunder, saying by acts, if not by words, "The Lord is yours, but I have no experience of His shepherdly care and protection."[2]

[1] Dr. James Wells, *Life of James Hood Wilson*, 291.
[2] *The Expository Times*, xxii. 304.

III.

Jehovah my Shepherd.

1. "The Lord is my *shepherd.*" The image, natural amongst a nation of shepherds, is first employed by Jacob (Gen. xlviii. 15, xlix. 24). There, as here, God is the Shepherd of the *individual* (cf. Ps. cxix. 176), still more frequently of His *people* (lxxviii. 52, lxxx. i.; Mic. vii. 14; Isa. lxiii. 13, and especially Ezek. xxxiv.): most beautifully and touchingly in Isa. xl. 11. So in the New Testament of Christ (John x. 1–16, xxi. 15–17; Heb. xiii. 20; 1 Pet. ii. 25, v. 4). To understand all the force of this image, we must remember what the Syrian shepherd was, how very unlike our modern shepherd.

2. Shepherd-life, as David knew it, was a life essentially emotional and devotional. Shepherdhood, as David exercised it, was a relation at once so affectionately solicitous and so ingeniously resourceful as to be akin to motherhood. For the sheep of Eastern lands live in their shepherd. He is the centre of their unity, the guarantee of their security, the pledge of their prosperity. For them, pastures and wells and paths and folds are all in him. Apart from him their condition is one of abject and pathetic helplessness. Should any sudden calamity tear him from them they are forthwith undone. Distressed and scattered, they stumble among the rocks, or bleed in the thorn-tangle, or flee, wild with fear, before the terror of the wolf. Hence a good shepherd never forsakes his sheep. He accompanies them by day and abides with them by night. In the morning he goes before them to lead them out, and in the evening, when he has gathered them into the fold, he lies down in their midst. Then as he views their still, white forms clustered about him in the darkness, his heart brims with a brooding tenderness.

> Upon the hills the winds are sharp and cold,
> The sweet young grasses wither on the wold,
> And we, O Lord, have wandered from Thy fold,
>   But evening brings us home.

Among the mists we stumbled and the rocks,
Where the brown lichen whitens and the fox
Watches the straggler from the scattered flocks,
  But evening brings us home.

The sharp thorns prick us, and our tender feet
Are cut and bleeding, and the lambs repeat
Their pitiful complaints—oh, rest is sweet,
  When evening brings us home.

We have been wounded by the hunter's darts,
Our eyes are very heavy, and our hearts
Search for Thy coming, when the light departs.
  At evening bring us home.

The darkness gathers, thro' the gloom no star
Rises to guide. We have wandered far,
Without Thy lamp we know not where we are.
  At evening bring us home.

The clouds are round us and the snowdrifts thicken,
O Thou, dear Shepherd, leave us not to sicken,
In the waste night, our tardy footsteps quicken.
  At evening bring us home.[1]

3. It was in anticipation of the time when His Son was to take our likeness upon Him, and die for us men, and for our salvation, that God revealed Himself to the Old Testament saints as "the Shepherd of Israel, leading Joseph like a flock." They rejoiced in the light that stretched toward them from the far-off day of Christ's appearing. Of him they read the sure words of prophecy, "He shall feed his flock like a shepherd: he shall gather the lambs with his arm, and carry them in his bosom, and shall gently lead those that are with young." We know how He, in one of the most touching of all His parables, applied this emblem to Himself, and thus gave it its true significance and beauty. "I am the good shepherd, and know my sheep, and am known of mine." "I am the good shepherd: the good shepherd giveth his life for the sheep."

¶ On this, the "Good Shepherd" Sunday, one's thoughts circulate round the significant symbol. The thought before me

[1] John Skelton.

at this moment is the completeness of His knowledge of the sheep, their ills, necessities, possibilities, all involving on the part of the Shepherd completeness of sacrifice, "perfect sympathy calling out the perfect remedy," as Westcott puts it. And one perceives the truth of this the more one's own sympathies are educated, and one's own life flows out.[1]

¶ It is cheering to remember that, for the sake of His own Name, and of His own glory, as well as for the sake of His great love, the full supply of all our needs is guaranteed by our relationship to Him as our Shepherd. A lean, scraggy sheep, with torn limbs and tattered fleece, would be small credit to the shepherd's care; but unless we will wander from Him, and will not remain restfully under His protection, there is no fear of such ever being our lot. We may lie down in peace, and sleep in safety, because the Shepherd of Israel neither slumbers nor sleeps. No lion or bear can ever surprise our ever-watchful Guardian, or overcome our Almighty Deliverer. He has once laid down His life for the sheep; but now He ever liveth to care for them, and to ensure to them all that is needful for this life, and for that which is to come.

"The Lord *is* my Shepherd." He saith not was; He saith not may be, or will be. "The Lord is my Shepherd"—is on Sunday, is on Monday, and is through every day of the week; is in January, and is in December, and in every month of the year; is at home, and is in China; is in peace, and is in war; in abundance, and in penury. Let us live in the joy of the truth here pointed out: "The Lord is my Shepherd; I shall not want"; and let us learn to trust for others as well as for ourselves. Not only are the sheep of the flock safe, but the little lambs—about which the ewes may be more solicitous than about their own safety—are all under the same guardian Eye, and the same Shepherd's care.[2]

4. The Lord is my Shepherd—what does that mean for me?

(1) God has the shepherd-heart, pulsing with pure and generous love—love that means grace and sacrifice.

(2) He has the shepherd-eye, that takes in the whole flock, and misses even the one poor sheep that wanders astray.

(3) He has the shepherd-nearness; not living far away, and hearing about us now and then through the report of His angels; He is about us and among us day and night.

[1] R. W. Corbet, *Letters from a Mystic of the Present Day,* 158.
[2] Hudson Taylor, *Choice Sayings,* 22.

(4) He has shepherd-knowledge, being acquainted with every-thing that concerns us, understanding our desires better than we do ourselves.

(5) He has shepherd-strength; He is "able to keep" us; and we need not fear the teeth of the lion or the paw of the bear, so long as we are under His defence.

(6) He has shepherd-faithfulness; and we may fully trust Him. *He* hath said, "I will never leave you, I will never for-sake you"; so that *we* may boldly say, "The Lord is my helper; I will not fear what man can do unto me."

(7) He has shepherd-tenderness, carrying the lambs in His arms and gathering them in His bosom. There is nothing that comes out into more wonderful relief in Scripture than this tenderness. A comforted saint is "like one whom his mother comforteth." In upholding His people God spreads underneath them "the everlasting arms." His pity is like unto a father's pity. In nurturing our life from feebleness to strength, "Thy gentleness hath made me great." His control is not that of the cold, sharp bit thrust between our teeth, and the compelling lash, but, "I will guide thee with mine eye." When He defends from the arrow and flying death, it is not by clothing in a shirt of mail, that pains and burdens, while it defends, the wearer; but, "He shall cover thee with his feathers"—could anything be softer and gentler?—"He shall cover thee with his feathers, and under his wings shalt thou trust." *That* is the God to whom David bids us look up.[1]

IV.

HIS PROVIDENCE.

1. "I shall not want." Coverdale's translation, used in the Prayer Book, is better, "Therefore can I lack nothing"; still better, as more literal, is Kay's, "I shall have no lack." The word is used in Deut. ii. 7 of Israel's "lacking nothing" *during its passage through the wilderness*; and in viii. 9, of the provision to be made for them *in Canaan*.

¶ "Want" was preferred by the translators of the A.V. because the word "lack" had in the meantime suffered deprecia-

[1] J. Culross, *God's Shepherd Care*, 19.

tion from the use of it as a common interpellation by stall-keepers to passers by: What d'ye lack, what d'ye lack?

We may observe by a comparison of other passages that *lack* is much rarer in the Bible of 1611 than in that of 1539. Thus in Judges xviii. 10; Luke xv. 14—

1539.	1611.
A place, which doth lacke no thyng that is in the worlde.	A place where there is no want of any thing, that is in the earth
And when he had spent all, ther arose a greate derth in all that lande, and he began to lacke.	And when he had spent all, there arose a mighty famine in that land, and he beganne to be in want.[1]

2. The shepherdly care of Jehovah makes every life a Divine plan. It redeems it from caprice. The tendency of our day is to reduce everything to law. Scientific men tell us that in the world of matter there is no such thing as chance. The unexpected does not happen. The universality of law is an accepted fact. The air we breathe, the water we drink, are composed of gases which, if mixed in slightly different proportions, would work our destruction. If the laboratory of nature were turned into a playground for lawless forces, what a chaos we should see! But there is no such thing as chance; and everything, from a molecule to a sun, is marshalled under law. But shall suns and systems have their appointed orbits, and human life be left to accident and caprice? Shall the soulless worlds of matter that drift through the infinite spaces have the personal leading of Jehovah, and all the hosts of men be allowed to wander uncared for and untended in the barren wilderness of time? No. Even of the stars it is said, "He calleth them all by name"; and we are of more value than many stars. They are but the furniture of His choice and many-chambered palace, but we are the children of His heart and His home. They are but waxing and waning splendours which come and go in the pauses of His breath, but we shall endure through all the years of the Most High.

3. But how shall we reconcile this care of God with what is called "natural law"? It is a conclusion of science that the order of nature is fixed and invariable; how can we reconcile this fixedness with the doctrine of present care? We neither *can* do this,

[1] J. Earle, *The Psalter of 1539*, 267.

nor *need* to do it. On the one side, science rests on its own proper basis, which is that of sense. Science receives nothing that does not rest ultimately on the evidence of sense, and knows only of the "natural." Take even astronomy, which is in some respects the grandest of the sciences, and you will find that it has no other foundation than this. On the other hand, the assurance of Divine loving-kindness and care rests on a spiritual foundation, of which the senses know nothing. We are brought in among things which "eye hath not seen, nor ear heard." The assurance of Divine loving-kindness and care rests on Divine revelation; and when men endeavour to destroy our confidence in the reality of the care by an argument drawn from science, that is to say, resting ultimately on sense, we can only reply, in the words of Jesus to the Sadducees, " Ye do err, not knowing the scriptures, nor the power of God."

¶ Never did I realize the power of Providence over human destiny as when I perceived how little man himself is able to control the act which most affects his own fate. For I cannot conceal from myself the fact that all my meditation can serve but little to guide me, seeing the future, which alone could give me a fixed point for my inquiry, is mercilessly hidden from my view. True indeed it is that we are *led*. Happily the Christian may add, "We are *well led*!" This indeed is our only true and logical consolation.[1]

¶ "And Elijah the Tishbite, who was of the inhabitants of Gilead, said unto Ahab, As the Lord God of Israel liveth, before whom I stand, there shall not be dew nor rain these years, but according to my word." Your modern philosophers have explained to you the absurdity of all that: you think ? . . . Do these modern scientific gentlemen fancy that nobody, before they were born, knew the laws of cloud and storm, or that the mighty human souls of former ages, who every one of them lived and died by prayer, and in it, did not know that in every petition framed on their lips they were asking for what was not only fore-ordained, but just as probably fore-*done* ? or that the mother, pausing to pray before she opens a letter from Alma or Balaclava, does not know that already he is saved for whom she prays, or already lies festering in his shroud ? The whole confidence and glory of prayer is in its appeal to a Father who knows our necessities before we ask, who knows our thoughts before they rise in our

[1] *Brother and Sister* (Memoir of Ernest and Henriette Renan), 131.

hearts, and whose decrees, as unalterable in the eternal future as in the eternal past, yet in the close verity of visible fact, bend, like reeds, before the fore-ordained and faithful prayers of His children.[1]

> O strong, upwelling prayers of faith,
> From inmost founts of life ye start,—
> The spirit's pulse, the vital breath
> Of soul and heart!
>
> From pastoral toil, from traffic's din,
> Alone, in crowds, at home, abroad,
> Unheard of man, ye enter in
> The ear of God.
>
> Ye brook no forced and measured tasks,
> Nor weary rote, nor formal chains;
> The simple heart, that freely asks
> In love, obtains.
>
> For man the living temple is:
> The mercy-seat and cherubim,
> And all the holy mysteries,
> He bears with him.
>
> And most avails the prayer of love,
> Which, wordless, shapes itself in deeds,
> And wearies Heaven for naught above
> Our common needs.[2]

4. There are two ways of not lacking a thing in this world. He lacks nothing who has everything. If one could take the stars from the sky, and the rivers from their beds, he might say, "I lack nothing." To get everything possible for the soul to want is one way of saying, "I want nothing." The better way is for a man to look up and bring his desires down to that which God sees fit to give him. This applies emphatically to things of faith. If I knew all the mysteries of God, I might say, "I lack no knowledge of God." But if, knowing only what God has told me, I let all the gaps in my knowledge go because He has not chosen to fill them, in a richer sense I may say, "I lack no knowledge of God."

[1] Ruskin, *On the Old Road.*   [2] J. G. Whittier, *The Hermit of the Thebaid.*

¶ God does not say He will supply every one of our wants, but He does say He will supply every one of our needs. The two words are not coincident in any one of our lives. Half of the difficulty in our lives is caused by letting our wants predominate and not keeping them within our grip.[1]

¶ I once said to a servant girl who had got into a good family, "Are you happy where you are?" She had got what for a servant was a good situation, and I shall not forget the quietly confident way in which with beaming face she said, "Oh yes, sir, I have £22 a year, *and all found.*" "The Lord is my shepherd," and all is found. "I shall not want." "All found." That was evidently more to her than the small sum total of the actual pounds. She dwelt upon that, and said with emphasis, "and all found."[2]

¶ The Oriental shepherd was always ahead of his sheep. He was down in front. He was eyes and ears, heart and brain for his flock. Any attack upon them had to take him into account. He was the defence force—the advance guard, that had to be measured and reckoned with. Now, what the Eastern shepherd was to his sheep, God is to His people. He is down in front, both as to time and place. He is in the to-morrows of our history. It is to-morrow that tyrannizes over men and fills them with dread. It is the unknown that paralyses the heart and puts such tension on the nerves. But once let the thought of God as Shepherd take its place among the certainties of our life, and straightway we are delivered from this thrall. The future is guaranteed. He is there already. All the to-morrows of our life have to pass Him before they can get to us. We literally take them from His hand. We step down into to-morrows that are filled and flooded with God. The deduction for the Psalmist was inevitable: "I shall not want." "Want" and "Jehovah" are mutually exclusive ideas. They cannot co-exist in the mind excepting in antithesis. They cancel each other. Jehovah stands for all a man needs for time and for eternity. Give a worried man, or a careworn woman, this assurance, and at once life takes on a different complexion, and moves upward to a higher plane. He who is not delivered from the fear of want can never touch the highest levels of life or achievement. Christ saw this when He said, "Be not anxious for the morrow," and assured His hearers that it was along the lines of fulfilled relations to God that life would find all its satisfaction and supply.[3]

[1] G. Beesley Austin.   [2] John McNeill.
[3] H. Howard, *The Shepherd Psalm*, 16.

When God shall ope the gates of gold,
The portals of the heavenly fold,
And bid His flock find pasture wide
Upon a new earth's green hillside—

What poor strayed sheep shall thither fare,
Black-smirched beneath the sunny air,
To wash away in living springs
The mud and mire of earthly things!

What lonely ewes with eyes forlorn,
With weary feet and fleeces torn,
To whose shorn back no wind was stayed,
Nor any rough ways smooth were made!

What happy little lambs shall leap
To those sad ewes and spattered sheep,
With gamesome feet and joyful eyes,
From years of play in Paradise!

The wind is chill, the hour is late;
Haste thee, dear Lord, undo the gate;
For grim wolf-sorrows prowling range
These bitter hills of chance and change:

And from the barren wilderness
With homeward face Thy flocks do press:
Their worn bells ring a jangled chime—
Shepherd, come forth, 'tis eventime! [1]

[1] May Byron, *The Wind on the Heath*, 28.

Rest, Refreshment, Restoration.

LITERATURE.

Armstrong (R. A.), *Memoir and Sermons*, 160.

Austin (G. B.), *The Beauty of Goodness*, 50, 98.

Banks (L. A.), *Sermons which have Won Souls*, 397.

Brooke (S. A.), *Sermons in St. James's Chapel*, 56.

Brooks (P.), *The Spiritual Man*, 281.

Cooke (G. A.), *The Progress of Revelation*, 105.

Culross (J.), *God's Shepherd Care*, 28.

Cumming (J. E.), *Consecrated Work*, 43.

Darlow (T. H.), *Via Sacra*, 205.

Fairbairn (A. M.), *Christ in the Centuries*, 69, 83.

Finlayson (T. C.), *The Divine Gentleness*, 223.

Freeman (J. D.), *Life on the Uplands*, 1.

Gray (W. H.), *Our Divine Shepherd*, 1.

Griffin (E. D.), *Plain Practical Sermons*, ii. 230.

Horne (C. S.), *The Soul's Awakening*, 131.

Howard (H.), *The Shepherd Psalm*, 1.

Jerdan (C.), *Pastures of Tender Grass*, 37.

Jones (J. M.), *The Cup of Cold Water*, 17.

Knight (W. A.), *The Song of Our Syrian Guest*, 1.

Levens (J. T.), *Clean Hands*, 92.

McFadyen (J. E.), *The City with Foundations*, 201.

      ,,   ,,   *Ten Studies in the Psalms*, 23.

Maclaren (A.), *Sermons Preached in Manchester*, i. 307.

McNeill (J.), *Regent Square Pulpit*, i. 241.

Newbolt (W. C. E.), *Penitence and Peace*, 77.

Parker (J.), *City Temple Pulpit*, vii. 270.

      ,,   ,,   *Studies in Texts*, iv. 183.

Price (A. C.), *Fifty Sermons*, i. 257.

Robertson (P. W.), *The Sacrament Sabbath*, 211.

Robertson (S.), *The Rope of Hair*, 79.

Sadler (T.), *Sermons for Children*, 180.

Smellie (A.), *In the Hour of Silence*, 142.

Smith (G. A.), *Four Psalms*, 1.

      ,,   ,,   *The Forgiveness of Sins*, 238.

Spurgeon (C. H.), *Metropolitan Tabernacle Pulpit*, xix. (1873) No. 1149.

Stalker (J.), *The Psalm of Psalms*, 37.

Talmage (T. De Witt), *Fifty Sermons*, ii. 151.

Vaughan (J.), *Sermons* (Brighton Pulpit), xii. (1875) Nos. 900,.901.

Watt (L. M.), *The Communion Table*, 137.

Christian Age, liii. 2 (Hepworth), 244 (Talmage).

Christian World Pulpit, xi. 401 (Bainton); xii. 5 (Bainton); xxi. 387 (Haines); xxxiii. 82 (Darnton); lxv. 232 (Parker); lxvii. 193 (Aked); lxxv. 36 (Balgarnie).

Church of England Magazine, lxix. 56 (Morton).

Rest, Refreshment, Restoration.

He maketh me to lie down in green pastures :
He leadeth me beside the still waters.
He restoreth my soul.—Ps. xxiii. 2, 3.

1. WE are apt to think about the Old Testament as if it were hard and rigid and rugged and severe and stern. Some people say, "I like the New Testament very much, but I do not care to read the Old Testament"; but right in the middle of the Old Testament shines the Twenty-third Psalm, as if it were put there in order that men might never dare to call that book harsh and hard and severe and stern. This Psalm is an outpouring of the soul to God, never matched in all the riches of the Christian day. It is the utterance of a soul absolutely unshaken and perfectly serene. There are times when everything in God's dealings with us seems to be stern and hard and bitter ; then, just as we are ready to cast ourselves away in despair, and feel toward God as toward a ruler whom we can simply fear but never love, there comes some manifestation of God that sets our soul to singing. The hardest and severest passages in the Old Testament find relief if we let the light shine on them from the Twenty-third Psalm.[1]

2. In the New Testament many of the expressions of deepest faith have their origin in this Psalm. "The Lord is my shepherd, I shall not want." See how one of the words which afterwards became the inheritance of the race first came to be used. Many words have passed into common use and are now used without any feeling of their sacred origin in the local circumstances out of which the Bible was first written. This is the case with the word "shepherd." David, the shepherd boy, had been back and

[1] Phillips Brooks, *The Spiritual Man*, 283.

forth over the fields of Judæa, and, in the care of those dependent on him, had learned to feel the care of the heavenly Father. It is a beautiful thing when the soul, from its own relationship towards dependent ones, comes to recognize the care of God. Taking up the lamb in his arms, David thought: So my heavenly Father will carry me through all the days of my life. Our Saviour said, " I am the good shepherd." He took the figure from the Old Testament, and when His disciples came to do the work He had done, the title " shepherd," or " pastor," became universal in Christian history. The pastors of the flock are they who try, in their weakness and inability, to do that which Christ did perfectly. David could find no word to describe more fully to his own mind the richness of the care that God had for his life, the absolute dependence of his life upon God's love, than that taken from his own daily occupation.

I.

REST.

" He maketh me to lie down in green pastures."

1. The green pastures, says Delitzsch, are pasture-grounds of fresh tender soft grass, where one lies at ease, and rest and enjoyment are combined. The word rendered " pastures " is the plural of a word which is used for a dwelling or homestead. In six of the twelve places where the word occurs, it is coupled with " wilderness "; and in three more it refers to pasturage. It evidently denotes, therefore, the richer, oasis-like spots, where a homestead would be fixed in a generally barren tract of land. We must banish from our minds the green fields of our country, enclosed with hedges or stone walls. In the East the barren uplands are all open and unfenced; and you never see a flock of sheep without the shepherd in charge of them. Everything depends upon the shepherd; he has to find out where the thin grass lurks beneath the rocks, where the precious fountain bubbles into the cistern, where shelter may be had from the scorching sun at noonday.

¶ Some time since I was driving across the Cornish moors, when my friend who was with me pointed to a greener slope between the rocky hills. "My father owned some land here when I was a boy," said he, "and many a time I have ridden over these moors looking for the sheep; I generally found them on that slope." "Why there?" I asked. Then he showed me how two high hills rose up and sheltered it from the north and east, and how the slope faced the south, so that they found it warmer, and the early young green grass grew there. Some time afterwards that pleasant picture of the hills happened to come back to my mind, and I turned wondering as to where His flock finds its resting-place. Very beautiful for situation is this Twenty-third Psalm. The Psalm before it begins with that dreadful cry, "My God, my God, why hast thou forsaken me?" Here is the hill of Calvary, with its mocking crowd, "They part my garments among them, and cast lots upon my vesture." His sheep have come over Calvary; they have passed under the Cross. Behind them rises that hill which for ever breaks the fierce storms that beat upon us. "Being justified by faith, we have peace with God through our Lord Jesus Christ": here is the calm, and overhead the blue sky where no storms gather. Then immediately after the Twenty-third Psalm comes that which tells of the hill of Zion with its splendours and shouts of triumph. "Lift up your heads, O ye gates; and be ye lift up, ye everlasting doors; and the King of glory shall come in." So sheltered lies the flock of the Good Shepherd, betwixt Calvary and Heaven, shut in from the angrier blasts, and dwelling in a land that looks towards the sunny south.[1]

2. Here is a promise, then, to the weary, of *repose*. Thank God this is not an age of idleness. Can we equally say, Thank God this is not an age of repose? It is almost the prevailing stamp which defines the character of the present day—its rest-lessness. Call it, if you will, impatience; call it hurry; certainly whatever is the opposite to repose.

> We see all sights from pole to pole,
>   And glance and rush and bustle by,
> And never once possess our soul
>   Before we die.

There is a deep craving within our spiritual nature for a true spiritual rest; not the rest of inactivity or sloth, but a calm,

[1] M. G. Pearse, in *The Sunday Magazine*, 1884, p. 605.

abiding peace, which shall be within us even in the midst of our labour. The full satisfaction of this craving is reserved for the future: "There remaineth a rest for the people of God." But there are seasons and opportunities of repose vouchsafed to us even now. Resting-days are given us, on which we may gather in our thoughts from the excitement of the world, and receive into our hearts that "peace which passeth understanding."

¶ There is probably no necessity more imperatively felt by the artist, no test more unfailing of the greatness of artistical treatment, than that of the appearance of repose; yet there is no quality whose semblance in matter is more difficult to define or illustrate. As opposed to passion, change, fulness, or laborious exertion, Repose is the especial and separating characteristic of the eternal mind and power. It is the "I am" of the Creator opposed to the "I become" of all creatures; it is the sign alike of the supreme knowledge which is incapable of surprise, the supreme power which is incapable of labour, the supreme volition which is incapable of change; it is the stillness of the beams of the eternal chambers laid upon the variable waters of ministering creatures.[1]

¶ I began Miss Martineau's book (*Feats on the Fiord*) at sunrise, and finished it a little after breakfast-time. It gave me a healthy glow of feeling, a more cheerful view of life. I believe the writer of that book would rejoice that she had soothed and invigorated one day of a wayworn, tired being in his path to the Still Country, where the heaviest-laden lays down his burden at last, and has rest. Yes, thank God! there is rest—many an interval of saddest, sweetest rest—even here, when it seems as if evening breezes from that other land, laden with fragrance, played upon the cheeks and lulled the heart. There are times, even on the stormy sea, when a gentle whisper breathes softly as of heaven, and sends into the soul a dream of ecstasy which can never again wholly die, even amidst the jar and whirl of waking life. How such whispers make the blood stop and the very flesh creep with a sense of mysterious communion ! How singularly such moments are the epochs of life—the few points that stand out prominently in the recollection after the flood of years has buried all the rest, as all the low shore disappears, leaving only a few rock-points visible at high tide![2]

[1] Ruskin, *Modern Painters* (*Works*, iv. 113).
[2] *Life and Letters of F. W. Robertson*, 204.

The universal instinct of repose,
The longing for confirmed tranquillity,
Inward and outward; humble, yet sublime:
The life where hope and memory are as one;
Where earth is quiet and her face unchanged
Save by the simplest toil of human hands
Or season's difference; the immortal Soul
Consistent in self-rule; and heaven revealed
To meditation in that quietness![1]

3. "He maketh me to lie down." The first thing that the shepherd does with the sheep in the morning is to make them "lie down in green pastures." How does he do it? Not by walking them and wearing them out, but by feeding them until they are satisfied. For sheep will go on walking long after they are weary, but the moment they are satisfied they will lie down. It may seem unlikely that early in the morning, as the very first thing in the day, the shepherd should be able to feed his flock so well that they will lie down satisfied. But that depends upon the pastures. If he gets them at once to green pastures, they will of their own accord—their appetites being sharpened by the morning air—eat and be satisfied, and lie down in a great content.

Now a day with the shepherd and his sheep in the uplands is the life of the believer with God. Its first act is the satisfaction of the soul with the things which He has provided. For the believer of to-day the great provision is the Lord Jesus Christ Himself. And no one who has tasted and seen how gracious the Lord is will deny that the very first experience of the goodness and mercy of God is well described in the first act of the Eastern shepherd's working-day,—"He maketh me to lie down in green pastures."

Where dost Thou feed Thy favoured sheep?
    O my Beloved, tell me where;
My soul within Thy pastures keep,
    And guard me with Thy tender care.
Too prone, alas! to turn aside,
    Too prone with alien flocks to stray;
Be Thou my shepherd, Thou my guide,
    And lead me in Thy heavenly way.

[1] Wordsworth, *The Excursion.*

If thou wouldst know, thou favoured one,
  Where soul-refreshing pastures be;
Feed on My words of truth alone,
  And walk with those who walk with Me.
I with the contrite spirit dwell;
  The broken heart is Mine abode;
Such spikenard yields a fragrant smell,
  And such are all the saints of God.[1]

¶ "Lie down and look at it," a friend once said to me when we were out together for a trip on the Grampians. The scenery around us, I need not say, was strikingly beautiful. There were mountain-tops tipped with snow, hillsides covered with purple heath, green valleys through which flowed the Earn with its tributaries, waving cornfields, and rich pasture lands on which the sheep and deer were feeding in the distance, making a picture which, when once seen, was not to be forgotten. Here and there, too, were ruins of ancient castles, dismantled and dilapidated, carrying one's thoughts back to the realm of history, and reminding one of times when might was right and those quiet glens were the scenes of war and bloodshed.

But my companion kept on calling my attention to shades of green in the fields, shades of purple on the moors, shades of blue in the sky. He was evidently absorbed in the picturesqueness of the scenery. At last I said to him, "You have got the painter's eye, and I have not; you can see a beauty in this landscape which altogether escapes me." "Well, perhaps so," he said, "but at all events I want to give *you* the painter's eye; just lie down and look at it." And never till that moment had I been conscious of the amazing difference which a slight change of attitude can effect in viewing the fields of Nature. Everything changed with the posture and the standpoint. I now understood, for the first time, the mystic charm which mountain scenery has for the poet's and the painter's eye; the ever-changing tints and shades of colour, in earth and sea and sky, transferred with such subtle power to the canvas, and fixed there, "a thing of beauty" and "a joy for ever." All this I had learnt by following my comrade's injunction—he made me to lie down in green pastures.[2]

(1) The first essential of this rest is *an assurance of safety.*— The stranger startles the flock, the watch-dog frightens it, the howl of the wild beast scatters it in panting terror. The confidence of the first line is the key to all the gladness of the Psalm—

[1] R. T. P. Pope.   [2] R. Balgarnie.

" The Lord is my shepherd." The whole song is born of assurance. Fear strikes all dumb, as when the hawk wheels overhead in the blue heavens and hushes instantly the music of the groves. Doubt spoils it all—" the little rift within the lute." Confidence, steadfast, unwavering confidence, is the very heart of this rest. There must be a great, deep, abiding conviction wrought into me that He is mine, and I am His.

¶ What if one who calls himself my friend should ask me to his house, and welcome me with many words, and entertain me with sumptuous show of hospitality, and give me a thousand tokens of his regard. He bids me make myself at home, and hopes I shall be comfortable; but as I am going to rest, he takes me aside. " This is a pleasant house, isn't it ? " " Very, indeed," say I ; " most pleasant. The design and arrangements are perfect, the views are charming, the gardens delightful; everything is complete." " I am glad you like it; I hope you will rest well "; and then his voice sinks to a whisper—" but there is just one thing I ought to mention, we are not quite sure about the foundations." " Then, sir," I say indignantly, " you may depend upon it I am not going to stay here." Sleep ! I couldn't. Why, the man's welcome to the place is cruel; the entertainment is a hideous mockery; the decorations and furniture are a madman's folly. No; give me some poor cottage with many discomforts, but where I do know that the foundations are right, and I should be much better off.[1]

(2) The next thing is *satisfaction*.—God becomes the answer to all our longings, the fulfilment of all our hopes. He fathoms and fills the uttermost deeps of our being. Our souls lie back on Him and are satisfied—abundantly satisfied, finding in Him their being's end and aim. God made the soul for Himself; He has begotten within it a thirst that all the waters of time can never quench. This thirst, rightly interpreted, is the grand distinctive mark of our high origin—the prophecy of our return to God.

The Psalm at this point reflects the comfort and peace of those happy souls who, in early life, have tasted and seen that God is good. Satisfied in the morning with His mercy, they rejoice and are glad all their days. To make an ideal beginning of our life we must go with the Good Shepherd early and spend the dewy

[1] M. G. Pearse, in *The Sunday Magazine*, 1884, p. 606.

morn with Him upon the meadows of His grace. For then the spiritual appetite is keen and the heart feeds hungrily on the fat pastures of God's love until it is nourished into a deep content. There are no lives that dwell in such a profundity of peace or hold within them such reserve and resource of spiritual power as those who can say, "Thou hast been my God from my youth."

¶ In the dark hours of our life all other sounds die away, and leave silence in our souls—silence that we may hear His voice. And it is a great step forwards in the Christian life, if one learns to say, "The Lord is my portion." Nothing teaches this as sorrow teaches. From it we learn the transitoriness of earthly things, the permanence of the eternal, the loving call of God; but also we learn the very hard lesson that God is really the only satisfaction for the soul.[1]

II.

REFRESHMENT.

"He leadeth me beside the still waters."

1. G. A. Smith renders it thus: "By waters of rest He refresheth me." This last verb, he says, is difficult to render in English; the original meaning was evidently to guide the flock to drink, from which it came to have the more general force of sustaining or nourishing.

It is the noontide hour. "Sunbeams like swords" are smiting the sheep. They pant with heat and burn with thirst. It is time for the shepherd to lead them to the drinking-place and cool them at the waters. He knows the way. All over these Judæan hills, at frequent intervals, there are deep, walled wells, whose waters never fail. A good shepherd carries in his mind a chart of every well in all his grazing area. These wells are his chief dependence. Were it not for them the country would be impossible for grazing purposes. For though there are many streams the sheep cannot safely drink from them.

At the well-mouth, with bared arms, the shepherd stands and plunges the bucket far down into the darkness, sinking it beneath

[1] Mrs. George J. Romanes, *The Hallowing of Sorrow.*

the waters and shattering the stillness which till now has brooded there. He plunges and draws. Swiftly the rope coils at his feet as the laden bucket rises responsive to the rhythmic movements of his sinewy arms. Into the trough he pours the sparkling contents. Again the bucket shoots into the darkness of the well; again, and yet again, and when the trough is filled he calls the thirsty sheep to come in groups and drink. The lambs first, afterwards the older members of the flock, till all are served and satisfied.

2. God leads the sheep by the still waters, where it may drink the cool, clear draught in safety, and not be scared or confused by the roar of the cataract; the devil would lead the sheep beside the turbulent rapids, where it can scarcely drink without danger of being carried down to the cataract which bewilders with its noise and foam. Think of all the pleasure of simple, innocent recreation; think of the joy which comes to us from the wonder and beauty of Nature; remember the pleasures of music, of poetry, of art; think of the calm joys of true friendship, and the delights which cluster around the pure affections of the home. All these are the refreshment and exhilaration of the cool, still waters. But think of the exciting pleasures of the gambler; think of the muddled brain of the drunkard singing his foolish song; think of the riotous, lascivious mirth of the casino; reflect on the half-insane glee of the rake who boasts of his debauchery: here you have the intoxication of the rapids and the cataract. And let us never forget that the rapids and the cataract are sometimes *only farther down in the very same stream* beside the still waters of which the Lord is leading His people.

We know how often in Scripture the emblem of water, as a purifying and refreshing element, is employed to represent the gracious operations of the Holy Spirit. "If any man thirst, let him come unto me, and drink . . . this spake he of the Spirit." This is the "pure river of water of life, clear as crystal, proceeding out of the throne of God and of the Lamb." When the Spirit receives of the things of Christ and shows them to the believer, longing to behold His power, His glory, and His beauty, or discovers to him his interest in the hopes and promises of His Word, witnessing with his spirit that he is a child of God, he is strengthened and revived as by a draught from that "well of water which springeth up unto everlasting life." To be led "beside the still waters" is to be "walking in the comfort of the Holy Ghost," to be enjoying holy and tranquil communion with Him, to have clear and enlarged and soul-satisfying discoveries of Christ and His work, to have the love of God shed abroad in our hearts, so that even amid outward tribulation we have inward peace. It is He who opens up "the wells of salvation," out of which the believer draws water with joy. Though often "in a dry and thirsty land where no water is," let him follow the leadings of his Shepherd, and the promise will be fulfilled, "When the poor and needy seek water, and there is none, and their tongue faileth for thirst, I the Lord will hear them, I the God of Israel will not forsake them. I will open rivers in high places, and fountains in the midst of the valleys: I will make the wilderness a pool of water, and the dry land springs of water." This is the rest wherewith He has caused the weary to rest, and this is the refreshing which comes down on the fainting soul as the dew of Hermon, and as the dew that descended on the mountains of Zion.

> Not always, Lord, in pastures green
>   The sheep at noon Thou feedest,
>   Where in the shade they lie
>   Within Thy watchful eye:
> Not always under skies serene
>   The white-fleeced flock Thou leadest.
>
> On rugged ways, with bleeding feet,
>   They leave their painful traces;
>   Through deserts drear they go,
>   Where wounding briers grow,
> And through dark valleys, where they meet
>   No quiet resting-places.
>
> Not always by the water still,
>   Or lonely wells palm-hidden,
>   Do they find happy rest,
>   And, in Thy presence blest,
> Delight themselves, and drink their fill
>   Of pleasures unforbidden.

Their track is worn on Sorrow's shore,
Where windy storms beat ever—
Their troubled course they keep,
Where deep calls unto deep;
So going till they hear the roar
Of the dark-flowing river.

But wheresoe'er their steps may be,
So Thou their path be guiding,
O be their portion mine!
Show me the secret sign,
That I may trace their way to Thee,
In Thee find rest abiding.

Slowly they gather to the fold,
Upon Thy holy mountain,—
There, resting round Thy feet,
They dread no storm nor heat,
And slake their thirst where Thou hast rolled
The stone from Life's full fountain.[1]

III.

RESTORATION.

"He restoreth my soul."

1. The words translated "he restoreth my soul" mean to bring the soul back again to itself, to bring the soul that has become unlike itself once more into a condition of equilibrium, and therefore to inspire with new life, to recreate. There are thus two possible interpretations.

(1) Restoration may mean bringing back that which has gone astray. We think at once of the parable of the Lost Sheep recorded in the Gospel of Luke. Yonder is a shepherd with a flock of an hundred sheep feeding around him. One of them wanders off unperceived, and is lost. Though ninety and nine remain, the good shepherd misses the lost *one*; he goes forth to seek it; having found it, perhaps far away in the wilderness or the mountain, and it may be near to nightfall, he brings it back with him to the rest of the flock. He does this most tenderly and lovingly. Though it has cost him toil and pain, he does not use it roughly; he does not scourge it before him, or drag it after

[1] J. Drummond Burns.

him; he does not leave it to hireling care; he lays it on his own shoulders, rejoicing, and so brings it home.

With just such tender, compassionate loving-kindness does the Lord the Shepherd bring back the wandering soul; He bears us no grudge for the toil and pain we have cost Him, but rejoices over us; He forsakes us not, nor leaves us to our own strength, till He has carried us across the threshold of celestial bliss, and set us down among the saints in light, the home-doors folding us in.

¶ In Deuteronomy (xxii. 1, 2) we read, "Thou shalt not see thy brother's ox or his sheep go astray, and hide thyself from them: thou shalt in any case bring them again unto thy brother. And if thy brother be not nigh unto thee, or if thou know him not, then thou shalt bring it unto thine own house, and it shall be with thee until thy brother seek after it, and thou shalt restore it to him again." This humane and honest custom still prevails among the shepherds of Palestine. Whoever finds a sheep, goat, or any other domestic animal straying on his land, secures it and informs the neighbours and shepherds with whom he is acquainted, or whom he may meet, that he found an animal straying on his property and that any one who has lost such and can prove ownership should come and take it. If one finds an animal straying on the highway the finder will send it to the public square of the nearest village or city, where generally some one will recognize whose property it is. Everybody who hears of the find relates the fact to everybody else with whom he is acquainted, and to every shepherd he meets if the animal is a sheep or a goat. Animals that have been bought and brought to a flock where they are strangers will sometimes stray away in search of their former companions and shepherd.[1]

¶ An evangelical hymn from this Psalm by Sir Henry W. Baker, the editor of "Hymns Ancient and Modern," is among the most generally appreciated in that collection. The Rev. J. Julian (*Dictionary of Hymnology*, v. "Baker") says: The last audible words which lingered on his dying lips were the third stanza of his exquisite rendering of the 23rd Psalm, "The King of Love my Shepherd is":—

> Perverse and foolish oft I strayed;
> But yet in love He sought me,
> And on His shoulder gently laid,
> And home rejoicing brought me.[2]

[1] A. F. Mamreov, *A Day with the Good Shepherd*, 68.
[2] J. Earle, *The Psalter of 1539*, 267.

¶ What a beautiful, comforting gospel that is in which the Lord Christ depicts Himself as the Good Shepherd, showing what a heart He has towards us poor sinners, and how we can do nothing towards our salvation! The sheep could not defend nor provide for itself, nor keep itself from going astray, if the shepherd did not continually guide it: and when it has gone astray and is lost, cannot find its way back again, nor come to its shepherd; but the shepherd himself must go after it and seek it until he find it; otherwise it would wander and be lost for ever. And when he has found it, he must lay it on his shoulder and carry it, lest it should again be frightened away from himself, and stray or be devoured by the wolf. So also is it with us. We could neither help nor counsel ourselves, nor come to rest and peace of conscience, nor escape the devil, death, and hell, if Christ Himself, by His Word, did not fetch us, and call us to Himself. And even when we have come to Him, and are in the faith, we cannot keep ourselves in it, except He lift and carry us by His Word and power, since the devil is everywhere, and at all times on the watch to do us harm. But Christ is a thousand times more willing and earnest to do all for His sheep than the best human shepherd.[1]

(2) But it seems more in keeping with the language used to understand restoration to be revival of fainting life. It may then be regarded as an anticipation of that profound saying of Jesus concerning His sheep: "I am come that they might have life, and that they might have it *more abundantly*"—a life ever enlarging in strength and depth and fulness and joy. The hot sun has been beating down upon the flock, and they are sorely exhausted; their "soul" is faint and weary, and the shepherd uses suitable means to refresh and restore them; and then he leads them in the right ways, known to himself, whither he would have them go.

¶ Christ shelters us from the heats of life in the shade of His own majestic Personality. The thought of restoration in the protecting shade of the Divine presence occurs repeatedly throughout the Scriptures. It strikes the keynote of the Ninety-first Psalm. "He that dwelleth in the secret place of the Most High shall abide under the shadow of the Almighty." It is the central idea in Psalm One Hundred and Twenty-One. "The Lord is thy shade upon thy right hand." It is in view of this that the promise follows:—"The sun shall not smite thee by day." Isaiah

[1] Martin Luther.

dwells upon the thought with evident delight. "For thou hast been a refuge from the storm, a shadow from the heat." Again, with the thought of the Divine presence in his mind he sings, "And there shall be a pavilion for a shadow in the daytime from the heat."[1]

2. Our Psalm is deepening in spirituality and becoming more inward as it proceeds. Hitherto the shepherd-care of Jehovah has been viewed merely in its relation to bodily needs. But man is something more than a body with a set of physical desires and appetites. He is a soul. There is that within him to which the temporal and material order is not correlated. There are sides of his being that Nature cannot touch. There are mountain peaks upon which her sunlight never falls, and slopes which all her verdure cannot clothe. There are spaces that her fulness cannot fill, and depths which her deepest plummet cannot sound. The eye wearies for sights more beautiful, and the ear for harmonies more sweet, and the heart for friendships more abiding and for joys more deep and full, than those of time. Man has a set of faculties which are accommodated with a merely temporal residence in the body, in order that they may find a preparatory school for the earlier stages of their development before being launched on the timeless ranges of the life to come. No view of life can be complete which does not take this side of man into account, and no provision can be regarded as complete which does not meet its needs. Nature is too poor to meet our deepest necessities. We possess a life higher and nobler than that which can be sustained by meat and drink. We hunger for bread that Nature never breaks to us. We thirst for waters that never gush from her springs.

¶ David had lived a full life. He had known the extremes of want and wealth. He had endured the tortures of physical hunger and thirst, and had moved amid all the splendours of an Oriental court. He had mingled freely with the affairs of State, and knew all its ambitions and temptations, its plots and counter-plots. He had proved the despiritualizing effects of a voluptuous court life, and the necessity for restoration of soul; for, like the body, the soul runs down. And David had found that there was but one way of recovering spiritual tone, and that was in fulfilling personal relations with a personal God. He—Jehovah—and He

[1] J. D. Freeman, *Life on the Uplands*, 51.

alone could reinforce him on the moral side, and so brace him up that he could say " No " to the clamour of unholy desire.[1]

(1) First among the means of "restoring" is God's *Word*, read, heard, meditated upon, hidden in the heart, conversed about, prayed over, loved, opened and applied by the Holy Spirit; with its revealings, instructions, records of experience, saintly examples, consolations, mighty spiritual energies, exceeding great and precious promises.

¶ The Bible is not a book that has guided only the lives of fools and women and babes. It has moulded the lives of the noblest, and made wise men like Carlyle, Bright, Gladstone, Tennyson, Shakespeare, and Milton as vessels of power and grace. It was for many generations the chief if not the only text-book of our Scottish sires; and those whose praises are in all the churches were made brave enough to live and strong enough to die, drawing deep draughts of grace and power from the stream of Holy Scripture. In the enfolding universalness in which its unity is found; in its deep power of truth-revealing, its uplifting and guiding grace, its ocean-song of majestic phrase and captivating words, the irresistibleness of the Divine within and about it, it vindicates its claim to be Literature, and the greatest utterance of Literature in the language of men.[2]

(2) Then there is the blessed intercourse of *prayer*, whereby the creature-spirit comes into immediate communion and fellow-ship with the Infinite Spirit. There is restoring for our souls in the very contact with God, and in the answer that He sends. Let experience declare. We have gone into our closets, and bowed our knees or cast ourselves on the floor, under an over-whelming sense of feebleness and prostration, like Elijah under the juniper tree, or David when he cried out, " My soul cleaveth unto the dust"; and, through the Divine intercourse of prayer, we have come forth strong and gladdened: and, through prayer as a daily habit (growing into a necessity of our being), we have found our life deepening and expanding, and filling with joy from year to year.

¶ Prayer is a spiritual exercise, and its results are spiritual. The men who know its fullest exercise are the men who are in a condition to talk about it. *Cuique suâ arte credendum est.* Says

---

[1] H. Howard, *The Shepherd Psalm*, 39.
[2] L. MacLean Watt, *Literature and Life*, 70.

Bagehot, and with entire truth : "The criterion of true beauty is
with those—they are not many—who have a sense of true beauty;
the criterion of true morality is with those who have a sense of
true morality; and the criterion of true religion is with those
who have a sense of true religion." It is so, emphatically, with
prayer.[1]

¶ How constantly through my life have I heard testimony of
the power that answers prayer. History everywhere confesses its
force. The Huguenots took possession of the Carolinas in the
name of God. William Penn settled Pennsylvania in the name
of God. The Pilgrim Fathers settled in New England in the
name of God. Preceding the first gun of Bunker Hill, at the
voice of prayer, all heads uncovered. In the war of 1812 an
officer came to General Andrew Jackson and said, "There is an
unusual noise in the camp; it ought to be stopped." The General
asked what this noise was. He was told it was the voice of prayer.
"God forbid that prayer and praise should be an unusual noise
in the camp," said General Jackson. "You had better go and
join them."[2]

(3) Then there is *praise*—the praise of the "great congregation"; the praise of the fireside, with the sweet child-voices
chiming in; the praise of solitude, ringing through the wood or
rising from the lonely fisherman's boat; the unheard praise of the
workshop or street, when we "carry music in our heart." And
its restoring efficacy is not less wonderful. When Israel chanted
that lofty song on "the shore of deliverance," when Paul and
Silas sang aloud in the dungeon at midnight, the very singing
uplifted their spirits, doubtless, into a higher region.

¶ Song lies nearer the centre of life than we think; and the
words were spoken from a true insight, "Give me the making of
a nation's songs, and I care not who makes its laws." In the
great revival of religion in New England last century, Jonathan
Edwards mentions, as a sign of the Spirit's work and an instru-
mentality He employed, "the great disposition to abound in the
Divine exercise of singing praises, not only in appointed solemn
meetings, but when Christians occasionally met together at each
other's houses." He even gives his approval, under certain
limitations, to the practice of singing psalms on the way to or
from public worship, and says it "would have a great tendency to
enliven, animate, and rejoice the souls of God's saints, and greatly

[1] J. Brierley, *Life and the Ideal*, 74.
[2] *Autobiography of Dr. Talmage*, 156.

to propagate vital religion." As a means of revival, the importance of praise is coming to be recognized more and more by all good men.[1]

> Praise is devotion fit for mighty minds,
>   The diff'ring world's agreeing sacrifice;
> Where Heaven divided faiths united finds:
>   But Prayer in various discords upward flies.
>
> For Prayer the ocean is, where diversely
>   Men steer their course, each to a sev'ral coast;
> Where all our interests so discordant be
>   That half beg winds by which the rest are lost.
>
> By Penitence when we ourselves forsake
>   'Tis but in wise design on piteous Heaven;
> In Praise we nobly give what God may take,
>   And are, without a beggar's blush, forgiven.[2]

(4) Then there is the *communion of saints*, in all its breadth, including not only our converse one with another, but our whole intercourse and fellowship in worship and service—communion marked by sympathy, love, joy, and full of spiritual impulse and strength.

¶ "I believe in the Communion of Saints." That cannot mean a very lukewarm interest in their welfare. If the body of Christ is one, and one of the members suffer, all suffer. Infantile and poorly educated as the Church in Uganda doubtless is, yet not a few children of God here have shown a strength of faith and resistance unto blood which their fellow-believers in Europe, to-day at least, know little or nothing of. I cannot but think that their heroism deserves the commendation of all true men of God throughout the world. It must be remembered, too, what their fellows are still suffering on account of the faith. All the evils of persecution, so vividly pictured in the end of Hebrews xi., are being bravely, yet meekly, endured to-day.[3]

3. What are the methods which God employs in this moral restoration of our souls?

(1) *He begins at the very beginning.*—Deep down in the heart of every man, wearied and weakened by sin, lies the instinct that

---

[1] J. Culross, *God's Shepherd Care*, 65.
[2] Sir W. Davenant, *Gondibert*, Canto vi.   [3] *Mackay of Uganda*, 324.

for him restoration can come only through beginning life again at the very beginning; and Christ is worshipped to-day by men as their Saviour, because He has a gospel and a power to satisfy this instinct. He said to men, come back and begin again at the beginning, and, trusting Him, they found they could. He did not do this in the merely negative way in which His Gospel has sometimes been misrepresented. He did not only say, Thy sins are forgiven thee; live out the rest of thy life, sparingly with the dregs thy prodigal past has spared thee. Nor only, Thou art free, go thy way. He did not leave men where their life had run to sand. He led them back to where life was a fountain. Sometimes He did this in the simplest way. When the woman who had sinned was left alone with Him, He did not only say, " Neither do I condemn thee," and so get rid of her. He added, " Go and sin no more." What an impossible order for poor mortals to receive! Yet to hear Christ say it is not only to hear the command but to feel its possibility. And why? Not because the soul is overborne by a magical influence, which works without respect to her own powers; but because Christ makes her feel that in forgiving her God infects her with His own yearning for her purity, constrains her faculties by His love, enlists her will among the highest forces of the Universe, and the purest personalities of her own kind, and above all trusts her—there is no more natural or moral power in all the Universe than that of trust—trusts her to do her best in the discipline and warfare that await her; trusts her to be loyal to Him, and trusts her capacity to overcome.

(2) *He awakens in us the conscience of the infinite difference between obedience and disobedience.*—If we carefully read the Gospels, we shall find that next to revealing the Father, our Lord insisted most upon the infinite difference between obedience and disobedience. On this His words are always stern and frequently awful. " Except your righteousness shall exceed the righteousness of the scribes and Pharisees, ye shall in no wise enter into the kingdom of heaven. Ye have heard that it was said to them of old time, Thou shalt not kill; and whosoever shall kill shall be in danger of the judgement: but I say unto you, that every one who is angry with his brother shall be in danger of the judgement." Can we, however sleepy or dull of conscience we may be, however

self-indulgent or flattered by the world—can we listen to words like these without a startling restoration of the soul? Yet it is not only the Lord's words but Himself who restoreth our soul. How He lived, even more than what He said, is our conscience. You know the plausible habit we all slide into of giving ourselves this or that indulgence because it is within our right, or because the tempter said it was natural. Then there rises before us the figure of the Son of God tempted even thus in the wilderness. And immediately we have power to see that a thing is not right to do merely because we can do it, or because it lies along the line of our natural appetites. And our soul is restored as nothing else could have restored it.

¶ I am to think of Jesus as the Good Shepherd who speaks to *me*. He calleth His own sheep by name. If I will, I can hear His voice in words spoken from the pulpit, in the conversation of friends, in the reading of devout books. Sometimes He speaks in sweet thoughts which come to me, in the tender touches of the Spirit of God in the soul. If He speaks to me, I must listen. How am I to listen for the Divine voice? To listen for Him I must hold the powers of my soul in restraint. I must keep myself in calmness and peace. External things are in movement. Without, is the noise of the world. If this noise is filling my soul, I cannot hear the voice of the Good Shepherd. The danger of excessive pleasure, excessive business, excessive work, is this— the powers of the soul become dissipated. I *must* keep some time for retirement, for watching over myself, for listening to the voice of the Good Shepherd; then—by His Holy Spirit—He will guide me. If He find me quiet, attentive, listening, then Jesus will teach me. "Speak, Lord; for thy servant heareth." I must follow His teachings, and obey His voice, if I am indeed to be "the lost sheep" found. I must be ready and generous, willing to make ventures, strong to make sacrifices. Sometimes He may call me to trial—I must endure it; to silence—I must refrain my lips; to speech—I must speak out. Dear Shepherd, whether the way Thou callest me to be smooth or rough, give me grace to follow. Alas! how often have I failed in this! How different would my spiritual state be, had I only obeyed. Obedience to the voice is better than sacrifice, but sacrifice must, indeed, often be the duty to which I am called if I practise obedience.[1]

¶ Obedience is not an easy thing to learn. We do not learn it by singing beautiful hymns about it; by repeating with

[1] Canon Knox Little, *Treasury of Meditation.*

devotion "Thy way, not mine, O Lord," or "My God, my Father, while I stray"; nor by hearing exhortations about it; but by practising it. Christ learned obedience by the things that He suffered; and we can learn in no other way.[1]

(3) *He reveals self-sacrifice as the only secret of the fulness of life.*—The restoration of the soul which Christ begins in us by forgiveness and the faith that we are the children of God, and which He makes so keen and quick by the example of His obedience and service—this restoration, He tells us, is perfected only through self-sacrifice. That is a discipline which has always been ready to suggest itself. Most moral systems inculcate it; and there never was a man in whose heart, however obscure or ignorant, the thought of it did not arise as a resource in danger or as compensation for sin. It has been preached by religion as penance; and many a man feeling the world to be intrinsically bad, or his own body very evil, has forsaken the one or mutilated the other. But to Jesus self-sacrifice was never a penalty or a narrower life. It was a glory and a greater life. He called men to it not of fear, nor for the purpose of appeasing the Deity, or of having their sins forgiven; but in freedom and for love's sake. He urged it not that men might save a miserable remnant of life by resigning the rest, but that through self-denial they might enter a larger conception of life, and a deeper enjoyment of their possibilities as sons of God. "He that findeth his life shall lose it, but he that loseth his life shall find it."

¶ Francis of Assisi was no truer follower of Jesus Christ in poverty and simplicity of life than was David Hill. They are kindred spirits indeed in their sweetness, purity, and loving-kindness, and in different ages and in different climes they were both possessed by the same dominant idea, to follow Jesus literally, and to witness for Him to men; and in this fact is the explanation of their similarity. A self-denying life is often called an ascetic one; the two things are different, though related. Self-denial is a means to an end, asceticism is an end in itself. The monastic conception of holiness was of purity attained by rigid self-discipline, and there it stopped. The New Testament ideal of holiness is of a perfect love—a love that denies self in order to bless others. The Lord Jesus Christ left His Father's throne, and came into this world, and lived the life of a poor working-man for

---

[1] Bishop G. H. S. Walpole, *Personality and Power*, 86.

our sakes, but He was no ascetic. Following Him, David Hill lived a life of poverty and self-denial, and his beautiful and holy renunciation was not practised in order to obtain saintliness for himself, but that he might win the Chinese to be saints.[1]

¶ When, after his great breakdown in health, Bishop Lightfoot returned for too short a time to work, he made a statement on the subject, in a public speech, of almost sublime manliness. He then hoped that he had regained, or would regain, his old vigour ; but he said, boldly and frankly, that if his overwork had meant a sacrifice of life, he would not have regretted it for a moment : " I should not have wished to recall the past, even if my illness had been fatal. For what, after all, is the individual life in the history of the Church ? Men may come and men may go—individual lives float down like straws on the surface of the waters till they are lost in the ocean of eternity ; but the broad, mighty, rolling stream of the Church itself—the cleansing, purifying, fertilizing tide of the River of God—flows on for ever and ever." That is really the secret of happiness—to dare to subordinate life and personal happiness and individual performance to an institution or a cause, and to be able to lose sight of petty aims and selfish considerations in the joy of manly service.[2]

[1] J. E. Hellier, *Life of David Hill*, 72.
[2] A. C. Benson, *The Leaves of the Tree*, 206.

Good Guidance.

LITERATURE.

Brooks (P.), *The Spiritual Man*, 281.

Burns (J. D.), *Memoir and Remains*, 293.

Clarke (G.), *From the Cross to the Crown*, 16.

Cooke (G. A.), *The Progress of Revelation*, 105.

Culross (J.), *God's Shepherd Care*, 74.

Duff (R. S.), *The Song of the Shepherd*, 81.

Finlayson (T. C.), *The Divine Gentleness*, 223.

Freeman (J. D.), *Life on the Uplands*, 63.

Gray (W. H.), *Our Divine Shepherd*, 1.

Griffin (E. D.), *Plain Practical Sermons*, ii. 230.

Howard (H.), *The Shepherd Psalm*, 46, 55.

Hunt (A. N.), *Sermons for the Christian Year*, i. 199.

Jerdan (C.), *Pastures of Tender Grass*, 37.

Jowett (J. H.), in *The Presbyterian* (Canada), Sept. 1, 1910.

Knight (W. A.), *The Song of Our Syrian Guest*, 1.

McFadyen (J. E.), *The City with Foundations*, 201.

    „   „   *Ten Studies in the Psalms*, 23.

McNeill (J.), *Regent Square Pulpit*, i. 241.

Mamreov (A. F.), *A Day with the Good Shepherd*, 44.

Matheson (G.), *Thoughts for Life's Journey*, 21.

Newbolt (W. C. E.), *Penitence and Peace*, 77.

Parker (J.), *City Temple Pulpit*, vii. 270.

Smith (G. A.), *Four Psalms*, 1.

Stalker (J.), *The Psalm of Psalms*, 57.

British Congregationalist, Feb. 27, 1908 (Jowett).

Christian World Pulpit, xii. 5 (Bainton); xxi. 387 (Haines); lxv. 232 (Parker).

Expository Times, iii. 329; xix. 51.

Sunday Magazine, 1892, p. 378 (Dale).

GOOD GUIDANCE.

He guideth me in the paths of righteousness for his name's sake.—
Ps. xxiii. 3.

1. "HE guideth me in the paths of righteousness for his name's
sake." There is an insinuating and pervasive calmness in the very
words, and the leisureliness of the long vowels induces something
of the serenity which breathes through the entire Psalm. We
cannot read them at a gallop. The words are gracious sedatives,
and minister to the fretful and irritable spirit. And therefore it
is well to have such restful passages ready at hand. Some people
have little medicine chests which they carry about on their journeys,
and to which they can turn in moments of sudden ailment or
accident. And would it not be possible for us to have an
analogous ministry for the spirit?—words for times of panic,
moral sedatives when we are inclined to become feverish; spiritual
refreshers and restoratives? Just to repeat them to ourselves
very quietly is a helpful means of grace.

And yet, although the words are very restful, this particular
passage is descriptive of life which is "on the move." We are on
the open road. We are in the midst of the ministry of change.
We are leaving one thing for another. The tents have been
struck, and we are on the march. We must not forget what
immediately precedes the words of our meditation. That is ever
the difficulty of any expositor who seeks to sever a portion of this
Psalm from the whole. Every part belongs to every other part.
It is dependent upon every other part for its true interpretation.
If we cut out a bit it will bleed. So we must take it in its vital
relationships. Look back to what precedes it. "He maketh me
to lie down in green pastures." How rich is the significance!
It speaks of treasure, and leisure, and pleasure; it is a combination of sustenance and rest. It is a stretch for the weary limbs

amid fat and juicy nutriment. "He leadeth me beside the still
waters." Again, how rich is the significance! We are led by
the waters of stillness where there are no dangerous floods,
where the cattle can stand knee-deep on the feverish day, and
slake their thirst. And so this is the environment of our text,
a steeping, nutritive rest. And what is the purpose of the rest?
It is just that we might be prepared for a more valiant walk in
the "paths of righteousness." We have been taken to the field of
rest in order that we may be equipped for the roads of activity.

> Oh, splendour in the east!
>   Oh, glory in the west!
> Who is it knows the least
>   Of all your joy and rest?
>
> Oh, yellow spring-time leaves,
>   Oh, golden autumn corn,
> Sweet glow of summer eves,
>   Red light of wintry morn!
>
> Mute snow upon the lands,
>   Glad sunshine of the Springs—
> Who is it understands
>   As ye do, silent things—
>
> How good it is to do,
>   How sweet it is to rest?
> God gave us both, who knew,
>   Not we, which gift was best.[1]

2. This is, according to the Authorized Version, the second
time the word "lead" occurs in this Psalm; but it is with a
totally different signification. The Authorized Version gives no
hint of any change of meaning, but the Revisers have substituted
the word "guide" for "lead" as an indication that the distinction
should be noted. The fact is that the word translated "leadeth"
in the first case implies something done *for* the Psalmist. He
is catered for, provisioned. The Septuagint says "fostered" or
"nurtured," so that the reference is primarily to the meeting of
physical needs; whereas the Hebrew word which lies behind the
second word "leadeth" implies something done *in* the Psalmist.

[1] Mrs. Stanford Harris.

¶ Wherever St. Francis and his six friends went, their sermons excited the greatest attention in peasant circles. Some would speak to them, asking what order they belonged to and whence they came. They answered that they were of no order, but were only "men from Assisi, who lived a life of penance." But if they were penitents, they were not for that reason shame-faced—with Francis at their head, who sang in French, praised and glorified God for His untiring goodness to them. "They were able to rejoice so much," says one of the biographers, "because they had abandoned so much." When they wandered in the spring sunshine, free as the birds in the sky, through the green vineyards of Mark Ancona, they could only thank the Almighty who had freed them from all the snares and deceits which those who love the world are subject to and suffer from so sadly.[1]

¶ On meeting with so many obstructing influences, I again laid the whole matter (of becoming a missionary) before my dear parents, and their reply was to this effect:—"Heretofore we feared to bias you, but now we must tell you why we praise God for the decision to which you have been led. Your father's heart was set upon being a minister, but other claims forced him to give it up. When you were given to them, your father and mother laid you upon the altar, their first-born, to be consecrated, if God saw fit, as a missionary of the Cross; and it has been their constant prayer that you might be prepared, qualified, and led to this very decision; and we pray with all our heart that the Lord may accept your offering, long spare you, and give you many souls from the heathen world for your hire." From that moment, every doubt as to my path of duty for ever vanished. I saw the hand of God very visibly, not only preparing me for, but now leading me to, the foreign mission field.[2]

I.

THAT WE ARE GUIDED.

"He guideth me."

1. There are few things more largely written in Scripture, or more evidently and certainly experienced in good men's lives, than the leading of God—leading which is partly outward and providential, partly inward and spiritual. To the man of the

[1] J. Jörgensen, *St. Francis of Assisi*, 68.   [2] *John G. Paton*, i. 92.

world, for whom nature is a veil that hides the face of God, and who walks by the sight of his eyes and the hearing of his ears, or at the best by natural reason, it is wholly unreal, visionary, impossible, Utopian—a beautiful fancy, and nothing more. To the man of faith, on the other hand, who is " as seeing him who is invisible," there is nothing more absolutely certain and worthy of confidence. To him, life is a course in which he may enjoy the guidance of the Infinite Wisdom and the Infinite Love: to him, Jehovah is " the Shepherd of Israel," who "leadeth Joseph like a flock"; who "bringeth the blind by a way that they know not"; in whose paths "the wayfaring men, though fools, shall not err." And so it is written, "The steps of a good man are ordered by the Lord": "In all thy ways acknowledge him, and he shall direct thy paths": "Commit thy way unto the Lord; trust also in him, and he shall bring it to pass": "I am the Lord thy God, who teacheth thee to profit, who leadeth thee by the way that thou shouldest go."

The fulness of meaning contained in the words, "He leadeth me," could not be known by Old Testament saints; could not be known till the Good Shepherd came and dwelt among us. Unlike what we are accustomed to, the Eastern shepherd literally "leads" his flock; he goes before them, and calls them by name, and they follow him: and this is what the Divine Shepherd has done. He has not merely marked out the way for us in His Word; He does not merely lead us by His providence and by the inward impulse of His Spirit; but He has also gone before us,—has given us an example that we should walk in His steps: and now our part is to follow Him; to reproduce His life among men; to be in the world even as He was in the world; so that we may be able to say, by no mere figure of speech, "I live; yet not I; but Christ liveth in me."

¶ Is God your leader?—or does He only rein you in? Are you personally conscious of the vast difference between these two experiences? It is well to be held back from sin, no doubt, but the joy of the God-directed, sanctified man, is certainly beyond that of the horse and mule which have no understanding, and whose mouth must be held in with bit and bridle.

There is no holiness of a radical sort without Divine, positive, everyday guidance. This differs not only in degree but in kind from negative restraint. The latter may be no more than the rebuke or cry of our own alarmed conscience. Laws written involuntarily upon our heart operate upon our fears. Guidance appeals to our faith.

" I will guide thee with mine eye " is a promise to God's people which goes far ahead of conscience, and so universally is it intended to be enjoyed that it was given even long before the coming of our Lord.

But there is no guidance of this highest kind without the eager and abiding desire for it—a desire strong enough in its faith and intensity to survive during the severest trial and suffering.

Direct, Divine, personal guidance is the privilege of the sanctified. There is a poise of the spirit which God, when truly sought, produces. It is without bias from "self" or other influence, and may be as sensitive to Divine impressions as the photographer's film is sensitive to the light. Its possession is rare, yet how to possess it is an open secret. The conditions are of the simplest order—a real preference for the will of God, and an approach to Him by our Lord Jesus Christ.

Inbred or inherited sin is no other than a born preference for our own way. Actual sin is the carrying out of this preference into practice. Holiness, on the other hand, is a " born-from-above " preference for the will of God, resulting in love and everyday good works. When the will of God is thus preferred and practised, sin has no longer a place within us!

God's perfect guidance is perfect holiness. He cannot guide us in, or into, sin. No wonder that Paul prayed, " That ye may be filled with the knowledge of his will "; or, that, living in the centre of it, John could exclaim, " Truly our fellowship is with the Father and with his Son Jesus Christ "; and again, " Whosoever abideth in him, sinneth not." [1]

2. The means and methods of Divine leadership are many. The Great Leader is like a wise human leader, and He adapts His ministries to the nature of the child and the character of the immediate need. Let us mention two or three of these varied methods of leadership as we find them in the Word of God.

(1) Here is the first: " And the Lord spake thus to me with a strong hand." It is the speech of a young prophet, and it describes a leading of God. Let us apprehend the figure. The counsel of the Lord has come to Isaiah like a strong hand, as some-

[1] F. W. Crossley, in *Life* by Rendel Harris, 165.

thing he could not escape. The intuition was laid upon him like an arrest. What was the nature of the counsel? He was called upon by the Lord to separate himself from his nation by a solemn act of detachment. He was commanded to confront his people, to oppose them, to leave the majority and stand alone. He was bidden to prophesy the unpleasant and even to predict defeat. We know how such men are regarded—they are denounced as unpatriotic, as devoid of national feeling and fraternal ambition. The young prophet shrinks from the task; he is tempted to silence and retirement; he meditates retreat; but the Word of the Lord came to him "with a strong hand." The imperative gave him no freedom; heaven laid hold on him with holy violence; the invisible gripped his conscience as a man's arm might be gripped, until it ached in the grasp. This was the kind of leading that came to Saul as he journeyed to Damascus. It was the kind of violent arrest that laid hold of John Bunyan as he played on Elstow green.

¶ Of dogma Cromwell rarely speaks. Religion to him is not dogma, but communion with a Being apart from dogma. "Seek the Lord and His face continually," he writes to Richard, his son: "let this be the business of your life and strength, and let all things be subservient and in order to this." To Richard Mayor, the father of his son's wife, he says: "Truly our work is neither from our own brains nor from our courage and strength; but we follow the Lord who goeth before, and gather what He scattereth, that so all may appear to be from Him." Such is ever the refrain, incessantly repeated, to his family, to the Parliament, on the homely occasions of domestic life, in the time of public peril, in the day of battle, in the day of crowning victory; this is the spirit by which his soul is possessed. All work is done by a Divine leading. He expresses lively indignation with the Scottish ministers, because they dared to speak of the battle of Dunbar, that marvellous dispensation, that mighty and strange appearance of God's, as a mere "event." [1]

(2) Here is a second method of leading: "I will guide thee with mine eye." How startling the change: We pass from the grip of the hand to the glance of an eye, from a grip as severe as a vice to a touch as gentle as light. We pass from a nipping frost to a soft and cheering sunbeam. We find the word in the

[1] John Morley, *Oliver Cromwell*, 55.

Thirty-second Psalm, and the Psalm itself provides us with the figure of violent contrast. "Be ye not as the horse or the mule." The mule is headlong and headstrong, and he is to be guided by the "strong hand." But the Lord would guide us by His eye. How exceedingly delicate is the guidance of a look! What tender intercourse can pass through the eyes! There is a whole language in their silent communion. But let it be marked that this eye-guidance implies very intimate fellowship. Eye-speech is the speech of lovers. We may be guided by a "strong hand" even when we are heedless of God; we can be guided by His eye only when we are gazing on God.

¶ "They looked unto him and were lightened." That is guidance by a look. Whilst they worshipped they received the light. Their minds were illuminated while they gazed. "They caught the ways of God," and they had a certain radiance of spirit which assured them that they had found the King's will. We cannot say much about the delicate experience through the clumsy medium of words. There are some communions for which ordinary language is altogether insufficient. Who can explain the message that passes between souls in love with one another; and who can describe the gentle communion of souls in love with God? But there is another instance of this delicate guidance of the eye: "Jesus turned and looked upon Peter." That, too, was a look from Lover to lover. I know that one of the lovers had failed, but his love was not quenched. He had failed at the test, but the love was still burning. And Jesus turned, and with a look of poignant anguish He led His disloyal disciple into tears, and penitence, and reconciliation, and humble communion, and liberty. Peter was guided by the eye of his Lord.[1]

¶ What meaning, what warning, what rebuke, what counsel, what love, the eye can flash forth—so subtly, so fully, so quickly, so certainly, so powerfully! At the fireside, for example, a mother can speak to her children by glances which the stranger cannot understand, and compared with which speech is slow and uncertain. The Lord *looked* on Peter, and he went out and wept bitterly.[2]

¶ The clergy of London were at first inclined to regard their new bishop (Dr. Temple) as cold and unsympathetic, not to say brusque and overbearing; but, with personal knowledge of him, the feeling quite wore away and was exchanged, all over the

---

[1] J. H. Jowett.   [2] J. Culross, *God's Shepherd Care*, 77.

diocese, for a universal conviction that under the masculine exterior there beat a heart of almost womanly tenderness. The clergy of Hackney will not forget how, on one occasion, when speaking of the supreme value of home influence as a preparation for Confirmation, he completely broke down in relating an early experience of his own about a fault, then corrected by his mother, which had never been repeated. "She said nothing: she only looked at me with a look of pained surprise; and I have never forgotten that look."[1]

> O Jesu, gone so far apart
> Only my heart can follow Thee,
> That look which pierced St. Peter's heart
> Turn now on me.
>
> Thou who dost search me thro' and thro'
> And mark the crooked ways I went,
> Look on me, Lord, and make me too
> Thy penitent.[2]

(3) There is leading by hindering. "After they were come to Mysia they assayed to go into Bithynia; but the spirit suffered them not." And what kind of leading was this? It was leading by impediment. It was guidance by prohibition. It was the ministry of the closed door. There came to the Apostle what the Friends would describe as a "stop in the mind." His thought was resisted and had no liberty. He felt that his purpose was secretly opposed by an invincible barrier. In certain directions he had no sense of spiritual freedom, and therefore he regarded that way as blocked. "The angel of the Lord stood in the way for an adversary."[3]

> A streamlet started, singing seaward-ho!
> But found across the path its fancy planned
> A stone which stopped it with the stern command,
> "Thus far and never farther shalt thou go."
> Then, where the tiny stream was wont to flow,
> A shining lake appeared with silver strand,
> Refreshing flower-strewn fields on either hand—
> Reflecting starry skies and sunset glow.

---

[1] *Frederick Temple, Archbishop of Canterbury*, ii. 16.
[2] Christina G. Rossetti.   [3] J. H. Jowett, in *The Presbyterian*, Sept. 1, 1910.

So oftentimes we find our progress stayed
By stones that bar the steps we fain had trod,
    Whereat we murmur with a sense of wrong;
Unmindful that by means like this is made
That sea of glass where stand the saints of God
    To sing the new and never-ending song.[1]

3. "He guideth *me*." Mark that word *me*. There is not only general guidance for the whole flock, but leading for each individual member of it. Will God really concern Himself about *me*, so insignificant, so poor and needy? The experience uttered in this verse answers, *Yes*. There is nothing that comes out more clearly in Scripture than the individual care granted to all who trust in God, exactly adapted to the various conditions and circumstances of each. The very hairs of the head are numbered.

That is the supreme wonder—the infinitely gracious God takes charge of thee and me! We are neither of us overlooked in the vast crowd. "I know my sheep." "He calleth his own sheep by name, and leadeth them out." So let me step out without fear, "Whither he doth lead—to the thirsty desert or the dewy mead."

II.

That We are Guided Aright.

"He guideth me in the paths of righteousness."

1. Here and there in the grazing country of Judæa the traveller will come upon narrow, well-worn paths. Generations of shepherds and myriads of flocks have trodden these old ways. They are the recognized highways, traversing the land from well to well and from fold to fold. To come upon one of these paths is to pick up a clue that leads out from the mazes of the wilderness to some familiar rendezvous. A competent shepherd has expert knowledge of all these paths. Only with this knowledge can he plan the day's pilgrimage with accuracy and preclude the danger of being overtaken with his flock by night in wild and undefended places.

The picture which we have before us now is that of the

[1] Ellen Thorneycroft Fowler, *Verses Wise and Otherwise*, 192.

shepherd guiding his rested and freshened flock along one of these old paths. It was a fortunate thing for the sheep that they had experienced the rest and refreshment of the well before they attempted the long strip of road that stretched before them now. Restoration there has conditioned them for sturdy climbing here. For these paths are often steep and stony, severely testing the flock's strength. Before the day is done and the night fold reached, they must make heavy draught upon their stored-up energy.

¶ A man in Glasgow translated the Psalms into broad Scotch, because he thought that broad Scotch had wonderful affinities in its idiom to simple, old-world Hebrew; and I think he was right. He said here, " He leadeth me in richt roddins." There are little bits of country-road that seem to lead nowhere, but the farmer needs them all and uses them all. Tourists, if they struck them, would find that they led nowhere; but the farmer uses them, and the shepherd uses them, and the dairymaid knows all about them for her charge. So with the Lord Jesus Christ. He leads us by little bits. He does not lay out a whole champaign of country, and cast us on the great highway. No; but He leads us along this sheep-track to-day, and another sheep-track to-morrow. And these tracks never lose themselves in the moor, for He will always be with us, and it will always be found that there was a track and a path, and that it was the right path. Literally translated, it is, " He leadeth me in the straight paths." They have an expected end and termination because He is Leader and He is Guide.[1]

2. *The paths of righteousness*—that is an admirable phrase, and yet it blurs the edge of the Psalmist's meaning. It is an interpretation of his words—an excellent interpretation, as far as it goes—rather than a translation. The Psalmist was writing as a poet, and he expressed his thought in a metaphor; the phrase strips off the imaginative clothing of the thought; explains the metaphor instead of reproducing it; and the explanation is incomplete. What the Psalmist says is that God will guide His flocks in the *right paths*, the *direct paths*, to their water and their pasture; so that the sheep will not follow tracks which will bring them no nearer to what they want to reach; they will not lose themselves and waste their strength. Or, dismissing the metaphor, he means that God will lead us by the surest and

[1] John McNeill.

safest ways to the blessedness and honour to which He has destined us. Of course, these paths are righteous paths, or the righteous God would not lead us in them; and only righteous paths can bring us to where God desires us to come.

¶ *Righteousness* has here no theological meaning. The Psalmist, as the above exposition has stated, is thinking of such desert paths as have an end and goal, to which they faultlessly lead the traveller: and in God's care of man their analogy is not the experience of justification and forgiveness, but the wider assurance that he who follows the will of God walks not in vain, that in the end he arrives, for all God's paths lead onward and lead home.[1]

¶ A mother, when teaching her little daughter the 23rd Psalm, was asked, "What are the paths of righteousness?" "Well, dear, you know the little tracks up and down the hills where the sheep tread?—those are called paths." One day, when out walking with her nurse, Muriel wandered away by herself up a hill. On being asked where she was going, she replied, "I'm walking in the paths of righteousness."[2]

> So many, many roads lie traced
>   Where wanderers may stray—
> Roads twining, weaving, interlaced,
>   Roads sorrowful and gay.
> Running through countryside and town
>   They climb the mountain steep,
> Through storied realms of far renown
>   Unceasingly they creep.
> When silver moonlight floods the nights—
>   O hark! across the sea
> These roads, the wanderer's delights,
>   Are calling you and me.
> Singing their challenge sweet and clear
>   For wanderers to roam;
> But, all at once, I only hear
>   The road that leads me home.[3]

3. While they are *paths of righteousness* they are something more. For a man may say, "I acknowledge that the great thing is to keep a good conscience, to do justly, love mercy, and walk humbly with my God. But I may do that, and yet miss my way. My life may be a succession, not of sins, but of blunders. I may

---

[1] G. A. Smith, *Four Psalms*, 19.   [2] W. Canton, *Children's Sayings*, 114.
[3] Alice Cary.

be misled through my own fault or the fault of other people, or through accident and misadventure. I may make nothing of my life; or, at any rate, I may make much less of it than I might have made. The great thing is to be righteous; but, without any moral blame, through defective information or defective judgment, I may make a wrong decision in one or two critical moments, and my whole life comes to be a miserable failure." But the Psalmist means that if a man is under God's guidance he will be protected from making a wrong decision in critical moments; he will not take the wrong track; he will be kept in the right path—the righteous path, no doubt; but also the path which will lead him to the successful achievement of the great ends of life. God's guidance keeps a man from sin; but it also keeps him from wasting his strength and failing to make the most of all his powers and opportunities.

¶ St. Paul in his Epistles and spirit is more than ever clear and dear to me. As soldiers cried once, "Oh, for one day of Dundee!" so do I feel disposed to cry, "Oh, for one day of Paul!" How he would puzzle and astonish and possibly pain our Churches, ay, us all, for he is far in advance of us all yet! But as Max Piccolomini, when wishing for an angel to show him the true and good, said, why should he wish this when he had his noble Thekla with him to speak what he felt; so much more surely you and I and all who seek the truth may have peace, with the loving, patient, and wise Spirit and Guide, who will search us and lead us into all truth! [1]

¶ I suppose that in all projects for doing service to mankind, a devout man may trust God to guide him in right paths. How much time and strength and thought and money and earnestness have been spent on schemes which were well meant, and which seemed full of promise, but which have come to nothing; schemes of religious and philanthropic work; schemes of moral, social, and economical reform; schemes which had very modest though very excellent aims; schemes which it was hoped might confer enduring good on great communities! With some men nothing seems to succeed. They have a genuine desire to serve God and man; and they work hard at the methods of service which they have chosen; but somehow they always miss their way; they achieve nothing; or, if now and then they have a success, their successes are only an occasional break in a monotonous procession

[1] *Memoir of Norman MacLeod*, ii. 193.

of failures. Other men hit on the right path and have the joy of seeing all they hoped for. The end is not yet; and it may be that the apparent failures of some men were necessary to the success of others; in any case, self-sacrificing to do good will not be forgotten in heaven. But for myself, I am less and less inclined to soothe my own disappointments by taking optimistic views of human life. I cannot resist the conviction that in the plain sense of the words a great deal of good work is wasted. It was well intended; God accepts it and thinks kindly of the man who did it; what was meant to be a " cup of cold water " given to a brother of Christ will not lose its reward, even though, through the clumsiness of the hand that offered it, the water was spilt before it reached the parched lips; but it would have been better if it had not been spilt; in the plain sense of the words, the water was wasted.[1]

4. These paths of righteousness to the righteous, *led* of God in them, are also in the highest sense paths of " pleasantness." *In the highest sense*—for to the selfish heart they are irksome, and oftentimes intensely disagreeable. But to one who has tasted the joy of walking with God and doing His will, the paths of righteousness have a delight which cannot be expressed. It is, indeed, a common thought, and has done much mischief, that the ways of the Lord are ways of gloom. In part it is the whisper of the devil in the heart; in part it is a deduction from the lives of some good men who, instead of " rejoicing in the Lord alway," have thought it their duty to " hang down the head like a bulrush, and to spread sackcloth and ashes under them"; and in part we have mistakenly embodied it in our religious teaching.

¶ Mr. Edmund Gosse's poem, " To Tusitala," addressed to Robert Louis Stevenson, reached him at Vailima three days before his death. It was the last piece of verse read by Stevenson, and it is the subject of the last letter he wrote on the last day of his life. The poem was read by Mr. Lloyd Osborne at the funeral. It is now printed in Mr. Gosse's *In Russet and Silver*. It concludes as follows :—

> By strange pathways God has brought you,
>   Tusitala,
> In strange webs of fortune sought you,
> Led you by strange moods and measures
> To this paradise of pleasures !

[1] R. W. Dale, in *The Sunday Magazine*, 1892, p. 38.

And the body-guard that sought you
To conduct you home to glory,—
Dark the oriflammes they carried,
In the mist their cohort tarried,—
They were Languor, Pain, and Sorrow,
        Tusitala!
Scarcely we endured their story
Trailing on from morn to morrow,
Such the devious roads they led you,
Such the error, such the vastness,
Such the cloud that overspread you,
Under exile bow'd and banish'd,
Lost, like Moses in the fastness,
Till we almost deem'd you vanished.
Vanish'd? Ay, that's still the trouble,
        Tusitala.
Though your tropic isle rejoices,
'Tis to us an Isle of Voices
Hollow like the elfin double
Cry of disembodied echoes,
Or an owlet's wicked laughter,
Or the cold and hornëd gecko's
Croaking from a ruined rafter,—
Voices these of things existing,
Yet incessantly resisting
Eyes and hands that follow after;
You are circled, as by magic,
In a surf-built palmy bubble,
        Tusitala;
Fate hath chosen, but the choice is
Half delectable, half tragic.
For we hear you speak, like Moses,
And we greet you back, enchanted,
But reply's no sooner granted,
Than the rifted cloudland closes.[1]

¶ My mother's unquestioning evangelical faith in the literal truth of the Bible placed me, as soon as I could conceive or think, in the presence of an unseen world ; and set my active analytic power early to work on the questions of conscience, free will, and responsibility, which are easily determined in days of innocence ; but are approached too often with prejudice, and always with disadvantage, after men become stupefied by the opinions, or tainted by the sins, of the outer world : while the gloom, and even

[1] J. A. Hammerton, *Stevensoniana*, 92.

terror, with which the restrictions of the Sunday, and the doctrines of the *Pilgrim's Progress*, the *Holy War*, and Quarles' *Emblems*, oppressed the seventh part of my time, was useful to me as the only form of vexation which I was called on to endure; and redeemed by the otherwise uninterrupted cheerfulness and tranquillity of a household wherein the common ways were all of pleasantness, and its single and strait path, of perfect peace.[1]

III.

THE ASSURANCE.

"For his name's sake."

1. The ground of the Psalmist's confidence that God will guide him aright is expressed in the words "for his name's sake." That phrase is the secret of God's kindness to us. God hath loved us with an everlasting love. Divine love springs from nothing external to God Himself. It is His very essence and being. "I do not this for your sakes, O house of Israel, but for mine holy name's sake." And here is our hope and inspiration. The love we do not cause we cannot change or destroy. Be our state what it may, we are still the objects of the love of God. Then with all our sins, if we throw ourselves on that absolute and boundless affection, we shall be both welcomed and blessed.

¶ Very falsely was it said, "Names do not change Things." Names do change Things; nay, for most part they are the only substance which mankind can discern in Things.[2]

2. A true name of old not only pointed out and identified, but also described. It did not merely turn our thoughts to a particular individual, but was significant—carried a meaning in it, declared something characteristic of the individual. Thus the dying Rachel called her boy *Benoni*, "the son of my sorrow"; and Hannah called hers *Samuel*, "asked of God," saying, "Because I have asked him of the Lord."

¶ The name of God not only distinguishes Him from other beings, but describes Him; tells who He is, and what He is; so that if we know His name, we know Himself. The name is much more glorious *for us* than it was for David. Marvellous dis-

---

[1] Ruskin, *Praeterita*, i. 224.   [2] Carlyle, *Miscellanies*, iv. 116.

closures have been made since his time, both in word and act;
above all, the name has been revealed in Jesus, so that "whosoever
hath seen him hath seen the Father also." I do not think that
David has in view the name as given to Abraham or to Moses; but
the name which he has used in the beginning of this Psalm—
the shepherd-name—which tells of care, love, guidance, defence,
fellowship, salvation.[1]

3. When God leads us in the paths of righteousness "for his
name's sake," it is implied that the reason for the leading is not in
us, but *in Himself*; He is true to His shepherd-name. It is a name
that He has taken to Himself; and He will not falsify, He will not
dishonour it. In all His dealings with me He will show forth
that He *is* my Shepherd. And this is why He leads me in the
paths of righteousness : it is " for his name's sake."

¶ We should have expected him to say, "God is leading me in
green pastures on account of the good life *I* have led." On the
contrary, he says, "God is leading me in green pastures to further
the good of other people—to minister to those who have *not* led a
good life." And I think the experience of the Psalmist will be
found true to all experience. I do not believe that any man is
led into prosperity or into adversity for the *sake* of that prosperity
or adversity ; it is always for the sake of God's name or holiness.
You pray for worldly wealth and it comes to you. Has God led
you into that wealth ? Yes, but not to reward your prayer.
Rather would I say that the prayer and the riches are both parts
of His guidance into a path of humanitarian righteousness where
you can minister to the sorrows of man. Why was Abraham
promised the land of Canaan ? As a reward for leaving Ur of the
Chaldees ? No, but with the view of making blessed all the
families of the earth. God did not give him the new country as
a recompense for leaving the old; He inspired him to leave the
old because He meant to give him the new.[2]

> There is a valley paved with tears,
>   Whose gates my soul must pass,
> And to dim sight it yet appears
>   Darkly as through a glass.
> But in its gloom faith sees a light
>   More glorious than the day;
> And all its tears are rainbow bright
>   When Calvary crowns the way.

[1] J. Culross, *God's Shepherd Care*, 90.
[2] George Matheson, *Thoughts for Life's Journey*, 21.

Jesus, my Lord, within that veil
  Thy footsteps still abide;
And can my heart grow faint or fail
  When I have these to guide?
Thy track is left upon the sand
  To point my way to Thee;
Thine echoes wake the silent land
  To strains of melody.

What though the path be all unknown?
  What though the way be drear?
Its shades I traverse not alone
  When steps of Thine are near.
Thy presence, ere it passed above,
  Suffused its desert air;
Thy hand has lit the torch of love,
  And left it burning there.[1]

[1] George Matheson, *Sacred Songs*, 86.

THE VALLEY OF THE SHADOW.

LITERATURE.

Brooks (P.), *The Spiritual Man*, 286.

Burns (J. D.), *Memoir and Remains*, 301.

Cooke (G. A.), *The Progress of Revelation*, 107.

Culross (J.), *God's Shepherd Care*, 93.

Drew (H.), *Death and the Hereafter*, 86.

Duff (R. S.), *The Song of the Shepherd*, 95.

Eyton (R.), *The Search for God*, 75.

Fairbairn (A. M.), *Christ in the Centuries*, 90.

Finlayson (T. C.), *The Divine Gentleness*, 240.

Freeman (J. D.), *Life on the Uplands*, 79.

Gray (W. H.), *Our Divine Shepherd*, 19.

How (W. W.), *Plain Words*, i. 45.

Howard (H.), *The Shepherd Psalm*, 65, 71.

Hutton (W. R.), *Low Spirits*, 188.

Jerdan (C.), *Pastures of Tender Grass*, 41.

Joseph (M.), *The Ideal in Judaism*, 121.

Knight (W. A.), *The Song of Our Syrian Guest*, 14.

Lonsdale (J.), *Sermons*, 248.

McFadyen (J. E.), *Ten Studies in the Psalms*, 23.

McNeill (J.), *Regent Square Pulpit*, i. 252.

Mamreov (A. F.), *A Day with the Good Shepherd*, 71, 75.

Newbolt (W. C. E.), *Penitence and Peace*, 115.

Parker (J.), *City Temple Pulpit*, v. 175.

Pearse (M. G.), *Parables and Pictures*, 68.

    „   „   *In the Banqueting House*, 143.

Phillips (S.), *The Heavenward Way*, 88.

Roberts (D.), *A Letter from Heaven*, 124.

Service (J.), *Sermons*, 243.

Smellie (A.), *In the Hour of Silence*, 142.

Spurgeon (C. H.), *Metropolitan Tabernacle Pulpit*, xxvii. (1881) No. 1595.

Stalker (J.), *The Psalm of Psalms*, 77.

Vaughan (J.), *Sermons* (Brighton Pulpit), New Ser., xv. No. 1031.

Voysey (C.), *Sermons*, xxiii. (1900) No. 20.

Christian World Pulpit, iv. 206 (Collyer); xxi. 387 (Haynes); lxv. 232 (Parker).

Church of England Magazine, xxiii. 272 (Kelk); xxix. 256 (Perkins); xxxiv. 24 (Hull); lx. 308 (Hull).

Expository Times, v. 288 (Clemens).

Preacher's Magazine, vi. 404 (Pearse).

The Valley of the Shadow.

Yea, though I walk through the valley of the shadow of death,
I will fear no evil ; for thou art with me :
Thy rod and thy staff, they comfort me.—Ps. xxiii. 4.

1. The various methods of God's leading of His flock, or rather, we should say, the various regions into which He leads them, are described in this Psalm in order. These are Rest, Work, Sorrow; and this series is so combined with the order of time that the past and the present are considered as the regions of rest and of work, while the future is anticipated as having in it the valley of the shadow of death.

2. The word rendered "valley" does not answer exactly to our English word, which suggests a pleasant lowland sweep bounded by sloping hillsides ; nor even to the modern Arabic "wady" or torrent-bed, filled in the rainy season and dry the rest of the year; it is rather, as its derivation indicates, a chasm or rent among the hills—like Gehenna—a deep, abrupt, faintly-lighted ravine with steep sides and narrow floor, the bushes almost meeting overhead. Some savage glen among the hills of Judah, familiar to David during his shepherd-life, may have supplied the image ; some deep narrow defile where the robber lurks and takes the flock at a disadvantage, or in which some fierce beast of prey has its lair. Of course in the failing light and blackening shades of dusk the gloom would be more than doubled.

¶ The wilderness of Judæa is not a barren waste of sand and land without water, as a major portion of the Occidental world believes it to be. "Wilderness," as the word is now understood, is altogether a misnomer. The "Wilds of Judæa" would be more correctly descriptive. The wilderness of Judæa is about forty miles long and ten miles broad. It stretches along the western coast of the Dead Sea and the southern portion of the Jordan

Valley. This land of plateaus rises by steps westward from twelve hundred to fifteen hundred feet. This district presents a series of chalky, flint-strewn eminences and small plains separated by narrow torrent beds, worn deep by the winter rains, and here and there by terrific rocky gorges forming gloomy precipitous rifts through the beds of limestone. These gorges are veritable " valleys of the shadow of death " ; for in these cragged mountains there are innumerable caves, both natural and hewn in the solid rock of the " everlasting hills " (Heb. iii. 6). In these caves still live numerous wild beasts. Lions have been extinct since the days of the Crusaders, who hunted and killed till they exterminated as much life as they could during their occupation of the country. Leopards are rare, and bears are now found only in the Lebanon ranges ; but hyenas, wolves, wildcats, and jackals still roam at will over the country, as also birds of prey, such as eagles and vultures of great size and strength and beauty. All these are the natural " enemies " of the flocks of sheep and goats.[1]

3. One word is translated " shadow of death " (Heb. *tsalmāveth*). The same word (differently punctuated) means " deep shadow " or " deep gloom." And it is practically certain that this is the word the Psalmist used, although the Ancient Versions and all the great English Versions take it in the former way. In any case, it is evident from the Psalm itself that the reference is not to death. The Psalm is a series of pictures of a believer's life, and confidences. And *after* " the valley of the shadow of death " comes " the prepared table," and " the anointed head,"—and " the mantling cup," and " goodness and mercy following to the end " ; —and then " the death," or rather no death at all, for it is leapt over, or left out as almost a thing which is not,—" Surely goodness and mercy shall follow me all the days of my life " : and then, without one break, " and I will dwell in the house of the Lord for ever." Driver's translation (in *The Parallel Psalter*) is, " Yea, though I walked in a ravine of deathly gloom, I would fear no evil."

To think only of dying is greatly to narrow the application of David's words ; especially *now*, under the dispensation of the Spirit. If death throws down tremendous shadow, Christ has brought life and immortality to light through the Gospel. As a rule, believers do not find the avenue to the other world dark ; on

[1] A. F. Mamreov, *A Day with the Good Shepherd*, 16.

the contrary, the eternal light flings its radiance on their path; the eternal peace attends them; the eternal love is shed abroad within their bosom; not seldom they rejoice with joy unspeakable and full of glory.

¶ John Bunyan knew the Bible well, and he also had an intimate knowledge of the Christian life. Where does he place "the Valley of the Shadow of Death" in *The Pilgrim's Progress*? Not at the very end of the pilgrimage,—he puts the bridgeless river there,—but in the middle of the pilgrim's way.[1]

¶ After this long misery of haunted loneliness (in the Valley of the Shadow of Death) there comes the infinite relief of the human voice, as Christian hears great words spoken by a man going before him. . . . The verse which the unseen man is repeating is from the 23rd Psalm, where there is as yet no word of ending, and the comfort comes simply from the fact that God is with the man. By and by the day breaks, and Bunyan, who was intensely sensitive to the changes of light and darkness, finds a deep satisfaction in the new light. His poems of sunrise are well worth consulting. There is in them that authentic note of true poetry which reminds us sometimes of Chaucer and sometimes of Spenser. They contain the finest touches in his printed poems. The verse that Christian utters is, "He hath turned the shadow of death into the morning": it is the same that is engraved upon the tombstone of Dr. Guthrie.[2]

4. But this need not lead us away from the associations with which our old translation has invested the words. For it is not only darkness that the poet is describing, but the darkness where death lurks for the poor sheep—the gorges, in whose deep shadows are the lairs of wild beasts, and the shepherd and his club are needed. It stands thus for every dismal and deadly passage through which the soul may pass, and, most of all, it is the Valley of the Shadow of Death. There God is with men no less than by the waters of repose, or along the successful paths of active life.

¶ One night, when I was a lad, lying in my bed at home, long ago, I awoke, and it was dark, and I heard a voice in the night— not a song, but I heard the voice of my mother as she lay upon her bed of pain. She was twenty-five years in the valley of the shadow of death. Her "light affliction" endured for a quarter of a century, but it was "but for a moment," seeing that it led to the

[1] C. Jerdan, *Pastures of Tender Grass*, 41.   [2] John Kelman, *The Road*, i. 150.

JOB–PS. XXX.—29

"eternal weight of glory." I shall never forget how the sound of her voice floated into my dark room and my disquieted heart— "Yea, though I walk through the valley"—think of it rising in the air at two o'clock on a dark winter morning with the wind howling round your house—"Yea, though I walk through the valley of the shadow of death, I will fear no evil; for thou art with me." [1]

¶ This verse is full of comfort; its very terms are reassuring. Death has become, certainly to us Christians, that which the Psalmist imagined here—only a shadow. It is dark, cold, gloomy, terrible, but only a shadow. So said Archbishop Laud on the scaffold: "Lord, I am coming as fast as I can. I know I must pass through the shadow of death before I can come to see Thee. But it is but *umbra mortis*, a shadow of death, a little darkness upon nature; but Thou, Lord, by Thy goodness, hast broken the jaws and the power of death." [2]

¶ I knew an old soldier who had served throughout the Peninsular War and at Waterloo, a plain, simple-minded man who had lived a blameless Christian life, and whose most noticeable characteristic, perhaps, was the singular elevation of his spirit in prayer. As his strength declined and he wore slowly away, his cheerfulness increased, and he would talk with solemn gladness about what lay before him. Dying had ceased to trouble him; he always called it "falling asleep." As I shook hands with him on the morning of his death, he said—and his face beamed with a most perfect serenity—"I have taken many a journey in my time; this morning I am taking the pleasantest journey of all— I am going home to my Father's house." [3]

I.

COURAGE.

"I will fear no evil."

1. Even when we know that Love leads us in, it is natural for our poor, weak human hearts to shrink and fear in the entering. Not the timid only, but those who are constitutionally brave. Not children only, but even strong men; and sometimes strong

---

[1] John McNeill, *Regent Square Pulpit*, i. 254.
[2] W. C. E. Newbolt, *Penitence and Peace*, 116.
[3] J. Culross, *God's Shepherd Care*, 100.

men more than children. "They *feared* as they entered the cloud "—bright though it was. Imagination peoples the darkness with shapes of terror. Somewhere or other there *may* be danger couching invisible in the gloom, watching its opportunity, and ready to spring forth upon us without warning; and even when there is none, our faithless hearts call up a thousand frightful possibilities; and our fears are none the less distressing that they are vague and shapeless, but rather all the more.

¶ David did not mean to say that he was devoid of all fear, but only that he would surmount it so as to go without fear wherever his Shepherd should lead him. This appears more clearly from the context. He says, in the first place, " I will fear no evil"; but immediately adding the reason of this, he openly acknowledges that he seeks a remedy against his fear in contemplating, and having his eyes fixed on, the staff of his Shepherd: " For thy staff and thy crook comfort me." [1]

¶ In the Manchester Art Gallery there is a famous picture by Briton Rivière, entitled " In Manus Tuas, Domine ! " of which the artist says : " I have failed indeed if the story does not carry some lesson to ourselves to-day, whatever be our doubts or fears." The message it conveys is the victory of faith. The picture represents a fair-haired young knight clad in armour, seated upon a white charger whose downcast head, quivering nostrils and quivering limbs denote intense fear. At the charger's feet there crouch three bloodhounds, also gazing before them in terror. Behind the knight is the forest glade through which he has passed, rich in green sward and sun-kissed paths, but the path in front is full of gloom and unknown terrors. In his fear the knight is at one with the trembling brutes, but he has that within him which raises him above them and gives him aid. It is faith. Lifting his sword before his face, it forms itself into a cross. " Into Thy hands, O Lord," he says, and goes forward. He conquers fear by faith, and by it, " though he walk through the valley of the shadow, he will fear no evil." [2]

2. What is the bearing of the Lord's flock in entering this valley ? It comes into view in these words, which one speaks for all, " I will fear no evil." Mark, it is a single voice that speaks, a man all alone, conscious only of the presence of God. I will go into the death-gloom without dread and palpitation of heart. There may be threatening, alarm, evil (tiger-like) watching its

[1] Calvin, *Psalms*, i. 395.   [2] J. Burns, *Illustrations from Art* (1912), 128.

opportunity, all around; curses flung out of the darkness by the enemy, as if they were yet unrepealed; but I shall not be disquieted or dismayed, for evil shall not be allowed to harm me, yea, rather shall be compelled to contribute to my well-being.

¶ Hardly any one, when the time comes, is really afraid of death. My sister said : " I have a great fear, but also a great hope." This is uncommon. My mother said : " I wonder whether I shall ever sit in the garden any more." I am glad to be nearer death for one reason—because I can see the problems of theology in a truer manner, and can get rid of illusions.[1]

¶ About this time Mr. Romanes drew up a paper, which is given here, as it may interest some readers :—

"18 CORNWALL TERRACE, REGENT'S PARK, LONDON, N.W.

" DEAR SIR OR MADAM, — While engaged in collecting materials for a work on Human Psychology, I have been surprised to find the greatness of the differences which obtain between different races, and even between different individuals of the same race, concerning sentiments which attach to the thoughts of death. With the view, if possible, of ascertaining the causes of such differences, I am addressing a copy of the appended questions to a large number of representative and average individuals of both sexes, various nationalities, creeds, occupations, etc. It would oblige me if you would be kind enough to further the object of my inquiry by answering some or all of these questions, and adding any remarks that may occur to you as bearing upon the subject—

" ' Do you regard the prospect of your own death (*a*) with indifference, (*b*) with dislike, (*c*) with dread, or (*d*) with inexpressible horror ?

" ' If you entertain any fear of death at all, is the cause of it (*a*) prospect of bodily suffering only, (*b*) dread of the unknown, (*c*) idea of loneliness and separation from friends, or (*d*), in addition to all or any of these, a peculiar horror of an indescribable kind ?

" ' Is the state of your belief with regard to a future life that of (*a*) virtual conviction that there is a future life, (*b*) suspended judgment inclining towards such belief, (*c*) suspended judgment inclining against such belief, or (*d*) virtual conviction that there is no such life ?

" ' Is your religious belief, if any, (*a*) of a vivid order, or (*b*) without much practical influence on your life and conduct ?

[1] *The Letters of Benjamin Jowett*, 247.

"'Can you trace any change in your feelings with regard to death as having taken place during the course of your life?

"'If ever you have been in danger of death, what were the circumstances, and what your feelings?'"[1]

¶ Most wonderful is it how largely and how variously this fearless confidence comes out in the Book of Psalms—not from the sanguine and untried, but from those who have had widest and profoundest experience—who have been in the valley and have come forth from it unhurt, yea, nobler and loftier spiritually. "Though an host should encamp against me, my heart shall not fear." "God is our refuge and strength, a very present help in trouble. Therefore will not we fear though the earth be removed, and though the mountains be carried into the midst of the sea." "Thou shalt not be afraid for the terror by night, nor for the arrow that flieth by day; nor for the pestilence that walketh in darkness; nor for the destruction that wasteth at noonday." "The Lord is thy keeper; the Lord is thy shade upon thy right hand. The sun shall not smite thee by day, nor the moon by night. The Lord shall preserve thee from all evil; he shall preserve thy soul: The Lord shall preserve thy going out and thy coming in from this time forth, and even for evermore."[2]

¶ I remember going down one night, about twelve o'clock, to the seaside, and I stood in the shadow of a gloomy wood. In the front of me for miles stretched the frith of the sea. Away across yonder were the Argyleshire hills, and up above them, again, the gloomy heavens, with here and there a star peeping out. It was like the valley of the shadow of death. The sea was lapping at my feet, and a gentle breeze was blowing over it, when suddenly I heard a sound. I listened and strained my ear, and that sound turned out to be the sound, first of all, of oars in the rowlocks— a dull, thumping sound as some fishermen urged their boat along its way. And still I listened, and what I heard was the sound of music; and as the boat came nearer, there was borne to me across the waves the sound of singing. Those fishermen were Christians, and even while tugging at the weary oar in the dark and lonely night they were cheering themselves with the songs of Zion.[3]

> There is a courage, a majestic thing
>   That springs forth from the brow of pain, full grown,
>   Minerva-like, and dares all dangers known.
> And all the threatening future yet may bring;

[1] *Life and Letters of George John Romanes*, 188.
[2] J. Culross, *God's Shepherd Care*, 106.   [3] John McNeill.

Crowned with the helmet of great suffering,
   Serene with that grand strength by martyrs shown
   When at the stake they die and make no moan,
And even as the flames leap up are heard to sing.
A courage so sublime and unafraid,
   It wears its sorrows like a coat of mail;
And Fate, the archer, passes by dismayed,
   Knowing his best barbed arrows needs must fail
To pierce a soul so armoured and arrayed
   That Death himself might look on it and quail.[1]

3. On what does this fearless courage rest? Not on the thought that there *is* no evil in the dark valley. That were false because groundless security. There may be evil great and manifold in the valley; evil that has the heart, if only it had the opportunity, to ruin us; tens of thousands setting themselves against us round about; the devil himself going about like a roaring lion seeking whom he may devour. Nor does it rest on the foolish fancy that we are able ourselves to cope with the evil. We cannot even *see* to defend ourselves, although we had the strength; and any fight in which we might engage were a fight in the dark. Our courage rests on our consciously enjoying the presence of Jehovah our Shepherd. All minor considerations are omitted here—such as, that others have been in the valley already, the hope of getting well through it, the thought that bright-harnessed angel-guards surround us, and so forth —and the soul fixes on this chief thing of all, the Shepherd's presence.

It is the love of Christ and trust in Him that alone can give true courage. For notice that there is no attempt made in the Psalm to paint death otherwise than it is, in itself evil, fearful, and appalling. But it is the love of Christ that gives the confidence, the courage that we need. The God who has fed us, the Good Shepherd who has guided us through so many perils, is true and staunch, and will not desert His sheep in the hour of danger. Having loved His own which were in the world, He loved them unto the end.

¶ Among Mr. Brown's duties as assistant to Edward Irving in London one was to visit the Sunday schools, once a month each,

---

[1] Ella Wheeler Wilcox, *Poems of Passion*, 145.

when one of the exercises was the repetition of metre Psalms. An
incident connected with this duty made such a deep impression
on him that more than sixty years afterwards, when he was in his
ninety-second year, he recorded the circumstances in a journal
conducted by the Young Men's Christian Association of Aberdeen.
A poor, sickly boy, too unwell to be out, had repeated the Twenty-
third Psalm.   Next month it was reported that he was dying, and
Mr. Brown went to see him, and found him in a miserable place—a
sort of drying loft.   The mother met him with tears in her eyes,
and told him that her boy had been speaking all night.   "What
has he been speaking about?" asked Mr. Brown.   "Well, sir, you
see I am a Roman Catholic, and I don't know your hymns, but it's
something about death's dark vale."   "Oh! my woman, I know
well what your boy has been speaking about; take me to him."
"On reaching his bed [Dr. Brown explained], I found it was a deal
box, and he was lying on straw.   'My dear boy,' I said, as he
looked up smiling, 'you are dying.'   'Yes, sir.'   'Are you afraid
to die?'   'No, sir.'   'Why?'   'Because I am going to Jesus.'
'But how do you know that you are going to Jesus?'   'Because
I love Him.'   It was a child's answer [said Dr. Brown], but it
was music to me."[1]

4. The spirit of the verse is that of fearless courage in going
forward to encounter the dark unknown.   It is not possible to
evade entering the valley; but it is possible to be in it and not
to fear realizing a Divine Presence in the gloom, aware of a love
and power on which we may securely count.   And so this verse,
breathed three thousand years ago from the heart of one whom
God had comforted, comes down through the ages as God's great
Fear not to His people when He leads them into the darkness;
rather, indeed, His great Fatherly assurance that all things shall
work together for their good.   It is laid up in the Book for the use
of all future ages, a promise and strength and joy for whatever
evil days may come.   Just like those snatches of song and sudden
bursts of exaltation that lie scattered throughout the Apocalypse
—like that great *Alleluia* which is to be uttered when the Lord
God Omnipotent reigneth—so this verse, mighty for the past, is
written for times still future, and lies waiting till there shall be
hearts and lips to sing it.

¶ The highest courage has its root in faith.   One may be bold
because he is ignorant or because he lacks sensitiveness; one may

[1] W. G. Blaikie, *David Brown, D.D., LL.D.*, 36.

be indifferent to danger because he is indifferent to fate; one may be brave from that instinctive pluck which focusses all a man's powers on the doing of the thing in hand, or the resolute holding of the place to which one has been assigned; but the quality which sees with clear intelligence all the possibilities of peril, which is sensitive to pain and loss, which loves life and light and the chances of work, and yet calmly faces calamity and death, is born of faith, and grows to splendid maturity by the nurture of faith.[1]

¶ Edward Irving returned to London to find himself forbidden to administer the Sacraments, for the act of deposition was a judicial act, depriving him of his authority as a minister. Though he was re-ordained by the apostles of his own Church, he never recovered from the blow. He accepted it with a humility which was the more touching from his confidence in his extraordinary powers. But his heart was broken. Slowly his life ebbed from him. His faith in his mission was unshaken; he believed in it with all the fervour and strength of his soul, and toiled still to gain for it the ear of the world; but in vain. In September 1834 he left London a dying man. Riding through Shropshire and Wales, and visiting his scattered congregations as he went, he reached Liverpool. In his touching letters to his wife are messages to his little daughter, Maggie, sent in the simply-told stories that he gleaned on his way. When other comforts had failed, and fame had fled, he clung to his Bible, and made the Psalms his constant companions. "How in the night seasons," he writes on October 12th, "the Psalms have been my consolations against the faintings of flesh and spirit."

At Liverpool he took ship and sailed for Glasgow. The end was near. For a few weeks he was able to preach, though, at forty-two, his gaunt gigantic frame bore all the marks of age and weakness. His face was wasted, his hair white, his voice broken, his eyes restless and unquiet. As November drew to its close, his feebleness increased, till it was evident that his life was rapidly passing away. His mind began to wander. Those who watched at his bedside could not understand the broken utterances spoken in an unknown tongue by his faltering voice. But at last it was found that he was repeating to himself in Hebrew, Psalm xxiii., "The Lord is my Shepherd." It was with something like its old power that the dying voice swelled as it uttered the glorious conviction, "Though I walk through the valley of the shadow of death, I will fear no evil." The last articulate words that fell from his lips were, "If I die, I die unto the

[1] H. W. Mabie, *The Life of the Spirit*, 120.

Lord. Amen." And with these he passed away at midnight on December 7th, 1834.[1]

II.

COMPANIONSHIP.

"For thou art with me."

1. Most men will agree that it is the loneliness of death that constitutes its chief dread. If we could die in families, in groups, in communities; if hand in hand we could move down the dark valley, hand in hand breast the dark river, hand in hand pass into the Paradise of God, then death would indeed lose much of its terror and gloom. But, alas! each must die for himself, even though he may die with others. Loved ones, however dear, can only see us off. The most they can do is to smooth our passage down to the edge of the shadow, and then wish us a good voyage as we embark. Last words have to be spoken, final leave has to be taken; and then alone, as far as human eye can see, and unattended, the soul must pass out into the night that men call death. So, indeed, it seems to our dull sight; but not to the Psalmist's. With a prophet's keen vision he pierces the veil, and, seeing no break in the sheltering care of the All-Fatherly hand, triumphantly declares that even the death-crisis cannot come between him and his Shepherd-Guide. "Thou art with me!"

¶ I remember being much struck with the remark made by a former Sabbath-school teacher of my own. His mother was a widow, and he lived with her. When the doctor told him he could not survive the night, he bade good-bye to all his friends; and after they had left the house, turning to his mother he said, "We will meet the king of terrors alone." Yet even she had to leave him *to die alone.* But they who have God as their Shepherd are not even then alone. The Son of God has promised that He will come again to take them to Himself; that where He is, there they may be also.[2]

¶ "Thou art with me." I have eagerly seized on this; for out of all the terrors which gather themselves into the name of

---

[1] R. E. Prothero, *The Psalms in Human Life,* 313.
[2] W. H. Gray, *Our Divine Shepherd,* 21.

death, one has stood forth as a champion-fear to terrify and daunt me.   It is the loneliness of death.   " I die alone." [1]

> Jesu, have mercy !
> 'Tis this new feeling, never felt before,
> (Be with me, Lord, in my extremity !)
> That I am going, that I am no more.
> 'Tis this strange innermost abandonment,
>   (Lover of souls ! great God ! I look to Thee,)
> This emptying out of each constituent
>   And natural force, by which I come to be.
> Pray for me, O my friends ; a visitant
>   Is knocking his dire summons at my door,
> The like of whom, to scare me and to daunt,
>   Has never, never come to me before.[2]

2. Loneliness is a thing which we must learn to face, in our work, in the separations of life, and in times of quiet.   Certainly, whether we like it or not, we must be alone in death, as far as this world is concerned.   And men preach to us detachment.   " Sit loosely to the world," they say, that the wrench may be less when it comes.   But the Good Shepherd says rather, learn attachment. It is His promise: " Fear not; I will be with thee."   It is our confidence: " I will fear no evil : for thou art with me."   It is more ; it is our joy : " Who shall separate us from the love of Christ ? " And is not this the true answer to our fears—How can I go to meet that shadow ?   How will my faith stand its cold embrace ? How shall I ever believe in the bright promise of a land beyond, when here all is dark ?   Let us ask rather—How am I going to meet the duty just before me ?   Is He with me now ?   Have I learned to find Him in the quiet hours of the day ?   Have I found His presence in desolating sorrow ?   Have I felt His hand in darkness and doubt ?   Have I found Him near me in prayer and Eucharist ?   If so, I need not look forward.   He is leading me on, step by step, and day by day.   He is habituating me, little by little, to the withdrawal of the light, and to utter trust in Him.   " Sufficient unto the day is the evil thereof."   There is grace given me for the new day's work ; there is grace given me under this desolating sorrow.   There is grace given me to live

---

[1] W. C. E. Newbolt, *Penitence and Peace*, 118.
[2] Newman, *Dream of Gerontius*.

well; when I need it, there will be grace given me to die well. "For thou art with me." Now is the time to make firm that companionship. To be still, and know that He is God. To find the guiding Hand in all its strength and security, amid the death and life of each day's hopes and fears. And then, when we enter the shadow, still it will be "with God onwards."

¶ What is it that a mother's love with its infinite tenderness and ministry should welcome us into the world, what is it that friendship and love should gladden life through all its days, if when we pass away from earth there be but an awful solitude, a horror of great darkness, where no hand grasps ours, and no voice cheers us? What is it that the sun should shine, or that earth should yield ten thousand things to meet my commonest needs, if these highest and deepest wants within me be all unmet, and I go forth perishing with hunger? If in what *is* there be any prophecy of what shall be, if the beneficence of the present is any promise and pledge of the future, surely it must be that love shall not fail us then—then when we need it most. All hope, all need, all the goodness and promise of every day do find their fulness in the words of our Lord: "I go to prepare a place for you. And if I go and prepare a place for you, I will come again, and receive you unto myself; that where I am, there ye may be also." [1]

3. Observe at this point the change in David's manner of address. Hitherto he has been speaking about the Lord the Shepherd in the third person; now as he moves into the sphere of darkness, like a child creeping closer to his father's side in the blackening gloom, he draws closer to God, and changes from "he" to "thou"! Instead of speaking *about* Him, he speaks directly *to* Him, as to one near and hearing. In the last verse of the Psalm it was "*He* leadeth me"; now, in the region of death-shadow, it is "*Thou* art with me." The change, I think, marks the energizing of faith, and its closer grip of the great Hand in the dark. What a conception it gives us of the greatness of God that He *hears*, really hears, this breathing of the heart, "Thou art with me." Think what multitudinous voices rise to the ear of God— voices of sin, distress, joy, praise, prayer — in whispers, groans, shrieks, hosannas—in all tones—in all languages—by night and by day—from the whole earth! And yet *my* feeble voice is not

---

[1] M. G. Pearse, *In the Banqueting House*, 145.

lost in the din, but reaches His ear, when I draw close to Him in the darkness, and breathe out my confidence, " Thou art with me." [1]

III.

COMFORT.

" Thy rod and thy staff, they comfort me."

1. The shepherd is as powerful as he is tender ; for he carries in his hand a great oak club to beat off the wild beasts. Even to-day " many adventures with wild beasts occur, not unlike that recounted by David (1 Sam. xvii. 34–36); for, though there are now no lions here, there are wolves in abundance ; and leopards and panthers, exceeding fierce, prowl about these wild wadies. They not unfrequently attack the flock in the very presence of the shepherd, and he must be ready to do battle at a moment's warning " (Thomson, *The Land and the Book*). The staff is different from the rod : on it the shepherd leans; with it in various ways he helps his sheep. So that rod and staff together symbolize the power and the affection of the Divine Shepherd. Well might the Psalmist point to them with pride and gladness, and say, " *They* are my consolation."

There are several places in which this word " rod " occurs that show us its meaning. The first is in Lev. xxvii. 32. The reference is to the numbering of the sheep, driving them into a corner, so that they can pass through a gap only one at a time, and the rod is dipped over them as they are counted. So the rod is the *symbol of possession.* Then, again, although the word is not used, there is the same thought in Jer. xxxiii. 10. It is the beautiful picture of Israel's restoration. " Again shall there be heard in this place, which ye say is desolate . . . the voice of joy, and the voice of gladness, the voice of the bridegroom, and the voice of the bride, and the voice of them that say, Praise the Lord of Hosts : for the Lord is good ; for his mercy endureth for ever : . . . in this place, which is desolate . . . shall be an habitation of shepherds causing their flocks to lie down . . . the flocks shall pass again under the hands of him that telleth them, saith the Lord." It is the picture of fullest and most assured possession.

[1] J. Culross, *God's Shepherd Care*, 113.

2. The rod and the staff are not by any means those of the
pilgrim, which would be a misleading sudden transition to a
different figure, but those of Jehovah the Shepherd as the means
of guidance and defence. The rod and staff in God's hand
comfort him, *i.e.* impart to him the feeling of security, and
therefore make him of good cheer. Even when he walks through
a narrow defile, dark and gloomy as the grave, where surprise and
disasters of every kind threaten him, he fears no misfortune.

¶ The staff of the mountaineer is often inscribed with the
names of his triumphs. And on this staff what triumphs are
written! Hold it and read what is written thereon: "Able to
save to the uttermost all that come to God by him." "Able to
keep us from falling." "Able to present us faultless before the
presence of his glory with exceeding joy." Here is no room for
fear. Here faith must sing her cheeriest, sweetest song: "Thy
rod and thy staff, they comfort me."[1]

3. The rod and staff are sometimes regarded as two names
for one object, used for different purposes. The more natural
meaning of the double phrase is, however, the more correct. The
shepherd carries both a *shebet*, a kind of club or mace slung by
the side and used as an offensive weapon when needed, and a
mish'eneth, a long straight pole carried in the hand and used
for climbing, for support, and for helping the sheep in various
ways.

¶ The shepherd's staff is not a crook, as painted by foreign
artists. The shepherds of Palestine never used a crook, nor do so
to-day. It is a camel-herder that carries a light cane with a
crook at one end, with which he catches the camel by hooking its
neck with the crook, and guides it by taps of the crook instead of
a halter when riding it.[2]

¶ Going before the flock, the shepherd beats the grass and
bushes with his staff to drive out the serpents lurking in the
paths. These reptiles usually glide quickly away and escape, but
occasionally one bolder than the rest will show fight. Then quick
as a flash the good shepherd strikes the serpent with his heavy-
headed club, taking care to crush its head, because a snake is not
fatally wounded whose head is not crushed, the vital organs being
situated, as with fishes, close to the head. Otherwise, even

[1] M. G. Pearse, *In the Banqueting House*, 152.
[2] A. F. Mamreov, *A Day with the Good Shepherd*, 27.

if cut in half, it is still capable of inflicting mortal injury by its sting.[1]

4. "They comfort me." What does "comfort" mean, as used in the Bible? It means *with strength. Comfortare* is to give strength, to comfort by increasing power; not to smooth and quiet and hush down, and say, "No, be quiet, be calm." That is not the Bible comfort; comfort in the Bible is to gird with strength, to strengthen, to stimulate. He is comforted, He is made strong enough to resume the war. "They comfort me"; they make me so strong that I take up Death, and in the great wrestle I fling him to the dust.

> Death! I know not what room you are abiding in,
>> But I will go my way,
>> Rejoicing day by day,
>> Nor will I flee or stay
> For fear I tread the path you may be hiding in.
>
> Death! I know not if my small barque be nearing you;
>> But if you are at sea,
>> Still there my sails float free;
>> "What is to be will be."
> Nor will I mar the happy voyage by fearing you.
>
> Death! I know not what hour or spot you wait for me;
>> My days untroubled flow,
>> Just trusting on I go,
>> For oh, I know, I know,
> Death is but Life that holds some glad new fate for me.[2]

¶ There came a critical moment in my life when I was sadly in need of comfort, but could see none anywhere. I could not at the moment lay my hands on my Bible, and I cast about in my mind for some passage of Scripture that would help me. Immediately there flashed into my mind the words, "The Lord is my shepherd; I shall not want." At first I turned from it almost with scorn. "Such a common text as that," I said to myself, "is not likely to do me any good." I tried hard to think of a more *recherché* one; but none would come, and at last it almost seemed as if there were no other text in the whole Bible. And finally I was reduced to saying, "Well, if I cannot think of any

[1] A. F. Mamreov, *A Day with the Good Shepherd*, 72.
[2] Ella Wheeler Wilcox, *Poems of Experience*, 29.

other text, I must try to get what little good I can out of this one," and I began to repeat to myself over and over, " The Lord is my shepherd; I shall not want." Suddenly, as I did so, the words were illuminated, and there poured out upon me such floods of comfort that I felt as if I could never have a trouble again.[1]

5. " *They* comfort me." "They " is emphatic, because they are *thy* rod and *thy* staff, says Perowne. Here we must regard " they," not as the personal pronoun, but as a survival of the older function of the word, *i.e.* as a demonstrative. It would be a good practice if we followed an example which has been set by some of the Germans, and printed such latent demonstratives in spaced type. This " they " is so essential, it is so distinct and emphatic in the Hebrew, Septuagint, Vulgate, and Jerome, that it is strange Coverdale should have overlooked it.[2]

6. And they bring me through. " Though I walk *through* the valley," says David. There are words, says Pearse, that are like the shells to which children listen, hearing the roll and murmuring of the sea; words like the crystal stones within whose depths are a thousand mysteries of beauty. Such is this word *through*. I listen—it is the music of the angels that I hear, faint and afar off. I look into the word, and the light breaks, soft and pure, the light of heaven. *Through,*—it is as when one goes through some Alpine tunnel—on this side the bleak heights, the glaciers, the snows and solitude of an eternal winter; then the darkness, on and on, until at last we come forth from the gloom. Suddenly about us breaks the light of Italy, the green slopes that face the sunny south, the olive trees, the vineyards, the pastures gay with a thousand flowers, the hills all musical with waterfalls, the fertile plains rich with all kinds of crops. *Through,*—there is a way out, another side.

¶ It is a tunnel, but only a tunnel, and, like all tunnels, it has light at both ends, and certainly it has light at that end to which you are travelling. Most of the railway stations, I notice, are entered through tunnels. I do not know why, but it so happens that coming into most of our London termini you shoot through a long, dreary, ghostly, rattling tunnel, and then there is the terminus, and your father there, or your wife there on the plat-

[1] Mrs. Pearsall Smith, *The God of all Comfort,* 45.
[2] J. Earle, *The Psalter of 1539,* 267.

form, and then the embrace and the kiss and the hearty welcome. We are going through the tunnel, and at the end of it is the terminus, and, please God, we shall soon be there. It is dark and noisome and spectral, and a little awesome and fearsome just now. Sing. Sing this Psalm of heart-confidence, and the shadows will become somewhat luminous with the light that is about to reveal itself—the light of heaven, our eternal home.[1]

> How should it be a fear
> To leave the spirit's house
> Where is our certain pain?
> The wide path waits and here
> We dully pine and drowse.
>
> The Fields, the illimitable Seas,
> The Snows and Storms and Suns
> Are for our own soul's foot.
> With them will be our ease
> When the free spirit runs
>
> Out from the gate at last.—
> O halting soul, to yield
> Unto this lovely change!
> To let the lot be cast—
> Be bold—and sure—and yield![2]

¶ When a child is born into the world, one of the most wonderful things to watch is how utterly it takes its surroundings for granted; it nestles to its mother's breast, it does not doubt that it is welcome; then, as it begins to perceive what is happening to it, to look round it with intelligence, it smiles, it understands love, it imitates words, it claims the rights of home and family; it has not the least sense of being a stranger or a sad exile; all that it sees belongs to it and is its own. So will it be with the new birth, I make no doubt; we shall enter upon the unseen world with the same sense of ease and security and possession; there will even be nothing to learn at first, nothing to inquire about, nothing to wonder at. We shall just fall into our new place unquestioning and unquestioned; it will be familiar and dear, our own place, our own circle. The child is never in any doubt as to who it is and where it is; and in the vast scheme of things, our little space of experience is assured to us for ever.[3]

[1] John McNeill.   [2] M. M'Neal-Sweeney, *Men of No Land*, 77.
[3] A. C. Benson, *Thy Rod and Thy Staff*, 60.

ENTERTAINMENT, ENJOYMENT, ENRICHMENT.

LITERATURE.

Burns (J. D.), *Memoir and Remains*, 305.

Clark (H. W.), *Laws of the Inner Kingdom*, 72.

Culross (J.), *God's Shepherd Care*, 121.

Duff (R. S.), *The Song of the Shepherd*, 111, 129, 143.

Freeman (J. D.), *Life on the Uplands*, 91.

Howard (H.), *The Shepherd Psalm*, 84.

Jowett (J. H.), *The Silver Lining*, 83.

Knight (W. A.), *The Song of Our Syrian Guest*, 16.

Newbolt (W. C. E.), *Penitence and Peace*, 131.

Pearse (M. G.), *In the Banqueting House*, 155.

Price (A. C.), *Fifty Sermons*, ii. 41.

Smith (D.), *The Pilgrim's Hospice*, 73.

Spurgeon (C. H.), *Metropolitan Tabernacle Pulpit*, xv. (1869) No. 874; xxi. (1875) No. 1222.

Stalker (J.), *The Psalm of Psalms*, 91.

Vaughan (J.), *Sermons* (Brighton Pulpit), x. (1873) No. 815.

Watkinson (W. L.), *Mistaken Signs*, 155.

Wynne (G. R.), *In Quietness and Confidence*, 123.

Christian World Pulpit, xx. 123 (Hammond).

Church Pulpit Year Book, viii. (1911) 78.

Churchman's Pulpit, Harvest Thanksgiving: xcvii. 61 (Hammond).

Homiletic Review, xlviii. 465 (Norris).

ENTERTAINMENT, ENJOYMENT, ENRICHMENT.

Thou preparest a table before me in the presence of mine enemies :
Thou hast anointed my head with oil ; my cup runneth over.

Ps. xxiii. 5.

1. WE all love to look at pictures of happiness and content. We linger over the pages which describe the peaceful Garden of Eden. We love to read about the courtship of Isaac and Jacob. We take up the Book of Ruth with the same emotion. We gaze with pleasure upon the picture of little Samuel, waking up and answering the call of God. We underscore such verses in the Bible as "Ho! every one that thirsteth" and "Come unto me all ye that labour and are heavy laden." We print the Beatitudes in large type. With much reading we soil those pages where words of comfort lie. The sacred page opens of itself at the fourteenth chapter of John, where these words meet us, "Let not your heart be troubled." Often do we turn to the joy-producing miracles. Well acquainted are we with the road to Bethany, with the resurrection morning, and with the picture painted in the 23rd Psalm.

Those poems in which the cup runs over are read the most and will live the longest. "The Deserted Village" cannot die, nor the "Cottar's Saturday Night," nor the "Village Blacksmith." The bright lines of happiness in the Greek and Latin poets draw us back to them again and again. We listen to men who lift us up with hopeful words. When a David sings "My cup runneth over," travellers stop to listen. The song of happiness will make some chord tremble in every human breast.

2. This Psalm seems to belong to the later years of David's life. There is a ripeness and maturity of experience in it, also a fulness in its tone of trust, and thankfulness, and hope. Youth could

hardly write in so rich and full and immortal a strain of the goodness and all-encompassing care of God. This sweet, serene, poetic strain of the man who had been taken from the sheepfolds, from following the ewes great with young, to be king over Israel, seems to have been sung when the sun in his life's day was beginning to descend, and the shadows were beginning to lengthen. There are some things which youth has that age has not. Youth has its energy, its buoyancy of spirit, its fervid impulses, its hopeful outlook, arising partly from inexperience of life, its fresh susceptibility to impressions from the scenes of nature and events of human life. It has these things which age has not, or has only in a feeble degree. But, on the other hand, age has something which youth has not. Where the life has been devout, thoughtful, righteous, godly, there is with the passing years growth of the soul in moral qualities and in the knowledge of the unfailing care and providence of God. A man then has a wider outlook upon the events and experiences of human life, and a richer store of inward peace and faith and hopeful assurance, and can sing a sweeter, loftier song of loyal, filial praise. As we pass from youth to old age, we lose something out of our life, but with the loss there may also be gain in those things which make life real and blessed. It was so with the shepherd king of Israel, when he sang of the Lord as his Shepherd and Helper.

3. It would seem at first sight as though this Psalm had been sung amid happy surroundings, so peaceful and calm and even joyous is its strain; but it is probable that it belongs to a dark and troublous period in his life — the period, indeed, when Absalom was in revolt. We are to picture the king as an exile, having fled from Jerusalem for refuge. Absalom, in his unfilial ambition, has won the hearts of the people, and now seeks to overthrow his father, and to ascend the throne and place the crown on his own brow. It is a shameful revolt. Upon the son who now plots against him the king has lavished all the affection of his noble and intense heart. The weight of this new trouble lies heavy upon him. The pain that is smiting his heart is sharp and cruel. His life is suddenly darkened, and black tempests— charged clouds of sorrow—fill his sky. And yet, while so much

trouble was in his life, he could still calmly see ánd realize God and the goodness of God.   You do not find any weak repining, fretful crying out against God, morbid dwelling upon the gloomy events that darken his life.   Anything but that.   His trouble did not blind him to the Almighty guidance and love around him.   His hands could still sweep the strings of his harp and draw forth tones of gratitude and hope.   Faith, trust, and love, with their .beautiful offspring, peace, joy, and serenity, were still strong in his soul.   He could look out over the whole range of his life—back upon the past, around him upon the present, onward into the future—and behold, throughout it all, the hand of one who was as a shepherd.   " The Lord is my shepherd; I shall not want.   He maketh me to lie down in green pastures : he leadeth me beside the still waters."

David was far more a victor than when he had slain Goliath and received the triumphant shouts of a rejoicing people.   It is in times of trouble that a man is tested.   That we see the goodness of God when there is no trouble to darken our way is very well, but the difficult thing is to see God in His fatherly love when sorrow, like a mountain mist, envelops us and intercepts our view.   How many fail in this !   They cannot recall how they have been led in green pastures and beside still streams. They cannot feel that they are guarded as sheep by a tender Shepherd.   They cannot hope that when they walk through the narrow, sunless ravine, where dangers lurk, they will feel a Divine rod and staff comforting them.   Trial conquers them, and drives them before it as a dismasted, rudderless ship is driven before the gale.   It is a great victory for the soul to rise above trial and pray, but it is a greater victory still for the soul to rise above trial and sing.[1]

4. There are three acts in one drama : (1) Entertainment— " Thou preparest a table before me in the presence of mine enemies "; (2) Enjoyment—" Thou anointest my head with oil "; (3) Enrichment—" My cup runneth over."

[1] T. Hammond.

I.

ENTERTAINMENT.

" Thou preparest a table before me in the presence of mine enemies."

i. The Table.

1. What a picture of peace it makes, this supper on the darkening wold, when the sheep feed richly on the guarded green! For now the dew is again upon the earth. The grass is moist. The air is incense-laden from the flowers which all day long have been breathing forth their fragrance. And the fold is near.

The analogy holds true in the experience of Christ's followers. The Shepherd and Bishop of our souls reserves His choicest swards for the delectation of our later days. Beulah Land lies near the bounds of life. It comes after the long march on the roads and the adventures in the glen. Let those who face the " sunset of life " lay this comfort on their hearts! The gospel is " a great supper," as well as a satisfying breakfast, for the soul. It opens into the richest enclosures toward the day's end. Our Shepherd surpasses Himself in the banquet which He spreads for His followers on the evening tablelands of life.[1]

2. Beyond question, the prepared table is an emblem of the provision divinely made and secured for the wants of our spiritual and immortal nature. The idea is expanded in those numerous passages, both in the Old Testament and in the New, which speak of the blessings of grace as a feast which the Lord of Hosts has prepared, and to which are invited even the poor and maimed and halt and blind from the streets and lanes of the city, and the homeless wanderers from the highways and hedges. " The meek shall eat and be satisfied; they shall praise the Lord that seek him." Just as the body is nourished by appropriate food, so the spiritual being is up-built by those blessings which God's free grace provides and bestows, and which we include under the name of salvation. There is enlarging knowledge of truth and enlarging capacity of apprehending it, the blossoming of all

[1] J. D. Freeman, *Life on the Uplands*, 92.

beautiful and holy affections, growing force and greatness of nature, deepening and expanding power.

3. There is fellowship at this table. You talk with a stranger on the highway, walking side by side in the same direction; you shake hands with an acquaintance in the street; you invite a friend to your table. The very eating of an ordinary meal together at the same table, even in our own country, is so far a seal of friendliness, and makes us feel nearer to one another; and so it was to a much greater extent in old days in the East, and, indeed, is still. There was something almost sacred in the common meal; and the guest felt that he could trust his entertainer's faithfulness to the utmost, as Sisera, after partaking of the hospitality of Jael, resigned himself to sleep in her tent with a feeling of perfect security. It was counted perfidy of the worst kind when one who had eaten another's bread proved unfaithful to him; and so David says in another Psalm, " Mine own familiar friend, in whom I trusted, which did eat of my bread, hath lifted up his heel against me." [1]

4. This idea of fellowship is prominent in the Sacrament of Holy Communion. We sit down together at the table of our heavenly Father; we take the bread as from the hand of the unseen Christ; we acknowledge our brotherhood, with all its high and sacred obligations, in the Divine family; we feel ourselves united, by closer ties than those of blood relationship, to all the children of God, some of whom are before the throne, and some struggling, and praying, and rejoicing here on earth.

¶ By fellowship is meant one-mindedness, sympathy, agreement. It is not the submission of a servant to a command because it is a command. It is more, much more, than this. It is the sympathy of the friend with the friend, seeing and appreciating his character and plans, and entering into them with real heart satisfaction. It is the " amen," the " so let it be," of the spirit. " I have not called you servants, but friends." To have this fellowship two things are needed : first, knowing our Master's will, and secondly, having that mind and spirit in us which necessarily sympathizes with it. It is delightful to stand in spirit *beside* Christ, and look outwards from that central point, and see things as He sees them. This is having His " light" and " life," and therefore so

---

[1] J. Culross, *God's Shepherd Care*, 128.

living and seeing as He does; and while we do so, He has fellow-ship with us! There is something very grand I think in this high calling, to be made partakers of Christ's mind and joy! It is such godlike treatment of creatures! It shows the immense benevolence of Christ, to create us so as to lift us up to this sublime position, to make us joint heirs with Himself in all this intellectual and moral greatness and blessedness.[1]

5. There is even more than this to be taken into account, in order to enter into the full significance of David's words here. If you sit down to eat at the table of an Eastern chief, if you should even taste his salt accidentally, you come thereby under his defence; and obligations of kindness and faithfulness are created which he would count it foulest dishonour not to own.

I sit down at Jehovah's table, which He has prepared before me in the presence of mine enemies. It is not merely that I find supply for all the wants of my spiritual and immortal nature, but I am Jehovah's guest; He has received me into His pavilion His tabernacle, His palace; He has set me at His table; thus He binds Himself to protect me; He covers me with His defence, and takes me into relations of friendship with Him; my enemies look on, and know that *my* cause is *His* cause, and that in reaching me for harm they must first pierce through His defence. Thus we perceive how the words are much more than a repetition, with change of figure, of the opening idea of the Psalm; and how they lay a foundation for the great confidence, "If God be for us, who can be against us?"[2]

¶ Chalmers came to know afterwards, from one of the chiefs, that again and again the murder of the whole missionary party had been determined, and that those appointed to do the deed had come once and again to the low fence which surrounded the rough mission home. They had only to step over it and rush in upon and murder the unarmed man and his wife. Had they done this they would have been hailed as heroes by local Suau opinion. But the same chief told Chalmers that at the low fence they were restrained by some mysterious thing which held them back. What was it? To the devout mind there can be no doubt. It was the restraining Hand of that God and Father in whom both His servants so firmly trusted, at whose call they had come

---

[1] Norman Macleod, in *Memoir*, by his brother, i. 328.
[2] J. Culross, *God's Shepherd Care*, 130.

to Suau, and for whose sake they were willing to lay down their lives.[1]

ii. The Enemies.

1. "In the presence of mine enemies"—it is the one note which has a suspicion of jar in this Psalm's music of content. Were it not for the sudden intrusion of this phrase, one might suppose that for the Psalmist the whole world had been so absolutely transformed that no element of ugliness or hostility remained: here alone does his eye, as it roams over the field, alight upon something which reminds him that opposition is not quite done with yet. With all this deep peace within him—with all these marvellous mercies of God around him—the enemies still keep their hostile watch and await their chance to attack and slay. Notwithstanding the sweetness and sufficiency of the feast, it is in the presence of foes that the feast is spread. The Psalmist's joy is not a joy that blinds him to the harder realities of life, not a joy that prevents him from feeling their presence or recognizing the danger they hold; and he beholds still the unlit spots upon his world where possibilities of tragedy and harm are gathered.

2. David sees himself in his tent on the plains of Bethlehem. There it rises covered with black skins, a rough-made dwelling-place, a shelter from the scorching heat of noon or the drenching dews of night; a place where he turns aside to eat his meals, and where he keeps his supply of food. Some day he sits in the door of the tent, the sheep moving quietly about him or lying down in the green pasture, when afar off in the distance he sees one flying for very life. David starts, and, shading his eyes, stands fixed, watching eagerly. For a moment the fugitive appears on the height of the limestone cliff, then leaps down the steep path and rushes on his way. Now on the height appears the enemy that pursues him—the avenger of blood. Instantly is hurled the spear that rattles on the rocks beside the hunted man. On comes the fugitive madly; a moment's hesitation, a falter, a slip will mean certain death. He has caught sight of the shepherd's tent, and makes for it. Now he has reached the plains, and the sheep scatter as the runner comes near. The avenger sees his last chance, and puts forth all his strength in

[1] R. Lovett, *James Chalmers*, 168.

pursuit. David stands lifting the folds of the tent. Another minute, and the man rushes within its folds, and falls fainting on the ground. Now he is safe. Here he is "the guest of God," as it is called to this day. The avenger has reached the tent door, and stands with eyes flashing in furious hatred, the hand grasping the hilt of the dagger. But no foot of an enemy dare come within the tent. Its folds are as buttressed walls. Within its kindly shade David kneels, and lifts the fainting man, and holds to his lips the cup of milk—the cup that runneth over. Now the languid eyes open. The man feels the arm that supports him; he hears the voice that comforts him. He sips the proffered cup. He starts as he catches sight of the avenger, then turns and blesses the kindly shelter and the friendly succour: "Thou preparest a table before me in the presence of mine enemies."[1]

¶ There was another sacrament no less reverend in Oriental eyes and no less potent for the ratification of a covenant than the blood of sacrifice. It was the sacrament of food. Let men once eat in company, sharing table and salt, and they were forthwith bound one to the other by an inviolable bond, yea, though they had aforetime been enemies and had eaten together only by accident or inadvertence. It is told of a Bedouin sheikh whose son had been slain by an unknown hand, that, while his sorrow was yet green, a stranger came to his tent craving food and rest, and was welcomed with the generous hospitality which obtains among the sons of the desert. As they communed, the sheikh discovered that the stranger was none other than the slayer of his son. His impulse was to rise and smite him; but the stranger had eaten from his dish and drunk from his cup, and the bond of hospitality restrained him. He sat in silence, his soul burning within him; and, when the meal was ended, he led him to his son's grave and told him who lay under the mound of sand; and he bade him haste away lest the lust for vengeance should prevail and drive him to sin against the sacred covenant of hospitality.[2]

> Dear Jesus! Thou camest, Thy glory forsaking,
>   In quest of Thy sheep that had wandered away.
> Sweet Jesus! true Shepherd! on me pity taking,
>   O draw me unto Thee no longer to stray.

[1] M. G. Pearse, *In the Banqueting House*, 160.
[2] D. Smith, *The Pilgrim's Hospice*, 73.

I am the lost sheep in misery lying;
  From Hell's mouth devouring, Jesus, me free.
If Thou cleanse me from sin in the blood of Thy dying,
  O Jesus, my soul's love Thy guerdon shall be.

Thou comfort of sadness, Thou heart of all gladness,
  Love, Fountain of grace, Delight of all lands,
Good Saviour, true Shepherd! from th' Enemy's madness
  Protect me, and pluck me at death from his hands.

Jesus, how fair Thou art, Spouse of my ravished heart,
  Than honey more sweet, more serene than the sun!
May Thy free grace relieve me, Thy mercy forgive me,
  Thy glory receive me when life's course is run.

3. The Psalmist did not close with the fourth verse, otherwise so natural a climax. For he knew that weariness and death are not the last enemies of man. He knew that the future is never the true man's only fear. He remembered the inexorableness of the past; he remembered that blood-guiltiness, which sheep never feel, is worse to men than death. As perchance one day he lifted his eyes from his sheep and saw a fugitive from the avenger of blood crossing the plain, while his sheep scattered right and left before this wild intruder into their quiet world,— so he felt his fair and gentle thoughts within him scattered by the visitation of his past; so he felt how rudely law breaks through our pious fancies, and must be dealt with before their peace can be secure; so he felt, as every true man has felt with him, that the religion, however bright and brave, which takes no account of sin, is the religion which has not a last nor a highest word for life.

(1) Here then is an enemy—*the sin of yesterday.* We cannot get away from it. When we have half forgotten it, and leave it slumbering in the rear, it is suddenly awake again, and, like a hound, it is baying at our heels. Some days are days of peculiar intensity, and the far-off experience draws near and assumes the vividness of an immediate act. Yesterday pursues to-day, and threatens it!

  O! I have passed a miserable night,
  So full of ugly sights, of ghastly dreams,

> That, as I am a Christian faithful man,
> I would not spend another such a night,
> Though 'twere to buy a world of happy days,
> So full of dismal terror was the time.

And what were the "ugly sights" which filled the time with "dismal terror"? They were the threatening presences of old sins, pursuing in full cry across the years! The affrighted experience is all foreshadowed by the Word of God. Whether we turn to the Old Testament or to the New Testament the awful succession is proclaimed as a primary law of the spiritual life. "Evil pursueth sinners." That sounds significant of desert-flight and hot pursuit!

So it is that David thinks of himself, but it is no more as the sheep that lie in the morning, calm by the green pasture. He sees himself not as one *led*, but as one pursued. The broken law has its avenger. Every sin tracks a man until it runs him down —nothing can turn it aside, nothing can stay it. That is the deepest need of the human heart—deliverance from sin. No help can avail us anything unless it can save us from our sins. The foe that destroys us is not in our circumstances, or misfortunes, or pains, or poverty—out of the heart comes the murderer that seeks to slay us. This is the strength and glory of our holy religion, that it never hides or lessens the black fact that we have sinned; and yet it provides for every man a Saviour. The figure fails us here, for lo, there comes forth One to greet us who gave Himself for us, the Just for the unjust, that He might bring us to God. With a new and fuller meaning we may say indeed: "This man receiveth sinners, and eateth with them."

¶ There is a resemblance in structure, if perhaps only superficial, between this Psalm and the fifteenth chapter of the Gospel of Luke. That chapter opens with the picture of a good shepherd, and closes with a view of the festal joy when the lost son is received back into his father's house. "Let us eat, and be merry," the father says ; "for this my son was dead, and is alive again; and was lost, and is found." In like manner, this Psalm begins by speaking of the Lord as our Shepherd, and ends by telling of the joy with which we are received at His table and made to dwell in His house. The verses already considered set forth the relation of God to His people as that of a shepherd to his flock, and bring into view His careful, thoughtful, patient, mighty, sheltering love on the one side, and their trusting helplessness on the other.[1]

> Wherever He may guide me,
>   No want shall turn me back;
> My Shepherd is beside me,
>   And nothing can I lack.
> His wisdom ever waketh,
>   His sight is never dim,—
> He knows the way He taketh,
>   And I will walk with Him.
>
> Green pastures are before me,
>   Which yet I have not seen;
> Bright skies will soon be o'er me,
>   Where the dark clouds have been.
> My hope I cannot measure,
>   My path to life is free,
> My Saviour has my treasure,
>   And He will walk with me.[2]

(2) Here is another enemy—*the temptation of to-day.* Yesterday is not the only menacing presence; there is the insidious seducer who stands by the wayside to-day. Sometimes he approaches in deceptive deliberateness; sometimes his advance is so stealthy that in a moment we are caught in his snare! At one time he comes near us like a fox; at other times he leaps upon us like a lion out of the thicket. At one time the menace is in our passions, and again it crouches very near our prayers! Now the enemy draws near in the heavy guise of carnality, "the lust of the flesh"; and now in the lighter robe of covetousness, "the lust of the eyes"; and now in the delicate garb of vanity, "the pride of life"! But in all the many guises it is the one foe. In the manifold suggestions there is one threat. "The enemy that sowed them is the devil." If I am awake I fear! If I move he follows! "When I would do good evil is present with me." "O wretched man that I am, who shall deliver me from the body of this death?" The soul is in the desert chased by the enemy of ever-present temptation.

¶ When you say, "Lead us not into temptation," you must in good earnest mean to avoid in your daily conduct those temptations which you have already suffered from. When you say,

[1] J. Culross, *God's Shepherd Care*, 121.   [2] A. L. Waring.

"Deliver us from evil," you must mean to struggle against that evil in your hearts, which you are conscious of, and which you pray to be forgiven.[1]

¶ There are temptations, commonly so called, which can be a trouble, even when they have ceased to be a dread, just at the moment when we are enjoying the beauty of the scene.

> It is a beauteous evening, calm and free;
> The holy time is quiet as a nun
> Breathless with adoration; the broad sun
> Is sinking down in its tranquillity;
> The gentleness of heaven is on the sea.

Just when all is peace and glory, there comes the ribald murmur of an evil thought, the haunting disquiet of some evil imagination. In a moment the vast unprotected surface of the mind is ruffled and clouded as with a storm-gust, and pitted with stinging suggestions of falling evil. Most certainly "those that trouble us" take the shape of evil thoughts.

Now it is not God's care to remove temptation, but to strengthen the tempted. He never promised to remove trouble; but He has promised to make anxiety out of the question. He never promised to remove pain; but He has promised to elevate it into a bearing, supporting cross. "He prepares a table before me in the presence of mine enemies," as they stand, like a lion greedy of his prey, casting their eyes down to the ground.[2]

¶ You must recollect all places have their temptations—nay, even the cloisters. Our very work here is to overcome ourselves and to be sensible of our hourly infirmities; to feel them keenly is but the necessary step towards overcoming them. Never expect to be without such while life lasts; if these were overcome, you would discover others, and that both because your eyes would see your real state of imperfection more clearly than now, and also because they are in a great measure a temptation of the Enemy, and he has temptations for all states, all occasions. He can turn whatever we do, whatever we do not do, into a temptation, as a skilful rhetorician turns anything into an argument.[3]

(3) Here is a third enemy—*the death that awaits us to-morrow.* "And I looked, and behold a pale horse: and his name that sat on him was Death, and Hell followed with him." Man seeks to banish that presence from his conscience, but he pathetically fails. The pale horse with his rider walks into our feasts! He

---

[1] Cardinal Newman.   [2] W. C. E. Newbolt, *Penitence and Peace*, 133.
[3] *Letters of J. H. Newman*, ii. 428.

forces himself into the wedding-day! "To love and to cherish
until death us do part!" We have almost agreed to exile his
name from our vocabulary. If we are obliged to refer to him we
hide the slaughter-house under rose-trees, we conceal the reality
under more pleasing euphemisms. I have become insured. What
for? Because to-morrow I may——— No, I do not speak in that
wise. I banish the word at the threshold. I do not mention
death or dying. How then? I have become insured, because
"if anything should happen to me——?" In such circumlocu-
tion do I seek to evade the rider upon the pale horse. Yet the
rider is coming nearer! To-morrow he will dismount at the door,
and his hand will be upon the latch! Shall we fear his pursuit?
"The terrors of death compassed me," cries the Psalmist.
"Through fear of death" they "were all their lifetime subject
to bondage," cries the Apostle of the New Covenant. It is an
enemy we must all meet. "The last enemy . . . is death."

"God is our refuge and strength, a very present help in time
of trouble." In the Lord our God is the fugitive's refuge. "In
the secret of his tabernacle shall he hide me." In the Lord our
God we are secure against the destructiveness of our yesterdays,
the menaces of to-day, and the darkening fears of the morrow.
Our enemies are stayed at the door! We are the Lord's guests,
and our sanctuary is inviolable![1]

> Goodness and mercy
>   Ever attend,
> Guidance and keeping
>   On to the end;
> Solace in sorrow,
>   Brightness in gloom,
> Light everlasting
>   Over the tomb.
>
> Counsel and comfort
>   Whate'er befall
> Thou wilt afford us,
>   Saviour, in all.
> Let Thy glad presence
>   Still with us dwell:
> Nothing shall harm us,
>   All shall be well.

[1] J. H. Jowett, *The Silver Lining*, 88.

> Faint yet pursuing,
>   Upwards we rise;
> See the bright city,
>   Yonder the prize!
> On to the haven,
>   To the calm shore,
> In the fair city
>   Safe evermore.[1]

II.

ENJOYMENT.

"Thou hast anointed my head with oil.'

1. If the figure of the shepherd and his sheep is still retained, as some hold, then the anointing refers to a singularly beautiful custom which the Eastern shepherd has. It is the last scene of the day. At the door of the sheepfold the shepherd stands, and the "rodding of the sheep" takes place. The shepherd stands turning his body to let the sheep pass: he is the door, as Christ said of Himself. With his rod he holds back the sheep while he inspects them one by one as they pass into the fold. He has the horn filled with olive oil, and he has cedar-tar, and he anoints a knee bruised on the rocks, or a side scratched by thorns. And here comes one that is not bruised, but is simply worn and exhausted; he bathes its face and head with the refreshing olive oil, and he takes the large two-handled cup and dips it brimming full from the vessel of water provided for that purpose, and he lets the weary sheep drink. There is nothing finer in the Psalm than this. God's care is not for the wounded only, but for the worn and weary also. "He anointeth my head with oil, my cup runneth over." [2]

It is an exquisite picture of Christ's tender grace as He stands to anoint and refresh the souls of believers when, weary and worn, they look up to Him in the gloaming of life's little day. No office which our Saviour performs is more precious and beautiful than this in which He touches His weary ones with balm, that they may retire with cool, clean souls to rest.

[1] Horatius Bonar.   [2] W. A. Knight, *The Song of Our Syrian Guest*, 19.

¶ On August 18, 1887, Dr. Ullathorne writes to a friend as follows: I have been visiting Cardinal Newman to-day. He is much wasted, but very cheerful. We had a long talk, but as I was rising to leave an action of his caused a scene I shall never forget. He said in low and humble accents, "My dear lord, will you do me a great favour?" "What is it?" I asked. He glided down on his knees, bent down his venerable head, and said, "Give me your blessing." What could I do with him before me in such a posture? I could not refuse without giving him great embarrassment. So I laid my hand on his head and said: "My dear Lord Cardinal, notwithstanding all laws to the contrary, I pray God to bless you, and that His Holy Spirit may be full in your heart." As I walked to the door, refusing to put on his biretta as he went with me, he said: "I have been indoors all my life, whilst you have battled for the Church in the world."[1]

¶ There comes to mind a great educationist. In the realms both of secondary and of higher education, he was a master. He wrought out for and established in two Canadian provinces their splendid system of free schools. In a third province he gave great impetus to the thought that resulted in the creation of a vigorous Christian university. For a brief period he stood at its head. Then, realizing that his strength was broken, he suddenly stepped aside. With a single step he passed from noon to twilight. Those of us who knew him intimately knew that the pain of the twilight was acute in his heart. But the compensations were sweet and satisfying. The Master held out to him the brimming cup of joy.

> Then purged with euphrasy and rue
> The visual nerve, for he had much to see.

And he told us what he saw in kindling speech. The fountain of song was unsealed within his heart. For the few years that were left to him he moved among us like a winged spirit. He was our nightingale singing in the twilight. He was our inspirationist, our prophet, our guide, philosopher, and friend. The beauty, the richness, the literary fruitfulness of those years were the marvel and delight of all who saw. In the twilight of his day God crowned him with loving-kindness and tender mercies; He satisfied his mouth with good things, so that his youth was renewed like the eagle's.[2]

---

[1] W. Ward, *Life of Cardinal Newman*, ii. 531.
[2] J. D. Freeman, *Life on the Uplands*, 106.

2. But the thought is not less beautiful if we adopt the usual view of the structure of the 23rd Psalm, that at the fifth verse the figure of a shepherd tending his sheep is replaced by that of a host welcoming and entertaining a guest. Now, at their feasts, when they wished to express joyous welcome of a guest, they would anoint his head with a fragrant oil. When Jesus sat at meat in the house of Simon the Pharisee, He took note of the omission of this observance: "My head with oil thou didst not anoint," as men do to bidden and welcome guests. In ordinary cases, it was done by a servant, as the guest took his place at table; in special cases, it was done by the master of the house himself. So it is here. Jehovah, as it were, pours oil on the head of him whom He has invited to His table, in token of His joyous welcome. I am received, not as with reluctant and half-compelled consent, but with all the joy of His gracious heart.

¶ Compared with us in the more sunless West and North, the old Hebrews had a much keener appreciation of everything fragrant, as we see in their plentiful use of incense and perfumed oils in their religious rites and services, and in all that we know of their social life. Even *we* can know the delightful charm of a clover field, or of a hillside covered with furze and heather, or of a garden in which a thousand flowers mingle and blend their perfume; but still greater is the charm to the children of the sun, who live in regions where

> Eternal summer dwells,
> And west winds, with musky wing,
> About the cedar alleys fling
> Nard and cassia's balmy smells.

We have only to turn over the leaves of the Bible, and we find a thousand illustrations of this love of fragrant substances among the Hebrews;—in the "sweet savour" that rose from Noah's sacrifice; in the "smell of a field which the Lord hath blessed"; in "the scent of waters"; in the "perpetual incense" offered every morning and evening in the tabernacle or temple; in the "oil of gladness" with which God has anointed the king; in the "holy oil" poured upon "one that is mighty"; in the "precious ointment" to which brotherly love is likened; in the prayer "set forth before God as incense"; in the "oil of joy" given for mourning; in the "name as ointment poured forth"; in the "incense and a pure offering" that shall be offered to God's name

in every place; in the "golden vials full of odours, which are the
prayers of saints."[1]

3. In Scripture anointing with oil is employed as an emblem
of the gracious influences of the Holy Spirit. "Ye have an
unction from the Holy One." "The anointing which ye have
received from him abideth in you." It is not only that there is
the hope of a *future* salvation possessed by the believer, but the
joy of a *present* salvation begun even now—not only the "earnest
of the Spirit," as the evidence that the inheritance is purchased,
but the purifying presence of the Spirit consciously preparing him
for its sacred delights and occupations. Christ is said to have
been "anointed with the oil of gladness above his fellows," but all
His fellows, every man in His own order, are partakers of it.

III.

ENRICHMENT.

"My cup runneth over."

When seated at His table, He puts a cup into my hand—the
cup of blessing, the cup of salvation; and it is not merely full
but overflowing. He can afford to fill it; for the "Fountain of
Jacob," the source of blessing, is inexhaustible. This overflowing
cup represents His abundant goodness. The year is crowned
with the goodness of God; the earth is full of it; but this is "the
goodness of *his house*," the goodness which He has laid up for
them that fear Him; and wrought for them that trust in Him
before the sons of men. It comprehends blessings of all sorts, all
gifts of His holy and loving heart, fitted to contribute to our well-
being and joy.

¶ If God were recognized at all times as the Giver and the
Gift, every natural meal would be truly sacramental in all degrees,
being recognized as the expression of Divine love in visible form,
the natural clothing and continent of spirit and life. All truth
would be realized as Divine truth, all labour as God's working
through His children, all needful rest and recreation as God's
Sabbath; every day the Lord's Day; every dwelling a Bethel,
and every man the Temple of the Lord in whom Christ dwells.[2]

[1] J. Culross, *God's Shepherd Care*, 131. [2] J. W. Farquhar.

1. Our cup of *natural blessings* is overflowing. We see this—

(1) In the *beauty* of creation as opposed to mere *utility*. The sad philosopher of antiquity confessed: "He hath made everything beautiful in his time"; and the poet of to-day rejoices: "All things have more than barren use." Some modern cynics have roundly abused nature and tried hard to show the seamy side of the rainbow, but the loveliness and grandeur of things are too much for them, and the poet's vocation is not yet gone. Our natural belief also in the spirituality and transcendence of the beautiful and sublime is too profound to be uprooted by the utilitarian, however ingeniously he may argue on the material and physiological. Everywhere we see nature passing beyond utility into that delightful something we call beauty, glory, grandeur. Sounds harmonize into music; colours glow until the round world seems a broad, unwasting iris; cries blend into songs; the earth breaks into blossoms; the sky kindles into stars.

> Nature never did betray
> The heart that loved her; 'tis her privilege,
> Through all the years of this our life, to lead
> From joy to joy: for she can so inform
> The mind that is within us, so impress
> With quietness and beauty, and so feed
> With lofty thoughts, that neither evil tongues,
> Rash judgments, nor the sneers of selfish men,
> Nor greetings where no kindness is, nor all
> The dreary intercourse of daily life,
> Shall e'er prevail against us, or disturb
> Our cheerful faith, that all which we behold
> Is full of blessings.[1]

(2) In the *abundance* of creation as opposed to mere *sufficiency*. "Thou preparest a table before me." And how richly is that table furnished! We have a school of political economists which is tormented by the dread of population outstripping the means of subsistence, and is ever warning society against the awful peril. What confusions of heart and understanding do all these ominous vaticinations betray, seeing we dwell in a world so rich and elastic!

¶ However the utilitarian may urge his sordid story, we cannot look at the superb dome of many-coloured glass above us,

[1] Wordsworth.

or ponder the vast panorama of earth and sea, full of pictures, poems, and symphonies which human art at best only darkly mirrors, without feeling that life inherits riches far beyond all material uses. The gorgeous garniture of the universe, at which the mere physicist stumbles, and which generations of metaphysicians fail to explain, is simply the overflow of our royal cup.[1]

¶ At one period of his life John Stuart Mill was distressed by the apprehension of the exhaustibility of musical combinations, but he came to see that the possibilities of original harmony are practically infinite. It would be a blessing if that school of economists with which Mill is identified could be brought to perceive that the possibilities of the world on every side are practically infinite.[2]

2. Our cup of *social blessings* is overflowing. God setteth the solitary in families. He has constituted society that the joy of life might be full. See the precious clusters which through this gracious arrangement are pressed into our cup!

First, perhaps, to strike the eye amongst the clusters of our Canaan is *Home*—the father's reason made silken by affection; the mother's voice sweeter than any music; the kindly strength of the brother; the fondness of the sister; the comeliness and sparkle of little children. *Friendship* is a kindred cluster englobing rich wine. Another fruition is *Philanthropy*, delicious as a fruit of Paradise plucked from some branch running over the wall. Then the eye longs to drink as well as the lip, and the ear to drink as well as the eye, so *Art* displays creations refreshing as the vineyard's purple wealth; the artist with marble and canvas unsealing fountains of beauty, the musician with pipe and string pouring streams of melody. *Science* shows the earth a great emerald cup whose fulness flashes over the jewelled lip. *Literature* is a polished staff bearing grapes beyond those of Eshcol. *Commerce* is a whole vine in itself, and we gaze at its embarrassing lavishment with amazed delight. "Fir trees, cedars and oaks ; silver, iron, tin, lead, and vessels of brass; horns of ivory and ebony; wheat, honey, oil, and balm; horses and horsemen, lambs, rams, and goats ; wine and white wool ; chests of rich apparel, bound with cords; emeralds, purple and broidered

[1] W. L. Watkinson, *Mistaken Signs*, 156,   [2] *Ibid.*

work, and fine linen, coral and agate ; cassia and calamus, with chief of all spices, and with all precious stones and gold." By our ships we are replenished and made very glorious in the midst of the seas. *Patriotism* is a first-rate grape whose generous blood gives to the spirit that unselfish glow which surpasses all sensual pleasure ; and the best wine runs last in that sentiment of *Humanity* which gives the crowning joy to the festival of life.

3. The munificence of God is revealed to the uttermost in the cup of *spiritual blessing*. The cup of salvation runs over. It was not the study of God just to save us, but to save us fully, over-flowingly.

¶ May 28, 1892. If spared till to-morrow I shall have finished the eighty-second year of my pilgrimage. When I read the other day that verse in Deut. ii. 7, " The Lord thy God hath blessed thee in all the works of thy hand ; these forty years he hath been with thee, thou hast lacked nothing," I said to myself, " These eighty-and-two years He has been with me," twice the time mentioned there, and I can truly say " I have lacked nothing." More than that, He has given me " that blessed hope," the prospect of being for ever in the kingdom with Him who has redeemed me by His blood. It was in the year 1830 that I found the Saviour, or rather that He found me, and laid me on His shoulders rejoicing, and I have never parted company with Him all these sixty-two years.[1]

> I praise Thee, while Thy providence
> In childhood frail I trace,
> For blessings given, ere dawning sense
> Could seek or scan Thy grace ;
>
> Blessings in boyhood's marvelling hour,
> Bright dreams and fancyings strange ;
> Blessings, when reason's awful power
> Gave thought a bolder range ;
>
> Blessings of friends, which to my door
> Unask'd, unhoped, have come ;
> And, choicer still, a countless store
> Of eager smiles at home.

[1] A. A. Bonar, *Heavenly Springs*, 206.

Yet, Lord, in memory's fondest place
I shrine those seasons sad,
When, looking up, I saw Thy face
In kind austereness clad.

I would not miss one sigh or tear,
Heart-pang, or throbbing brow;
Sweet was the chastisement severe,
And sweet its memory now.

Yes! let the fragrant scars abide,
Love-tokens in Thy stead,
Faint shadows of the spear-pierced side,
And thorn-encompass'd head.

And such Thy tender force be still,
When self would swerve or stray,
Shaping to truth the froward will
Along Thy narrow way.

Deny me wealth; far, far remove
The lure of power or name;
Hope thrives in straits, in weakness love,
And faith in this world's shame.[1]

(1) We see it *in the pardon of sin.*—God does not forgive sin
with measure and constraint, but graciously multiplies pardons.
The overflowing cup is the sign of a grand welcome, of a cordial
friendship, of a most hearty love. The forgiveness of God is not
official, arithmetical, hesitating, but free and full beyond all compare. "He will abundantly pardon. For my thoughts are not
your thoughts, neither are your ways my ways, saith the Lord.
For as the heavens are higher than the earth, so are my ways
higher than your ways, and my thoughts than your thoughts."

¶ If God had not told a man that his sins are forgiven, it would
be presumption in him to believe that they are forgiven; but if
God has told him that they are forgiven, then the presumption
consists in disbelieving it or doubting it.[2]

¶ During the visit to Cañon City, Colo., in 1899, the Governor
of the State, hearing that Mr. Moody was to speak at the peni-
tentiary on Thanksgiving Day, wrote him, enclosing a pardon for

[1] Cardinal Newman.   [2] Thomas Erskine of Linlathen.

a woman who had already served about three years. Seven years more were before her. Mr. Moody was greatly pleased to be the bearer of the message. The woman was quite unaware of the prospective good fortune. At the close of the address, Mr. Moody produced a document, saying, " I have a pardon in my hands for one of the prisoners before me." He had intended to make some further remarks, but immediately he saw the strain caused by the announcement was so severe that he dared not go on. Calling the name, he said, " Will the party come forward and accept the Governor's Thanksgiving gift ? "

The woman hesitated a moment, then arose, uttered a shriek, and, crossing her arms over her breast, fell sobbing and laughing across the lap of the woman next her. Again she arose, staggered a short distance, and again fell at the feet of the matron of the prison, burying her head in the matron's lap. The excitement was so intense that Mr. Moody would not do more than make a very brief application of the scene to illustrate God's offer of pardon and peace.

Afterward he said that should such interest or excitement be manifest in connection with any of his meetings—when men and women accepted the pardon offered for all sin—he would be accused of extreme fanaticism and undue working on the emotions. Strange that men prize more highly the pardon of a fellow-man than the forgiveness of their God ![1]

(2) We see it also in *the sanctification of the soul.*—We are saved by Christ not merely from ruin, but into a surpassing perfection of life. The Psalmist prayed: " Purge me with hyssop, and I shall be clean: wash me, and I shall be whiter than snow." What is whiter than snow ? We have white clouds, flowers, foam, shells ; but in the whole realm of nature we know nothing whiter than snow. Are we then to dismiss the Psalmist's aspiration as so much Oriental rhetoric ? The highest poetry contains the deepest truth, and we must seek lovingly for great meanings in expressions which are really a Divine rhetoric. Is not the truth here, that grace gives our spirit a perfection beyond all perfection found in nature ? Science declares that in things most perfect there is some imperfection, that there is an ideal perfection which nature rarely or never reaches, that the most exquisite organs lack theoretical harmony and finish. Rude matter does not attain all the delicacy of the Divine thought, and the naturalist

[1] W. R. Moody, *The Life of Dwight L. Moody,* 281.

with the Psalmist complains: "I have seen an end of all perfection." But the human spirit aspires to a truthfulness, purity, and beauty beyond that of the physical universe, it pants to be whiter than snow; and this sublimest aspiration of our being is destined to attainment in Jesus Christ.

(3) There is, last of all, boundless provision *in Christ Jesus.* —History tells that an ancient king granted pardon to some criminals under sentence of death, but when these discharged malefactors applied for relief at the palace gates the king refused them, protesting: "I granted you life, but did not promise you bread." This is not the theory of the Gospel; Christ not only saves from destruction, but opens to the soul sources of rich strengthening and endless satisfaction. "In this mountain shall the Lord of hosts make unto all people a feast of fat things, a feast of wines on the lees, of fat things full of marrow, of wines on the lees well refined." This prediction is grandly accomplished in Him in whom "dwelleth all the fulness of the Godhead bodily." The Gospel of Christ is not a scheme meeting a certain dreadful exigency and then of no further significance; it is the fullest revelation of the Divine truth and love and holiness, on which the spirits of the just shall feed and feast for ever.

> Heart of Christ, O cup most golden,
>   Taking of thy cordial blest,
> Soon the sorrowful are folden
>   In a gentle healthful rest:
> Thou anxieties art easing,
> Pains implacable appeasing:
> Grief is comforted by love;
> O, what wine is there like love?
>
> Heart of Christ, O cup most golden,
>   Liberty from thee we win;
> We who drink, no more are holden
>   By the shameful cords of sin;
> Pledge of mercy's sure forgiving,
> Powers for a holy living,—
> These, thou cup of love, are thine;
> Love, thou art the mightiest wine.[1]

¶ "It passeth knowledge." It overflows the heart. The saint sometimes cries with Fletcher: "Lord, stay Thine hand, or the

---

[1] T. T. Lynch, *The Rivulet*, 87.

vessel will break." As in certain parts of Australia the abundance of flowers fills the air with sweetness until it becomes painful to the senses, so does the saint sometimes so vividly realize the grand all-encompassing love of God that the soul is overwhelmed with the mingled pain and bliss, and only finds vent in adoring tears.

> Joy through our swimming eyes doth break,
> And mean the thanks we cannot speak.[1]

¶ Annually when the ice breaks up in Russia the Czar goes in state to drink of the River Neva; and, having drunk, it was long the custom for the Czar to return the cup to his attendants full of gold, but year by year the cup became so much larger that at length a stipulated sum was paid instead of the old largesse. But however large the vessel we bring to God, and however much it increases in capacity with the discipline of years, God shall still make it to overflow with that peace and love and joy which is better than rubies and much fine gold. Let us pray

> Open the fountain from above,
> And let it our full souls o'erflow.[2]

4. How is our cup to be kept overflowing?

(1) *By keeping it always under the spring.*—The cup stands under the spring, and the spring keeps running into it, and so the cup runs over, but it will not run over long if you take it from where the springs pours into it. It is our unwisdom that we forsake the fountain of living waters and apply to the world's broken cisterns. We say in the old proverb, "Let well alone," but we forget this practical maxim with regard to the highest good. If your cup runs over, hear Christ say, "Abide in me." David had a mind to keep his cup where it was, and he said, "I will dwell in the house of the Lord for ever."

(2) *By drinking fully.*—"My cup runs over, then let me, at any rate, drink all I can. If I cannot drink it all as it flows away, let me get all I can." "Drink," said the spouse, "yea, drink abundantly, O my beloved." The Master's message at the communion table always is, "Take, eat!" and again, "Drink ye, drink ye all of it." Oftentimes, when the Lord saith to us, "Seek ye my face," we answer, "But, Lord, I am unworthy to do so." The proper answer is, "Thy face, Lord, will I seek."

[1] W. L. Watkinson, *Mistaken Signs*, 165.　　　[2] *Ibid.* 168.

(3) *By communicating to others.*—If your cup runs over, call in your friends to get the overflow. Let others participate in that which you do not wish to monopolize or intercept. Christian people ought to be like the cascades seen in brooks and rivers, always running over and so causing other falls, which again by their joyful excess cause fresh cascades, and beauty is joyfully multiplied. Are not those fountains fair to look upon where the overflow of an upper basin causes the next to fall in a silver shower, and that again produces another glassy sheet of water? If God fills one of us, it is that we may bless others; if He gives His ministering servants sweet fellowship with Him, it is that their words may encourage others to seek the same fellowship; and if their hearers get a portion of meat, it is that they may carry a portion home.

> O look, my soul, and see
>   How thy cup doth overflow!
> Think of the love so free
>   Which fills it for thee so!
>
> Let fall no tears therein
>   Of self-will or of doubt;
> There may be tears for sin,
>   But sinful tears keep out.
>
> What lies within? Life, health,
>   Friends—here, or gone before;
> Promise of heavenly wealth,
>   Of earthly, some small store;
>
> Power to act thy part
>   In earth's great labour-field;
> Grace which should make thy heart
>   An hundred-fold to yield.
>
> The drops that overflow
>   Shine in the morning sun,
> And catch the evening glow,
>   When each day's work is done.
>
> And if there mingle there
>   Some drops of darker hue,
> What colour would all bear
>   If all were but thy due?

What God's own wisdom planned,
Is it not right and meet?
Shall aught come from His hand,
And not to thee seem sweet?

Pursuit and Permanence.

Literature.

Binney (T.), in *The Pulpit*, lxvii. 29.
Burns (J. D.), *Memoir and Remains*, 308.
Culross (J.), *God's Shepherd Care*, 141.
Cunningham (W.), *Sermons*, 1.
Duff (R. S.), *The Song of the Shepherd*, 157.
Freeman (J. D.), *Life on the Uplands*, 113, 131.
Howard (H.), *The Shepherd Psalm*, 91, 98, 105.
Landels (W.), *Until the Day Break*, 33.
McFadyen (J. E.), *The Divine Pursuit*, 201.
Macmillan (H.), *The Mystery of Grace*, 135.
Matheson (G.), *Rests by the River*, 50.
Melvill (H.), *Fifty Sermons*, 31.
Munger (T. T.), *The Appeal to Life*, 67.
Newbolt (W. C. E.), *Penitence and Peace*, 142.
Pike (J. K.), *Unfailing Goodness and Mercy*, 1.
Price (A. C.), *Fifty Sermons*, vii. 169.
Stalker (J.), *The Psalm of Psalms*, 107.
Tipple (S. A.), *Sunday Mornings at Norwood*, 233.
British Weekly Pulpit, i. 597 (Macmillan).
Christian World Pulpit, xx. 123 (Hammond).

PURSUIT AND PERMANENCE.

**Surely goodness and mercy shall follow me all the days of my life:
And I will dwell in the house of the Lord for ever.—Ps. xxiii. 6.**

1. THE phrase of the poet, that "this wise world is mainly right,"
has no better illustration than the use it makes of this 23rd
Psalm. There is no other form of words which it holds so
dear, except perhaps the Lord's Prayer; but if that has a superior
majesty, this has a deeper tenderness; if one is Divine, the other
is perfectly human, and its "touch of nature makes the whole
world kin."

2. It was probably written by David, not while he was a
shepherd-boy, but after an experience of life, and perhaps during
the very stress of it. For a shepherd-boy does not sing of flocks
and pastures, even if he be a true poet, but of things that he has
dreamed yet not seen, imagined but not realized. Hence youthful poetry is of things afar off, while the poetry of men is of
things near at hand and close to their life—the daisies under their
feet, and the hills that rise from their doors. The young, when
they express themselves, are full of sentimentality; that is, feeling
not yet turned into reality under experience; but there is no
sentimentality here—only solid wisdom, won by experience and
poured out as feeling. The shepherd-boy becomes a warrior and
king; life presses hard on him; he covers it in its widest extremes,
tastes all its joy and bitterness; his heart is full and empty; he
loves and loves; he is hunted like a partridge and he rules over
nations; he digs deep pits for himself into which he falls, but rises
out of them and soars to heaven. David's nature was broad and
apparently contradictory, and every phase of his character, every
impulse of his heart, had its outward history. Into but few lives
was so much life crowded; few have touched it at so many points,

for he not only passed through vast changes of fortune, but he had a life of the heart and of the spirit correspondingly vast and various; and so his experience of life may be said to be universal, which cannot be said of Cæsar or Napoleon—men whose lives outwardly correspond to his.   Hence, when some stress of circumstance was heavy upon him and faith rose superior to it, or perchance when the whole lesson of life had been gone over and he grasped its full meaning, he sang this hymn of faith and content.

¶ This Psalm of reminiscence is not simply a leap over intervening years into the first of them, but, starting thence with a metaphor, it is a review of life and an estimate of it; it is an interpretation of life.   On looking it over and summing it up, the author states his view of life; *his* life, indeed, but what man ever had a better right to pronounce on life in general? If life is evil, he certainly ought to have known it. If life is good, he had abundant chance to prove it by tasting it in all its widest variety.   We are not to read these words of flowing sweetness as we listen to soothing music, a lullaby in infancy and a death-song in age, but as a judgment on human life.   It is Oriental, but it is logical; it is objective, but it goes to the centre; it is simple, but it is universal; it is one life, but it may be all lives.   It is not the picture of life as allotted and necessary, but as achieved.   Live your life aright and interpret it aright, and see if it is not what you find here.[1]

3. The Psalm now passes from faith and gratitude forward to hope.   The preceding part of it contemplates the past mainly; this closing verse contemplates only the future.   We see a man going through life with goodness and mercy, like angel-guardians, following him, and home full in view.   It supplies an illustration of the way in which "experience worketh hope." David has reposed his trust in the Lord, and surrendered himself to His holy and loving will; he has had proof of His faithfulness and mercy and all-sufficiency in the ever-varying circumstances of many years, and so he hopes in Him for the days or years to come; and as a bird sings forth its pleasant song even in the faint noontide from the coolness and greenness of sheltering leaves, his soul sings forth its joyful hope in God.   "Because thou *hast been* my help, therefore in the shadow of thy wings will I rejoice."

[1] T. T. Munger, *The Appeal to Life*, 69.

This verse coming at the end of the Psalm is full of blessing. It is like the great "Lo, I am with you alway, even unto the end of the world. Amen." After the falls of the third verse, after the fears of the fourth, after the temptations of the fifth, still it is "goodness and mercy" that he has to think of. "My song shall be alway of the lovingkindness of the Lord: with my mouth will I ever be shewing thy truth from one generation to another."[1]

> Thou Heart! why dost thou lift thy voice?
>   The birds are mute; the skies are dark;
> Nor doth a living thing rejoice;
>   Nor doth a living creature hark;
>   Yet thou art singing in the dark.
>
> How small thou art; how poor and frail;
>   Thy prime is past; thy friends are chill;
> Yet as thou hadst not any ail
>   Throughout the storm thou liftest still
>   A praise that winter cannot chill.
>
> Then sang that happy Heart reply:
>   "God lives, God loves, and hears me sing.
> How warm, how safe, how glad am I,
>   In shelter 'neath His spreading wing,
>   And there I cannot choose but sing."[2]

I.

The Pursuit.

"Surely goodness and mercy shall follow me all the days of my life."

1. *Goodness and mercy.*—At once these words, "goodness and mercy," attract our attention. It was "goodness and mercy" that led us first out of the fold, with an aim and object in life. There was "goodness and mercy" in that shelter from the noontide heat. But now it is "goodness and mercy" all the days of my life. And we think of grace, which is not only preventing and accompanying, but also subsequent. We owe a

---

[1] W. C. E. Newbolt, *Penitence and Peace*, 142.   [2] D. C. Dandridge, *Rose Brake*.

great deal to the grace that comes after, the grace that follows us; not only the grace that gives us the wish to do what is right, not only the grace that starts us and helps us in what is right, but also the grace that helps us to finish.

Here is that striking characteristic of the love of God Almighty which comes out in all His dealings with us, namely, its completeness. "Having loved his own which were in the world, he loved them unto the end." Creative love, which placed man in the world, did not exhaust the goodness of God towards him: redemptive love met him when he fell. And as if redemptive love itself were not sufficient, sanctifying love came in to fill up where redemptive love seemed to lack. So it is with each single soul. God completes His work.

¶ Perfect the day shall be, when it is of all men understood that the beauty of Holiness must be in labour as well as in rest. Nay! *more*, if it may be, in labour; in our strength, rather than in our weakness; and in the choice of what we shall work for through the six days, and may know to be good at their evening time, than in the choice of what we pray for on the seventh, of reward or repose. With the multitude that keep holiday, we may perhaps sometimes vainly have gone up to the house of the Lord, and vainly there asked for what we fancied would be mercy; but for the few who labour as their Lord would have them, the mercy needs no seeking, and their wide home no hallowing. Surely goodness and mercy shall *follow* them, *all* the days of their life; and they shall dwell in the house of the Lord—FOR EVER.[1]

¶ Ought not we who bear the name of Jesus to ask ourselves whether we are keeping pace in new purposes and answering with devotion God's summoning gifts and challenging mercies? When the year is old or the year is young, and we think of the passing of life, it is a good thing to ask whether our trees justify the room they take and the nourishment they get in the Master's vineyard. Is your tree standing because "it brings forth more fruit"? or is it because of the mercy, the hope, the patience, of the Lord who intercedes,—"Spare it yet another year; it may be it will bear fruit"? Let the goodness of God lead us to repentance and a better return in fruitfulness and fidelity for His loving care.[2]

¶ No gloomy foreboding as to a dark and unknown future— no dread of the King of Terrors—no doubts as to his acceptance

---

[1] Ruskin, *Lectures on Art*, § 96 (*Works*, xx. 94).
[2] M. D. Babcock, *Thoughts for Every-Day Living*, 36.

in Christ, obscured the radiance of his setting sun. In the same letter, written within six weeks of his death, when he was in good health, James Haldane thus affectionately addresses his eldest son in London, as if anticipating that his years (now eighty-three) were numbered: "This is the last day of the year, and the last letter I shall write this year. My life has been wonderfully preserved, much beyond the usual course of nature. Goodness and mercy have followed me all the days of my life, and, without the shadow of boasting, I can add, I shall dwell in the house of the Lord for ever. May the blessing of God Almighty rest on you and yours!"[1]

Enough that blessings undeserved
   Have marked my erring track;—
That wheresoe'er my feet have swerved,
   His chastening turned me back;—

That more and more a Providence
   Of love is understood,
Making the springs of time and sense
   Sweet with eternal good;

That death seems but a covered way
   Which opens into light,
Wherein no blinded child can stray
   Beyond the Father's sight;—

That care and trial seem at last,
   Through Memory's sunset air,
Like mountain-ranges overpast;
   In purple distance fair—

That all the jarring notes of life
   Seem blending in a psalm,
And all the angles of its strife
   Slow rounding into calm.

And so the shadows fall apart,
   And so the west-winds play;
And all the windows of my heart
   I open to the day.[2]

---

[1] A. Haldane, *The Lives of Robert and James Haldane*, 640.
[2] Whittier, *My Psalm*.

2. The Psalmist's hope is uttered in a twofold form of speech. First and in general, it is the hope of "goodness and mercy"; "*goodness*," including all that contributes to our well-being, temporal and spiritual, and "satisfies" the wants of our nature,— not mere cold beneficence that chills us while it aids, but having a heart of lovingkindness; "*mercy*," including all the manifestations of His favour, whether as compassion, forbearance, long-suffering, deliverance, forgiving love, help in time of need, or whatever else may be named—all that it glorifies God to bestow, and blesses us to receive.

¶ There is a touching story of Lord Westbury which Sir William Gull told me. He was dying of a painful disease, and said to Sir William and Sir James Paget, "Surely this is, if ever there was, a case for Euthanasia, or the happy despatch." They argued with him that their duty was to preserve life, and on the following day he said, "I suppose you are right. I have been thinking over the story of what the Roundhead said when he met the Royalist in heaven. He was surprised at his presence, and asked him how it had come about. The Royalist answered—

> Between the saddle and the ground
> I mercy sought and mercy found.

I suppose you think that might be my case." [1]

(1) We may compare Goodness to an angel with a radiant countenance, bright as the sun, ever beaming with smiles that shed gladness all around her. She has a light and buoyant step, and movements musical as the chiming of marriage bells. Flowers grow where she treads, and springs of living water flow to refresh the thirsty ground. She has a full and yet open hand, for while always dispensing her gifts, her store is never exhausted.

We connect her ministry with the brightest times in our history, when all is manifestly going well with us. We see it most clearly in what may be called the summer of the soul, when the sky is bright and the air balmy, and the flowers open their petals to the sun, and the grass grows upon the mountains, and the pastures are covered with flocks, and the valleys with corn. We see her presence in the home, when health and happiness are there, when she covers the table, and makes our slumbers light and refreshing, and sweetens the intercourse of brothers and sisters, and

[1] Sir Algernon West, *Recollections*, i. 304.

gladdens the hearts of parents with the welfare and well-doing of their children, and endows them all with health and strength.

And if sometimes Goodness veils her brightness and appears in such guise that men may not be conscious of her presence, in what may be called the wintry season of the soul, and there is less radiance on her countenance, and less music in her tread, and an apparently less liberal dispensation of her gifts; even then to the eye of faith her features are the same, and the same blessed ends are promoted by her gentle, holy ministry. There is the same kindness in her heart, although it be not so visibly manifested; the same words of blessing on her lips, although the ear hears them less distinctly; the same expression on her countenance, although it be somewhat veiled; the same benefactions bestowed by her hand, although they be not so sweet to the taste. A stronger faith would see the essential features under the dim disguise, and share in the Psalmist's assurance that Goodness as well as Mercy follows all the good man's steps.[1]

¶ When Jacob looks at the coat of his darling son dedaubed with blood, a horror of great darkness falls upon his mind. He rends his garments. His anguish is pitiful. His hopes are crushed. The light of his life is gone out. He puts on sackcloth, and mourns for his son many days. He "refuses to be comforted." He sees nothing before him but a set grey life, and then the dreariness of Sheol. He will follow his son into the darkness. His faith in God is not so grandly steadfast as that of Abraham, who believed that

> Even the hour that darkest seemeth
> Will His changeless goodness prove.

Men of stronger faith have learned to answer even such questions as, "Is this thy son's coat?" without rending their garments and refusing to be comforted. Richard Cameron's head and hands were carried to his old father, Allen Cameron. "Do you know them?" asked the cruel men who wished to add grief to the father's sorrow. And he took them on his knee, and bent over them, and kissed them, and said, "I know them! I know them! They are my son's, my dear son's." And then, weeping and yet praising, he went on, "It is the Lord! Good is the will of the Lord, who cannot wrong me and mine, but has made goodness and mercy to follow us all our days."[2]

[1] W. Landels.   [2] J. Strachan, *Hebrew Ideals*, ii. 94.

(2) Mercy is closely allied to Goodness, and closely resembles her, as twin sisters frequently resemble each other, although she exercises her ministry chiefly under different circumstances, and in slightly different ways. She is less buoyant and radiant than the other, with more gravity and tenderness of manner. Her eye is tearful, as if she were ever ready to weep with those that weep, and her lips tremulous with pity. She has a noiseless step, and a soft, gentle touch, and a voice that falls like music on the dull ear of sorrow. With whispered consolation on her lips, and a cordial in her hands, her favourite haunts are chambers of sickness, or prison cells, or closets where souls groan in secret under heavy loads of sin and woe; and there, in her mild accents, she bids the guilty be of good cheer because their sins are forgiven, and with her strong though gentle hand lifts the burden from the heavy laden, and with her fragrant ointment tenderly heals the broken in heart and binds up their wounds. She is seen more frequently in the shade than in the sunshine, and exercises her ministry most when some darkly brooding sorrow hangs over the individual or the family or the nation's heart. When Goodness puts on her veil, and works behind her disguise so that men know her not, then is Mercy often employed most actively in furthering her gracious designs. Her ministries are more specific than those of Goodness, and confined to a more limited sphere, a preparedness of heart being necessary to fit men for receiving them. But withal they are not less spontaneously, or freely, or cheerfully exercised.

> The quality of mercy is not straind,
> It droppeth as the gentle rain from heaven
> Upon the place beneath.

Unpurchased, oftentimes unsolicited, Mercy pays her visits and impart her benefactions; and those who have profited most by her ministry are sometimes those who never thought of her till they found her by their side.[1]

¶ I have a very great confidence indeed in the kindness of God towards us. I do believe if we shall find ourselves mistaken on either side in Eternity, it will be in finding God more merciful than we expected.[2]

[1] W. Landels.   [2] *Life of Charles Loring Brace*, 83.

¶ Miss R. having told Dr. Duncan that a young man had said at a meeting that "there was not mercy in God from everlasting —there could not be mercy till there was misery," he said, "God is unchangeable; mercy is an attribute of God. The man is confounding mercy with the exercise of mercy. There could not be the exercise of mercy till there was misery; but God was always a merciful God. You might as well say that there could not be justice in God till there were creatures towards whom to exercise punitive justice."[1]

> Silent, alone! The river seeks the sea,
>   The dewdrop on the rose desires its sun!
> Oh, prisoned Soul, shalt thou alone be free?
>   Shalt thou escape the curse of death and birth
>   And merge thy sorrows in oblivion?
>   Thou, thou alone of all the living earth?
>
> Silent, alone! I know when next the dawn
>   Shall cast its vision through the desert sea
> And find me not, the sword that I have drawn
>   Shall flash between the twilights, and a word
>   Shall praise what I was not but strove to be,
>   Saying: "Behold the mercy of the Lord."[2]

3. "Goodness and mercy *shall follow me.*" It is a strong word that the Psalmist uses, the strong fierce word *pursue*—the very word used of the pursuit of the enemy in battle. It is as if God's love were so eager to find the man that it was determined to run him down. Look! there they are, two blessed and gentle figures, Love and Pity, angels twain, on the heels of every man, running and resolved to find him. And when they find him, and bring him into the quiet tent, as the guest of God, is it any wonder that he longs to dwell there "throughout the length of days"?

He pursues us with the zeal of a foe, and the love of a Father; pursues us "throughout the length of days" with a Divine impatience that is never faint and never weary. He is not content to follow us; He pursues us, because He means to find us. Behind the loneliest man is a lovely apparition; nay, no apparition, but angels twain, Goodness and Mercy, shielding and urging him

---

[1] *Memoir of John Duncan, LL.D.*, 422.
[2] George Cabot Lodge, *Poems and Dramas*, i. 55.

on. Will he not turn round and look at them ? For not to smite, but to bless, are the hands uplifted behind him. Had the powers that pursue us not been Goodness and Mercy, they would have slain us long ago, as cumberers of the ground.[1]

¶ When night came the church was packed. "Now, beloved friends," said the preacher, "if you will turn to the third chapter of John and the sixteenth verse, you will find my text." He preached the most extraordinary sermon from that verse. He did not divide the text into "secondly" and "thirdly" and "fourthly"; he just took the whole verse, and then went through the Bible from Genesis to Revelation to prove that in all ages God loved the world. I never knew up to that time that God loved us so much. This heart of mine began to thaw out; I could not keep back the tears. It was like news from a far country: I just drank it in. So did the crowded congregation. I tell you there is one thing that draws above everything else in this world, and that is *love*.[2]

¶ How many unsatisfied hearts there are, tired of their own tired question, "Who will show us any good?" Nor are they only the hearts which have tried the less pure springs of earthly happiness and rest. Not long ago there died a man eminent in scientific knowledge and achievement, who towards the close of his comparatively brief life was brought back from remote mental wanderings to God in Christ. I refer to the late Mr. George Romanes. He was a man of blameless morals, exemplary in every personal duty; and he seemed constrained, to his own infinite unhappiness, to disbelieve in God. He tried, in this sad condition, to make life satisfactory without Him. He gave himself up fully to his own refined and elevated line of thought and work. He was a diligent and masterly observer and enquirer amidst the mysteries of nature, and a kindly and unselfish man besides. But was he satisfied? Listen to his own avowal: "I felt as if I were trying to feed a starving man with light confectionery." It would not do. Nothing would do but the living God. He sought, he felt, he knelt his way back to Him, and he was satisfied at last.[3]

4. The idea of goodness and mercy following a man is exceedingly beautiful and suggestive. There is a phrase in the Bible, with which we are familiar, which speaks of the "preventing

[1] J. E. McFadyen, *The Divine Pursuit*, 201.
[2] *The Life of Dwight L. Moody*, 127.
[3] Bishop H. C. G. Moule, *All in Christ*, 204.

mercies" of God, this word "prevent" formerly meaning not to hinder, as it does now, but simply to go before—God's mercies outrunning our necessities, going before them to anticipate and provide for them. It is in this sense that we usually think of the goodness and mercy of God, as going before us to prepare our way and provide for our wants. But in our deeper moods we feel that we need quite as much that goodness and mercy should follow us. Our greatest troubles are ever those which belong to our past, which come from the things that are behind us, which we are striving to forget. Our march through life is like the march of an army through a hostile region. While we are conquering and possessing the present, we are leaving unsubdued enemies, and unconquered fortresses, and old inveterate habits of sin behind us, that will assuredly rise up and trouble us again. Our past is not dead and buried; it is waiting for us in some future ambush of our life.

How precious in such an experience are the words of the text, assuring us that God is following us—not as the American Indian follows upon the trail of his enemy to slay him, not as the avenger of blood follows in his awful vendetta upon the track of the manslayer, but with goodness and mercy! He cries to us as we hasten away from Him in the sullenness and unbelief which sin produces—"I, even I, am he that blotteth out thy transgressions for mine own sake, and will not remember thy sins." He can cast our sins behind His back; remove them as far as east is from the west. He can follow us as Jesus followed Peter when he cut off Malchus's ear with the sword, to heal the wounds we have inflicted, to redress the wrongs we have committed, to neutralize the consequences of our folly, ignorance, or sin. He can gather up all our woeful past in His boundless mercy, and enable us as little children to enter His kingdom again. He can separate us from the debasing associations of our sin, give us a sense of recovered freedom and enlargement of heart, and enable us to begin anew, without the disabilities of former days clinging like fetters about our feet and impeding our steps.

¶ The Psalmist does not ask that blessings shall continue to lead him, but that goodness and mercy shall follow him. They are not to be the guides of his life, but the consequences of his life. He is to go his way as well as he can, through the pastures and valleys of experience, and after him there are to follow more goodness and more mercy. Perhaps he is still thinking of the Oriental shepherd in whose name the Psalm began. " The Lord," he has said, " is my shepherd"; and in the East the shepherd goes before, and the sheep hear his voice and follow him. Thus the man who has been blessed of God is to go steadily on, and behind him, like a flock of sheep, will follow the good thoughts and merciful deeds of a better world.

Such is the Psalmist's picture of the blessed life. The man who thus goes his way up and down the hills of experience does not have to look behind him to watch for goodness and mercy; they know his voice and follow him. He meets his obstacles and reverses, and as he looks ahead, life may not appear good or merciful; but what he is concerned about is the consequence of his life, and he goes his way bravely to clear the path for goodness and mercy to follow. Says Whittier—

> The blessings of his quiet life,
> Fell round us like the dew,
> And kind thoughts where his footsteps pressed
> Like fairy blossoms grew.

It was a figure which Jesus Himself liked to use. He did not expect to get much mercy from the world : He prayed that after Him might follow a world of mercy. " For their sakes," He said, " I sanctify myself; that they also might be sanctified through the truth." " I am the good shepherd; the good shepherd giveth his life for the sheep." Here is the self-respecting, rational end of any modern psalm of praise: " Thou hast led me through many blessings, among green pastures, and by still waters. I do not ask for more of this quiet peace. I ask for strength to go my way bravely along the path of duty, so that after me it shall be easier to do right and to be merciful, and goodness and mercy shall follow me all the days of my life." [1]

> I asked my God to go before
> To light with signs the unknown shore
> And lift the latch of every door;
> He said, " I *follow* thee."

> I asked Him to prepare my way
> By kindling each uncertain ray
> And turning darkness into day;
> He said, " I *follow* thee."

[1] F. G. Peabody, *Mornings in the College Chapel*, ii. 36.

He bade me linger not till light
Had touched with gold the morning height,
But to begin my course by night,
   And day would follow me.

He told me when my hours were dark
To wait not the revealing spark,
But breast the flood in duty's ark,
   And peace should follow me.

Therefore, O Lord, at Thy command
I go to seek the unknown land,
Content, though barren be the sand,
   If Thou shalt follow me.

I go by night, I go alone,
I sleep upon a couch of stone;
But nightly visions shall atone
   If Thou shalt follow me.

I sow the seed in lowly ground,
I sow in faith and hear no sound;
Yet in full months it may be found
   That Thou hast followed me.[1]

¶ There is a mercy which goes before us, and there is a mercy which follows us. The one is the clearing of our own path; the other is the clearing of a path for our brother man. There is an expression, "May your path be strewn with flowers!" That may mean one or other of two things. It may be the wish that you may be called to tread a flowery way, or it may be the wish that when you tread the thorny way you may leave flowers where you have passed. The latter is the Psalmist's aspiration, and it is the nobler aspiration. It is an aspiration which can come only from a "restored soul." *Any* man can desire to be cradled in green pastures and led by quiet waters. But to desire that my life may *make* the pastures green, to desire that my life may *make* the waters quiet—that is a Divine prayer, a Christlike prayer. There is a prosperity for which every good man is bound to pray. It is finely expressed, I think, in a line of Tennyson's "Maud"—

Her feet have touched the meadows, and have left the
   daisies rosy.

[1] G. Matheson, *Sacred Songs*, 10.

The daisies were not rosy in advance; they became rosy by the feet touching them. It was the footsteps themselves that exerted a transforming power; they created a flowery path for *future* travellers; goodness and mercy *followed* them.[1]

5. The hope uttered here has no element of doubt mingling with it. This is indicated by the word "surely." Here is not only hope, but the full assurance of it. When our hope rests on an earthly friend, it is necessarily more or less troubled, because our friend may change, his love may grow cold, his power may fail, he may forget us in his own distractions, he may die, or in some one of a thousand ways we may pass out of the sphere within which alone he can help us; but there is no such element of disturbance and unquietness in the hope we repose in God; it is, it has reason to be, assured hope. Instead of "*surely*," some commentators make it "*only*"—"only goodness and mercy shall follow me"; just as in the 73rd Psalm they read, "God is good and only good—nothing but good—to Israel, even to such as are of a clean heart." Nothing but goodness and mercy *shall pursue me*. What a contrast to the lot of the wicked man, pursued by the angel of judgment (xxxv. 6), hunted by calamity (cxl. 11).

6. "All the days of my life." A continuance of grace and strength is needed every hour till the close. Often is the saint surprised by severe trial even when nearing home, like a vessel which has safely weathered the storms of a voyage and seems past all danger, but is nevertheless wrecked almost in entering port. Above all such fear of failing at last the believer's confidence triumphs in the assurance that He whom he has known and trusted will never leave his side.

¶ Grace being an endowment above the strength of nature, what is it else, but young glory? For that the knowledge of the one will lead us by the hand unto the knowledge of the other: as glory is grace in the bloom and fullest vigour, so grace is glory in the bud and first spring-time; the one is holiness begun, the other holiness perfected; the one is the beholding of God darkly, as through a glass, the other, beholding Him face to face.[2]

[1] G. Matheson, *Rests by the River*, 50.   [2] Andrew Wellwood.

II.

PERMANENCE.

"I will dwell in the house of the Lord for ever."

1. Not only are Goodness and Mercy—these two white-robed messengers of God—to follow us instead of the avenger of blood, but we are to dwell in the house of the Lord for ever. The man-slayer who fled to one of the old cities of refuge in Palestine had not only the right of asylum there, safety from the vengeance of the friends of the murdered man, but also the right of citizenship. Though he did not by birth belong to the city to which he fled, and had no possession in it; though his crime had made him an outcast from his own city and inheritance, his very necessity constituted a title to be received as a citizen in the new dwelling-place. And by the merciful provision of the Mosaic law, his very misery and danger raised him from the condition of a stranger and a fugitive, to be an associate with the priests of God in their holiest services.

But great as were the privileges which he enjoyed in the city of refuge, they were only temporary. He was only to dwell there till his case should be investigated by the proper authorities, or at the utmost till the death of the man who happened to be high priest at the time. He must then, if pronounced guilty, be given up to the just doom connected with his crime, or, if found innocent, depart to his own home. But it is not so with the house of the Lord, to which the Psalmist refers. David knew that the sanctuary on Zion would be a secure place of refuge ; and often did he long with an intense yearning for its privileges, and contrast the miserable spiritual privations of his exile in the wilderness with the means of grace which he used to enjoy. But even if he had been restored to the sanctuary, he could not have said of it, " This is my rest for ever : here will I dwell ; for I have desired it."

¶ At Cadiz, in Spain, above the entrance of the Casa di Misericordia, or House of Refuge, is carved the inscription in the words of the one hundred and thirty-second Psalm—" This is my rest : here will I dwell." The ear misses the two familiar words of the Psalm " for ever." A friend has told me that as he looked up one day at the inscription and noticed the omission, the Superior, who happened to be near, with a smile explained the reason. "This Casa," he said, "is the rest of the poor—but not for ever." [1]

2. David must have looked beyond the earthly sanctuary to the city which hath foundations, whose builder and maker is God; beyond the dark valley of the shadow of death to the house not made with hands, eternal in the heavens. There alone should he be everlastingly safe and blessed.

We also fled to this house of the Lord for safety in a time of sore distress; and we have found in it the true rest of life. We were driven by stress of trial and danger into it when all other refuge failed us, and we looked on our right hand and viewed, but there were none to know or help us; and now so blessed are we in it that we would not leave it if we could. No sin can accuse us there; no death can snatch us from its joy. Nothing can shake the security, nothing can mar the peace, of those who dwell thus in the house of the Lord. Goodness and mercy have wiped away all the evils of our life, and converted them into good. And "neither death, nor life, nor angels, nor principalities, nor powers, nor things present, nor things to come, nor height, nor depth, nor any other creature, shall be able to separate us from the love of God, which is in Christ Jesus our Lord."

3. But the dwelling does not begin when the "days of our life" are ended; the two are simultaneous, and go on together. There is indeed no termination to the dwelling in God's house, it reaches into eternity and never ceases; but it begins at present, and runs parallel with our enjoyment of God's goodness and mercy. It is the "one thing" that David says elsewhere he desired of the Lord, and would seek after all the days of his life, and that inspired such Psalms as the Sixty-third and Eighty-fourth, which express so wonderfully the soul's longing for conscious fellowship with God.

We see the faith and feeling of the man expand and en-large, till they embrace the great and ultimate future of the life that is to be; and he says, I feel that I have been led onwards to that. These capacities and affections of mine, the stirring of a

[1] H. Macmillan, *The Mystery of Grace*, 148.

spiritual life within me, were never made to find their perfection
here.   I carry within myself, in my own religious consciousness,
a prophecy, an earnest of something greater than the life which
now is ; and I believe that "I will dwell in the house of the Lord
for ever," and that the goodness and the mercy that have followed
me hitherto, and which, I believe, will follow me still, shall
effloresce and bear fruit in the upper world, in the blessedness
which is prepared for the people of God.   I believe it ! I believe
that I shall pass away from the rich satisfactions of the spiritual
life here, which, however rich, are still mingled.   I am still in the
presence of my enemies ; and though they do not hurt me or come
near me, still they suggest feelings, thoughts, that partake of fear,
and occasion a necessity for watchfulness, and for the exercise of
duties from which I shall one day be delivered.   I shall pass away
from the feast here, rich as it is, to a richer and a better ; for I
shall " sit down at the marriage supper of the Lamb."   Or—to
change the figure, and go back to the previous picture—I believe,
reasoning from the past and the present to that which is to come,
that I shall pass away from this lower scene, these verdant and
pleasant pastures, only to find myself, in a higher world, one of
that flock of which it is said—" For the Lamb which is in the
midst of the throne shall feed them, and shall lead them unto living
fountains of waters : and they shall hunger no more, neither thirst
any more ; neither shall the sun light on them, nor any heat."
" Surely goodness and mercy shall follow me all the days of my
life : and I will dwell in the house of the Lord for ever."

> None other Lamb, none other Name,
>   None other Hope in heaven or earth or sea,
> None other Hiding-place from guilt and shame,
>   None beside Thee.
>
> My faith burns low, my hope burns low,
>   Only my heart's desire cries out in me
> By the deep thunder of its want and woe,
>   Cries out to Thee.
>
> Lord, Thou art Life tho' I be dead,
>   Love's Fire Thou art however cold I be :
> Nor heaven have I, nor place to lay my head,
>   Nor home, but Thee.[1]

[1] Christina G. Rossetti.

4. "For ever"—literally, "throughout the length of days": what a wonderful phrase! To one who knows God to be the Shepherd of his life, the valley of the deep shadow will only lead from the green pastures and the quiet waters of earth to the pastures more green and the waters more quiet of heaven. For this Jesus of ours has Himself been through the valley of the deepest shadow, and He came out on the other side, and said: "Peace be unto you!" Shall we not then take heart, as we yield ourselves to the guidance of our Shepherd, who is good and wise and strong, to whom belong the pastures on this side of death and the pastures on that? And so throughout the length of days we shall praise Him—all our days in the world that now is, and then in the world everlasting.

¶ Jesus utilizes the great parable of the Family for the last time; and as He had invested Fatherhood and Sonhood with their highest meaning so He now spiritualizes Home. What Mary's cottage at Bethany had been to the little company during the Holy Week, with its quiet rest after the daily turmoil of Jerusalem; what some humble house on the shore of Galilee was to St. John, with its associations of Salome; what the great Temple was to the pious Jews, with its Presence of the Eternal, that on the higher scale was Heaven. Jesus availed Himself of a wealth of tender recollections and placed Heaven in the heart of humanity when He said, "My Father's House."[1]

[1] John Watson, *The Mind of the Master.*